Private Governance and Public Authority

At a time of significant concern ⟨…⟩ global
economy, businesses are eager to ⟨display⟩ responsible corporate practices.
While rulemaking for these practices was once the prerogative of states,
businesses and civil society actors are increasingly engaged in creating
private rulemaking instruments, such as eco-labeling and certification
schemes, to govern corporate behavior. When does a public authority
intervene in such private governance and reassert the primacy of public
policy? Renckens develops a new theory of public-private regulatory interactions and argues that when and how a public authority intervenes in
private governance depends on the economic benefits to domestic producers that such intervention generates and the degree of fragmentation of
private governance schemes. Drawing on European Union policymaking
on organic agriculture, biofuels, fisheries, and fair trade, he exposes the
political-economic conflicts between private and public rule makers and
the strategic nature of regulating sustainability in a global economy.

STEFAN RENCKENS is Assistant Professor in the Political Science Department of the University of Toronto. His research examines the political
economy of transnational private sustainability governance and public-
private governance interactions. He holds a Ph.D. in Global Environmental
Politics from Yale University. His Ph.D. dissertation received the American
Political Science Association's best dissertation award in Science, Technology, and Environmental Politics (2015). He also holds master's degrees in
political science, economic policy, and conflict and peace studies. He has
received research grants from the Canadian Social Sciences and Humanities
Research Council, the U.S. National Science Foundation, and the Research
Foundation Flanders.

BUSINESS AND PUBLIC POLICY

Series Editor
Aseem Prakash, *University of Washington*

Series Board
Sarah Brooks, *Ohio State University*
David Coen, *University College London*
Nathan Jensen, *University of Texas at Austin*
Christophe Knill, *Ludwig-Maximilians-University Munich*
David Konisky, *Indiana University*
David Levi Faur, *Hebrew University of Jerusalem*
Layna Mosley, *University of North Carolina at Chapel Hill*
Abraham Newman, *Georgetown University*
Leonard Seabrooke, *Copenhagen Business School*
Mike Vandenberg, *Vanderbilt University*
Edward Walker, *University of California, Los Angeles*
Henry Yeung, *Singapore National University*

This series aims to play a pioneering role in shaping the emerging field of business and public policy. *Business and Public Policy* focuses on two central questions. First, how does public policy influence business strategy, operations, organization, and governance, and with what consequences for both business and society? Second, how do businesses themselves influence policy institutions, policy processes, and other policy actors and with what outcomes?

Other books in the series

TIMOTHY WERNER, *Public Forces and Private Politics in American Big Business*

HEVINA S. DASHWOOD, *The Rise of Global Corporate Social Responsibility: Mining and the Spread of Global Norms*

LLEWELYN HUGHES, *Globalizing Oil: Firms and Oil Market Governance in France, Japan, and the United States*

EDWARD T. WALKER, *Grassroots for Hire: Public Affairs Consultants in American Democracy*

CHRISTIAN R. THAUER, *The Managerial Sources of Corporate Social Responsibility: The Spread of Global Standards*

KIYOTERU TSUTSUI & ALWYN LIM (Editors), *Corporate Social Responsibility in a Globalizing World*

Private Governance and Public Authority

Regulating Sustainability in a Global Economy

STEFAN RENCKENS
University of Toronto

CAMBRIDGE
UNIVERSITY PRESS

CAMBRIDGE
UNIVERSITY PRESS

University Printing House, Cambridge CB2 8BS, United Kingdom

One Liberty Plaza, 20th Floor, New York, NY 10006, USA

477 Williamstown Road, Port Melbourne, VIC 3207, Australia

314-321, 3rd Floor, Plot 3, Splendor Forum, Jasola District Centre, New Delhi - 110025, India

103 Penang Road, #05-06/07, Visioncrest Commercial, Singapore 238467

Cambridge University Press is part of the University of Cambridge.

It furthers the University's mission by disseminating knowledge in the pursuit of
education, learning and research at the highest international levels of excellence.

www.cambridge.org
Information on this title: www.cambridge.org/9781108748483
DOI: 10.1017/9781108781015

First published 2020
First paperback edition 2022

A catalogue record for this publication is available from the British Library

ISBN 978-1-108-49047-4 Hardback
ISBN 978-1-108-74848-3 Paperback

Contents

Figures

Tables

Acknowledgments

A tremendous number of people have helped in shaping this book project. Special thanks go to Ben Cashore, my PhD supervisor at Yale University, and Hans Bruyninckx, my co-supervisor, whose inexhaustible sources of creativity, unconventional thinking, and constructive encouragement have guided me throughout my academic career. This book has further benefited enormously from the guidance of my other two dissertation committee members, Frances Rosenbluth and Tim Büthe, whose challenging comments encouraged me to continuously rethink my assumptions.

Since our graduate school days in New Haven, Graeme Auld has been a colleague and friend who has offered intellectual and personal support to this project. At the University of Toronto, I am grateful to Steven Bernstein, Matt Hoffmann, Grace Skogstad, and Phil Triadafilopoulos, who commented on several draft chapters. I am also indebted to my other colleagues at Yale, Toronto, and the University of Leuven for offering an intellectually stimulating and caring environment.

Special thanks go to Aseem Prakash and John Haslam at Cambridge University Press for their belief in this book.

I want to thank the many people I was able to interview and who have generously offered their precious time and insights. Without them, this book would not have been possible.

I gratefully acknowledge financial support from the University of Toronto Scarborough, the Yale School of Forestry and Environmental Studies, the Yale Graduate School of Arts and Sciences, the Yale MacMillan Center for International and Area Studies, the US National Science Foundation, and the Belgian American Educational Foundation.

I want to thank all my friends in Belgium, who have continued to support me ever since I embarked on my graduate studies journey in the USA. Special thanks go to Wim, Joris, Tom, Pieter, and Bart, who make every trip back home an adventure.

I am forever grateful to my family. My mom and dad have supported me throughout all my personal and professional endeavors. I would not have succeeded without their unconditional love. My brother Kris, sister-in-law Tina, and nieces Marie and Nora have been a huge support and masters in keeping everything we do in perspective. Bedankt aan jullie allemaal!

I am eternally grateful to my wife, Cory, who has been an ardent supporter and loving companion for the past twelve years: You rock. Finally, I want to thank my son, Elliot, for his love and joyfulness: Your laugh beats everything; you are the future.

Abbreviations

2BSvs	Biomass Biofuels Sustainability voluntary scheme
4C	Common Code for the Coffee Community
ACP	Africa, the Caribbean, and the Pacific
AIPCE-CEP	European Fish Processors Association – European Federation of National Organisations of Importers and Exporters of Fish
ASC	Aquaculture Stewardship Council
BAP	Best Aquaculture Practices
C.A.F.E.	Coffee and Farmer Equity Practices
CAP	Common Agricultural Policy
CFP	Common Fisheries Policy
CME	coordinated market economy
CO_2	carbon dioxide
COGECA	General Confederation of Agricultural Cooperatives in the European Union
COM	Common Organization of the Market
COPA	Committee of Professional Agricultural Organisations
CSR	corporate social responsibility
DG	Directorate-General of the European Commission
EBB	European Biodiesel Board
ECF	European Coffee Federation
EEB	European Environmental Bureau
EESC	European Economic and Social Committee
EFTA	European Fair Trade Association

ETFP	Ethical Trade Fact-finding Process
GLOBALG.A.P.	Global Good Agricultural Practices
FAO	Food and Agriculture Organization of the United Nations
FLO	Fairtrade Labelling Organizations International / Fairtrade International
FSC	Forest Stewardship Council
FTAO	Fair Trade Advocacy Office
GAA	Global Aquaculture Alliance
GATT	General Agreement on Tariffs and Trade
GBEP	Global Bioenergy Partnership
GHG	greenhouse gas
GIZ	German Society for International Cooperation
GSSI	Global Sustainable Seafood Initiative
IFAT	International Federation of Alternative Trade/International Fair Trade Association
IFOAM	International Federation of Organic Agriculture Movements
ILO	International Labour Organization
ILUC	indirect land-use change
IOAS	International Organic Accreditation Service
IRFM	Iceland Responsible Fisheries Management scheme
ISCC	International Sustainability and Carbon Certification
ISEAL	International Social and Environmental Accreditation and Labelling Alliance
ISO	International Organization for Standardization
ISPO	Indonesian Sustainable Palm Oil System
IUCN	International Union for Conservation of Nature
LME	liberal market economy
LowCVP	Low Carbon Vehicle Partnership
MSC	Marine Stewardship Council
NEWS!	Network of European World Shops

NGO	nongovernmental organization
npr-PPM	non-product-related process or production method
NTA 8080	Netherlands Technical Agreement 8080
OECD	Organization for Economic Co-operation and Development
RBSA	Abengoa RED Bioenergy Sustainability Assurance
RED	Renewable Energy Directive
RFA	Renewable Fuels Agency
RSB	Roundtable on Sustainable Biofuels / Roundtable on Sustainable Biomaterials
RSPO	Roundtable on Sustainable Palm Oil
RTFO	Renewable Transport Fuels Obligation
RTRS	Round Table on Responsible Soy
SAN	Sustainable Agriculture Network
SQC	Scottish Quality Farm Assured Combinable Crops
STAP	Sustainable Trade Action Plan
TBT	Technical Barriers to Trade
UAA	utilizable agricultural area
UNDP	United Nations Development Programme
UNEP	United Nations Environment Programme
WFTO	World Fair Trade Organization
WTO	World Trade Organization
WWF	World Wide Fund for Nature

1 | Introduction
Public–Private Governance Interactions

Ensuring the sustainability of global production processes and supply chains is an increasing concern in many sectors. The production of agricultural commodities such as sugar, coffee, or soy, for example, has been associated with adverse environmental and social impacts, including land degradation, deforestation, and labor exploitation (High Level Panel of Experts, 2013; UNDP, 2016). These commodities travel several thousand miles and cross multiple borders before they end up in the hands of consumers, who are often unaware of the origins of the products they buy and the practices that were used to produce them.

States and international organizations have long since attempted to address sustainability in supply chains. However, they have had many difficulties, and on numerous occasions blatantly failed to comprehensively regulate global production processes. Weak regulations, feeble law enforcement, and ineffective domestic institutions often inhibit countries from effectively addressing environmental problems domestically (McDermott et al., 2010; Steinberg and VanDeveer, 2012). The cross-boundary nature of supply chains renders action by any one country difficult. Effective international coordination has been hard to come by as well. Multilateral environmental and trade agreements attempting to address the negative externalities of global economic integration have often had insufficient impact to reverse trends of large-scale resource depletion and pollution (Young, 2011). Furthermore, voluntary public efforts such as the Guidelines for Multinational Enterprises, developed by the Organization for Economic Co-operation and Development (OECD), or the United Nations (UN) Global Compact, have received mixed reviews as well (Berliner and Prakash, 2015; Bernhagen and Mitchell, 2010; Ruggie and Nelson, 2015; Schuler, 2008).

Over the last three decades, a private form of governance has firmly established itself as an alternative means to address sustainability concerns.[1] On products, in stores, on company websites, and in corporate advertising we can see the results of such private governance in the form of a plethora of eco-labels and other types of sustainability claims. These private initiatives cover a diverse set of products ranging from produce and seafood to clothing, jewelry, and paper and wood products (Bartley, 2003; Bloomfield, 2017; Cashore et al., 2004; Fransen, 2011; Gulbrandsen, 2009).[2] Non-state actors rather than governments develop the rules on which these sustainability claims rest. Many businesses and industry associations have developed codes of conduct for which they monitor compliance themselves, giving rise to "self-regulation" (Haufler, 2001). Initiatives that are more recent often encompass coalitions of corporate and civil society actors to establish the rules, while employing an independent auditor to verify compliance and grant formal "certification" to the compliant business. Governments in some instances have been a partner in the rulemaking process in a larger multi-stakeholder setting, yet private governance does not derive its authority from the state and has largely developed outside of the purview of governments (Cashore, 2002). Many private governance schemes, moreover, are transnational in the sense that they are not confined to the boundaries of a given state or polity.

Firms engage with this type of private governance as a new form of corporate social responsibility (CSR) (Auld et al., 2008). This new CSR goes well beyond Milton Friedman's famous adage that the "social responsibility of business is to increase its profits" (Friedman, 1970) and CSR's traditional manifestation as corporate philanthropy. In its new incarnation as private governance, CSR aims to directly address the adverse impacts of the core productive activities of firms. If stringent enough, the sustainability rules can induce changes in corporate behavior and be costly to firms, while also potentially offering market benefits in the form of enhanced reputations or price premiums for their sustainably produced products (Potoski and Prakash, 2009).

Building on these expected sustainability and market benefits, some scholars have ascribed a transformational potential to private governance (e.g., Bernstein and Cashore, 2007; Cashore et al., 2007; Pattberg, 2007; Ruggie, 2004). This view highlights the potential of private governance to either complement or provide an alternative to public regulation. This is the case because private governance has particularly thrived in areas where international or domestic rules are lacking or have proven insufficiently effective. As a result, these scholars situate private governance in the context of the prominent use of market-based environmental solutions and "liberal environmentalism" (Bernstein, 2001), and see it as part of a Polanyian effort to re-embed markets in rules (Polanyi, 2001 [1944]). It is exemplary of the current age of "regulatory capitalism" (Levi-Faur, 2005), part of which implies "using markets as regulatory mechanisms, as opposed to the neoliberal schema of markets as the antithesis of regulation"(Braithwaite, 2008: 7).

Other scholars are more critical of private governance. They argue that rulemaking is still dominated by states – and at the international level by the most powerful states – while private governance emerges as a second-best outcome (Drezner, 2007: 81–87). Critics also dismiss private governance as corporate "greenwashing" that is used to obscure destructive corporate practices. Private governance is put down as an exponent of neoliberal economic ideology and the "myths" of the green economy, which merely intends to enhance corporate structural and discursive power at the expense of the regulatory capacity of the state (e.g., Cutler, 2006; Dauvergne and Lister, 2013; Lipschutz, 2005; Scott et al., 2009; Sklair, 2001; Wright and Nyberg, 2014). The market-based logic of private governance and its focus on green consumerism is seen to perpetuate a capitalist, growth-focused rationale ultimately considered destructive to the environment and social relations. As Paterson (2010: 362) aptly phrased it, instead of private governance being "the second half of a Polanyian 'double movement', where social actors 're-embed' markets in rules … [i]t is rather that the development of rules is the condition of possibility for market actors to realize profits and accumulate capital."

Whether one embraces a transformational or a more critical perspective on private governance, both positions beg the question of whether there is a role for governments in steering or regulating private governance. From a transformational perspective, one could argue that there is no role for the state. Business has the expertise to improve production processes itself, and the cooperation with civil society actors provides the required credibility to private governance. At most, states could get involved to support the optimal functioning of private governance by ensuring a stable regulatory and institutional framework, such as through secure property rights and enforceable contract law, and by facilitating and incentivizing companies to engage with private governance (Cashore, 2002; Ebeling and Yasué, 2009).

The critical perspective on private governance offers a clearer rationale for interventions by public authorities. Why would states leave the market to its own devices and allow private actors to define sustainability? This is an important question, since, while in some instances the markets for sustainable products are niche markets, in others there is rapid growth. In fisheries, for example, one of the most prominent private governance schemes, the Marine Stewardship Council (MSC), claimed to cover "nearly 14% of the global wild marine catch" in 2017, in a market for certified seafood products that is worth six billion dollars annually (MSC, 2017b: 4). For cocoa production, the three main private governance schemes – Fairtrade, Rainforest Alliance, and UTZ Certified – together certified over 38 percent of global production in 2015 (International Trade Center, 2017). Indeed, in many sectors we observe the emergence of several competing private governance schemes, which indicates there is a market demand for "green" products and a willingness by firms to invest resources in this market. These dynamics could elicit government intervention to more actively steer private governance efforts, possibly improve their credibility and effectiveness, or even take over private governance and reestablish the primacy of politics (Abbott and Snidal, 2009b; Hospes, 2014).

This book addresses the topic of public interventions in private governance by asking the following research questions: What are the conditions under which a public authority will regulate private governance? What form will these regulatory interventions take? And what are the implications of such interventions for the nature and functioning of private governance and the larger policy field? I assess these questions based on an examination of (non)interventions in private governance in four issue areas in the European Union (EU): organic agriculture, biofuels production, fair trade, and fisheries. The main argument the book develops is that variation in the EU's regulatory interventions in private governance can be explained by the interaction of two variables: the benefits that regulatory interventions offer domestic producers by publicly differentiating products based on their sustainability characteristics, and the degree to which public interventions can solve problems that result from a fragmentation of the private governance market. The book shows that interest representation and lobbying by private governance schemes – a topic the literature has overlooked so far – play an important role in bringing about these regulatory dynamics. Furthermore, the book argues that the EU's interventions have had a dual regulatory effect. On the one hand, they have leveled the playing field and raised the bar for some private governance schemes, while excluding clearly fraudulent and underperforming private schemes. On the other hand, the EU has aimed to design the interventions in such a way as to not directly undermine the functioning or regulatory nature of private governance. This outcome results in several possibilities for future policy learning and policy diffusion, whereby private governance innovations can, over time, make their way into public policy.

Public intervention in private governance is an area of study that has not yet received much systematic scholarly attention. As I will discuss further shortly, the EU offers an ideal polity to examine such interventions. The EU has extensive regulatory competences in issue areas that have witnessed the emergence of private governance; it is a global leader in sustainability regulation, and it has experience with engaging private actors through the use of new governance instruments. The central task of the book is to use the European experience to develop an explanatory framework for understanding the political economy of regulatory interactions between private governance and public authority in the context of a global economy.

Standards and Procedural Regulations

To answer the research questions that are at the heart of this book I assess, for each of the four cases, whether and why the EU has intervened in two key features of private governance's functioning (Auld, 2014b: 4). The first feature comprises the capacity to develop standards of appropriate business behavior. In the context of this book, these standards detail the practices that are permitted or prohibited in the production process of a good. I refer to a public intervention in this standard-setting feature as "standards regulation." Standards regulation not only encompasses substantive rulemaking around production processes, but also an intervention by a public authority that regulates the way compliance with the standard is communicated to a broader audience. This communication can occur in the form of an on-product label or some other indication of sustainability. These consumer communication instruments are part of standards regulation, since they function as the exteriorization of the substantive sustainability standard.

The second key feature of private governance's functioning comprises the way private governance schemes organize themselves by the governance procedures they use. These procedures can encompass a variety of elements, such as the practices that private governance schemes employ to develop and revise a substantive standard; the rules regarding the composition of a private scheme's membership; the relationship between a private scheme and the company seeking compliance with the substantive standard; the relationship between a private scheme and the auditor that verifies compliance; and the accreditation of the auditors. I will refer to public interventions in these private governance procedures as "procedural regulation."

The dependent variable of this study – EU interventions in the form of standards and/or procedural regulation, or the absence of intervention – bears some relation to existing concepts in the literature, as I will also discuss further. The interventions could be considered a form of "orchestration," as defined by Abbott et al. (2015), whereby public actors use intermediaries such as private governance schemes to indirectly govern their rule targets, who are, in most cases, producers. However, the authority relationships between public authority and private governance as examined in this book are more hierarchical than those covered by the general orchestration concept of Abbott et al.'s 2015 edited volume. In that respect, the public interventions discussed in this book are more akin to Abbott and Snidal's (2009b, 2010) earlier and more specific concept of "directive orchestration," which entails a state or international organization imposing its sovereign authority directly on private governance through mandatory rules. Furthermore, the private governance schemes discussed in this book are all examples of what Green (2014) has coined "entrepreneurial private authority." She contrasts this type of private authority with "delegated private authority" that entails the state-based delegation of policy functions to private actors. As the empirical chapters will show, this book discusses instances in which these two types of private authority are merged. Through its interventions, the EU may enroll private governance schemes by delegating responsibilities to them and regulating this delegation (Black, 2003). This type of delegation, as a result, forms an extension of Green's model of delegation, since it entails a delegation to entrepreneurial authority, thereby combining the two types of private authority.

The ways in which standards and procedural regulations are designed can vary. Public intervention could be minimal, in that it entails little public infringement on how private governance schemes substantively regulate their rule targets and organize their governance procedures. At the other extreme, a public authority can "take over" and very stringently describe what sustainability in an issue area substantively entails, and how private governance schemes need to organize themselves; this leaves private schemes no space to develop standards or procedures as they see fit. While these different *degrees* of public intervention have important ramifications for the continued functioning of private governance, this book is, in the first instance, committed to explaining the *form* of public intervention: standards and/or procedural regulation, or their absence altogether. In the final chapter, the book addresses the issue of degrees of intervention when discussing how public interventions in the different issue areas have impacted on private governance: Did the interventions lead to a complete takeover by the EU, or is there still space left (and how much) for private actors to govern as they see fit?

Empirical Puzzle

The empirical puzzle this book addresses is why the EU has intervened extensively in private governance in some issue areas, while in others it has decided not to do so. In the cases of organic agriculture and biofuels production, the EU has intervened with both standards and procedural regulations, while it has not (yet) intervened at all in the areas of fair trade and fisheries.

Organic agriculture is a prominent example of public intervention in private governance. Organic agricultural practices date back to the first half of the twentieth century, when small-scale farmers first developed these farming methods. In the late 1960s and early 1970s, private certification and eco-labeling initiatives formalized these practices. Their intent was to create larger knowledge networks, spread information about agricultural practices that were considered an alternative to large-scale industrial farming, and provide quality products for which farmers could get broader market recognition. Throughout the 1980s and early 1990s, governments started to get involved with organic agriculture as well. Policymakers attempted to support and define organic agriculture and started to integrate this new policy domain into existing agricultural policy. In European countries, for example, this happened in France in 1980, in Denmark in 1987, and in Spain in 1989 (Lampkin, Foster, and Padel, 1999; Lampkin, Foster, Padel, et al., 1999).

In 1991, legislative action was taken at the level of the EU.[3] This intervention resulted in the EU providing a formal definition of organic agriculture, thereby specifying the production processes that operators needed to comply with when claiming to be engaged in organic agriculture. The EU initially suggested that operators use the indication of "organic farming–EEC Control System" on products to show that the operators had complied with EU rules. In later revisions of the policy, an EU on-product organic label was created, as well as additional indications, such as "EU/non-EU agriculture," to provide information on whether the agricultural raw material is farmed in the EU or in third countries.

In addition to such standards regulation, the EU has developed procedural regulation. The EU's policy provides for the delegation to private auditors of the verification of the public standard. These auditors have to comply with certain criteria, such as third-party auditing, which over time have become stricter and more encompassing. Especially early on, this intervention directly affected private governance schemes since, in many instances, private standard-setting organizations had not yet been strictly separated from audit organizations. In later revisions of the policy, the EU also devised rules for non-EU auditors that verify compliance of products with the EU rules in third countries.

A second prominent case of the EU intervening in private governance by means of both standards and procedural regulations is biofuels production. Private governance schemes addressing the sustainable production of biofuels have been emerging since the early 2000s. While some of the private schemes cover biofuels in general, others focus on particular crops, such as soy, sugarcane, or palm oil. In 2003, the EU promulgated legislation in support of biofuels production, but without interfering with private governance. The policy was based on an overall positive outlook on the biofuels sector's future development and its contribution to the EU's sustainability and climate policies. In 2009, however, the EU partly reversed course and created both standards and procedural regulations. The EU established a set of sustainability criteria for biofuels sold in the European market; these criteria cover greenhouse gas (GHG) emissions savings from biofuels production and the types of land on which biofuels can be grown. Furthermore, the EU developed what is called a "meta-standard" approach, which requires that an operator who wants to show compliance with the EU biofuels sustainability criteria can do so with certification by an EU-approved private governance scheme. This approach has resulted in private governance schemes adopting the EU standard almost word for word and having their entire functioning (i.e., the way they organize and engage in certification and monitoring compliance), scrutinized and approved by the EU before they can operate in the European market.

Public interventions in private governance, as in the cases of organic agriculture and biofuels production, are certainly not the norm. In this book, I examine two cases of nonintervention. The first case covers fair trade. Private governance schemes dealing with fair trade have existed since at least the late 1980s.[4] Over the years, EU policymakers have engaged in several discussions on how to respond to private governance in this issue area. Both public policymakers and private actors have many times called for EU interventions in the form of both standards and procedural regulations. Yet, on two separate occasions (in 1999 and 2009), the EU explicitly decided not to intervene in this issue area. Moreover, even though the debate reemerges at times, EU policymakers consider interventions in the near future highly unlikely.

The second case of nonintervention is fisheries. Private fisheries governance emerged in the early 1990s. As in the fair trade case, the EU has so far not intervened. Yet unlike fair trade, the fisheries policy area is still in flux, and an EU intervention is within the realm of possibility in the near future. For the last two decades, policymakers have been discussing possible EU regulatory interventions. While a legislative proposal on procedural regulation was developed around 2008–2009, it failed to materialize due to a confluence of events, including European elections in 2009 and a reform of the EU's Common Fisheries Policy (CFP) between 2009 and 2013. Since this reform concluded, a new round of discussions on regulating private fisheries governance was started. At the time of writing, however, no decision had been taken.

Table 1.1 *EU interventions in private governance*

	Private Governance Emergence	EU Public Regulation
Organic Agriculture	Early 1970s	1991 Standards and procedural regulations
Biofuels	Early 2000s	2009 Standards and procedural regulations
Fisheries	Early 1990s	2008–2009 Unreleased proposal for procedural regulation 2017 No intervention yet
Fair Trade	Late 1980s	1999 Explicit decision against intervention 2009 Explicit decision against intervention

The Argument

What explains these divergent regulatory interventions in private governance? Why did the EU intervene with both standards and procedural regulations in the cases of organic agriculture and biofuels production, while it decided not to intervene (yet) in private governance in the areas of fisheries and fair trade? In this book, I argue that the variation in these public regulatory interventions can be explained by the interaction of two explanatory variables: the domestic benefits of product differentiation by a public authority in support of domestic producers, and the fragmentation of the private governance market, which may result in second-order information asymmetry problems, or trade and competitive distortions.

First, I argue that a public authority will intervene in private governance to support its domestic producers, which are the rule targets of private governance. Since participation in private governance provides firms with access to the market for certified goods, a public authority can have an incentive to facilitate access to this market for its domestic producers and hence increase their global competitiveness. Public intervention in private governance, therefore, can be geared toward producers who are already engaged in sustainable production, or toward developing new opportunities for those not yet involved. This will be a particularly useful strategy when the public authority expects that such intervention will contribute to attaining public sustainability goals, or when the market for sustainably produced goods has large growth potential. Furthermore, an intervention can be appealing when existing private governance schemes are not a good fit for domestic producers. This is the case, for example, when the private rules or compliance procedures are too strict or not adapted to the local conditions in which the producers operate. Finally, creating a first-mover advantage can motivate public interventions. In this way, a public authority can target foreign governments that are likely to intervene in private governance in their home markets or are already doing so, and that thereby may offer advantages to competitors of domestic producers.

Alternatively, there are several reasons why a public authority will choose a noninterventionist approach. First, domestic producers may consider the adjustment costs too high for complying with public rules. Such costs will make it more difficult for producers to access the market for sustainably produced goods and potentially place them at a competitive disadvantage compared to foreign firms. Second, this opposition to public intervention can be reinforced when policy communities that have a preference for the status quo, and are opposed to public interventions, dominate the regulatory process. Finally, policy constraints imposed by the international trade regime can stimulate nonintervention. These constraints on private sustainability governance are controversial, since there is continued uncertainty around the conditions under which rules for production processes are considered discriminatory, as is the extent to which public authorities can reference, endorse, or incorporate private governance that embodies such rules.

My second argument is that a public authority will intervene in private governance when a fragmented private governance market results in problems related to information asymmetries or trade and competitive distortions. Fragmentation here refers to diversity in the characteristics of private governance schemes. This diversity can relate to the quality, stringency or scope of private standards, or the type of producers that private schemes target. In addition, diversity results from private schemes exhibiting different procedural features, such as their compliance verification procedures or rules around stakeholder involvement.

There are two main reasons for a public authority to intervene in a fragmented private governance market. First, fragmentation can result in information asymmetries that can be resolved with public intervention. One of the rationales behind the emergence of private governance has been to address information asymmetry problems between producers and interested stakeholders (such as consumers and activists) around the sustainability of corporate production practices. Private governance instruments – certification and labeling, for instance – intend to elucidate CSR practices that may otherwise remain hidden. Yet, second-order information asymmetries can emerge when it is unclear to actors in the supply chain how the different private initiatives compare to one another in terms of standards or procedural characteristics. This lack of clarity can cause confusion when producers or consumers do not know which private governance scheme to trust or rely on, which may subsequently result in legitimacy problems and undermine the credibility of all private governance schemes in an issue area. This situation is particularly prone to being problematized by actors who are disadvantaged by false or unsubstantiated claims in the market, or by those private schemes and operators that have adopted more stringent standards and procedural features.

Second, fragmentation of the private governance market can result in trade and competitive distortions. Differences in standards or governance procedures among private schemes operating in local markets (in the EU this can mean both subnationally and in specific Member States only), can hinder cross-border market access or prevent a product from being recertified under a scheme in a different market. A product that performs according to the rules of a local private governance scheme may not see these rules and accompanying sustainability claims accepted when it is traded outside of the market where the local scheme operates. This implies that the product has difficulty being marketed under its original scheme, while it also may preclude the product from being acknowledged by a local scheme operating in the importing territory. Such market access difficulties offer a potent incentive for a public authority to intervene, particularly in a polity like the EU's, where the single market is a key institution.

To reduce the likelihood of public intervention, the market could solve the fragmentation problems by means of private coordination or harmonization. This could occur, for example, by private governance schemes mutually recognizing one another, or by private schemes creating an umbrella program with harmonized standards and procedural rules. Absent such private coordination, however, a public authority may intervene to structure the fragmented market.

Applied to the specific EU context, the book highlights the importance of the European Commission as a policy entrepreneur for private governance regulation. Across the cases, the Commission has been instrumental in developing and pushing forward proposals in favor of, or against interventions in private governance, and thus has been a receptive venue for initiating public intervention. Furthermore, since the Commission's position on intervention is shaped by its anticipation of policymaking obstacles in the other decision-making institutions of the EU, stakeholder input to anticipate these obstacles is crucial. Particularly relevant in this respect are the relative openness of the EU system of interest representation to diverse interests; the emergence of new interest coalitions supporting or opposing interventions; and the historical domination of some issues areas by strong policy communities, both at the EU and the Member State level.

The interactions between the incentives for a public authority to intervene in private governance (i.e., support for domestic producers and a fragmented private governance market) will determine the form the public regulatory intervention takes, with both standards and procedural regulations in principle able to contribute to ensuring domestic benefits and addressing market fragmentation. To start, since claims of sustainability need to be supported by a set of rules, standards regulation will be developed to support domestic producers. This regulation will, in the first instance, take the form of a public definition of sustainable production. Such a public standard can be supplemented with a public label (as the exteriorization of the public standard) to further inform consumers and steer demand for sustainably produced products. In addition, standards regulation can create order in the private governance market by harmonizing substantive standards and labels. A public harmonization of standards can weed out false or unsubstantiated claims in the market, enhance the credibility of the entire private governance market, and ensure that as soon as a product complies with the public standard, all private governance schemes need to recognize it as such. A common public label can in addition be employed to increase consumer recognition and further facilitate the free flow of goods, either in addition to, or as the replacement for, private labels. Procedural regulation can equally serve to reduce fragmentation and harmonize private governance schemes, and to make it easier for producers to be certified and distinguish themselves from competitors. It can, thereby, increase confidence in the market, ensure the comparability among schemes, and provide a common baseline to benchmark private schemes. Moreover, procedural regulation is particularly relevant when the verification of compliance with a public standard is delegated to private governance schemes and the latter are directly integrated into public policy.

Once in place, a public authority like the EU is likely to further deepen public interventions. Advancements in the private governance market will at least partly drive the incremental expansion of standards and procedural regulations. Private governance schemes experimenting with new rules and governance procedures or filling policy gaps left open by the initial public intervention, provide learning opportunities for policymakers at relatively low cost. Furthermore, over time, the norms around good practices and credible private governance have evolved. At least in the EU, public policymakers are expected to adapt regulatory interventions in private governance to reflect some of these norms.

Finally, the book argues that the regulatory impacts of the EU's interventions in private governance have been twofold: On the one hand, the interventions have been significant in terms of restructuring the private governance field by requiring private schemes to adjust their standards and practices. On the other hand, the EU's interventions were not intended to fundamentally challenge or undermine the regulatory or governing authority of private schemes. The EU's interventions have overall been supportive of, and at times even deferential to, private governance. The cases of nonintervention in this book equally highlight the strategic nature of public responses to private governance. By giving governance space to private governance schemes, possibilities are opened for spillovers and dynamic interactions between public policy and private governance. Moreover, given public authorities' engagement with private governance, any analysis of sustainability impacts of private governance needs to take into account these interactions and the impacts of public interventions on private governance.

Researching Private Governance and Public Authority Interactions

The main contribution of this book's analysis is that it explains variation in *direct* public regulatory interventions in private governance. Studies on the interactions between public and private governance are still in their infancy and previous research has almost exclusively examined indirect or facilitative interventions by public authorities. While these studies help us better understand the ways in which public authorities are involved in fostering private governance, they tell us little about the conditions under which states will reassert their public authority.

Public Authority in Private Governance Research

As a relatively young field of study, private governance research has spent its formative years studying the emergence, development, and significance of private governance. For researchers outside of the field, it often appears as if private governance scholars turned their backs on the state and only recently shifted gears to "bring the state back in" (cf. Evans et al., 1985b). The state, however, never left. Even in early descriptive and explanatory work on the topic, the state was always present, even though at times somewhat too implicitly.

Scholars studying private governance have consistently situated their research in the context of the broader debate on the role of the state in an era of globalization, the increasing importance of non-state actors in world politics, and the shift from "government" to "governance" (Nye and Keohane, 1971a, 1971b; Rosenau and Czempiel, 1992). The forces of economic globalization and rapid technological change have shown the limits of states to govern global commercial activities (Castells, 2000, 2004; Cerny, 1997; Scholte, 2005). Since the dawn of the 1980s, the state has increasingly shied away from a hierarchical command-and-control role and instead has turned its attention to facilitating the functioning of markets, rather than strictly regulating and controlling them (even though neoliberal "deregulation" could better be described as "reregulation," but in a different form than before). This shift in the functioning of the state opened up space for a larger rulemaking role for non-state actors, such as business and nongovernmental organizations (NGOs) (Auld et al., 2009; Cashore, 2002;

Cutler et al., 1999a; Knill and Lehmkuhl, 2002; Mol and Spaargaren, 2006).

Building on this framing of private governance as having developed in direct relation to a redefined state, studies on private governance emphasize both passive and active relationships between public authority and private governance. From a more passive point of view, scholars have mainly explored the complementarity and substitutability of public and private governance. Early work, for example, highlighted that broader CSR standards were already embedded in public law and discussed the similarities between public and private governance and their potential substitutability (de la Cuesta González and Martinez, 2004; McBarnet et al., 2007; Meidinger, 2001; Rametsteiner, 2002; Wood and Johannson, 2008). Scholars have, in that respect, also argued that gaps in public governance have particularly stimulated the emergence of private governance, as mentioned earlier (Auld et al., 2009; Cashore et al., 2011). Yet private governance need not only emerge in situations where state or intergovernmental regulation is absent. Instead, scholars have found that private governance can develop to supplement existing (inter)governmental regulation. This can occur by private rules working symbiotically with existing public regulation, or by incorporating public rules. In this way, private governance can reinforce the authority of state-based regulation, but also potentially undermine the further strengthening of public authority (Abbott et al., 2016; Green, 2013; Green and Auld, 2017; Gulbrandsen, 2005; Levin et al., 2009; Renckens, 2015).

A fruitful field of study has developed around the linkages between domestic political variables and private governance and CSR. One set of studies focuses on the role of domestic institutions – in particular by contrasting liberal and coordinated market economies (Hall and Soskice, 2001) – in fostering CSR (Fransen, 2013). Some scholars argue that firms' CSR initiatives act as substitutes for domestic institutionalized forms of solidarity and stakeholder participation. As a result, they find that liberal market economies (LME) exhibit more, and more explicit forms of CSR than coordinated market economies (CME) (Jackson and Apostolakou, 2010; Kinderman, 2012; Matten and Moon, 2008). Others, however, argue that CSR activities mirror national institutions. Firms in CMEs, as a result, should be more involved in CSR since their activities reflect corporatist arrangements and strong welfare-state institutions (Campbell, 2007; Gjølberg, 2009;

Midttun et al., 2006). In contrast to both these substitution and the mirroring arguments, Brown and Knudsen (2015) have argued that market pressures and competitive concerns determine firms' CSR practices more than domestic institutions.

Another set of studies linking domestic variables and private governance addresses the effects of the public regulatory and governance environment on private governance. For example, several studies on the environmental management systems developed by the International Organization for Standardization (ISO) (such as ISO 14001) find that regulatory relief or flexibility, (perceptions of) strong public regulatory institutions, and more stringent domestic regulations lead firms to participate more in private governance (Berliner and Prakash, 2014; Delmas, 2002; Potoski and Prakash, 2004; Prakash and Potoski, 2006b). In addition, some scholars argue that the threat of public regulation increases corporate engagement with private governance and self-regulation (Haufler, 2001; Werner, 2012). These factors affect the cost-benefit ratio of participation in private governance, which implies that information provided on these costs and benefits will also be an important determinant of firms' participation (Kollman and Prakash, 2002). Cashore et al. (2004), moreover, argue that when the public regulatory process is more open to nonbusiness interests, firms are more likely to support more stringent private governance initiatives, while Ebeling and Yasué (2009) find that better government enforcement of legislation increases corporate participation with private governance. In contrast, Marx and Cuypers (2010) find that the corporate uptake of certification is not dependent on good governance indicators, such as the rule of law or regulatory quality, even in countries from the global South. Similarly, Espach (2006, 2009) argues that the regulatory environment (regulatory threat or stringency) cannot explain the variation in private governance uptake in countries from the global South. Prakash and Potoski (2014), nonetheless, find that private governance may compensate for less stringent public environmental regulations in that the effectiveness of private governance in reducing pollution is higher when domestic regulations are less stringent. Yet, contradictions between private standards and national laws may also prevent the effective implementation of private standards (Malets, 2015).

The finding that private governance may rely on the proper functioning of public governance has led some scholars to conclude that the true potential of private governance may only be realized in concrete interaction with public institutions and regulation (Bartley, 2011; Büthe, 2010; Cashore et al., 2007; Cashore and Stone, 2012; D'Hollander and Marx, 2014; Locke, 2013; Mayer and Gereffi, 2010; Overdevest and Zeitlin, 2014). Research that addresses more active engagement of public authorities with private governance can be divided broadly into two main streams, highlighting indirect or direct interventions.

First, most studies have examined indirect interventions, what Abbott and Snidal (2009b, 2010) have called "facilitative orchestration." This type of public engagement refers to low-interventionist domestic or international governmental support for private governance. This support can take several forms (Knudsen and Moon, 2017; Steurer, 2010). In some instances, governments have provided material or financial support to facilitate the development of private governance. In the 1990s in the forestry sector, for example, the government of the United Kingdom (UK) assisted in the development of a national certification standard against which the Forest Stewardship Council (FSC) as a private governance scheme could certify firms. Similarly, in Sweden, the government created legislation that fostered negotiations between the forest industry and environmental NGOs to develop a sustainable forest certification standard (Bell and Hindmoor, 2012: 152–153; Boström, 2003; Cashore et al., 2004; Gale and Haward, 2011; Gulbrandsen, 2004). In other instances, governments have provided financial assistance to companies to get certified by private governance schemes; have recognized certification as a credible policy tool by mandating the compliance of public operations with private standards (e.g., by having public forests certified by private governance schemes); or acted as an information clearing house and diffused knowledge on private governance (Abbott, 2012; Cashore et al., 2006b; Overdevest, 2010). States, in some instances, have also been directly involved in the standard-setting processes of private governance schemes as part of a multi-stakeholder approach (Ponte, 2014). In these cases, states are not the dominant standard-setting actors and do not require or enforce compliance with the rules. Finally, recent research has argued that the domestic institutional context (LME v. CME; political and legal systems) shapes the type of supportive governmental CSR policies that will emerge (Knudsen, 2018; Knudsen et al., 2015).

Second, these facilitative interactions are complemented with what Abbott and Snidal (2009b, 2010) have coined "directive orchestration," which is closest to the topic of this book. This more direct type of public intervention entails states imposing their sovereign authority on private governance. States do this by requiring private governance schemes to adhere to a mandatory substantive or procedural baseline; incorporating private governance in government programs; giving benefits to firms dependent on participation in a private governance scheme (e.g., in public procurement); or developing public voluntary programs (Abbott and Snidal, 2009b). Examples of such public activities have been identified in several sectors, such as forestry, fisheries, and palm oil (Foley and Havice, 2016; Giessen et al., 2016; Gulbrandsen, 2014; Hospes, 2014; Lister, 2011).

Systematic research on direct public interventions, however, is still in its infancy. Testable explanatory frameworks for direct regulatory interventions have not yet been developed. In addition, case studies are often based on positive cases only and highly sector-specific. It is to this part of the literature, therefore, that this book contributes.

Research Contributions and Design

The main contributions of this book are fourfold. First, the analysis disaggregates direct public regulatory interventions in private governance into two forms: standards and procedural regulations. These two types of regulation relate to two separate features of private governance, namely its standard-setting activities and its organizational functioning. While these features are widely discussed in the literature, the focus on explaining public interventions in them, in the form of standards and procedural regulations, is new. This specification allows for a more targeted analysis of direct public interventions by not considering them as one end of a continuum that includes both direct and indirect interventions (cf. Knudsen and Moon, 2017; Lister, 2011), but rather as phenomena to be explained in their own right.

A second contribution of the book is the development of a more nuanced understanding of the political agency of private governance. The active role of private governance schemes in shaping public policy, and private schemes acting more like traditional interest groups, has not received attention so far. While the literature has recognized that private governance schemes are organizations with specific interests, scholars have analyzed these interests from the perspective of power dynamics between different actors involved in the development of private governance or from the perspective of the relationships that private governance schemes have with their competitors. An analysis of the political interests of private governance, therefore, forms an integral part of this book's focus. The analysis elucidates how policy-related activities of private governance schemes shape both their political environment and their own institutional evolution. The empirical analysis shows that private governance lobbying influences the political calculations around support for domestic producers and around the problems resulting from the fragmentation of the private governance market. In addition, it shows how private governance adapts to public interventions to ensure its continued relevance. The improved understanding of private governance lobbying, as a result, will have practical relevance for both private governance practitioners and public policymakers.

Third, the comparative analysis of four diverse issue areas provides an important supplement to the literature on public–private governance interactions. The four case study areas were chosen based on two main selection criteria to ensure comparability across cases. Initially, this book examines private governance for which compliance incentives are market-based. This means that these private governance schemes depend on market demand and support from various nodes in the supply chain for their survival and authority. Therefore, multiple private schemes can compete with one another, while using divergent rules for similar products or production processes, and on that basis vie for the support of actors along the supply chain. This situation can be contrasted with non-market-based private governance, such as the development of harmonized technical standards for electrical and electronic products as performed by the International Electrotechnical Commission, or similar product standardization as overseen by ISO. As Büthe and Mattli (2011) explain, the authority of these organizations in coordinating the harmonization of standards is not disputed, and the basis for harmonization is economic efficiency and the reduction of transaction costs. Public authorities likely interact differently with market-based versus non-market-based private governance, hence the need to clearly distinguish them in a study on public–private governance interactions.

The next case-selection criterion relates to the fact that this book deals with private governance schemes that focus on process standards that describe how a product is produced. Excluded from the analysis, therefore, are private governance schemes dealing with product standards that relate to inherent characteristics of a product. An example of the latter is energy efficiency certification. In that case, a private governance scheme informs the customer about how energy efficient a product is. It does not, however, provide information on so-called credence attributes that are characteristics of a product that the consumer cannot evaluate even after its consumption (Darby and Karni, 1973). Environmental, social, or other conditions under which a product is produced are such credence attributes. Since this difference between product and process standards may influence both consumer and governmental responses to private governance schemes, this book only examines one type of standards, namely process standards.[5]

The final contribution of this book is that it offers a theoretical framework that is testable and potentially generalizable to other issue areas and polities. While public interventions in private governance are by no means EU-specific phenomena, the focus of this book on the EU is motivated by the fact that the EU provides an ideal political setting for researching interactions between public and private governance. From its inception as the European Coal and Steel Community almost seventy years ago, the EU has developed into an important rulemaking polity. Since the early 1970s, it has established a wide range of policies on the environment and sustainable development, areas in which private governance particularly has emerged. Environmental policy has become a core EU policy area, covering the vast amount of the Member States' legislation in this area (Knill and Liefferink, 2013). After the late 1980s, EU policymakers also increasingly committed to sustainable development as a horizontal policy goal (Pallemaerts, 2013). In addition to its regulatory capacity, the EU has experience with the use of nonhierarchical policy instruments, some of which entail the direct involvement of private actors (Eberlein and Kerwer, 2004; Héritier and Rhodes, 2011; Holzinger et al., 2006; Jordan, Benson, et al., 2013; Jordan et al., 2003; Jordan et al., 2005). These elements taken together make the EU a fruitful environment for observing and examining interactions between public and private governance in different issue areas.

As the EU is a unique polity – not a typical state, federal polity, or international organization – we cannot assume that similar dynamics, as discussed in this book, are at play in other polities. The theoretical argument of the book is indeed derived from the four issue areas and has been developed based on within-case analysis and cross-case comparison. This means that the cases are not intended to formally test the theoretical framework. In particular, the cases represent extreme outcomes, in the sense that in the cases of organic agriculture and biofuels production, both standards and procedural regulations were established, while in the cases of fair trade and fisheries, no regulation has yet been developed. The inclusion of these "negative cases" (i.e., cases in which interventions could have occurred but did not) is important from an explanatory standpoint (cf. Mahoney and Goertz, 2004). They offer crucial insights into the policy dynamics surrounding a potential intervention, thereby highlighting the divergent paths taken by policymakers. The inclusion of this variation improves our understanding of public authorities' interventions and increases our confidence in the explanatory power of the independent variables.[6]

This case-selection procedure also implies that cases of either standards or procedural regulation are not directly included in the analysis. As mentioned, however, the fisheries case offers crucial insights into the potential development of procedural regulation. As I will explain more elaborately in Chapter 6, the EU's intervention in the fisheries case was for a long time (and to a certain degree still is) geared toward establishing procedural regulation. This outcome has until now not materialized. Nonetheless, the policy discussions in this issue area provide valuable insights into the dynamics surrounding the development of procedural regulation as a stand-alone type of intervention. In addition, within the boundaries of the case-selection criteria, as outlined, there has been to my knowledge, no EU intervention that involves standards regulation without procedural regulation. Considering the relatively short history of public interventions in private governance, this is not entirely surprising. Empirical research on new and emerging processes (like the ones described in this book) shows that not all possible types of processes can necessarily be directly observed and examined. Yet, recent developments in the fisheries case again offer important insights in this respect, which shed light on the theoretical logic behind the development of standards regulation as a type of intervention. Furthermore, in the final chapter, I will relax the restriction of only assessing EU-level dynamics by also examining public interventions in private governance at the national and international levels to further tease out the logic behind the theoretical framework and assess the generalizability of the book's analysis beyond the EU level.

The analysis relies on a variety of information sources. EU legislation and related policy documents are key sources of information. Most of these documents are publicly available on the websites of the various EU institutions, or through the archived web pages as stored by the Internet Archive's Wayback Machine.[7] In addition to official sources, I gathered documents from private governance schemes, interest organizations, and other relevant stakeholders in the policymaking process. I also conducted seventy-five semi-structured interviews (see Appendix) with interviewees who included policymakers and their staff members, representatives from private governance schemes, interest groups and stakeholder organizations, and experts.[8] Interviews were conducted in person, via Skype, or by telephone between July 2010 and June 2016. Together with primary and secondary literature, these sources were used to provide an historical account of the policymaking processes and to assess the coevolution of public and private governance in the various issue areas.

Outline of the Book

The remainder of the book proceeds as follows: Chapter 2 discusses the theoretical framework. The chapter begins by reviewing the political agency of private governance and comparing it to that of traditional interest groups. It then discusses each of the two main explanatory variables: domestic support for product differentiation and the fragmentation of the private governance market. It highlights how the rationales to intervene in private governance are expressed in the European policymaking processes; how interactions of the variables result in regulatory outcomes; and how the interventions evolve over time.

Chapters 3–6 provide empirics on the EU's regulatory interventions in each of the four issue areas: organic agriculture (Chapter 3), biofuels (Chapter 4), fair trade (Chapter 5), and fisheries (Chapter 6). The empirical chapters are all structured similarly. They begin with an historical overview of the development of private governance in the issue area. These accounts highlight similarities and differences among private governance schemes and provide key insights into what the private governance fields looked like in the period before the EU intervened or considered intervening. Subsequently, the chapters outline the historical development of public policy initiatives and legislative efforts that have resulted either in EU interventions, or the absence of them, in private governance. The chapters show that in all issue areas, discussions about how to respond to private governance started not long after the first private initiatives saw the light of day. Even though discussions around possible interventions often took quite a long time, the empirical accounts elucidate that the shadow of state sovereignty has always been looming. It is a part of the story that is often absent in accounts of private governance. A key task of these empirical chapters, therefore, is to bring to the fore the prevalence of the policy discussions around private governance and their dynamic interactions with the evolution of private schemes in each of the issue areas.

The final chapter of the book offers a comparative perspective on the research findings from each of the issue areas and discusses the impacts of the EU's regulatory interventions on the nature and functioning of private governance. The chapter then returns to the question of the generalizability of the research findings by drawing insights from developments beyond the EU level of policymaking. It closes with a discussion of avenues for further research.

2 | Explaining Public Interventions in Private Governance

Private governance is not a recent phenomenon; neither is state intervention to regulate it. One prominent example takes us back to the medieval period in Europe. The *lex mercatoria*, or law merchant, was a private legal framework that developed around the eleventh century in Europe to structure long-distance trade. As Cutler (2003: 8) explains, the law merchant "operated to support a predominantly private commercial order, generating merchant laws and institutions that operated outside the local political economy of the period." Besides rules governing long-distance trade for which local laws were not applicable, the framework encompassed a dispute resolution mechanism with autonomous merchant courts to settle disputes (Milgrom et al., 1990). The rise of territorial states and capitalist economies, initially with a mercantilist outlook, shifted authority relations between public and private actors from the seventeenth century onward. States integrated commercial law into domestic legal systems to establish uniform national control, thereby reflecting local rulers' interests in domestic wealth accumulation. While differences across countries resulted in different degrees of integration, merchant law did not disappear completely. Some scholars have highlighted its reemergence in a transnational form in the twentieth century as well (Cutler, 2003).

A few centuries after these state interventions in merchant law, we again observe state interventions in private governance for reasons that are equally related to concerns about domestic economic conditions and harmonization. Unlike merchant law, the cases in this book deal with a regulatory type of private governance that addresses negative externalities of production processes. State interventions in private rulemaking should not be surprising. Private governance, after all, entails private actors encroaching on the regulatory domain previously occupied exclusively by public authorities. We should therefore expect incursions in the opposite direction as well, since private governance does not operate in a regulatory or jurisdictional vacuum. Even when private governance emerges to address public governance gaps, public rules usually exist for the broader issue areas in which private governance operates. As a result, public intervention is a possibility that in principle can be acted upon at any particular moment in time. The shadow of public sovereign authority, in other words, is always looming (cf. Héritier and Eckert, 2008). Yet, we still know very little about the conditions under which a public authority will intervene in private governance and the form that such an intervention will take.

This chapter develops an explanatory framework to examine these conditions and relate them to the type of regulation – standards and procedural regulations – a public authority adopts when intervening in private governance. I argue that the type of regulation a public authority adopts depends on the interplay of two variables: the domestic benefits of product differentiation and the fragmentation of the private governance market. These variables relate to the fact that on the one hand, a public authority may intervene in the market for sustainably certified goods to improve the competitive position of domestic producers that are the main rule targets of private governance schemes. On the other hand, a public authority may intervene to structure the private governance market in order to overcome problems resulting from a fragmented market, including supply chain confusion, a lack of credibility of existing private governance schemes, and trade and competitive distortions. While this chapter mainly discusses the explanatory framework in general terms – thereby referring to "public authority" as a generic term – the European setting forms the basis for the framework. The chapter, therefore, also discusses how the rationales for public intervention play out in the context of the EU's decision-making processes.

An analysis of public regulatory interventions in private governance implies that we move beyond merely analyzing rule-based interactions between public policy and private governance. In the literature, such rule-based analyses have dominated. Scholars have, for example, examined whether there is evidence of rule diffusion between private governance and public policy, and whether public and private rules are complementary or competitive (e.g., Cashore et al., 2007; Green, 2017; Green and Auld, 2017; Mills, 2016). An analysis of public policymaking on private governance, however, calls for a more actor-oriented perspective. In the policymaking process, various types of interest groups attempt to influence the regulatory output. Specifically, for the cases discussed in this book, this entails attempts to influence the political calculations around support for domestic economic interests and the fragmentation of the private governance market. Yet, while scholars have long studied traditional interest groups, such as civil society organizations and business associations, they have not yet explicitly studied private governance schemes as interest groups. Considering that public interventions in the form of standards or procedural regulations directly affect private governance schemes, and potentially interfere with their core governance activities, we can expect active interest representation by, or on behalf of, private governance schemes. Therefore, the chapter commences by briefly discussing private governance interest representation before explaining in more detail the logic behind the conditions for a public authority's regulatory interventions in private governance.

The Political Agency of Private Governance

Scholars generally conceptualize private governance as comprising novel systems of rules and compliance verification procedures. Yet, the organizations that develop these rules and procedures have agency and interests that they want to express politically. The literature has addressed agency and interest formation in private governance predominantly from an intraorganizational and an inter-scheme perspective. Scholars have found, for example, that the founders and funders of a private governance scheme impact the scheme's institutional design and problem focus (Auld, 2014b; Bartley, 2007a). Furthermore, outside audiences such as civil society or industry organizations that are not involved in the development of a particular private governance scheme, may also have an interest in the functioning of existing schemes. These audiences can influence the formulation or reformulation of private schemes' rules and procedures through stakeholder dialogues and critical assessments of the functioning or effectiveness of a private scheme. Alternatively, they can play a role in the development of competing or complementary private initiatives (Auld, 2014b; Auld and Renckens, 2017; Cashore, 2002). Interactions among private schemes, moreover, can result in isomorphic tendencies whereby schemes adopt similar types of substantive rules or procedural characteristics (Auld, 2014b; but see Fransen, 2011; Overdevest, 2010). Finally, scholars have assessed how private meta-governance organizations, which govern like-minded private governance schemes (such as the ISEAL Alliance[1]), shape a private governance field through their ideological differences and organizational interests (Fransen, 2015; Loconto and Fouilleux, 2014).

Apart from these intra- and inter-scheme interests, private governance schemes also develop interests with respect to the policy environment in which they operate. It is most likely that such attention to public policy is not immediately present in the early stages of a private governance scheme's existence.[2] A private scheme will first invest in developing standards, designing a verification system and internal governance procedures, and increasing the participation of its regulatory targets. Once the scheme has more firmly established itself in a regulatory area, interest formation around public policy is more likely. Such a shift in focus toward public policy, therefore, can be considered part of the "professionalization" of a private governance scheme as an interest group (cf. Klüver and Saurugger, 2013).

Most of the private governance schemes covered in this book exhibit the features that scholars identify as characteristic of interest groups. Beyers et al. (2008) argue that three features are central in this respect: organization, political interests, and informality. First, private governance schemes have formal organizational features through which to structure their political activities. These organizational features distinguish interest groups from less formally organized civil society movements or public opinion. Not all private governance schemes, however, are interest "groups" per se, since they are not "aggregating (or grouping) the preferences of some constituency (individuals, firms or organisations)" (Beyers et al., 2008: 1108–1109). Rather, they are interest "organizations," much like individual firms or institutions (such as universities or hospitals) that are studied by interest group scholars as being "equivalent to interest groups" (Beyers et al., 2008: 1108).

The second feature that private governance schemes share with interest groups is that they possess political interests, in that they can aim to influence public policy outcomes. As mentioned, most private schemes will likely not focus on influencing public policy in the early stages of their development. Rather, they develop these interests by degree and transform from latent or "potential" interest organizations into active ones (Truman, 1951). The incentives for this transformation can be multiple. The focus of this book will be on the triggers that relate to actions (or nonactions) by a public authority, and changes in market conditions, both in the market for goods and the market for private governance schemes.

Finally, Beyers et al. refer to informality as a third key feature of interest groups. This feature entails that interest groups do not have the intention to "seek political office or compete in elections" (Beyers et al., 2008: 1108). Instead, they seek to "pursue their [political] goals through frequent informal interactions with politicians and bureaucrats" (Beyers et al., 2008: 1106–1107). Klüver (2013b: 6) translates this feature into what she calls "private status," which implies that "interest groups are not seeking public office and that they are not public institutions which are funded and subject to the state." To a large degree, private governance schemes display these features of informality and private status. In some instances, state actors have been involved in the formative stages of private governance schemes, or they remain involved as stakeholders. Yet, those schemes' private status is guaranteed by them not having been created or run solely by states, while their governing authority is also not derived from the state, but from the market (Cashore, 2002).

Considering these similarities with the way interest group scholars have conceptualized societal actors as interest groups, one can expect private governance schemes to take up activities with which interest groups traditionally engage, such as political interest representation and lobbying. Despite these similarities, however, private governance schemes are distinct from traditional interest groups, which justifies identifying them as a new type of interest group. There are two main reasons for this. First, private governance schemes often embody "Baptist-bootlegger coalitions" of business and NGOs (Yandle, 1983, 2011). These actors in the coalition represent both economic and socio-environmental interests, which support the same goal or policy (e.g., sustainable production) for different reasons (e.g., profit versus normative reasons). Traditional interest groups, in contrast, only embody one of these interests. Corporations, business associations, NGOs, and consumer organizations all represent a particular interest, but it would be difficult to argue convincingly that they encompass both economic and broader societal interests. While "single-interest" private governance schemes do exist (i.e., those that are established solely by individual corporations, business associations, or NGOs), a norm has emerged that private governance schemes must include multiple stakeholders, or some semblance of a representation of diverse interests in their governance structures, in order to be considered legitimate (Auld et al., 2015; Bernstein, 2011; Dingwerth and Pattberg, 2009; Mena and Palazzo, 2012).

Since private governance schemes can claim to represent a diverse set of interests, they may be more influential than traditional interest groups. Drawing from the EU context, Klüver (2013b), for example, argues that three types of goods determine interest groups' influence: policy-relevant information, citizen support, and economic power. Unlike traditional interest groups, private governance schemes can potentially provide all three of these goods at once. First, building on their core regulatory activities, private governance schemes have policy-relevant information concerning rules about sustainable production processes and the verification of such rules. The schemes develop and implement these rules and as the empirical chapters will show, policymakers can learn from innovations in private rulemaking when devising public policy. Second, private governance schemes can claim to represent citizen interests because of the involvement of civil society groups as founders or participating stakeholders. The legitimacy of private governance schemes is indeed at least partly based on the participation of civil society groups in their internal governance processes. Finally, private governance schemes embody economic power through the producers and other business organizations that are involved in the schemes as regulatory targets, founders, or participating stakeholders. The economic power of private governance schemes may differ greatly depending on their level of corporate uptake. Yet, the fact that private schemes specifically address corporate sustainability and target economic operators, results in them inherently possessing the potential to represent economic power.

As private governance schemes can potentially provide these three goods at once, they may have a strong voice in the policy process, with policymakers explicitly seeking their input on and support for public interventions. In addition, we can expect that the content of a private scheme's rules and procedures and its position in the market, will further determine its policy influence. Schemes conforming to norms of rigorous standard-setting and verification (such as expert-based standard-setting, or independent third-party auditing) (Potoski and Prakash, 2009; van der Ven, 2015), and schemes with a larger market share, can have a stronger voice in the policy process due to their

perceived legitimacy and authority. These features of private governance schemes are considered important since "trust and credibility
have emerged as the strongest lobbying currency in Brussels" (Coen
and Richardson, 2009: 7).

A second reason why private governance schemes are distinct from
traditional interest groups builds on the observation that private
schemes can provide policy-relevant information on sustainability
rules and verification procedures. This feature of private governance
schemes implies that their organizational interests extend beyond the
details of any particular public policy option. As political actors with
policy preferences, private governance schemes may lobby governments for many of the same reasons as traditional interest groups,
including to provide expert knowledge, to seek policy change or pre-
serve policy continuity, and to attain (material) benefits (Beyers et al.,
2008). However, their interests also encompass their own governance
space – the autonomy to govern their regulatory targets and organize
their governance approach as they see fit. Unlike traditional interest
groups, private governance schemes bring to the table a particular set
of rules and governance practices to which certain societal actors – the
regulatory targets – adhere, and others, such as consumers or civil
society actors, defer. This compliance and deference forms the basis
on which private governance has acquired governing authority (Cashore, 2002; Green, 2014). Since public policy interventions may entail
an intrusion into this private governance space, private schemes are
confronted with a potential conflict of governing authority on which
they will likely act. In other words, they will defend their own survival
as governors.

While traditional interest groups are equally concerned with their
organizational survival (Lowery, 2007; Schmitter and Streeck, 1999),
the difference with private governance schemes is that the latter aim to
survive as rulemaking governors (cf. Avant et al., 2010). Moreover, the
funders and founders of private governance schemes, as well as their
regulatory targets, have vested interests in the survival of these schemes
as rule makers. These actors, as a result, may act on behalf of private
governance schemes when lobbying public authorities. This can occur,
for example, when the private schemes do not yet have the capacity
(resources, personnel) to do so. Firms, NGOs, and other actors associated with a private scheme may already be more engaged with interest
representation and lobbying and hence, act on a private scheme's

behalf. Moreover, private governance has become a significant commercial undertaking. Schemes can demand fees for membership, or for the use of their on-product label. In addition, private governance has provided a boost to the sector of independent auditors that get paid to verify firms' compliance with private rules (Auld and Renckens, 2019).

As a result, one can expect that private governance schemes, when targeting public policy, will strive to arrive at a policy outcome that allows them sufficient freedom to continue to perform and retain their preexisting governance functions and authority. Such an endeavor will entail bargaining over the implications of public interventions and opposition against intervention, when private governance schemes' governance space is being threatened.

Analyzing private governance interest representation is important, since a potential loss of private governance space resulting from public intervention can be considered a private equivalent to "sovereignty costs." As discussed in the international relations literature on legalization and delegation (Abbott and Snidal, 2000), sovereignty costs refer to costs that states incur when devising international hard law, which is defined as mandatory, precise, and entailing the delegation of interpretation and implementation functions. These sovereignty costs amount to a reduction of decision-making authority for individual states and "more fundamental encroachments on state sovereignty" when "international arrangements impinge on the relations between a state and its citizens or territory, the traditional hallmarks of (Westphalian) sovereignty" (Abbott and Snidal, 2000: 436–437). When discussing both the directive and facilitative orchestration of private governance by international organizations, however, Abbott and Snidal argue that "[w]hile firms, NGOs and RSS [regulatory standard-setting] schemes are protective of their independence, they do not suffer the 'sovereignty costs' experienced by states in the face of supranational authority" (Abbott and Snidal, 2010: 326). In contrast to Abbott and Snidal, I argue that private governance schemes do incur such costs when a public authority intervenes to regulate their functioning. Even if both private governance schemes and public authorities have an interest in such regulation, and they attempt to find a compromise between public and private governing authority, public regulatory intervention nonetheless implies that private governance schemes incur deliberate costs to their functioning in the form of limitations to their private governance space.

The conceptualization of private governance schemes as interest groups is important for the further development of the explanatory framework to follow. The reason is that the interest representation activities of private governance schemes – like those of traditional interest groups – can influence policymakers' decisions on regulatory interventions. They do this by changing the political calculations around the domestic benefits of product differentiation and the fragmentation of the private governance market, the two main explanatory variables discussed in this book. The chapter now turns to the logic of these two variables.

Domestic Benefits of Product Differentiation

One of the core rationales of private governance is the creation of a market for products that carry claims about the social and environmental impacts of their production processes. Private governance schemes attempt to address a specific market failure, namely an information asymmetry in the supply chain (Akerlof, 1970; Rametsteiner, 2002). Business uses private governance to inform stakeholders about its sustainability activities. Stakeholders are not always able to correctly assess the quality of a business' CSR efforts, especially when certain product features such as the conditions under which goods are produced are impossible to determine, even after consumption (so-called credence goods) (Darby and Karni, 1973).[3] Private governance addresses this supply chain information asymmetry by signaling product features, and by doing so, assists in distinguishing responsible businesses and responsibly produced goods from their less sustainable competitors. It provides information on unobservable product features and thereby limits the search and information costs of economic actors downstream in the supply chain.

Private governance aims to garner support for such product differentiation in different parts of the supply chain – from the producer all the way to the consumer – by offering or promising market access, price premiums, and improved reputations; by engaging in naming-and-shaming campaigns; and by appealing to the ethical consciousness of consumers (Baron, 2009; Cashore, 2002; Prakash and Potoski, 2006b). While initially not imposing their sovereign rulemaking authority on private governance, public authorities can structure product differentiation – and thereby engage in market-creating behavior – by providing explicit public support for the development of a market for sustainably produced goods.

Why would a public authority be interested in intervening for this reason? This section develops the argument that public authorities base their support for product differentiation on furthering the causes and competitive positions of the domestic regulatory targets of private governance, which in most cases are comprised of producers in the upstream part of the supply chain.[4] Public authorities can do this by using both standards and procedural regulations to ensure that producers can credibly distinguish themselves from noncompliant competitors, in particular, non-domestic ones. Note that in the context of this book, "domestic" transcends the traditional boundaries of the nation-state and refers to the European Union as a whole, encompassing a combination of EU-level interests (as expressed by the European Commission and the European Parliament) and national interests (as expressed by the Member States in the Council of Ministers and the European Council).

Supporting Domestic Producers

There are several incentives for a public authority to support domestic producers. Initially, intervention can aim to provide explicit support to producers that are already involved in sustainable production, or that at least differentiate their products based on such claims. These producers contribute to the provision of public goods, such as sustainability and environmental improvement. Policies in support of responsible producers are a concrete way in which public authorities can garner further support for their broader sustainability goals (Knudsen and Moon, 2017: 187), and these contributions are highly valued by a public authority like the EU. With more than 400 pieces of environmental legislation, the EU is responsible for the vast majority of its Member States' policies in this area (Delreux and Happaerts, 2016). Producers may also welcome some degree of protection, for example, in the form of a legal baseline standard to distinguish their products more clearly from less performing products in the market, whether produced domestically or imported. Similarly, they may be able to convince more consumers of the veracity of their claims when the private governance scheme they use adheres to publicly defined procedural criteria.

Next, public support for product differentiation allows new producers to become involved with sustainable production. Public support can provide diversification opportunities to producers by enlarging the market for sustainably produced goods. If niche markets for sustainable goods already exist, public support can offer those markets an opportunity to mature, which further contributes to broader environmental and sustainability goals. A public authority will particularly act on this opportunity when market demand for sustainably produced products is evident or expected in the future. Market demand may be the result of changing consumer preferences, civil society pressure, or a more generally increased social awareness about sustainability. This market growth potential is crucial to attracting producers to invest in changing their production practices and for them to enjoy the network effects of doing so (such as through enhanced reputations) (cf. Gulbrandsen, 2004; Prakash and Potoski, 2006b: 17–25). In addition, offering diversification opportunities can be strategically opportune to compensate a group of producers for a past or expected future loss. This loss can have resulted, for example, from a policy change in another issue area that reduced financial support to producers or that resulted in additional costs to an industry. Offering new diversification opportunities can even ensure the survival of an industry – in particular, precarious sectors like agriculture. In this way, regulatory policies can be employed for (re)distributive purposes.

Finally, public support may be a response to other countries acquiring a first-mover advantage or to the expectation that other countries may intervene to this end, which could negatively affect the competitive position of domestic producers. This is particularly the case when the foreign market is an important export market. Following the logic of Vogel's (1995, 1997) "California effect," or "trading up," argument, a public standard developed in an important export market may force exporters to this market to adopt this standard when there is a credible threat of market access restrictions. While often applied to product standards, Vogel argues that the logic may hold for production standards in particular when related to natural resources (Greenhill et al., 2009; Prakash and Potoski, 2006a; Vogel, 1997: 564). Since firms will not necessarily develop different production processes for different markets, they will adopt the export market's standard for products sold in the domestic market as well. Yet, this adoption may place these firms in a competitively disadvantageous position compared with other domestic companies not impacted by the foreign standard. As a result, export-oriented firms have an interest in pressuring domestic regulators to adjust the home standard to that of the foreign market. They will likely receive support from environmental NGOs for this effort, thereby creating Baptist-bootlegger coalitions. The possibility of a first-mover advantage and preventing an adjustment to a foreign standard, therefore, may create a powerful incentive for a public authority to intervene in support of domestic producers. As a large market, a polity like the EU could use this advantage to externalize its regulation and shape regulation globally (Bach and Newman, 2007; Damro, 2012).

These rationales for public intervention can be a direct result of the functioning of existing private governance schemes. Instead of intervening, a public authority could choose to assist domestic producers with gaining access to private governance schemes. A common response from public authorities, for instance, has been to carry part of the costs for producers to be certified (Cashore et al., 2006a; Lister, 2011). Existing private governance schemes, however, may be ill-suited for domestic producers. The schemes may be too strict, not credible enough in the market, or not adapted to local socioeconomic, cultural, or climatic realities. Furthermore, as Auld (2014b: 13–14) has shown, market demand may prevent private schemes from opening up their program to more participants, since producers that were early adopters want to reap the profit benefits of participation without sharing them with their competitors. In these circumstances, a public authority may want to intervene to facilitate certification for domestic producers.

Private governance schemes can also be supportive of public interventions in these situations. Public intervention can provide a stepping stone for producers to engage with private governance schemes that are stricter or more encompassing, and for which there is a particular demand in the market. In that respect, a public intervention can provide the basis for an enlarged future clientele for private governance schemes. The latter then have an incentive to lobby policymakers and to have them adopt a public standard or procedural rules that are close to or compatible with their private standards and procedures. A private governance scheme will withdraw support for public intervention when it disadvantages the scheme. This can be the case when a public authority creates a public standard or scheme that directly competes with private schemes, favors certain private schemes over others, or limits the overall functioning of private governance.

Mitigating Domestic Support

Despite these rationales for public intervention based on product differentiation, three factors will decrease the likelihood of an intervention. First, public intervention in support of domestic producers is less likely when the adjustment costs for producers are considered too high. Such costs refer to the changes that producers need to make to comply with public sustainable production rules and governance procedures. The level at which public sustainability rules are set has distributional implications and will be subject to political conflict, which may prevent public intervention altogether. On the one hand, adjustment costs are related to the existing private rules in the market. Similar to private governance schemes, producers that are already operating according to a particular set of private rules will want public authorities to adopt those rules, or will prefer public rules that are at least as stringent as the private ones with which they are already complying. Producers operating according to weaker or less encompassing rules, and producers opposed to public intervention, will want to avoid (strict) public rules. For them, the adjustment costs to meet strict public rules may be too high, and such rules may lead to producers being pushed out of the market. On the other hand, the level of the adjustment costs is related to existing legislation that requires producers to meet a certain level of sustainability. Producers may oppose public rules intended to further differentiate the market for sustainable products when these rules are stricter than existing legislation, or entail additional changes to production processes. This will particularly be the case when the existing legal rules are already imposing significant costs and producers are struggling to comply. Hence, existing requirements may place limits on the growth potential of the market for sustainably produced goods.

For a public intervention to have the desired effect, therefore, adjustment costs need to be sufficiently low; otherwise, too few producers will be able to shift toward more sustainable production practices. A public authority can attempt to alleviate adjustment costs by providing technical or financial support. This assistance is necessary when producers face significant costs to adhere to (even minimal) public rules, or when such rules favor foreign producers that are already producing according to higher standards and are thereby threatening the competitiveness of domestic producers. A public authority, as a result, can decide not to intervene when doing so would in fact undermine domestic production opportunities and when it would not sufficiently compensate adjustment costs.

Second, considering that public regulatory interventions have distributional impacts, the extent to which certain interests dominate the regulatory process and their preferences for the status quo, will influence the likelihood of public intervention. A traditional argument is that concentrated interests (such as business interests) are better able to persuade policymakers to grant them higher prices or market entry in exchange for campaign funding or votes (Peltzman, 1976, 1989; Stigler, 1971). In this respect, scholars have also referred to the "structural dependence of the state on capital," the "structural power" of business, and the "privileged position" of business with respect to the state (Lindblom, 1977; Przeworski and Wallerstein, 1988). Since the state relies on investments for economic growth, and politicians rely on the economy doing well to be reelected, the expectation is that public policy will cater to the demands of business. Diffuse interests (such as consumer interests) in contrast, have difficulty competing with business interests. Groups representing diffuse interests are less successful in acquiring specific benefits from policymakers since they face higher collective action costs, and find it more difficult to organize themselves and disseminate information (Mattli and Woods, 2009; Olson, 1965).

Despite this potential bias toward business interests, environmental and sustainability policies in a private governance context are somewhat distinct issue areas. The reason is that, in these issue areas, policymaking is often not the simplistic opposition of the interests of business versus those of civil society. Producers are also pitted against one another: Producers that engage with private governance are pitted against those that do not. And within the group of the engaged producers, there are potential conflicts depending on the private governance scheme they choose to partner with. On this basis, producers will participate in diverse coalitions with civil society actors. We can assume that environmental NGOs will look favorably upon producers that support sustainable production practices and credible private governance schemes; this facilitates the emergence of new producer-civic interest coalitions. Indeed, as I have just argued, private governance schemes often embody such Baptist-bootlegger coalitions and they can claim to represent producers with a vested interest in sustainable production. Taken together, the political activities of these actors and coalitions in comparison to more traditional and status quo–oriented interests, and policymakers' responsiveness to their policy demands, will therefore influence the likelihood of public intervention.

Finally, interventions by a public authority in support of domestic producers are constrained by the international trade regime under the World Trade Organization (WTO), which guards against undue protectionism and trade discrimination. The principle of nondiscrimination prevents the discrimination of "like" products from different trading partners (granting them most-favored-nation status), and prevents discrimination between domestic and foreign "like" products (national treatment principle). The international trade regime does allow general exceptions for public policy purposes, such as those related to protecting "human, animal or plant life or health," and to the "conservation of exhaustible natural resources" (WTO, 2017a, 2017b).

However, it remains uncertain how, and the extent to which, the rules of the WTO constrain private governance and public authorities using or referencing private governance. For the purposes of this book, the main issue is whether trade discrimination is allowed based on non-product-related processes or production methods (npr-PPMs). The question is "whether products may be treated differently because of the way in which they have been produced even if the production method used does not leave a trace in the final product, i.e. even if the physical characteristics of the final product remain identical" (WTO, 2017b). Establishing the "likeness" of products produced with different production methods that do not leave a trace is difficult, and the WTO recommends a case-by-case approach in this regard (WTO, 2017b). Many private governance schemes include substantive rules pertaining to npr-PPMs, such as on animal welfare, or on the environmental management of natural resources. Critics have argued that private governance may create nontariff trade barriers on this basis. This is the case, for example, when retailers demand compliance with specific private standards (Fuchs et al., 2009; Pattberg, 2006). The ambiguity is then centered around whether the WTO rules (and in particular the rules of the Technical Barriers to Trade [TBT] Agreement) apply when public authorities reference, endorse, or incorporate private governance (Bernstein and Hannah, 2008: 585–592; Botterill and Daugbjerg, 2011: 495–498; WTO, 2018).

This uncertainty regarding the applicability of WTO rules can prevent interventions by public authorities. It can prevent them from establishing a sustainable production standard or from enrolling private governance as a public policy instrument. Exporting countries can use this uncertainty strategically. If a country's exports would be negatively affected by another country's regulatory interventions in private governance, a threat to challenge the regulating country under the WTO dispute resolution mechanism could be sufficient to prevent interventions to occur in the first place. The fact that there are no concrete precedents in this respect contributes to the uncertainty.

In summary, when a public authority considers product differentiation, as originally provided by private governance, to be beneficial to domestic producers, there is a higher likelihood of public intervention. These benefits can relate to supporting producers already engaged in sustainable production, creating diversification opportunities for producers, or establishing or responding to a first-mover advantage with respect to other polities. This support to domestic producers is appealing to policymakers, since in this way they can support existing public sustainability goals, foster growth markets of sustainably produced products, and become global regulatory shapers. Producers, civil society actors, and private governance schemes may for different reasons offer support for such public interventions. However, the likelihood of public intervention decreases when producers face adjustment costs that are considered too high, when status quo–oriented interests dominate the regulatory process, and when there is uncertainty around whether public interventions will violate the rules of the international trade regime.

Fragmentation of the Private Governance Market

The second variable that explains public intervention in private governance is the fragmentation of the private governance market. I refer to a "market" since any private actor can, in principle, develop its own private governance initiative, while the voluntary nature of such initiatives implies that producers can freely decide to sign on to existing schemes, creating what Vogel (2005) has called a "market for virtue." A fragmented private governance market is defined as encompassing a diverse set of private governance schemes in terms of their governance characteristics, such as the stringency of their standards, their verification procedures, and stakeholder involvement, and in terms of the sheer number of schemes operating in the market and their relationship to each other (e.g., complementary or competitive). The argument developed in this section is that a larger fragmentation of the private governance market will increase the likelihood of public intervention when fragmentation results in second-order information asymmetries, or in trade and competitive distortions. A public authority can achieve harmonization of a fragmented market by imposing either a public substantive standard or public procedural rules, depending on which of these will more likely tackle the cause of the fragmentation.

Addressing Market Fragmentation

Second-order information asymmetries are the primary reason why a fragmented private governance market increases the likelihood of public intervention. These asymmetries at the level of the market for private governance schemes arise from the fact that individual private schemes each attempt to address information asymmetries in the supply chain, as discussed. A private governance market that is fragmented creates an additional market failure (hence a second-order effect). This is the case because fragmentation confronts producers and downstream businesses, stakeholders, and consumers with diverse claims about products' sustainability features and with different types of private governance schemes making these claims. Second-order information asymmetries exist when it is unclear (or unknown) how different private governance schemes compare in terms of the stringency and scope of their standards, internal governance procedures, or compliance verification processes.

Several adverse effects follow from this uncertainty, which may warrant public intervention. First, while private governance intends to reduce the transaction costs for producers and downstream businesses and consumers, a fragmented market may again increase transaction costs. Producers and other stakeholders need to invest time and resources in acquiring information on the content and quality of private governance schemes. This situation may lead to a duplication of certification efforts by rule targets, if different segments of a market have different preferences for private schemes. Next, fragmentation can create opportunities for firms to engage in forum shopping among the different schemes. Firms can use the confusion around private sustainability claims to choose compliance with less stringent schemes, thereby potentially compromising effective environmental improvements. Lastly, and as a result of this forum shopping, uncertainty and confusion about private sustainability claims can create problems of legitimacy for individual schemes, and eventually undermine the credibility of an entire field of private governance schemes. This can also lead to attempts by business, NGOs, and private governance schemes to undermine the credibility of competing schemes (Abbott and Snidal, 2009b: 551; Bernstein and Cashore, 2007).

Another reason for a fragmented private governance market to increase the likelihood of public intervention is that fragmentation can lead to distortions in trade and competition. These distortions emerge when differences among private governance schemes hinder products certified by a scheme in one market from having access to a market in another region or country. When there exists strong consumer or supply chain recognition of a particular scheme in a given market, the marketing and sale of products under a different scheme from outside that market may be difficult. Furthermore, private schemes may not acknowledge outside schemes when they rely on different standards or governance procedures. By not allowing the marketing of imported products under a local scheme, private governance schemes intend to retain their scheme-specific characteristics and position in their local market. In either of these situations, a public authority may want to intervene to facilitate trade and improve competitive conditions by harmonizing or coordinating sustainability standards and governance procedures.

These trade and competitive distortions are particularly relevant for federal or federal-like polities such as the EU, with strongly integrated markets. The emergence of subnational or Member State–specific private governance schemes can offer a strong incentive for public regulatory intervention. The distortions that result from a fragmented private governance market may need to be addressed to safeguard the unity of the internal market. These harmonization efforts can either be a direct response to private governance fragmentation or a response to public authorities at a lower political level responding to such fragmentation. The latter situation occurs when diverse private governance schemes operate within one polity, and the fragmentation is addressed by a public authority engaging in harmonization efforts at the subnational or Member State level. These public responses can subsequently lead to trade and competitive distortions, and elicit a demand for harmonization at the higher federal or supranational level.

Private governance schemes and their associated stakeholders (producers, NGOs, funders) can strategically support public interventions addressing fragmentation. They can problematize fragmentation when private governance schemes with unsubstantiated claims or substandard procedures populate the market. In that way, private schemes can try to outlaw or restrict market access to competitors, the goal being to arrive at a monopolistic, or at minimum, an oligopolistic private governance market structure. Even identifying the possibility of fragmentation in the future, when no such situation currently exists, may be used to elicit public intervention. In particular, we can expect the problematization of fragmentation to be exercised by more credible or legitimate private governance schemes, namely those schemes whose standards and procedural features are such that they are not considered greenwash (cf. Auld et al., 2008; Dingwerth and Pattberg, 2009; Potoski and Prakash, 2009; van der Ven, 2015). Such schemes will have an interest in banning from the market all clearly fraudulent private governance schemes in order to prevent the legitimization of underperforming schemes.

Irrespective of whether the drivers of public intervention are second-order information asymmetries or trade and competitive distortions, a public authority will again have to take into account the external constraints imposed by the international trade regime. Since both standards and procedural regulations can be employed to overcome fragmentation and harmonize the market, the same restrictions apply as discussed earlier.

Private Solutions to Market Fragmentation

Apart from problematizing fragmentation and supporting public intervention, actors in the private governance market can attempt to provide private solutions to fragmentation problems. That is, regardless of the source of the fragmentation problems in the private governance market, private actors can reduce the likelihood of public intervention in several ways (Cafaggi and Janczuk, 2010; den Hertog, 2010; Werner, 2012: 152–154). First, private governance schemes can engage in mutual recognition requiring that schemes acknowledge one another's standards and governance procedures as equivalent, without them having to be the same. The benefit is that products that comply with private governance scheme A's requirements would also be allowed to be certified under and use the on-product label of private scheme B. This solution can be convenient for firms, since it prevents them from having to be certified multiple times when marketing their products in different markets.

Next, a more far-reaching type of coordination among private governance schemes consists of a harmonization of their respective standards and procedural features. This harmonization can be done on a one-by-one basis between individual schemes, or by developing an umbrella program that covers many similar schemes. The creation of Fairtrade Labelling Organizations International (FLO) in 1997, as Chapter 5 discusses, is an example of such a harmonization effort. This initiative brought together seventeen national fair trade labeling initiatives under one overarching scheme. As an alternative to such issue-based harmonization, private governance schemes can establish an umbrella program that develops a standard for private governance schemes in the form of a standard-for-standards (Glasbergen, 2011). Private schemes can use membership of the overarching institution and compliance with its standards and governance procedures as a signaling device. One example of such a program is the ISEAL Alliance. ISEAL is a partnership between several transnational certification programs and accreditation bodies. It was established in 2002 with the aim of developing a set of good practices to assist private governance schemes in creating sustainability standards and properly designing their procedural features (Bernstein and van der Ven, 2017).[5]

Several barriers to private governance convergence and overarching coordination exist, which may again increase the likelihood of public intervention. Fransen (2011) and Auld (2014b), for example, attribute these barriers to conflicts between schemes based on their varied problem definitions and solutions, and their organizational interests. The latter type of conflict refers to founders' vested interests in retaining the specific character and market advantage of a given private governance scheme. These conflicts are a direct result of the negotiated nature of private schemes' emergence, whereby various types of stakeholders establish a delicate compromise between socio-environmental and economic concerns (cf. Bartley, 2007b). Coordination efforts with other schemes may threaten this compromise, since they will inevitably result in the (partial) loss of a private scheme's (geographic or issue-based) identity and consumer recognition.

Yet, private governance schemes may actively oppose public interventions that intend to address a lack of private coordination. Schemes can argue that public intervention aimed at harmonizing the market for private schemes by means of common public standards or procedures will eliminate more than just differences in the stringency of private standards or procedural characteristics. Private governance market fragmentation may be the direct result of schemes developing according to different private governance logics, giving them different functions in the market (Auld, 2014a; Auld et al., 2015). Some private schemes, for example, start with the intention of empowering marginalized producers in the global political economy (called a "logic of empowerment"). This starting point results in these schemes placing a larger emphasis on certain problem definitions and solutions, such as community building and local-level stakeholder engagement. Other schemes start from a more commercial, "big business" CSR perspective. This approach entails that private schemes have broader economic interests whereby they have to placate the interests of powerful economic actors, such as retailers or big brands. In that respect, these schemes will place a higher value on issues such as consistency in control mechanisms and product quality (a "logic of control"). Harmonizing these diverse approaches by means of a public intervention may lead to the elimination of these more fundamental differences among private governance schemes, which can result in an overall downgraded and less effective private governance market.

Thus, fragmentation should be considered a relative concept, the value of which is in the eye of the beholder (Biermann et al., 2009: 17–18). The fragmentation of the private governance market cannot necessarily be determined on the basis of the number of schemes alone. What matters is the quality or nature of the fragmentation. How the private schemes relate to one another in terms of issues they address and how they address them will result in fragmentation being considered more or less problematic. In other words, the framing of fragmentation as a problem and the receptiveness of policymakers to a particular framing, will influence the likelihood of public intervention in private governance.

In summary, there is a higher likelihood of public intervention when the fragmentation of the private governance market results in second-order information asymmetries or trade and competitive distortions. Fragmentation can result in confusion in the supply chain around the sustainability claims that are made, thereby increasing transaction costs, fostering forum shopping, and undermining the legitimacy of individual private governance schemes as well as the entire market. Furthermore, trade and competitive distortions emerge from differences among private governance schemes that can hinder market access and commercial cooperation among schemes. Private schemes and stakeholders can problematize this fragmentation in an attempt to achieve market dominance. Regardless of the source of the fragmentation, a public authority will still need to take into account the restrictions imposed by the international trade regime. The likelihood of public intervention is reduced, however, when private governance schemes are able to structure a fragmented market themselves by means of mutual recognition, the harmonization of standards and procedural features, or the creation of a meta-governance institution. In addition, private schemes can invoke divergent logics of private governance functioning and their place in the market to justify a certain level of market fragmentation, and thereby stave off public intervention. Table 2.1 summarizes the rationales for public interventions.

EU Policymaking Dynamics

How are these rationales to intervene in private governance expressed in the European policymaking processes? To start, it is necessary to acknowledge that the EU decision-making processes differ across the issue areas. This implies that not all EU institutions play an equally important role at all times. The cases in this book deal with regulatory policies and in all the issue areas the European Commission has the monopoly on proposing legislation. Until the 2007 Treaty of Lisbon, which entered into force in December 2009, the Council of Ministers had the sole competence to legislate in the cases of organic agriculture and fisheries, which fall under the Common Agricultural Policy (CAP) and the Common Fisheries Policy, respectively. The European Parliament was involved in these decision-making processes on a consultative basis, which meant that the Council of Ministers could not make a

Table 2.1 *Rationales for public regulatory interventions*

	Increasing Likelihood of Public Intervention	Decreasing Likelihood of Public Intervention
Domestic benefits of product differentiation	– Support for existing sustainable production and creation of new diversification opportunities, especially when there is market growth potential – First-mover advantage	– High adjustment costs for producers – Dominant status quo interests – Possibility of international trade regime violations
Fragmentation of the private governance market	– Second-order information asymmetries – Trade and competitive distortions	– Private governance coordination – Divergent private governance logics – Possibility of international trade regime violations

decision until the Parliament had offered its position on a legislative proposal, although the Council was not bound by the Parliament's position. Since the Lisbon Treaty, the European Parliament has had co-decision competence in these two issue areas, making it an equal player with the Council of Ministers in the decision-making process. For the biofuels and the fair trade cases discussed in this book, this co-decision procedure has consistently applied, even before 2009. However, as we will see, not all cases have proceeded to the full legislative process, as the European Commission did not always put forward formal legislative proposals.

The European Commission, indeed, plays a central role. For both the Common Agricultural Policy and the Common Fisheries policy, the European Commission has a strong policymaking role, considering its agenda-setting function is embedded in the European treaties

(Churchill and Owen, 2010; Roederer-Rynning, 2015; Wallace and Reh, 2015: 99–102). Furthermore, both for regulatory policies in general (Majone, 1994) and production-process regulations specifically (Pollack, 1997; Young and Wallace, 2000: 24–25; Zito, 2005), scholars have argued that the European Commission often plays the important role of policy entrepreneur or policy activist. Since process-based regulations imposed by Member States do not generally lead to trade barriers (and hence violate EU internal market principles), and since the EU treaties do not cover private process-based regulations (as the ones discussed in this book do), there is no strong treaty-based incentive for public intervention (Ankersmith, 2017: 81–95, 105–108; Pollack, 1997; Scharpf, 1996).[6] Yet, in the capacity of policy entrepreneur or policy activist, the European Commission can put these issues on the agenda and push legislation forward for internal market or other reasons. Once the European Commission sets the legislative process in motion, policy change is very likely (Eising, Rasch, and Rozbicka, 2017: 941; Klüver, 2013a: 60). For example, in issues related to social and environmental concerns, the European Commission has in the past taken up this activist or entrepreneurial role, especially earlier on in the EU's existence. It has done so to address competitive distortions resulting from process-based regulations, to level the playing field for operators, and to further non-internal market causes, such as the increase of environmental protection or the expansion of its own competences and authority with respect to the other EU institutions (in particular the Council of Ministers) (Pollack, 1997; Tallberg, 2007: 197). Policymaking around private governance therefore fits with this profile. Even though private governance has existed for several decades, it is still a relatively new and even a niche issue for a public authority like the EU to deal with. This is certainly the case for the issue areas discussed in this book. Except for organic agriculture, the initial policymaking discussions started between the late 1990s and early 2000s. Furthermore, the cases deal with environmental and sustainability issues, while also being primarily about market regulation and market growth. The European Commission is therefore receptive to taking on the role of policy entrepreneur on these issues.[7]

A common expectation in the literature is that the European Commission, as a strategic actor, formulates proposals that can receive the support of other key institutional actors in the decision-making process (Dür et al., 2015: 957; Naurin, 2015: 145; Princen, 2007: 33).

Stakeholder input is one way in which the European Commission gains insights in the potential obstacles toward getting a legislative proposal through the decision-making process, both in the Council of Ministers and the European Parliament (Klüver, 2013a: 61–63; Thomson, 2015: 201–202). The European Commission has a tradition of information gathering and broad consultations to inform and build support for its proposals, and through which it can gauge stakeholder groups' preferences. This process involves organizing workshops and conferences, establishing expert groups, developing formal and informal stakeholder consultations, and direct lobbying by interest groups (Broscheid and Coen, 2007; Kohler-Koch and Finke, 2007; Thatcher, 2015: 311; Young, 2006: 384). Bunea (2013: 552) argues in this respect that the pre-legislative and information-gathering stages that are dominated by the European Commission offer the "most favourable points of the policymaking process during which interest organizations can affect the content of European legislation." By doing so, the European Commission forms a receptive venue for these interests to be heard (Princen, 2012).

The novel and niche character of developing regulation for private governance, furthermore, allows for the formation of new interest coalitions between policymakers and interest groups, including coalitions that encompass interest groups that are not part of traditional policy communities (Peterson, 2009: 112–113; Richardson, 2015: 11–15). While scholars have argued that business interests are dominant in the EU policymaking process, the story is more complex with respect to sustainability policies. Studies of the EU-level system of interest representation have characterized it as a pluralist environment (Eising, 2008), with some qualifying it as an "elite pluralism" (Coen, 1997). This latter characterization is based on increased interactions between the European Commission and certain privileged groups, in particular economic interests and large firms. Scholars have, furthermore, found that groups representing business interests are by far the best represented groups at the EU level (Aspinwall and Greenwood, 1998; Wonka et al., 2010), even though this bias may vary over time and across sectors and issue areas (Berkhout et al., 2018; Coen and Katsaitis, 2013). This business bias, however, does not necessarily mean that industry will always have the upper hand (Klüver, 2013b). Mahoney (2008: 189–204), for example, finds that both business and civil society groups can attain their policy goals, yet business is relatively more successful since it is, more often than other interest groups, in favor of the status quo. Furthermore, Beyers and Kerremans (2012) argue that business actors engage more frequently in multilevel lobbying (i.e., lobbying at both the Member State and the EU level) compared to civil society actors, and may therefore have higher chances of lobbying success. Dür et al. (2015), on the other hand, find that business is only more successful when the issue is less conflictual and when the European Parliament has less legislative power. Indeed, researchers have found that EU regulatory policy outcomes often reflect civic interests, with European Commission activism frequently playing an important part in bringing this about (Pollack, 1997; Vogel, 2012; Young and Wallace, 2000).

Despite potential biases, a simplistic opposition of business versus civic interests does not usually characterize policymaking on sustainability issues, as mentioned. Therefore, while scholars of EU policymaking often start from the assumption that "on market-regulating issues, the dividing line is often between business and non-business groups representing environmental, health, consumer, or labor interests" (Dür et al., 2015: 957), this is not necessarily the case for private governance issues. While business may in certain situations have the upper hand in the EU, private governance schemes and actors that can speak on behalf of or in support of private governance, such as participating producers and civil society stakeholders, can also have a strong voice in the policy process and in time even dominate this process. The engagement of these actors, in particular at the agenda-setting and policy-formulation stages, and their positions toward public intervention, are important in shaping the policy process. Private governance schemes can influence the framing of the problem and the proposed solutions in terms of policy options as a result of their regulatory expertise, and the fact that they embody Baptist-bootlegger coalitions of producers' and civic interests. Apart from the European Commission, these capabilities may particularly benefit private governance schemes in targeting the European Parliament. The Parliament is historically considered the institution most likely in favor of new and more stringent environmental and sustainability policies, even though less radically so more recently (Burns et al., 2013; Dionigi, 2017; Pollack, 1997). As Dionigi (2017: 2) argues, "[i]f [interest groups] did not manage to have their views reflected in the Commission's texts, the EP [European Parliament] arena gives them a second chance to attempt to sway the legislation in their preferred direction." Nonetheless, the Parliament's influence on the decision-making process, even with co-decision, is in general "less than some researchers have argued ... or practitioners have hoped for" (Rittberger and Thomas, 2015: 111).

The relative influence on the policymaking process of private governance schemes as new interest groups and of the new interest coalitions they shape, also depends on the prior existence of strong policy communities, which are the highly integrated, stable, and exclusive networks of state and non-state actors that dominate a policy area (Rhodes and Marsh, 1992: 13–14). Certain sectors are more likely to be dominated by such communities and as a result, may be better protected for historical reasons. This is particularly the case for agriculture, which is relevant for three of the case study areas analyzed in this book. While the agricultural sector's share in the EU's gross domestic product is about 1 percent, policies related to agriculture are highly politically relevant. The Common Agricultural Policy, for example, takes up about 40 percent of the EU's budget (European Commission, 2012a, 2017a). Strong lobbies have developed around this policy area, and farming more generally (i.e., outside of the CAP context), and they have acquired a dominant position in policy communities at the European as well as the Member State level (Daugbjerg, 1999, 2012; Rieger, 2005). Similarly, the Common Fisheries Policy is a politically highly relevant policy area. The EU market for fishery and aquaculture products is the largest in the world, even though these sectors contributed less than 1 percent to the European gross domestic product and provided less than 0.5 percent of EU jobs in 2008. There are strong local concentrations, though, with Spain, for example, accounting for 25 percent of total employment in the fisheries sector in the EU (Ernst & Young et al., 2008: 2; European Commission, 2016b: 17; 2016e: 12; FAO, 2016: 3, 35). Interest groups in this policy domain are therefore more fragmented. This has hindered the creation of influential EU-level fishing industry associations and supported strong locally embedded interest groups and policy communities. These groups mainly lobby governments at the national level, with EU-level lobbying being a relatively less important route of interest representation (Churchill and Owen, 2010: 28; Lequesne, 2005).

These historically strong interests, whether at the EU or Member State level, may defend the status quo against EU interventions, which would result in more sustainable, but likely more costly production practices. As mentioned, the state of existing environmental and sustainability regulation in the issue areas will affect whether there will be opposition to intervention. Relevant in this respect, as the empirical chapters will show, is the introduction of more EU environmental regulations for farmers and fisheries. Overcoming potential opposition from these status quo interests that in the EU are more likely to mobilize and win (Bunea, 2013; Eising, Rasch, Rozbicka, et al., 2017; Mahoney, 2008), or the absence of such opposition altogether, are important conditions for successful EU interventions in private governance.

Since for national interest groups the main lobbying route is through the national government (Eising, Rasch, Rozbicka, et al., 2017), important Member States in a given issue area are crucial actors in the policymaking process. The policy positions of relevant Member States, therefore, will be taken into account early on in the policy-formulation phase. For example, countries for which a given sector is economically important (such as fisheries in Spain, for instance), and whose producers would face high adjustment costs from EU intervention, are key veto players. As well, scholars have found that economic interests and strong sectoral lobbies influence the positions that Member States take in the Council of Ministers more than the ideological position or partisan composition of the government (Bailer, 2011; Bailer et al., 2015; Churchill and Owen, 2010: 23). The fragmentation of fisheries interests, for example, complicates the positions that governments take in the Council of Ministers, since policymakers have to cater to various local economic demands. In some important producer states, such as France and the Netherlands, interest formation is also more centralized (among other things due to corporatist institutions), which gives local interests an even stronger position in the policy process (Lequesne, 2005). The influence of these national lobby groups, therefore, is particularly important since it is common practice in the EU's Council of Ministers to achieve consensus. Depending on the policy area, official voting procedures in the Council may vary. Yet, while there is an historical trend away from unanimity and toward qualified majority, the de facto consensus norm provides significant power to certain positions (Heisenberg, 2005; Tsebelis, 2013). As Naurin (2015: 145) argues, "[t]he apparent consensus procedure makes it possible for the smaller states to give concessions to the larger ones without losing face," while it "makes it possible for the more powerful actors to take advantage of their power resources and push for concessions." Nonetheless, Germany, France, and the United Kingdom, being the "Big 3," are somewhat distinct. Naurin (2015: 151) argues that this is the case since "they are less dependent on European solutions to economic and political problems generally" and "their power resources make them less vulnerable to reputational costs among negotiating peers in Brussels." This implies that these Member States' policy positions carry specific weight in the policymaking process.

The Form of Public Intervention in Private Governance

How do the two explanatory variables – domestic benefits of product differentiation and fragmentation of the private governance market – interact to produce a regulatory outcome? Table 2.2 presents the types of regulation that will be developed based on the interactions between the two variables: no regulation, either standards or procedural regulation, and both standards and procedural regulations.

When both domestic benefits and fragmentation are low, intervening public regulation will not emerge. In this situation, there are no incentives to intervene and the status quo of no regulation will hold.

Alternatively, when both domestic benefits from intervention are high and a fragmented market is creating problems that public intervention can solve, both standards and procedural regulations will emerge. Considering both types of regulation can be employed to ensure domestic benefits and address fragmentation, their use will be

Table 2.2 *The form of public intervention in private governance*

		Domestic Benefits of Product Differentiation	
		Low	High
Fragmentation of the private governance market	Low	No regulation	Standards regulation
	High	Procedural regulation	Standards and procedural regulations

mutually reinforcing. Standards regulation ensures domestic producers can credibly differentiate their products in the market, distinguishing them from imports in particular, while contributing to sustainability as a public good. It allows for the creation of a standard adjusted to the local context with which a sufficient number of domestic producers can comply, and which is authoritative and credible, since a public authority created it. In order to inform consumers and steer demand, a public label or some other indication of sustainability, can complement a public standard. Simultaneously, standards regulation addresses the harmonization of substantive rules across private governance schemes and thereby mitigates information asymmetries and trade or competitive distortions. Standards regulation can weed out false claims in the market or schemes with insufficiently stringent standards (i.e., addressing greenwashing) and enhance the credibility of the entire private governance market. A public standard, in addition, can ensure that as soon as a product complies with that standard, all private governance schemes operating in the market need to recognize it as such. Consumer information instruments, such as a public label, can further harmonize the market and enhance consumer recognition and trust.

Procedural regulation complements standards regulation with the aim of harmonizing the private governance market and facilitating the certification of producers that will be able to distinguish themselves from competitors. Procedural regulation ensures that private governance schemes employ similar internal private governance procedures and verification processes, and that they are all equally adapted to local sensitivities and regulations (e.g., regarding accreditation rules), while also limiting variation across schemes and improving harmonization, trustworthiness, and comparability. Such coordination through procedural regulation is particularly relevant when a public authority enrolls private actors in public policy to perform compliance assessments of a public substantive standard (Black, 2003; Tosun et al., 2016). This is done by enrolling private auditors or complete private governance schemes. Procedural regulation in this case ensures compliance verification is standardized, for example, by requiring independence of the auditor from private rule-setting organizations. While this independence is becoming the norm (Auld et al., 2015; Dingwerth and Pattberg, 2009), it is not a given. Even well-established schemes, such as Fairtrade International, originally considered the performance of audits to be an in-house activity, and only later in their organizational development delegated this task to an independent audit organization (Auld et al., 2015). Private governance schemes can be enrolled in their entirety as well, when a public authority considers being certified by a particular private governance scheme as equivalent to complying with public regulation. Procedural regulation will in this case ensure that the private governance scheme is equipped with the necessary organizational and regulatory capacity to perform its delegated functions (Bach and Newman, 2007; Evans et al., 1985a; Knill and Lehmkuhl, 2002; Skocpol, 1985).

Delegating compliance verification to private schemes can provide significant advantages to public authorities. One important benefit is the potential to save on policy costs (Hawkins et al., 2006; Keefer and Stasavage, 2003; Kiewiet and McCubbins, 1991). Private schemes have certification expertise that is costly for public agencies to develop and maintain. Furthermore, delegation can provide a useful tool for public authorities to verify compliance of imported products with public sustainability criteria (Verbruggen, 2013). Since it is difficult for government agencies to assess compliance in a foreign jurisdiction, certification by private schemes that have been approved by the importing polity as being credible and legitimate can significantly increase the extraterritorial reach of a public authority.

Since delegation to private governance schemes implies explicitly bestowing legitimacy on such schemes, this option requires an extension of the model of private authority as developed by Green (2014). She distinguishes two types of private authority, which she terms delegated and entrepreneurial private authority. Delegated private authority emerges when international organizations or states in some collective capacity delegate policy functions to private actors based on the common interests of great powers, and through a focal institution in a particular issue area. Entrepreneurial private authority, on the other hand, refers to private governance schemes, as conceptualized in this book. This type of authority emerges, Green argues, when delegated authority is not feasible. Therefore, delegation as discussed in this book represents an extension of Green's model, since it implies a public authority delegating verification functions to entrepreneurial private authority. In that respect, it merges delegated and entrepreneurial authority, an option that is not included in Green's theory.

In addition, this type of delegation should not be conflated with orchestration (see for example, Schleifer, 2013). Orchestration, as defined by Abbott et al. (2015), entails a mode of governance that indirectly addresses rule targets through the voluntary engagement of intermediaries (e.g., private governance schemes). Enrolling private governance schemes through delegation, in contrast, implies a higher degree of authoritative control by public actors over the intermediaries by directly regulating their functioning and behavior. In other words, while rule targets are still indirectly targeted, the relationship between the principal (i.e., the public authority) and the agent (i.e., the private governance scheme) is more direct and hierarchical than would be the case in an orchestration relationship.

For the skew-diagonal combinations of Table 2.2, only one type of regulation will emerge, which represents a trade-off between standards and procedural regulations. First, when the fragmentation of the private governance market is high, but domestic benefits of product differentiation are low, procedural regulation will be developed. While standards regulation could assist in tackling fragmentation, there is little incentive to create it due to the absence of domestic benefits of product differentiation, which in the first instance relies on sustainability standards. Domestic producers are not expected to gain from public differentiation and there is no direct need for creating a first-mover advantage. This situation can be the result of potential negative impacts of standards regulation on domestic producers due to adjustment costs being too high, opposition from status quo interests, or concerns about WTO violations. Procedural regulation remains as an instrument to address fragmentation. It will bring at least some structure to the private governance market by addressing information asymmetries and trade and competitive barriers through harmonizing the procedural aspects of private governance schemes.

Second, when market fragmentation is low but domestic benefits of product differentiation are high, standards regulation will be developed. In this case, neither standards nor procedural regulation is demanded to deal with problems related to a fragmented private governance market. This is likely the case when there exists only one, or one dominant private governance scheme, potentially as a result of prior private governance coordination or harmonization. In addition, this situation can emerge when a small number of schemes exist that are well organized, and that defend their differences toward the public authority based on them representing different governance logics, for which harmonization is neither desirable nor feasible. Private schemes will, as a result, actively oppose the development of public regulation for these reasons and if necessary, adjust their functioning accordingly. Yet, since product differentiation is nonetheless expected to be of assistance to domestic producers, public support can be expected to take the form of standards regulation. Considering only one or a few credible private schemes exist, a possible policy response could have been to assist producers in becoming certified with these existing schemes. The logic for establishing a separate public standard, then, is that the one or few existing schemes are not considered a good fit for domestic producers (for example, because private standards are too strict, or not adjusted to local conditions), and a public standard can better assist them in differentiating their products.

Adjustments to Standards and Procedural Regulations

Public interventions in private governance are expected to be sticky and have path-dependent effects (Pierson, 2004). The interventions create vested interests, which benefit from the rules that have been established, and which will defend their continued existence against opponents that intend to reverse the regulatory course (Mattli and Seddon, 2015; Richardson, 2015: 24–25). This applies to both standards and procedural regulations.

Once a public authority has intervened with standards regulation, there is a strong possibility that eventually the standard will be adapted and even expanded in breadth or made stricter. These adjustments can be the result of an increased availability of scientific evidence regarding the sustainability implications of business behavior, the use of new practices to address sustainability issues, or the emergence of new issues. These dynamics have strategic implications for private governance schemes. From a public authority's perspective, private governance schemes can be considered "experimenters" that progressively adjust their standards or introduce new principles to regulate productive practices. Private schemes can do this relatively easily. At least compared to a public authority, they are in general considered to have more flexibility in rule reformulation, even though a multi-stakeholder setting may limit this flexibility due to the multiple interests that need to be taken into account (Abbott and Snidal, 2009a). A public authority can then assess the degree to which new rules developed by private schemes are successful in terms of producers' ability to comply. If the implementation of the rules is successful, or if the rules are considered acceptable to firms, a public authority can adjust the public standard accordingly (Green and Auld, 2017). Alternatively, when a public intervention fails to address certain issues, for example due to a lack of political agreement or institutional constraints (such as WTO constraints), private governance can be considered to be a "gap filler." Private governance can serve as a forum to develop standards for excluded issues, just as many private governance schemes originally emerged in areas where state regulation was lacking. The inability by private governance to close such gaps, however, may eventually provide a political rationale for a public authority to step in again and try to address the issue. A new political context with new governing parties, evolving political interests, or a change in norms, makes this possibility more likely.

As it happens with standards regulation, public authorities will likely adapt procedural regulation and make it stricter as well. This dynamic is evident from an historical perspective. Over the years, the norms about appropriate procedures for private governance have become more pronounced. They include, for example, the independence of standard-setters from auditors, the independence of both of these organizations from the entity being audited, and the independent accreditation of auditors. While some private governance schemes adopted such principles early on, others did not. Other examples of evolving norms include the expectation of diversity in stakeholder representation and participatory governance processes, which also have been adopted unequally by private governance schemes (Dingwerth and Pattberg, 2009; Potoski and Prakash, 2009; van der Ven, 2015). However, there have been growing pressures (from market and non-market actors) to comply with these norms (Auld et al., 2015). Since the norms have changed – and likely will continue to change – a public authority will attempt to adjust its regulatory interventions accordingly.

For all these reasons, public interventions in private governance will likely gradually become more interventionist. While the incentives to do this and the decision-making hurdles to achieve this may differ across jurisdictions, at least for the EU such adjustments are expected. This expectation results from the EU's strong regulatory focus and its periodic policy reviews that ensure discussions over a policy issue will be revisited at regular intervals. This is one reason why private governance schemes in particular may initially be wary of public interventions and defend their governance space. Yet, once public interventions are in place, private schemes will adapt to this new situation and develop strategies and capacities to fit the interventions (Pierson, 2004: 34–35).

Public policy reversal, furthermore, is costly and takes time. Once standards or procedural regulations have been developed, it would take exceptional circumstances or exogenous shocks (Baumgartner and Jones, 1993; Sabatier and Jenkins-Smith, 1993) to reverse these policies. Policy reversion is not impossible, however, considering the existence of self-undermining policy feedback mechanisms, which can lead to the demise of a given policy (Jordan, Bauer, et al., 2013; Skogstad, 2017). One feature of the EU that can foster such a self-undermining dynamic is the institutionalized policy reviews. Hence, while such reviews may lead to the gradual deepening of a public intervention, they can equally result in policy reversion.

Conclusion

Why and how does a public authority intervene in private governance? This chapter has outlined an explanatory framework to answer these questions. Considering public policymaking elicits the mobilization of a diverse set of interests, the chapter started with an exploration of private governance schemes as interest groups. The literature has largely overlooked the mobilization of private schemes around public policy and has not yet conceptualized these schemes as interest groups. Private governance schemes are similar to traditional interest groups in terms of their organization, political interests, and informality (or private status). However, private schemes are also different for two main reasons: They can claim to represent both economic and societal interests, and apart from acting on policy-specific interests, they have an interest in defending their own private governance space.

The logic behind public regulatory interventions in private governance builds on two main variables. First, public intervention occurs when publicly differentiating products based on their sustainability characteristics is beneficial to domestic producers. Second, a public authority intervenes when a fragmented private governance market creates second-order information asymmetry problems or leads to trade and competitive distortions. The form that public intervention takes – no regulation, or standards and/or procedural regulation – is the result of the interaction of these two variables.

In the empirical chapters that follow, I will outline how the empirical evidence supports the claims made in this chapter by examining the historical coevolution of public and private governance in four issue areas. In particular, the chapters will assess how the rationales for public intervention, as offered in Table 2.1, play out in the interactions between EU policymakers and relevant stakeholders. Several expectations in terms of actors' strategic behavior follow from these rationales. First, the analysis involves assessing whether and how policymakers (and in particular the European Commission) reference support for domestic producers. It is expected that policymakers refer to supporting existing sustainable producers, in particular, since they contribute to public sustainability goals; to expanding a market for sustainable products because it has growth potential, possibly in order to compensate certain producers for past policy decisions; and to creating a first-mover advantage with respect to other polities that are or may be developing public interventions. Second, with respect to fragmentation, it is expected that policymakers act on the observation that a too-diverse set of sustainability claims in the market results in supply chain confusion, or a lack of legitimacy of the private governance field; and that a diversity of private schemes leads to certified products having difficulty accessing certain Member States' markets or being recertified by schemes operating in these markets.

Considering the European Commission invests in stakeholder input before it develops a proposal, the empirical chapters will assess the extent to which domestic producers (directly or through national governments), private governance schemes, or other relevant stakeholders offer support for and actively lobby in favor of EU intervention for all the aforementioned reasons. Specifically, one would expect to see new interest coalitions between the European Commission and these actors. Considering the central position of the European Commission in the policy process, it is also expected that the Commission develops proposals detailing the type of intervention (no regulation, standards and/or procedural regulation), while the policy discussions following the presentation of the legislative proposals deal with deliberations about the degree of public intervention.

At the same time, the arguments against public interventions imply that policymakers – and again in particular the European

Commission – rationalize nonintervention by referring to difficulties that producers may encounter in adjusting to an intervention, in particular by referring to existing legislation with which these producers already have to comply. Producers are expected to actively lobby against intervention for this reason, and these positions will carry more weight when coming from countries that are important producer countries in an issue area. Opposition to intervention will also more likely occur when a strongly developed policy community, which is opposed to additional public interventions, operates in a given policy area. One would expect these interests to prove relatively more successful in the areas of organic agriculture and fisheries prior to 2009, when the European Parliament only had consultative, and not yet co-decision, competences. Moreover, policymakers can defend nonintervention by referring to the uncertainty regarding violating WTO rules. Finally, policymakers can argue that intervention is not warranted when private governance schemes have engaged in private coordination or harmonization efforts. Private schemes will also lobby policymakers with this argument. In the absence of private harmonization or coordination, private schemes will argue against public intervention when differences between the schemes are based on divergent private governance logics.

The empirical chapters will show that many of the discussions around potential EU interventions often surfaced not too long after the first private governance schemes emerged in an issue area. While policy discussions often take many years to conclude and involve a lot of back and forth among the various EU institutions and stakeholders, the chapters elucidate one thing very clearly: that the shadow of state sovereignty and public authority has always been looming. It is a story that often remains untold in accounts of private governance and one that this book intends to uncover.

3 | Organic Agriculture

Agriculture has been a central policy domain of the European Union since 1962, when the then six Member States of the European Economic Community established the Common Agricultural Policy. The CAP aims to provide "affordable food for EU citizens and a fair standard of living for farmers" (European Commission, 2017a: 5). With 11 million farms and 22 million farm-related jobs, agriculture is a relatively small sector on an EU scale. Yet, agricultural policy is a defining feature of the EU, since it is currently responsible for about 40 percent of the EU's budget, down from a staggering 75 percent in the mid-1980s (European Commission, 2017a: 4, 7). While the CAP was originally predominantly aimed at ensuring the free movement of agricultural goods and supporting agricultural development, the policy's goals have shifted over the years. Since the late 1980s, there has been a more explicit focus on sustainability, with policymakers acknowledging that the increasing industrialization and scale enlargement of agricultural production had adverse environmental impacts.

The EU's policy on organic agriculture developed around the same time that this broader reorientation of agricultural policy was underway. Several conditions favorable to EU intervention, both in terms of domestic benefits of product differentiation and fragmentation of the private governance market, mutually reinforced one another to result in the EU establishing both standards and procedural regulations. The EU's regulatory intervention in this issue area is the oldest of all the cases discussed in this book, and the roots of the intervention can be traced back to the mid-1980s. Prior to the EU's intervention, principles and standards for organic agriculture had been developed by farmers and private organizations – going back as far as 1928 – and by several Member States since the early 1980s. Direct lobbying by the International Federation of Organic Agriculture Movements (IFOAM) brought the issue of regulating organic agriculture to the attention of the European Commission that recognized the opportunity to create a policy that would address several issues at once. An organic agricultural policy would create opportunities to expand domestic agricultural production and contribute to rural development at a time when the EU's CAP was being steered away from price support of agricultural production. In addition, such a policy could meet increasing consumer interest in organic products, contribute to making the CAP more sustainable, and create a first-mover advantage, especially with respect to the USA. Finally, the policy could address the fragmentation of both private claims and organic policies developed at the level of the Member States. While IFOAM had engaged in some form of private harmonization, there were still considerable differences among schemes due to divergent local interpretations of the IFOAM standards. Furthermore, the organic movement highlighted fragmentation as becoming problematic. The market contained multiple claims regarding "organic," "natural," or "wholesome" products. These terms were used liberally to refer to different ways of engaging with sustainable agriculture, yet not all of them were equally truthful or rigorously monitored.

While the strong policy community that had developed around agricultural policy at the time could have derailed the process, the discussions on organic agriculture created a new interest coalition that did not contain traditional agricultural lobbies. Instead, stakeholders supportive of public intervention in organic agricultural governance dominated the coalition, which created the space for the European Commission to propose and the Council of Ministers to adopt, the organic agriculture legislation. These supporters included IFOAM, national organic movements, Member States that had developed national organic regulations (such as the United Kingdom and France), private governance schemes, and the European Parliament.

Considering the expected benefits to domestic producers and the fragmentation of the market, the 1991 EU legislation – hereinafter referred to as the Organic Agriculture Regulation – combined standards and procedural regulations. The Regulation established a harmonized framework for the production, inspection, and labeling of all agricultural foodstuffs intended to be indicated as organic. The Regulation provided a legal definition of the organic agriculture concept, which the European Commission directly based on the private standards that IFOAM had developed in the 1980s. Furthermore, the Regulation included the possibility for Member States to delegate verification responsibilities to private auditors, many of whom had developed their own private standard or had close relations with standard-setting organizations. Initially, EU approval rules for the accreditation of auditors were minimal and only referred to the availability of sufficient resources and the independence of the auditors. By 1995, however, the EU would require formal compliance with EU-level accreditation rules.

Over the years, policymakers would significantly expand the organic agricultural policy; for example, standards regulation incrementally broadened to include a wider range of product categories, with the public standards often using evolutions in private standard-setting as their basis. While some of these policy changes were relatively uncontested, others were deeply divisive. This was particularly the case in the mid-2000s when the European Commission responded to the continued fragmentation of the private governance market with proposals to enforce mutual recognition of private schemes. While these proposals aimed to significantly curtail private governance space, private schemes vehemently defended their right to differentiate. Several Member States (including France, Germany, and the United Kingdom) and the European Parliament supported the schemes in their position. The compromise outcome was the introduction of a mandatory EU public label to harmonize the market, and expanded procedural regulation, including stricter rules on the independence and accreditation of private auditors. This new policy, which was promulgated in 2007, is still in place. A revision process was started in 2014, but had not concluded at the time of writing.

Transnational Private Governance and Organic Agriculture

The historical origins of organic agriculture and the standardization of organic practices as we know them today lie in various movements that date back to the early twentieth century. The movements developed under several headings, including "biodynamic" farming (Rudolf Steiner, Germany, 1913), "natural" agriculture (Ewald Könemann, Germany, 1925), "organic" farming (Albert Howard, India/United Kingdom, 1940), and "biological" farming (Hans Peter Rusch and Hans Müller, Switzerland, 1940s) (Baillieux and Scharpé, 1994: 4–5; Langman, 1992; Vogt, 2007). All of these movements focused on ideas and concerns that are still embodied in what is today called organic agriculture. Central to these ideas are a focus on a biological concept of soil fertility, concerns for environmental degradation, animal welfare, and human welfare and health, and, as a result, prescriptions to eliminate mineral fertilizers and synthetic pesticides (Vogt, 2007: 9).

Arguably the first private governance initiative in this area was the Demeter biodynamic label, which was established in Germany in 1928 (Demeter, 2017; Vossenaar, 2003). Demeter's approach, copied by several cooperatives in Switzerland, encompassed establishing norms and guidelines for responsible farming that it was hoped, would foster the development of a distinct philosophy on agricultural practices. It was not until the 1970s, however, that more formal processes of inspection and certification were promoted as additional ways to disseminate organic agricultural practices. The first example of this new orientation was a private certification program established by the Soil Association in the United Kingdom in 1973, based on organic agricultural standards that it had started developing in 1967 (Lampkin, Foster, Padel, et al., 1999: 85–86; Soil Association, 2013). This formalization of organic practices aimed to improve the financial viability of organic farmers. Before this time, the relationship between farmer and consumer was more direct and personal, and farmers were still very closely connected to the pioneers of the organic movement (Schmid, 2007). Confronted with an increasingly globalized and impersonal market as well as a "prevailing economic climate, dominated by the European Union's (EU's) Common Agricultural Policy, [that] was extremely hostile to low-input and sustainable production systems" (Concord and Holden, 2007: 194), the Soil Association offered standardization and monitoring as a means to foster price premiums and appeal to consumers who shared its principles of organic farming. Over the years, this trend continued, with concerns over product differentiation in a growing market stimulating the proliferation of standard-setting organizations and auditors. As Schmid (2007: 158) explains, "[o]ne can say (at the risk of simplification) that in the pioneer phase the standards brought organic farmers together, whereas later the standards seemed to divide them. More and more private standard-setting organizations exist with different standards, each claiming that it has additional or more detailed requirements."

By the time the EU's 1991 Organic Agriculture Regulation was promulgated, eight Member States – Belgium, Germany, Denmark, the United Kingdom, Ireland, Italy, Luxembourg, and Portugal – had witnessed the emergence of private governance schemes. Farmers' associations, umbrella industry organizations, audit organizations, and retailers all developed private organic standards and on-product logos. At that time, only three Member States – France (1980), Denmark (1987), and Spain (1989) – had national legal definitions of "organic," while the United Kingdom had established a nonlegal national definition in 1987 (Lampkin, Foster, and Padel, 1999; Lampkin, Foster, Padel, et al., 1999: 83–86).

From the outset, organic agriculture movements and standard-setters recognized the benefits of international cooperation. In 1972, IFOAM was established by five organizations: the Soil Association from the United Kingdom, the Biodynamic Association from Sweden, the Soil Association of South Africa, Rodale Press from the USA, and the French Nature et Progrès. By 2017, the IFOAM network had increased to include more than 800 members from over 100 countries, making it arguably the largest federation in this issue area (IFOAM, 2017). The original aim of IFOAM was not so much to strictly control the concrete practices of organic farming, but rather to exchange information on different practices and empower producers by creating a worldwide knowledge network (Audet and Gendron, 2012; Geier, 1997; Langman, 1992).

In 1980, IFOAM developed its Basic Standards. It had become clear by then that, due to increased international trade in organic products, there was a need for an international definition of organic agriculture and an organic guarantee system (Geier, 2007). The Basic Standards, which are reviewed biannually, provide a baseline of the principles of organic farming in the form of a "standard-for-standards" for private standard-setters. They are, therefore, not designed as a proper certification standard (Commins, 2003: 78). Private standard-setters, as a result, have developed their own interpretations of organic agricultural standards based on IFOAM's Basic Standards to accommodate local cultural and climatic circumstances. In addition, they have established their own accompanying on-product logos.

IFOAM developed an IFOAM Seal for accreditation in 1999 that read "IFOAM Accredited." It could be used by auditors that were accredited by the International Organic Accreditation Service (IOAS), and on products from operators certified by IOAS-accredited auditors (Commins, 2003: 76). The IOAS was established in 1997 as an independent NGO to accredit auditors against the IFOAM standards. It is the successor of the IFOAM Accreditation Program Board, which was established in 1992 and was not formally independent from IFOAM (Commins, 2005). In 2011, IFOAM presented a new logo, the Global Organic Mark, as part of the reform of its Organic Guarantee System (IFOAM, 2011).

Over the years, the field of private organic agricultural governance has witnessed a significant degree of professionalization. It has evolved from organizations that developed as producer and consumer groups for which certification only entailed one of many activities, to a commercially driven enterprise with companies specifically engaging in certification activities (Vossenaar, 2003: 13). In 2010, for example, eighty-four certification schemes for organic agriculture were operating in the EU Member States (Areté, 2010: 9–16). Private standards are often more detailed than national or EU rules, yet not necessarily more restrictive. In countries that have a long organic farming tradition the differences are most pronounced and private standards in these countries more often include areas that EU rules do not cover. Overall, Schmid et al. (2007: 10, 20, 52) found that while there is limited disagreement about the general concept of what constitutes organic agriculture, differences are mainly situated in technical aspects at the implementation stage.

The organic agricultural sector is continuously growing, yet still quite small (Figure 3.1). In 1985, less than 0.1 percent of the total

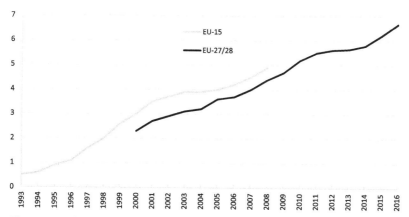

Figure 3.1 Share of organic area in the UAA in the EU (%) (1993–2016).
Sources: European Commission (2010a), Eurostat (2016)[1]

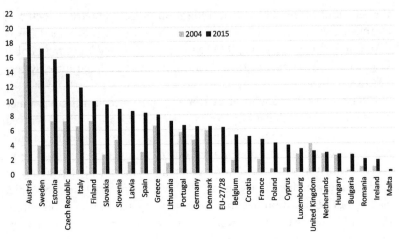

Figure 3.2 Share of organic area in the UAA in the EU Member States (%)
(2004 and 2015).
Source: Eurostat (2016)

utilizable agricultural area (UAA) in the EU was certified organic. By
2002, because of the EU's policies discussed shortly, this figure had
risen to 3.7 percent, with organic production accounting for about
2 percent of total agricultural output. By 2008, the organic agricultural
sector amounted to 4.3 percent of total UAA, with the fastest growth in
the twelve Central and Eastern European countries that joined the EU
between 2004 and 2007 (European Commission, 2004d, 2010a; Stolze
and Lampkin, 2009). A quarter century after the EU 1991 Organic
Agriculture Regulation, the share of organic agriculture in the total
UAA was still only 6.7 percent (European Commission, 2016d: 10;
Eurostat, 2016).

Disaggregated to the national level, significant differences exist
(Figure 3.2). In Austria, organic agriculture is most developed and in
2004 covered 16 percent of UAA and 20 percent in 2015. Following
Austria are Sweden and Estonia; in Sweden, the share of the organic
area increased from 4 to 17 percent of UAA between 2004 and 2015,
and in Estonia, from 7 to 16 percent in that period. At the same time,
while in 2004 eighteen of the twenty-seven Member States were at a
level below 5 percent of UAA, in 2015 this was still the case for twelve
of the twenty-eight Member States. The fifteen countries that were EU
Member States before 2004 hold the vast majority of both the organic

land (78 percent) and the organic farms (81 percent), even though the thirteen newest Member States in Central and Eastern Europe are catching up, with a 12 percent yearly growth in organic area between 2002 and 2015 (European Commission, 2016d: 5–10; Eurostat, 2010: 10; 2016).

Despite increasing domestic production, imports are an important part of Member States' consumption patterns.[2] In Austria, for example, imports have been estimated to account for about 50 percent of organic products consumption. For the United Kingdom and France, this figure has been estimated to be 30 percent, and for Italy around 20 percent. The EU as a whole is considered a net importer of organic products (Schönning, 2007).

Not only in terms of agricultural area, but also household expenses, the market for organic products remains a niche market. Organic products accounted for 1.9 percent of household food expenses in the EU-15 in 2007. More than 80 percent of organic food expenses occur in only four Member States: Germany, the United Kingdom, France, and Italy. The size of the organic food market in these countries, however, differs considerably: from 3.7 percent of the total food market in Germany to 2.7 percent in the United Kingdom, 1.4 percent in France, and 1 percent in Italy (European Commission, 2010a: 40–41). In this regard, Janssen and Hamm (2012a) note that studies have shown that "scepticism and uncertainty towards organic logos and certification schemes" limit consumers' purchases of organic products, since they "often lack knowledge on organic certification and agricultural practices" (Janssen and Hamm, 2012a: 337).

This lack of knowledge may be linked to the way organic products have been marketed and presented to consumers, by means which have changed significantly over the years (Aschemann et al., 2007: 126–135). Direct marketing from farmers to consumers was very common early in the development of the organic agricultural sector. From the 1970s onward, more specialized retail shops for organic products emerged and became the dominant distribution channel. This trend coincided with the aforementioned shift toward increased standardization and monitoring by private governance schemes. When the supply of organic products grew from the 1980s onward, the structure of the market changed accordingly. On one hand, there has been a trend toward an increased concentration of organic companies. Whereas in earlier times, cooperatives and smaller pioneering companies dominated the market; they have either expanded or merged to become large companies in order to survive in an increasingly competitive market; or they have been bought by large multinationals. As Aschemann et al. (2007: 134) note, "[g]lobal players such as Coca-Cola, Groupe Danone, Heinz, General Mills, Nestlé and McDonalds are taking part in the organic market today." On the other hand, regular retailers have become more powerful. When the increase in the supply of organic products succeeded the distribution capacity of the specialized shops, organic farmers' cooperatives, especially in Germany and the United Kingdom, started to create direct links to supermarkets that could offer organic products at lower prices due to lower distribution costs. Many retailers developed their own organic brand, which increased their market power, while also creating sales challenges due to consumer confusion around the distinct features of organic products and their labeling. EU policy has attempted to both stimulate and harmonize this market. It is to this policy that we now turn.

Public Authority Stepping In: Initial Standards and Procedural Regulations (1980s–2000)

In 1991, the EU promulgated its first Organic Agriculture Regulation that encompassed both standards and procedural regulations for private governance. The 1991 Regulation was the result of a clear policy evolution. Initially, policymakers considered organic farming a niche market better left to its own devices. Over time, however, policymakers came to acknowledge – under the influence of the organic agricultural sector – that organic production could play a distinct role in the larger agricultural policy domain and that private governance in this issue area needed to be regulated.

Up to the early 1980s, the EU favored a gradual development of the organic agricultural sector at its own pace due to its small size. Policymakers had no intention of setting specific rules for organic products beyond potentially limiting advertising claims regarding the "biological" or "organic" nature of products (European Parliament, 1980). The framework within which organic production was approached was one of a concern over food quality (Lynggaard, 2006: 106). Organic farming was not directly considered as being related to more profound environmental or sustainability issues.

From the mid-1980s onward, policy support for organic agriculture became increasingly linked to the first major reform of the CAP. This reform, the so-called MacSharry reform, was concluded in 1992 and explicitly included more attention to environmental conservation as a general objective (Baillieux and Scharpé, 1994: 1; Lynggaard, 2006). European policymakers increasingly considered protection of the environment and the "greening" of the EU's CAP important goals in and of themselves (European Commission, 1985a: 6). In this respect, the European Commission referred among other things, to the detrimental effects of the use of pesticides and chemical fertilizers and to the impacts of intensive livestock production (European Commission, 1985b: 50–51). In addition to environmental concerns, the CAP reform encompassed objectives that went beyond mere market support (in particular, price support) for traditional agriculture, including rural development and product quality. As Le Guillou and Scharpé explain, "by the late 1980s [the CAP] had broadly achieved its original aim of generating agricultural productivity gains so as to make the European Community largely self-sufficient for its food supply" (Le Guillou and Scharpé, 2000: 3).

In 1985, the European Commission first announced its intention to introduce a legislative framework to ensure the free movement of organically grown products and to provide the increasing group of consumers interested in organic products with satisfactory product guarantees (European Commission, 1985a: 14). The Commission's legislative proposal of 1989 contained both standards and procedural regulations, the main elements of which would be retained in the 1991 Organic Agriculture Regulation (Council of the European Communities, 1991; European Commission, 1989).

Convergence of Public and Private Interests

Important for the development of the 1991 Organic Agriculture Regulation was a convergence of interests between the organic agriculture movement and EU policymakers. The original impetus for the EU's regulatory intervention is situated in direct interactions between IFOAM representatives and the European Commissioner for Agriculture, Frans Andriessen, starting in 1985 (Ott and Desbrosses, 2013). The United Kingdom and France's Ministries of Agriculture, under the influence of their respective national organic movements, provided

Table 3.1 *EU policy on private organic agricultural governance*

Year	Title	Main Elements
1991	Council Regulation (EEC) No. 2092/91 of June 24, 1991 on Organic Production of Agricultural Products	– Legal definition of organic agriculture – Possibility to delegate verification responsibilities to private auditors, approved by Member State – Private logos allowed, in addition to "organic farming–EEC Control System" on the label
1995	Council Regulation (EC) No. 1935/95 of June 22, 1995 Amending Regulation (EEC) No. 2092/91	– Auditors need to comply with standard EN 45011 or ISO Guide 65
2000	Commission Regulation (EC) No. 331/2000 of December 17, 1999 Amending Annex V to Council Regulation (EEC) No 2092/91	– Creation of voluntary EU organic logo
2004	European Action Plan for Organic Food and Farming	– Twenty-one actions related to, inter alia: improving information provision to consumers and recognition of the EU logo; harmonizing organic standards; increasing coordination among auditors, and between auditors and competent public authorities; developing an accreditation system for auditors
2007	Council Regulation (EC) No. 834/2007 of June 29, 2007 on Organic Production and Labeling of Organic Products	– Auditors need to be accredited to EN 45011 or ISO Guide 65 – New EU logo made mandatory for all prepackaged food produced within the EU

support for these efforts (Gibbon, 2008: 569). The organic agriculture movements believed that EU regulatory intervention would be a useful means to open up new markets. EU rules would officially recognize organic agriculture as a distinct and credible alternative to traditional agricultural practices and give it a stronger position in the market. Additionally, official recognition would create opportunities for EU financial support for the conversion of farms to organic agriculture, including technical and training assistance. This support for farmers would facilitate their taking the risk to engage in the transition to organic farming and thus open up more production opportunities, especially in Member States where organic farming was in the initial stages of development. This financial incentive had earlier been important in some Member States where the organic agriculture movements had already recognized the usefulness of national-level regulation (Baillieux and Scharpé, 1994: 20–21; Gibbon, 2008: 567).[3] In the United Kingdom, for example, the Conservative government had supported a change in domestic agricultural policy and considered organic farming a solution for problems related to environmental and consumer welfare concerns and decreasing prices. Public regulatory initiatives in other countries, such as France, Denmark, Spain, and the Netherlands also received support based on a combination of concerns around the environmental impacts of traditional agriculture and the economic benefits of organic production (Lynggaard, 2006: 133–135).

EU-level policymakers equally believed that the diversification of agricultural production to organic farming would provide new economic benefits and serve rural development objectives (Baillieux and Scharpé, 1994: 1). The fact that consumers were increasingly demanding organically grown products and had shown a willingness to pay a price premium should have appealed to EU farmers, the European Commission argued. In that context, the Commission urged farmers to satisfy these consumer demands "before farmers outside the Community do so" (European Commission, 1985a: 14). In the late 1980s, for example, the USA was considering creating national organic farming standards, which in 1990 led to the Organic Foods Production Act, a piece of legislation that mandated the US Department of Agriculture to develop those standards (Dimitri and Oberholtzer, 2005).[4]

The emergence of private standards in a majority of the Member States, with often more than one private standard operating in each country, further contributed to nurturing a rationale for EU

intervention. The 1991 Organic Agriculture Regulation clearly identified several objectives in this regard, such as overcoming consumer
confusion, creating fair competition, and increasing transparency in
the market for organic products. The relative lack of harmonization of
private governance schemes and the proliferation of (sometimes ques-
tionable) standards and claims, created several market failures that EU
intervention intended to address.

First, private governance harmonization was too limited to overcome the proliferation of private standards. IFOAM was initially
established in 1972 as a network of organic agriculture organizations
based on a logic of empowerment (Auld et al., 2015), and was focused
on creating a knowledge network to exchange information on organic
farming (Audet and Gendron, 2012; Geier, 1997; Langman, 1992).
The IFOAM Basic Standards signified a shift toward a larger focus on
verifying compliance with standards and on the consistency of claims.
However, IFOAM only provided a baseline in the form of a standard-
for-standards, which private standard-setters could adjust to fit local
climatic or cultural circumstances. Gibbon (2008: 567) argues that
these differences made it difficult to harmonize private standards without governmental intervention. This harmonization occurred first at
the national level in a few Member States, which created the basis for
trade barriers. EU intervention was, in that regard, geared toward
harmonizing the internal market.

Second, the proliferation of private standards led to dishonest and
confusing claims in the market. There were complaints that economic
operators were using the concept "organic" fraudulently, in that they
would use the concept when they were not certified. In addition, there
was a lack of differentiation between claims about "organic," "natural," and "wholesome" products (Baillieux and Scharpé, 1994: 9; Le
Guillou and Scharpé, 2000: 5). The inability of consumers to verify
these claims, while paying higher prices for products carrying the
claims, created a clear incentive to intervene (EESC, 1990). This problem of dishonest and confusing claims had long been recognized.
A report by the European Parliament's Committee on Regional Policy
and Regional Planning, for example, argued as early as 1981 that the
future development of "'ecologically sound' products ... could be
jeopardized by unfair commercial practices whereby it is suggested
that a product is 'ecologically sound', although in fact it is not"
(European Parliament, 1981: 20). As a solution, the Committee

suggested EU legislation to deal with this issue. In 1986, after the European Commission developed its legislative proposal, the European Parliament reiterated this position, calling for both substantive criteria and an EU label to identify compliant products (European Parliament, 1986: 8).

A focus on countering false claims in the market was one more reason for the organic agricultural lobby to support public rules, first at the national level in Member States and later at the EU level. Yet, while the organic agriculture movement was clearly interested in having the EU engage in the market, it also recognized the challenges of governmental involvement. One representative of a private organic certification organization noted that the position of the organic agriculture movement had always been a bit "schizophrenic."[5] This was due to the trade-off between the benefits from EU recognition and the potential loss of control over the certification process that would inevitably result. Private governance schemes were concerned about this loss and wanted to limit it as much as possible. There existed many local interpretations of the practices of organic farming in what basically was a "split-prone movement" (Gibbon, 2006: 27) that made it hard to agree on common rules beyond the IFOAM Standards.

Despite these reservations, the overall convergence of interests between EU policymakers and the organic agriculture movement generated a new interest coalition in the debate on agricultural policy. This coalition gathered around the idea of organic farming as a nonconventional type of agriculture that could contribute to rural development, environmental protection, and food quality. The traditional agricultural policy community had historically been dominated institutionally by the European Commission and the Council of Agricultural Ministers, with the latter institution being "generally ... status quo-minded" (Daugbjerg, 2012: 92). The European Parliament played a less significant role since agricultural policy followed the consultation procedure, wherein the Parliament is consulted, without it having a final say in the legislative outcome.[6] Moschitz and Stolze (2007) further argue that traditional interest groups, and in particular the agricultural lobby represented by the Committee of Professional Agricultural Organisations (COPA) and the General Confederation of Agricultural Cooperatives (COGECA), had relatively little influence on the CAP reforms in the 1980s and 1990s. The new interest coalition around organic farming, as Michelsen (2001: 9) observed, "did not include many members of the dominant coalition in agricultural policy." Most importantly, COPA-COGECA did not show much interest in organic agriculture's niche-market status. National interest groups did influence national agricultural policy, and in that way, promoted their interests in the Council of Ministers. Yet, the influence of COPA-COGECA as the main European peak association – while still more important compared to other interest groups – was "debatable" (Moschitz and Stolze, 2007: 7). This situation would largely persist during further developments in organic agricultural policy throughout the 2000s (Gibbon, 2008).

The organic agriculture movement's main interest organization, IFOAM, had the largest influence on the 1991 Regulation. IFOAM had organized itself to this end and heavily lobbied the European institutions. In 1987, IFOAM established a delegation to lobby the European Commission about including organic farming in the CAP reform. In 1990, IFOAM developed the IFOAM EU Working Group (in 2002 renamed IFOAM EU Group) to create a permanent representation of the organic agriculture movements in Brussels (Geier, 1997; Schlüter and Blake, 2009). The lobbying efforts paid off, as the IFOAM Basic Standards formed the basis for the 1991 Regulation (Organic World, 2010). As Gibbon (2008: 569) notes:

The main actors in establishing Regulation 2092/91 were leaders in DG AGRI [Directorate-General Agriculture] and in IFOAM. Writing the regulation mainly involved drawing on expertise within IFOAM and the EU Commission's Legal Services ... This [Legal Services] decided to use the IFOAM Basic Standard as a model, for two reasons. Firstly, this standard appeared to be the most comprehensive and systematic available at the time. Secondly, Legal Services was impressed by the fact that IFOAM incorporated practitioners from across the entire EU, and could be construed as speaking in the name of European rather than national interests. Consequently, where Legal Services found the IFOAM Basic Standard confusing, it consulted IFOAM directly for clarification.

One of the main consequences of IFOAM's success in having the EU adopt its standards as the basis for the 1991 Regulation, as Geier (2007: 183–184) argues, was that IFOAM succeeded in ensuring that the EU Regulation would not define organic products based on the characteristics of the end product (e.g., free of chemical residues), but on the nature of the production process. The Organic Agriculture

Regulation was part of a larger set of policies that emerged in the early 1990s that all dealt with the quality of agricultural products (Le Guillou and Scharpé, 2000: 10). Yet, a focus that was merely on product features would have undermined the further development of the organic products market. It would have misrepresented a key characteristic of the organic agriculture movement, which is the promotion of an alternative way of engaging with nature and land for agricultural purposes. This goes beyond mere product qualities and encompasses the production process in particular. IFOAM lobbying the European Commission was crucial to having this concern included in the 1991 Regulation.

The 1991 Organic Agriculture Regulation

The EU promulgated Regulation 2092/91 on the organic production of agricultural products in June 1991 (Council of the European Communities, 1991). While the intention originally had been to develop a Directive – a type of legislation that Member States need to transpose into national law that allows for flexibility in how stated goals are reached – the European Commission instead opted for a Regulation, which is immediately legally binding in its entirety. According to people involved with IFOAM at the time, the choice for a Regulation was the result of the national organic agriculture movement representatives all supporting the IFOAM standards as the basis for EU legislation (Klein and Winickoff, 2011: 165; Ott and Desbrosses, 2013).

The 1991 Regulation established a harmonized framework for the production, inspection, and labeling of all agricultural foodstuffs that were to be designated as "organic." It created a legal definition of the concept of organic agriculture by specifying the allowed production methods and inputs. The Regulation also established a verification procedure, whereby Member States were required to set up an inspection system operated by designated public inspection authorities and/or by approved private organizations. The Regulation thereby explicitly allowed for the delegation of verification responsibilities to private auditors that first needed to be approved and supervised by a public agency in the Member State in which they intended to operate. The approval of private auditors was dependent on, inter alia, the "availability of appropriate resources in the form of qualified staff, administrative and technical facilities, inspection experience and reliability," and the "objectivity of the inspection body vis-à-vis the operators subject to its inspection." The option to delegate verification responsibilities to private auditors has been popular, with most Member States having engaged with such delegation. This can be explained by the fact that existing administrative capacity with respect to organic agricultural practices was rather poor in the Member States (Lampkin, Foster, Padel, et al., 1999: 86–87).[7] In 1993, for example, nine of the twelve Member States had either a system of approved private auditors (five in total), or a mixed system of a designated public inspection authority and approved private auditors (four in total) (Baillieux and Scharpé, 1994: 30–34). By 2013, this number had increased to twenty-two out of twenty-seven, with eighteen Member States having a purely private system, four countries a mixed system, and the remaining five a purely public system (European Commission, 2013c).[8]

With respect to labeling, the 1991 Regulation allowed the indication "organic farming–EEC Control System" on the label of a product, as well as the name and registered logo of the auditor. In this way, private certifiers could still benefit from consumer recognition of their logos. The Regulation, however, did explicitly prohibit any indication on the product that it is of superior quality compared to other, nonorganic products.

Finally, the 1991 Regulation stipulated that there could be only one route by which imported products could be marketed as organic within the European market. A country could be placed on a list indicating it had production and inspection rules equivalent to those of the EU Regulation. The Commission reserved for itself the right to have its experts perform on-the-spot examinations in an applicant country (European Commission, 1992a, 1992b). Very few countries, however, were ever included on the list. By mid-2006, there were only seven such countries, and since 1991, only nine countries had ever appeared on the list.[9]

The 1991 Organic Agriculture Regulation, in summary, encompassed both standards and procedural regulations, while leaving considerable governance space for private actors. Recall that this was the first time that EU policymakers had so closely interacted with private governance. While the EU made full use of private governance expertise by allowing Member States to delegate verification responsibilities to private actors, the standard-setting authority of private governance schemes was not fundamentally challenged or limited. Certifying against stricter or different private standards was still allowed, as long as the EU public baseline was met. Similarly, there were no restrictions on the use of private labels. As we will see, however, EU policymakers would soon experience the downside of this elaborate private governance space and would try to crack down on it in the run-up to a revised Organic Agriculture Regulation in 2007.

Incremental Revisions to the 1991 Regulation

After the promulgation of the 1991 Regulation, two important changes were made, one related to procedural regulation, and the other to standards regulation. First, Council Regulation 1935/95 of June 22, 1995, stipulated that from January 1, 1998, onward, all auditors needed to comply with the 1989 European Committee for Standardization's EN 45011 standard, with the intent of ensuring independent inspections. This standard is the European version of ISO Guide 65 on accreditation requirements for "bodies operating product certification systems" (Council of the European Union, 1995). While formal accreditation was not necessary, some Member States did make accreditation a formal requirement (Rundgren, 2002: 4).

Second, in 1999 the European Commission introduced an EU organic logo. Operators could use the logo on a voluntary basis when products were sold directly by a producer in sealed packaging, or placed on the market as prepackaged foodstuffs. The logo would allow "operators to increase the credibility of their products among the consumers in the European Union as well as a better identification of these products" (European Commission, 2000a: 1). The idea of an EU logo had already been proposed by the European Commission in 1993 (European Commission, 1993). While the European Parliament and the Council of Ministers supported this initiative, the various institutions differed on the timing and the urgency of the introduction of the logo, which delayed concrete action (Council of the European Union, 1995: 6; European Parliament, 1994a). The debate on an EU organic logo resurfaced when the European Commission in 1996 announced its legislative proposal to include livestock production in the Organic Agriculture Regulation (European Commission, 1996b, 1998a; European Parliament, 1997, 1999; Rogers, 1997). It took until 1999 before the European Commission finally introduced the voluntary logo as part of a larger effort on logos, which included logos for geographic indication and designations of origin.

Confronting the Authority of Private Governance Schemes (2000–2013)

In 2004, the EU initiated a process to revise the 1991 Organic Agriculture Regulation. The review process started with the development of the European Action Plan for Organic Food and Farming. The initial impetus for developing the plan was given at a conference in Denmark in 2001, after which the idea was taken up by the Council of Ministers of Agriculture (Danish Ministry of Food, 2001; European Commission, 2002b). Policymakers at the time recognized the importance of standards development at the private level, and they emphasized that new parameters for additional organic farming standards should be developed at the private (as well as the national) level first. EU harmonized standards would only be further developed on a needs basis (European Commission, 2002b: 12–13). In addition to standards development, policymakers were also contemplating making the EU organic logo mandatory, since the voluntary logo was little known to consumers (Council of the European Union, 2003a; European Commission, 2002b: 18; Fischler, 2004; Madelin, 2004). The Action Plan for Organic Food and Farming contained twenty-one actions related to, inter alia: improving information provision and consumer recognition of the EU logo; researching additional organic standards for wine and aquaculture; increasing coordination among audit bodies and between these bodies and competent public authorities; and developing a dedicated accreditation system for auditors (European Commission, 2004c). The latter two items in particular were indicative of problems in the verification system that would lead to severe conflicts between EU policymakers and the organic movement in the years to come.

A Clash between Public Authority and Private Governance

Following the development of the Action Plan, and with the 2004 elections resulting in a new European Commission and European Parliament, the Commission adopted a proposal for a complete overhaul of the 1991 Regulation in December 2005. The revision was intended to simplify the 1991 Regulation, which had been amended several times over the years. While the 1991 Regulation was considered a "labeling" regulation focused mainly on the conditions under which the "organic" claim could be made on products, the revision was aimed at more clearly identifying and defining the broader objectives and principles of organic farming.

Furthermore, policy developments in Member States had created problems for the uniformity of the EU's policy. Over the years, several Member States had allowed exceptions to some EU rules and decided not to implement others in order to adapt the policy to local circumstances and facilitate implementation (Gibbon, 2008: 564–565). The European Commission's proposal for a new regulation intended to shift away from such "legislation by derogation" in the direction of providing a "transparent strictly regulated mechanism [for] allowing less strict rules" (European Commission, 2005f: 3).[10]

Besides these more general intentions for reform, the Commission's proposal explicitly targeted three problems with private governance that had developed over the years and was clearly intended to severely limit private governance space. The first problem the European Commission intended to address was the growing divergence in the way Member States monitored private governance schemes. While the 1991 Regulation offered Member States the option of delegating the verification of compliance with the EU's organic agriculture rules to private auditors, it did not clearly specify how auditors needed to be regulated. This lack of regulatory oversight resulted in significant differences across Member States in the rigor with which auditors were monitored (Rundgren, 2002).[11] For example, accreditation of auditors to EN 45011, as mentioned, was required in some Member States, but not in others. As a result, this situation was problematic since the organizational capacity of auditors was not assured. In addition, their independence was not guaranteed either. Besides verifying compliance with the EU rules, many private auditors were also certifying against private standards. While this was not necessarily problematic, stronger oversight was warranted, since many auditors had historically close ties to specific private standard-setters, or were standard-setters themselves.

Second, aside from the aforementioned derogations by Member States, the European Commission also considered "upward divergence" of rules an important problem. This type of divergence entailed stricter rules being used in private governance schemes or in national legislation predominantly driven by private schemes active in the country (Gibbon, 2008: 564–565). While private governance schemes were required to take the EU standard as their baseline, they were also allowed to establish stricter or more comprehensive standards. Considering their prior independent governance activities, private schemes indeed gained legitimacy in the market on this basis. Since private governance schemes were more dominant in some countries than others, this situation created differences among the Member States that the Commission wanted to keep in check.

Third, and partly as a result of these differences, there was a lack of mutual recognition among private standards. The 1991 Regulation had intended to harmonize the market, facilitate trade, and create fair competition. However, several of the private governance schemes and auditors failed to recognize other private standards and refused to market under their own private logos products certified against those other standards. Considering that consumers in several Member States were strongly attached to logos from their domestic markets, it was particularly difficult for foreign operators to sell products that did not carry a local logo (European Commission, 2002b: 17–18).[12] In Sweden, for example, KRAV Kontrol would only recertify products that were originally certified by auditors accredited by IOAS, which was a minority. It thereby excluded many products from acquiring the KRAV label. This was problematic, since KRAV had a de facto monopoly in the Swedish market. A similar situation existed with Skal in the Netherlands, which had a monopoly since it had been given the status of governmental inspection authority by law (Gibbon, 2008: 565; Rundgren, 2002). These problems around mutual recognition of private governance schemes had already existed for quite a while and were partly responsible for the EU developing the voluntary organic logo in 2000 (Alemanno, 2009: 99).

In the eyes of many EU policymakers, private actors' governing authority in combination with the lack of private coordination and harmonization across national borders came into conflict with arguably one of the most important EU institutions: the internal market. In its 2005 proposal for a revised Regulation, therefore, the European Commission proposed to limit the authority of private governance. It tried to do this in three main ways. First, to prevent audit bodies from not recognizing certain private standards, the Commission's proposal stipulated that when a "control body has assessed and certified conformity with organic standards equivalent to those" of another control body, the latter "may not refuse to grant certificates or the use of its mark of conformity for any product" (European Commission, 2005f: 28). The burden of proof for demonstrating the nonequivalence of private standards would fall on the shoulders of the auditor that refused to grant the certificate or logo. The main goal of this provision was to "improve the free circulation of organic goods by ensuring that EU rules guarantee the highest standards," and to reinforce "mutual recognition of standards" (European Commission, 2005e). This position was supported by the agricultural lobby, which had highlighted this problem in the context of the 2004 Action Plan for Organic Food and Farming (COPA-COGECA, 2002a, 2005).

Second, the European Commission's proposal prohibited "[g]eneral claims that a particular set of private or national organic standards is stricter, more organic or otherwise superior to the rules laid down in this Regulation, or to any other set of organic standards" (European Commission, 2005f: 26). In this way, the Commission attempted to promote a "single concept" of organic production (European Commission, 2005f: 7). To further support this goal, the proposal expressed "the ambition for a high harmonization level" by limiting national derogations and upward divergence, since a "high harmonization level further reduces the room for private logos and marks of conformity" (European Commission, 2005f: 7).

Finally, to more strictly control private auditors and private labeling, the proposal suggested that auditors should comply with EN 45011 or ISO Guide 65, while it also mandated that an organic product's label indicate the auditor's code number. Furthermore, in case the EU logo – which was still voluntary – was not used, the label would also need to indicate "EU-ORGANIC" (or the equivalent in the Member State's language) (European Commission, 2005f: 26–27).

These attempts by the European Commission to regulate private governance more strictly proved very contentious. To start with, the organic agriculture movement, represented by the IFOAM EU Group, did not agree with the Commission's blaming of private standard-setters for the internal market problems and its attempts to "curb the influence of those control bodies operating to private standards" (Blake, 2009: 19). Instead, IFOAM argued that "[i]f there is a problem with the internal market, then private labels may be a symptom of this, but they are not its cause" (IFOAM EU Group, 2005b). IFOAM situated these causes with "the biological (and therefore the geographical- and climatic-dependent) nature of agriculture, the differences throughout the EU between less and more developed organic sectors, between the support regimes for organic farming and between the expectations of organic consumers" (IFOAM EU Group, 2005b).

The organic agriculture movement was particularly opposed to any restrictions on the labeling and advertisement of organic products (IFOAM EU Group, 2006b). IFOAM interpreted these proposals as contradicting "the functioning of a free market, with competition in quality possible as well as the competition in price" (IFOAM EU Group, 2006c: 7). Furthermore, IFOAM heavily opposed the Commission's proposal to limit private auditors setting their own standards and issuing their own logos:

Control bodies do not necessarily have or set their own standards, but may be licensed to inspect to the standards of a standard-setting body under the conditions set by that body. For others, their "mark of conformity" is a certification mark with strict legal obligations and controls. It would be entirely inappropriate, and may have conflicting legal implications, for this regulation to interfere in either of these processes. In any event, this would in practice be a confiscation of the value of and confidence in the private labels and result in a regulation not only being the base line, but also removing all other initiatives of quality differences, and voluntarily adopted production standards and market development. It is important that the different standards owners have the right to decide what is required to fulfil [sic] their standards (IFOAM EU Group, 2006c: 8).

In this respect, the organic agriculture movement argued explicitly for the right to product differentiation based on private standards, the right of private governance schemes to refuse recertification, and the right to oppose mutual recognition. Overall, IFOAM strongly contested the Commission proposal's underlying message "that private label organisations are responsible for stifling a vibrant European organic market" (IFOAM EU Group, 2006a). Some feared the proposal would be the "death knell" for the development of organic agriculture (KRAV, 2006), while others considered it an expression of "strong arm tactics," which "belongs more to a command-economy than a market-economy" (Rundgren, 2006).

The opposition from the organic agriculture movement was not merely informed by the concrete proposals of the European Commission. There existed a longer-standing dissatisfaction with the sector's decreased influence on European policymaking (Rundgren, 2001). The organic agriculture movement felt that its standard-setting capacity had been undermined by increasing governmental interventions. At the time of the 2004 Action Plan for Organic Food and Farming, for example, the movement already feared that the ultimate goal of the European Commission was to replace private standards with EU ones (IFOAM EU Group, 2004). The radical nature of the Commission's 2005 proposal for a new regulation did little to lessen that fear. While the organic agriculture movement acknowledged the need to revise the 1991 Regulation – in particular, in terms of making the Regulation simpler and more transparent (IFOAM EU Group, 2006b) – it was much less content with its own role in the process. There was, for example, a feeling that the European Commission was trying to rush through the revision in a very short time, with only limited possibilities for stakeholder involvement (Schlüter and Blake, 2009).[13]

The organic agriculture movement received support for its opposition to the Commission's proposal from the European Parliament, in particular the Parliament's Committee on Agriculture and Rural Development. For example, the Committee promoted the right of private governance schemes to provide information that their standards are "more specific as compared to the rules" of the 1991 Regulation or other organic standards (European Parliament, 2006e: 44; 2006k: 41). Furthermore, it argued against the Commission that there was no consumer confusion and that private governance schemes were not creating internal market problems. In addition, the Committee did not see the need for further EU interventions for harmonization, and said, "[p]rovided that the labeling and advertising of such products are based on specific and verifiable facts, it is unthinkable that the operation of private associations which function effectively, supplying clearly identified products, should be undermined in favour of a common EU label" (European Parliament, 2007c: 59).

Besides this substantive contention, there was a broader institutional power play at work. Recall that at the time the European Parliament had no co-decision competence on agricultural matters and only needed to be consulted in the revision process. IFOAM, therefore, argued that because the European Commission's proposal touched on consumer issues, this needed to be added to the legal base of the proposal. The co-decision procedure would then apply, making the Parliament a full-fledged co-legislator (IFOAM EU Group, 2005b). Similarly, the Parliament argued that the proposal touched on internal market issues (Article 95 of the Treaty establishing the European Community), which would give the Parliament more power "in possible negotiations on the implementing rules which are not included in the legislative proposal and are planned to be adopted by commitology [sic] procedure" (European Parliament, 2006e: 6). Mariann Fischer Boel, the EU Commissioner for Agriculture, however, argued that the use of co-decision in agricultural issues should not be discussed on a case-by-case basis but required a broader debate. Therefore, she was not willing to accept the Parliament's proposal (European Parliament, 2007a). For similar reasons, the Council of Ministers was unwilling to give more power to the European Parliament (European Parliament, 2007b).

Resolving Fragmentation and Conflicts of Authority: The 2007 Organic Agriculture Regulation

None of the controversial proposals of the European Commission that were aimed at limiting private actors' governance space were retained in the 2007 Organic Agriculture Regulation. Through active negotiations in and mediation by the Council of Ministers, the proposed articles were deleted or significantly changed. This outcome was most notably the result of compromise-seeking actions by Austria and Finland, which held the presidency of the Council of Ministers in the spring and fall of 2006, respectively, and of interventions by the German and French delegations (Council of the European Union, 2006b, 2006c, 2006d, 2006e, 2006f). The results of these actions were twofold. On the one hand, the restrictions on private governance as originally proposed by the European Commission were removed. The conflicts of authority between public and private governance were thereby mitigated by allowing private governance actors to retain their space to govern organic agricultural practices. On the other hand, to increase the harmonization of practices and reduce the negative effects of the fragmentation of the private governance market, the EU introduced a mandatory organic logo and required the accreditation of auditors to EN 45011 or ISO Guide 65 (both since 2012 replaced by ISO 17065).

The idea of transforming the EU logo from a voluntary to a mandatory one was not new. The discussion on the role of organic logos in the EU market had started well before the revision process of the 1991 Regulation was initiated. The problems associated with both private logos and the voluntary EU logo had been acknowledged in the early 2000s, when policymakers considered the availability of different logos to create a "logo jungle" that needed to be "cleaned up" (Danish Ministry of Food, 2001: 13). Experts mentioned, for example, that in the eyes of European consumers, products with the voluntary EU logo conveyed the message that "this is a product backed by the European Union and not that organic products are products which are different from the rest of the market" (Danish Ministry of Food, 2001: 154). This interpretation was partly the result of the similar design of the EU organic logo and the logos for geographic indication and designations of origin (European Commission, 1998b). Furthermore, by the early 2000s, Member States were acknowledging the intra-Community trade issues that resulted from the non-harmonization of private standards and from private governance schemes often requiring compliance with additional rules beyond the EU baseline. Nonetheless, the added value of having private logos operating in the market was not questioned at the time (Council of the European Union, 2002d: 2).

Transforming the voluntary EU logo into a mandatory one was an integral part of this larger debate on organic logos. In 2002, for example, Commissioner for Agriculture Fischler already favored a mandatory logo, in particular to facilitate trade with third countries for organic products produced according to equivalent standards (Council of the European Union, 2003a). In preparation of the 2004 European Action Plan on Organic Food and Farming, the European Commission had indeed suggested making the EU logo mandatory, based on the idea that a uniform logo would increase consumer recognition, while this would not necessarily mean restricting the use of, or prohibiting, other existing logos (European Commission, 2002b: 18; Fischler, 2004; Madelin, 2004). Not all Member States, however, supported the potentially compulsory nature of an EU logo (Council of the European Union, 2003a). In the Action Plan, the European Commission, therefore, did not propose making the label mandatory, and considered improved information and promotion campaigns for the voluntary logo appropriate alternative measures (European

Commission, 2004d). During the 2001 Denmark conference where the Action Plan was conceived, experts had indeed identified the lack of such consumer information campaigns as one of the main problems with the voluntary EU logo (Danish Ministry of Food, 2001: 188; cf. Janssen and Hamm, 2012a). The Council of Ministers supported the European Commission in its approach of not excluding the use of other logos – both national and private – yet stressed that a legislative framework was necessary to ensure the free movement of organic products, considering the existence of parallel standards and inspection systems at the EU, national, and private levels (Council of the European Union, 2004).

In the 2005 proposal for a new regulation, the European Commission again did not introduce a mandatory logo, since some Member States and stakeholders considered this would entail an "excessive EC interference in commercial freedom" (European Commission, 2005f: 5). The organic agriculture movement was also weary of a compulsory EU logo, stressing the importance of consumer recognition of already existing private and national logos (IFOAM EU Group, 2004). Moreover, it opposed the use of the indication "EU-ORGANIC," as proposed by the European Commission, since this would place "more emphasis on 'EU' than on 'ORGANIC, [sic] it might lead to consumer confusion if the product is imported from outside the EU and it undermines the emphasis on local production that should be at the heart of organic farming" (IFOAM EU Group, 2006c: 7). For similar reasons, the traditional agricultural lobby opposed both a compulsory EU logo and the indication "EU-ORGANIC" on imported products (COPA-COGECA, 2006b). Instead, it lobbied for the use of a more specific indication of origin (EU/non-EU), which would be included in the final 2007 Regulation (Gibbon, 2008: 577).

The aforementioned conflicts about the European Commission's proposals to limit private actors' governance space in the revised Organic Agriculture Regulation became entangled entirely with the discussion on the EU logo. Throughout 2006, there were intense debates in the Council of Ministers on whether an indication of "EU-ORGANIC" should be mandatory in case the voluntary EU logo was not used, or whether the logo itself needed to be mandatory. From mid-2006 onward, a majority in the Council of Ministers supported the idea of a mandatory logo for EU-produced organic products, while retaining the strict constraints on private governance as proposed by the European Commission. Several compromise papers from the Austrian and Finnish presidencies reflected this majority position (Council of the European Union, 2006a, 2006b, 2006e). Commissioner for Agriculture Mariann Fischer Boel supported this position and the mandatory EU logo became a political priority of hers (Council of the European Union, 2006a).[14] Germany and France, however, explicitly opposed this proposal. In addition, they demanded the deletion of the articles that prohibited private governance schemes from claiming to use stricter standards and that inhibited the use of private logos (Council of the European Union, 2006c). By taking this stance, these two countries, as well as the United Kingdom, were explicitly defending the strong position of their national and private labels in their domestic markets.[15]

The final compromise, proposed by the Finnish presidency of the Council of Ministers, was threefold (Council of the European Union, 2006d). First, a redesigned EU logo was made mandatory for prepackaged food produced in the EU, including the indication of "EU agriculture" or "non-EU agriculture" to indicate the geographical origins of the raw materials. These measures were intended to put forward more vigorously the idea of a single market and to facilitate trade.

Second, the 2007 Regulation explicitly recognizes that "[n]ational and private logos may be used in the labelling, presentation and advertising of products which satisfy the requirements" of the new Regulation (Council of the European Union, 2007b: 17). Third, the originally proposed articles limiting private actors' governance space were deleted. Partly compensating for this, the new Regulation mentions that (as is the case for public control authorities) private auditors cannot prohibit or restrict the certification of organic products that have been controlled by an auditor in another Member State when the products comply with the new Regulation. While attempting to safeguard the free movement of organic products, the Regulation does not impose any limitations on the use of private logos.

This compromise emerged late in the discussions on the new Regulation, and the decision on the EU logo in particular has been challenged. Some private governance schemes have expressed the fear that these provisions may undermine the role of private governance schemes as standards innovators, since the EU rules and logo represent "'lowest-common-denominator standards" and "will work against national values, regional identity, local markets and the connection between producers and consumers" (Soil Association Standards Board, 2008). Moreover, private schemes have argued that the mandatory EU logo may further increase consumer confusion (Blake, 2009: 19).

In addition to this compromise, the 2007 Regulation addressed the lack of independence of standard-setting organizations and auditors, and the differences across private governance schemes and Member States in the accreditation requirements for auditors. The Regulation mandates compulsory accreditation to EN 45011 or ISO Guide 65 to tackle these issues. By the time the 2004 European Action Plan on Organic Food and Farming was being prepared, the European Commission had already proposed mandatory accreditation (European Commission, 2002b: 21), and experts had emphasized the need for the harmonization of inspection methods (Danish Ministry of Food, 2001: 93). Furthermore, in the Action Plan, the Commission had proposed to officially recognize international accreditation systems, such as that of IFOAM (European Commission, 2004d). The Commission had even initiated talks with IOAS in 2004 (IFOAM EU Group, 2004). IFOAM supported this proposal, as did the European Parliament's Committee on Agriculture and Rural Development (European Parliament, 2007c: 73, 88–89). IFOAM argued that while EN 45011 accreditation could be useful, there was variation in accreditation across countries, so it suggested private accreditation to ensure consistency among Member States, in addition to national accreditation systems (IFOAM EU Group, 2005a: 14; 2005b). A reference to the IFOAM accreditation system and IOAS, however, was not retained in the 2007 Regulation.

A final element in the 2007 revision was the change to the import regime that now includes two routes for importing organic products; this has implications for private governance. The first route considers imports of *compliant* products, which means that the production and inspection rules applied in the third country are the same as those of the EU Regulation. The European Commission will approve auditors (EU-based or external) that can certify against such compliant standards and will establish a list of these auditors. The second route applies when the production and verification standards in the third country are *equivalent* to the EU's rules. Imports are allowed when the European Commission has placed the country in question on a third-country equivalence list, or when the auditor (EU-based or external) has been approved and placed on an auditor-equivalence list.[16] At the end of

2008, the same seven countries as during the previous import regime were on the third-country list (European Commission, 2008a), while by mid-2012 the total had increased to eleven (Abay et al., 2011; European Commission, 2012h).[17] The first thirty auditors considered for guaranteeing equivalence were approved late 2011 and by July 2012, when the system entered into force, the number had increased to fifty-three (European Commission, 2012e; Mattsson, 2011).

In this context of the auditor approval process, a reference to international accreditation systems reemerged. In the European Commission's guidelines on the initial assessment of auditors seeking approval to verify equivalence of organic standards, the Commission explicitly referred to the possibility of "an international supervisory or accreditation body that is specialised in organic agriculture" to provide the assessment report that confirms equivalence with the EU rules (European Commission, 2008c). As it turned out, twenty-two of the thirty auditors that were first approved had been accredited by IOAS. They were mainly small auditors from outside the EU that in the past had had difficulty in getting access to the EU market (Mattsson, 2011). According to Rundgren (2011), this approval was a major victory, since IOAS had to fight for recognition, especially against national accreditation bodies "that are often considered 'competent by default.'"

Conclusion

The EU's interventions in private organic agricultural governance have produced both standards and procedural regulations resulting from the interacting dynamics of a fragmented private governance market and domestic benefits of product differentiation. Standard-setting for organic agricultural practices emerged as an innovative instrument in the 1960s, based on guidelines and principles developed by farmers from the early twentieth century onward. The development of international standards by IFOAM was an early attempt to harmonize the private governance field. This harmonization process, however, resulted in a standard-for-standards that allowed private governance schemes significant leeway, both regarding substantive standards and procedural rules. The resulting second-order information asymmetries in the form of supply chain confusion and the persistence of false and unreliable claims in the market provided a credible rationale for EU intervention, which was for that reason also supported by the organic agriculture movement itself. Moreover, policymakers feared that initial public interventions in a few Member States could create market distortions and inconsistencies in organic certification practices.

In addition to these market fragmentation problems, policymakers and the organic agriculture movement alike envisioned EU intervention providing opportunities for both traditional farmers and those already engaged in organic farming. An EU organic agricultural policy would provide new diversification opportunities and contribute to rural development at a time when the EU was reforming the CAP and moving away from direct price support for agricultural products. Furthermore, EU recognition of organic farming would result in more secure market support and strengthen domestic organic production when other jurisdictions, like the USA, were also considering establishing organic standards.

Particularly important for the EU's intervention was the overall absence of the traditional EU agricultural lobby in the policy discussions and the strong presence of IFOAM as the mouthpiece of organic agricultural interests. IFOAM's central position resulted in the EU using the IFOAM Basic Standards as the foundation for its new public standard and in integrating private verification of the public standard in the new policy. Overall, the EU's policy allowed private actors considerable private governance space, which made the organic agriculture movement feel recognized as experimenter in its efforts to improve and verify organic agricultural practices. Indeed, the EU expanded its substantive standards several times based on standards originally developed by private governance schemes.

In the early 2000s, continued problems related to the fragmentation of the private governance market resulted in a strong willingness on the side of the European Commission to impose its authority further. These problems encompassed a lack of organizational separation between private standard-setters and auditors, which was partly due to Member States differentially monitoring private schemes; stricter standards used by private governance schemes leading to claims of "better quality" organic products; and an accompanying lack of mutual recognition among private schemes. While the European Commission wanted to address these problems by significantly curtailing the governance space of private actors, strong opposition from private governance schemes, IFOAM, and key Member States largely prevented a significant public intervention. Nonetheless, both standards and procedural regulations were strengthened further by the introduction of a mandatory EU organic logo and mandatory accreditation of private auditors against European or international standards.

While the organic agricultural policy has been in place since 1991, the practice of organic farming is still not widely diffused. In 2016, the total UAA in the EU that was certified was still only 6.7 percent, with wide variation across Member States. The lack of an overall EU-level target may be partly to blame. While some Member States established such targets over the years, an EU target could have further supported the uptake of organic agriculture. With consumer interest bound to increase in the years ahead, we can expect the market to grow. However, concrete targets could stimulate faster market growth. Such targets are indeed a useful policy instrument, as we will see in the next chapter on biofuels.

4 | Biofuels

Biofuels are renewable energy sources that people have used for many centuries in cooking, heating, and illumination. Policies supporting their development and use in transport, however, were only established relatively recently. Crop-based, or "first-generation," biofuels for transport exist in two main types: bioethanol is produced from crops such as sugarcane and corn and can be blended with gasoline; biodiesel is made from vegetable oils, such as rapeseed oil, soy oil, and palm oil, and is blended with diesel. "Advanced" biofuels, in contrast, are made from nonfood crops, wastes, and algae, among other things, but many of them are not yet commercially viable.

Policy attention to the use of biofuels developed in the EU in the 1980s, yet policymakers did not establish a dedicated policy stimulating a domestic crop-based biofuels market until 2003, when the EU set voluntary biofuels targets for Member States to replace conventional fuels. For a long time, both policymakers and many stakeholders considered biofuels beneficial energy sources, since they could contribute to decarbonizing the transport system and achieving GHG emissions-reductions targets. In recent years, however, research on the life cycle of crop-based biofuels has revealed that they are all but the climate-friendly fuels they were once thought to be.

Private governance schemes dealing with the sustainability of crop-based biofuels emerged in the early 2000s. They have developed into a mature market for schemes covering both biofuels in general and specific crops, such as soy, sugarcane, and palm oil. Similar to the organic agriculture case, the EU has developed both standards and procedural regulations in the 2009 Renewable Energy Directive (RED) because of mutually reinforcing dynamics related to domestic benefits of product differentiation and a fragmented private governance market. The EU's policy has evolved quite significantly by degree. The 2003 biofuels policy did not directly address private governance and the sustainability of biofuels. The policy was based on the expectation that biofuels would provide both economic and environmental benefits, by contributing to the development of a new EU market and offering GHG emissions-reductions benefits.

Shortly after establishing this policy, however, policymakers started to pay more attention to the increasing evidence of the detrimental impacts to sustainability of biofuels production. This development shifted the perception of biofuels from economic and environmental panaceas to devils-in-disguise, thereby threatening the newly developed EU biofuels industry. Stakeholder consultations organized by the European Commission showed support for the development of sustainability criteria. Environmental NGOs increasingly highlighted the detrimental impacts, therein supported by the European Parliament, which has co-decision competence in this issue area. NGOs linked the development of sustainability criteria to the European Commission's proposal to establish a mandatory biofuels production target that would further stimulate the EU biofuels market. Biofuels producers and farmers supported this target, yet they were much less convinced additional sustainability criteria were necessary, given that their products, unlike imported biofuels, already had to comply with European agro-environmental rules. This opposition was overcome in the end when the biofuels industry came to acknowledge that without a policy intervention to ensure the sustainability of European crop-based biofuels, the sector would have quickly fallen out of grace and its very existence threatened. Several of the Member States (such as the United Kingdom, the Netherlands, and Germany) had already started to take action in this respect, as had non-EU countries such as the USA.

Considering the nascent state of the private governance market by the mid-2000s, the European Commission initially envisioned developing a purely public biofuels certification scheme. However, actors closely involved with the development of private schemes, in particular the World Wide Fund for Nature (WWF) and the aforementioned Member States, highlighted the ongoing proliferation of private governance schemes, which were engaged in differentiating the market by covering different crops as well as biofuels in general. Moreover, these actors identified the attractiveness of using private schemes to verify compliance with public sustainability rules. They lobbied for the introduction of a so-called meta-standard approach, whereby operators would use approved private governance schemes to show compliance with the EU's sustainability criteria. By doing so, private schemes could contribute to reducing policy-implementation costs and increase the EU's policy reach through the verification of compliance of non-EU biofuels with EU sustainability criteria. The European Commission adopted this approach in its legislative proposal, which in the end resulted in the full-scale integration of private governance into the EU's biofuels policy. Before being allowed to operate on the market, private schemes now need to integrate the sustainability criteria into their private standard and comply with several procedural criteria, and on that basis, gain approval from the European Commission.

The main discussions between the European Commission, the Council of Ministers, and the European Parliament, in the end, centered on the content of the sustainability criteria and on circumventing concerns over violating WTO rules. These debates resulted in the sustainability criteria focusing on GHG emissions savings and the types of land on which to grow biofuels crops, while excluding social, food safety, and indirect land-use change (ILUC) criteria. Policymakers counted on private schemes to fill these policy gaps. Furthermore, they addressed possible WTO violations by allowing noncertified biofuels to enter the EU market, while only counting those compliant with the EU sustainability criteria for national biofuels targets and tax support.

In 2015, the EU adjusted its procedural regulation for private governance schemes. Since the approval process of private schemes lacked transparency and the market for private schemes remained fragmented, the Parliament requested stricter procedural rules and mutual recognition. While more reporting requirements were imposed on private schemes, the European Commission successfully defended its approval process of private schemes and the schemes' right to further differentiate themselves once they were approved. The future of biofuels is, nonetheless, highly uncertain. While the revision of the RED, which started in late 2016, had not yet concluded at the time of writing, overall support for crop-based biofuels has decreased significantly. Considering the limited availability of advanced biofuels, the future of biofuels as a credible renewable energy alternative may be in peril.

Transnational Private Governance and Biofuels Production

Transnational private governance schemes for sustainable biofuels production began in the early 2000s, with a focus on rules covering environmentally and socially responsible production, GHG emissions savings, and supply chain traceability. While some schemes cover biofuels in general, others have specialized in standards for a particular crop, such as soy, palm oil, or sugarcane. These crop-specific schemes are not only certifying products to be used as biofuels, but also used for other purposes, such as in food products or cosmetics.

The earliest transnational private governance scheme developed from 2001 onward, when WWF commenced talks with several business actors on a certification program for palm oil. Officially launched in April 2004, the Roundtable on Sustainable Palm Oil (RSPO) developed a first set of principles and criteria in 2005, a full certification system in 2007, and a supply chain tracking system in 2009 (RSPO, 2012, 2014a). Several other initiatives emerged soon after, with WWF playing a role in all of them. These schemes include the Round Table on Responsible Soy (RTRS), which was initiated in 2004 and launched in 2006; Bonsucro (formerly the Better Sugarcane Initiative), which was established in 2005; the Roundtable on Sustainable Biomaterials (RSB; formerly the Roundtable on Sustainable Biofuels), which was developed from 2006 onward; and the International Sustainability and Carbon Certification (ISCC) program, which was initiated in 2007 and formally established in 2010.

Characteristic of all these schemes is that they have been established as multi-stakeholder initiatives. The participants commonly include actors from several stages of the supply chain, and environmental and social NGOs.[1] A multi-stakeholder composition, however, does not ensure that power imbalances and unequal representation are absent. For instance, some schemes are considered to be driven more by industry interests, even though imbalances have been adjusted by giving a diverse set of stakeholders a voice, as was the case with ISCC (Ponte, 2014).

Alongside these transnational multi-stakeholder schemes, other types of initiatives have been established as well.[2] Individual companies, for example, have created certification programs that they use for their own supply chain. One example is the program developed in 2007 by Greenergy, a United Kingdom–based fuels supplier, which covers sugarcane-based ethanol in Brazil (Greenergy, 2008).[3] Other business-driven initiatives include national industry programs that emerged as farm- and food-quality assurance schemes and started covering biofuels crops. Examples are the UK Red Tractor Scheme, which was developed in 2000 as an umbrella program for several existing United Kingdom–based quality assurance labels, and the Scottish Quality Farm Assured Combinable Crops (SQC) scheme that was develop in 1994 (Assured Food Standards, 2014; SQC, 2016).

Efforts to harmonize private biofuels sustainability schemes did not occur before the EU developed its 2009 biofuels policy. From its inception, however, RSB intended to play such a harmonizing role. The first draft of its standard ("Version Zero") of August 2008 was explicitly based on work done by other initiatives, including RSPO, the Better Sugarcane Initiative, and the Cramer Commission. The latter was an expert group set up by the Dutch government, which in 2007 developed a set of criteria for the sustainable production of biofuels. The RSB draft standard mentioned that "RSB remains committed to incorporating and recognizing other sustainability standards work, and to harmonizing and reducing any eventual reporting burdens as much as possible" (RSB, 2008: 2). Initially, the formal recognition of other private governance schemes only occurred for non-biofuels-specific programs, such as the schemes of the Sustainable Agriculture Network (SAN) and the FSC. In 2014 only, it added Bonsucro as the first biofuels-specific program (RSB, 2014a).

Other harmonization initiatives have not been successful either, at least not prior to the development of the EU's biofuels policy. Examples of such initiatives are the Global Bioenergy Partnership (GBEP), a public-private partnership initiated at the 2005 Gleneagles G8+5 summit, and the International Biofuels Forum, a joint project of Brazil, China, India, South Africa, the USA, and the European Commission, which was established in 2007 (Bastos Lima and Gupta, 2013). While GBEP in 2011 launched a set of sustainability indicators, these indicators cannot be used to certify sustainable biofuels. Instead, they are merely intended to identify elements that could go into defining what sustainability means in the context of biofuels production. The same counts for ISO standard 13065, which was released in 2015 (Renckens et al., 2017).

The EU's policies on sustainable biofuels have had a significant impact on the development of both the market for biofuels and the market for private governance schemes. Considering this close connection, this chapter will first discuss these policies before further elaborating on the current and potential future state of the field of private governance schemes.

EU Policy and the Development of a European Biofuels Market (1980s–2003)

Parallel to the emergence of private governance schemes, the EU developed its initial policy on biofuels. The first fully developed piece of EU legislation to support biofuels production was not promulgated until 2003 and it did not directly address the sustainability of biofuels production. The political dynamics surrounding the 2003 legislation, however, and in particular the positive outlook toward the expected environmental benefits of biofuels, provide crucial insights into the subsequent development of biofuels legislation that did include private sustainability governance for biofuels.

The origins of the EU's biofuels policy go as far back as the mid-1980s, when support for the development of renewable energy sources was a central part of the EU's energy policy (Council of the European Communities, 1985, 1986; European Parliament and Council of the European Union, 2009b). The goals of the policy included the diversification of energy sources; the reduction of the dependence on foreign imports; rural development; and the balancing of energy and environmental concerns, as well as reducing energy consumption and the use of hydrocarbons and increasing energy efficiency. While still in their infancy, biofuels received attention early in this context. In 1985, for example, the Council of Ministers allowed blending ethanol with gasoline, up to a maximum of 5 percent of the total volume (Council of the European Communities, 1985). At the same time, broader policy support, such as subsidies or tax credits for agricultural production, was almost nonexistent, as the cost of producing ethanol was considered too high (European Commission, 1985b: 33–38).

The environmental benefits of renewable energy sources such as biofuels were more heavily emphasized from the mid-1990s onward, including commitments to increase their production and use. In several documents, the European Commission suggested increasing the share of renewable energy in the overall energy mix to 12 percent by 2010 (European Commission, 1995, 1996a, 1997a). Increasing the share of biofuels in transport was an integral part of this strategy. In a 1997 white paper on renewable energy, for example, the Commission linked environmental and economic concerns by highlighting that "[f]uture development of biofuels will have to be based mostly on production in Europe" (European Commission, 1997a: 38). In particular,

Table 4.1 *EU policy on private biofuels governance*

Year	Title	Main Elements
2003	Directive 2003/30/EC of May 8, 2003 on the Promotion of the Use of Biofuels or Other Renewable Fuels for Transport	– National voluntary targets for biofuels for transport, with reference values of 2 percent by the end of 2005 and 5.75 percent by the end of 2010 – Priority can be given to promoting biofuels showing "good cost-effective environmental balance"
2009	Directive 2009/28/EC of April 23, 2009 on the Promotion of the Use of Energy from Renewable Sources	– Mandatory national target of 10 percent renewable energy for transport – Sustainability criteria for biofuels production relating to GHG emissions savings, restrictions on land use for biofuels production, and EU agro-environmental requirements – Private governance schemes can be used to show compliance with the sustainability criteria after having been approved by the European Commission
2010	European Commission Communication on Voluntary Schemes and Default Values in the EU Biofuels and Bioliquids Sustainability Scheme	– Outlines Commission's approval process of private governance schemes and ways of showing compliance with standards and procedural requirements
2015	Directive (EU) 2015/1513 of September 9, 2015 Amending Directive 2009/28/EC	– Private governance schemes need to provide yearly information on auditors used, their accreditation, and audit processes – Mandatory mutual recognition of national and private governance schemes

the white paper mentioned that there was a need to reduce biofuels production costs, which were at the time estimated to be three times higher than those of conventional fuels (European Commission, 1997a: 16–17). In 1998, the European Parliament underscored this direction by suggesting a target of 2 percent biofuels in fuel consumption by 2003 (European Parliament, 1998e).

The development of more ambitious goals for biofuels characterized the early 2000s. In a green paper in 2000 on a European strategy for energy security, the European Commission suggested increasing the share of biofuels (as well as other substitute fuels, such as hydrogen) to 20 percent of total fuel consumption by 2020 as part of a strategy to reduce GHG emissions and improve security of supply (European Commission, 2000b). While direct support for the nonfood agricultural sector and tax differentiation in favor of biofuels were possible options, the European Commission faced several obstacles, such as public opinion resistance to more agricultural subsidies and restrictions on subsidies for certain agricultural products under international agreements (such as the Blair House Agreement with the USA). Instead, the European Commission argued that the simplest way of promoting biofuels was through ensuring that a certain percentage of biofuels was used as transportation fuel using blending mandates (European Commission, 2001a: 6–8).

Together with this green paper, the European Commission launched a proposal for a directive on the promotion of biofuels for transport. The proposal contained mandatory targets for Member States: By 2005, biofuels were to count for 2 percent of all gasoline and diesel sold for transport purposes (calculated on the basis of energy content), and this target was to increase to 5.75 percent by 2010 (European Commission, 2001c). The European Commission specifically emphasized the economic benefits of creating a domestic biofuels market. It argued that binding targets would "lead to an increased demand for biofuels in the internal market, which will provide EU-wide market opportunities for companies"(European Commission, 2001a: 29). In addition, the European Commission expected that biofuels targets would provide additional opportunities for developing the rural economy (European Commission, 2001b: 87; 2001c: 205). In particular, the Commission argued that it would "facilitate the absorption of the agricultural sector of the new Member States in the Common Agricultural Policy" (European Commission, 2001a: 6) once these ten countries joined the EU in 2004. The 2003 Biofuels Directive was indeed linked to the EU's agricultural policy through the 2003 reform of the CAP. This reform aimed to consolidate the EU's prior shift from price support toward income support by delinking financial aid from the crops that are produced, and to further encourage the development of the rural economy. The reform promoted the production of biofuels by introducing a special "aid for energy crops" program and by allowing "set aside" land – land that in earlier reforms had been mandated to be taken out of production – to be used for growing energy crops (European Commission, 2001b, 2001c, 2005a; Taylor, 2007).

The farmers' lobby COPA-COGECA strongly supported the European Commission's strategy, including the focus on setting targets for biofuels production. COPA-COGECA argued that considering the availability of land and its productivity, "European agriculture is already able to produce biofuels at a large scale" (COPA-COGECA, 2002b: 4). Since the high cost of production had been prohibitive in the deployment of biofuels, however, farmers expected the EU to provide financial support. The European Commission estimated this production cost at more than €5 billion annually, once reaching more than 5 percent substitution of fossil fuels by biofuels (European Commission, 2001a: 6). Compared to conventional diesel, for example, which at the time cost €200–250 per 1,000 liters, the cost of biodiesel was twice as high, estimated at €500 per 1,000 liters (European Commission, 2001a: 22).

Policymakers, furthermore, linked the expected economic benefits of biofuels production to the expected environmental benefits. Franz Fischler, who was European Commissioner for Agriculture, Rural Development, and Fisheries when the 2003 Biofuels Directive was negotiated, highlighted this close relationship between the economy and ecology when he stated that "[t]he production of bioenergy can offer new sources of farm income. It could become a concrete demonstration of a sustainable, multifunctional agriculture" (Hart's European Fuels News, 2001). There was indeed much optimism. The European Commission considered biofuels carbon dioxide (CO_2) neutral when the crops were grown domestically, even though it acknowledged that the full biofuels production process created CO_2 emissions as well (European Commission, 2001a: 5, 22–23). COPA-COGECA estimated in that regard, the agricultural sector could contribute greatly to reducing GHG emissions; implementing the proposed targets could double the sector's contribution to 11.7 percent (COPA-COGECA, 2002b). As a result, in addition to biofuels' potential to support local agricultural interests, the European Commission, the Council of Ministers, and the farmers' lobby found biofuels attractive from an environmental point of view and framed their approval as part of an effort to comply with the Kyoto Protocol (COPA-COGECA, 2002b; Council of the European Union, 2002a). This positive attitude toward biofuels was shared by other stakeholders, including some NGOs that also believed biofuels could be supported, considering their environmental benefits.[4]

Other EU institutions, such as the European Parliament and the European Economic and Social Committee (EESC) – a consultative body representing employers and employees – more directly emphasized the potentially adverse environmental impacts of biofuels production and use. In its review of the European Commission's proposal for a biofuels directive, the EESC explicitly highlighted the need to further study these environmental impacts (EESC, 2002). The European Parliament, in addition, called on the European Commission to assess in detail the life cycle of biofuels, their CO_2 benefits, and sustainable farming practices before considering increases in the biofuels targets. The European Parliament also called on Member States to submit reports to the European Commission in which they would elaborate on the environmental impacts of the measures taken to reach the biofuels targets, including information on land use, pesticide use, protection of watercourses, energy efficiency, and emissions of GHGs (European Commission, 2002a; European Parliament, 2002a, 2002b).

Due to the opposition from agricultural and industry interests and the overall positive outlook toward biofuels, most of these references to environmental criteria were not retained in the final 2003 Biofuels Directive, and none were made mandatory as far as the production of biofuels was concerned (Economist Intelligence Unit, 2003). The compromise between the European Parliament and the Council of Ministers on the new Directive, however, did not lose sight of potentially negative environmental impacts altogether. The Directive stipulated that the report the Commission would draft by late 2006 on the progress made in Member States would contain environmentally related information. This information would include the environmental impacts of further increasing the share of biofuels, a life cycle perspective on biofuels use, and the sustainability of the biofuels crops, including land use, the intensity of cultivation, the use of pesticides, and CO_2 emissions (European Parliament and Council of the European Union, 2003).

Equally important as the absence of environmental production criteria was the compromise that was reached on the biofuels targets. Throughout the negotiations on the Directive several Member States, including Germany, the United Kingdom, and Denmark, expressed reservations concerning the introduction of mandatory targets and granting tax benefits to biofuels production. Other Member States with plenty of land to grow biofuels crops such as Italy, Spain, and Austria, were in favor of mandatory targets (Council of the European Union, 2002c, 2003c; Gough, 2002; Peckham and Glunt, 2003; Peckham and Gough, 2002). The compromise that was reached specified that voluntary (or "indicative") targets would replace the proposed mandatory targets. Member States were free to set their own targets, with a minimum of 2 percent biofuels in the transport sector's fuel mix by 2005, and 5.75 percent by 2010. To achieve this compromise, Member States opposing mandatory targets had effectively hijacked negotiations on a related directive, which dealt with allowing total or partial exemptions or reductions in the level of taxation for biofuels (Council of the European Union, 2003b). Even though no Member State was explicitly opposed to this tax directive, several had vetoed progress on this directive until the proposal of mandatory targets in the Biofuels Directive was abandoned (European Parliament, 2003; Peckham and Gough, 2002).[5]

From the Devil-in-Disguise to Sustainably Certified Biofuels (2003–2010)

The 2003 Biofuels Directive did not put an end to discussions on the sustainability of crop-based biofuels. To the contrary, ensuing discussions on support for biofuels were characterized by intense debates about the potentially negative environmental and social impacts of biofuels production. New evidence and scientific research were used to frame biofuels as the devil-in-disguise. Unlike those for the 2003 Directive, the policy discussions on biofuels became more fully integrated with the discussions on renewable energy sources and climate change (European Commission, 2007d). By 2009, this energy-climate nexus resulted in the integration of the biofuels policy into a broader renewable energy directive and the integration of this directive into a broader climate and energy package. This package was shaped by heads of state and government during the March 2007 European Council meeting (Council of the European Union, 2007c), formally presented by the European Commission at the beginning of 2008, and finalized by the European Parliament and the Council of Ministers by mid-2009 in anticipation of the December 2009 UN climate change summit in Copenhagen (Parker and Karlsson, 2010).[6] The package's overall goal was to define and implement the EU's ambitious 2020 targets of a 20 percent reduction in GHG emissions from 1990 levels (with the possibility of raising this to 30 percent in the event of a global agreement in which other major economies would agree to comparable reductions), and a 20 percent share of renewable energy sources in energy consumption.[7] It was in the context of this latter target that biofuels were discussed; the discussion resulted in the creation of both standards and procedural regulations for private governance schemes.

The Road toward Standards and Procedural Regulations

The initial impetus for the development of both standards and procedural regulations was located in proposals by the European Commission to update the 2003 Biofuels Directive. In February–March 2005, the European Commission's Directorate-General (DG) Transport and Energy organized an online public consultation on the forthcoming EU Biomass Action Plan. The responses to the questionnaire provided support for the development of a sustainability standard for bioenergy. The sustainability rules were envisioned to focus on promoting the "energy, environmental and cost efficient use of the available bioresource," which could include the creation of an "assessment system with clear criteria," such as "high energy and cost efficiency, large GHG savings, no generation of waste, [and] soil and water protection" (Kavalov and Peteves, 2005: 9). In its response to the consultation, WWF already highlighted the importance of biofuels sustainability certification and EU coordination in this respect (WWF, 2005).

The 2005 Biomass Action Plan and the 2006 EU Strategy for Biofuels further developed the idea of creating sustainability criteria for biofuels. In the 2005 Action Plan, for example, the European

Commission proposed to change the 2003 Biofuels Directive so that "through a system of certificates, only biofuels whose cultivation complies with minimum sustainability standards will count towards the targets" (European Commission, 2005a: 9; 2006c). Considering the nascent state of the private governance market dealing with sustainable biofuels, the European Commission seemed to envision the certification system as a public scheme, even though in the 2005 Biomass Action Plan it mentioned that the system "would need to be developed in line with other initiatives for certification of agricultural and forestry produce and could require EU support in its introduction" (European Commission, 2005a: 40). The European Parliament supported the development of an EU mandatory certification system, which had to be nondiscriminatory to imported biofuels in order to avoid WTO disputes (European Parliament, 2006f, 2006h). The Parliament, furthermore, suggested that the system should address the whole life cycle of biofuels production. It would thereby not only tackle GHG emissions but also biodiversity, water resources, land-use change, and social issues such as rising food prices and the displacement of people. In addition, the Parliament suggested that biofuels that were not certified would neither count toward national targets, nor be eligible for subsidies or tax exemptions (European Parliament, 2008d).

Throughout these discussions, environmental NGOs put pressure on the European institutions to adopt stringent sustainability rules.[8] They initially linked their demand for these rules to a European Commission suggestion to replace the existing voluntary biofuels targets with mandatory ones. The NGOs argued that standards addressing the adverse effects of biofuels production had to accompany the mandatory targets. If not, the EU's policy in support of biofuels would lose its credibility given increasing scientific evidence of such detrimental impacts.

The idea to replace voluntary with mandatory biofuels targets had emerged in the immediate aftermath of the promulgation of the 2003 Biofuels Directive. From 2005 onward, it became clear that Member States would not reach the voluntary national targets, a failure that formed the main message of the 2007 Biofuels Progress Report (European Commission, 2007b; Londo et al., 2006). Recall that the 2003 Directive had set a reference value of 2 percent biofuels in the transport sector's fuel mix in 2005 and 5.75 percent in 2010.

Table 4.2 *Biofuels shares and voluntary targets in the EU-25 (2003–2005)*

Member State	Biofuels Share 2003 (%)	Biofuels Share 2004 (%)	Biofuels Share 2005 (%)	National Voluntary Target 2005 (%)
Austria	0.06	0.06	0.93	2.50
Belgium	0.00	0.00	0.00	2.00
Cyprus	0.00	0.00	0.00	1.00
Czech Republic	1.09	1.00	0.05	3.70
Denmark	0.00	0.00	n/a	0.10
Estonia	0.00	0.00	0.00	2.00
Finland	0.11	0.11	n/a	0.10
France	0.67	0.67	0.97	2.00
Germany	1.21	1.72	3.75	2.00
Greece	0.00	0.00	n/a	0.70
Hungary	0.00	0.00	0.07	0.60
Ireland	0.00	0.00	0.05	0.06
Italy	0.50	0.50	0.51	1.00
Latvia	0.22	0.07	0.33	2.00
Lithuania	0.00	0.02	0.72	2.00
Luxembourg	0.00	0.02	0.02	0.00
Malta	0.02	0.10	0.52	0.30
Netherlands	0.03	0.01	0.02	2.00
Poland	0.49	0.30	0.48	0.50
Portugal	0.00	0.00	0.00	2.00
Slovakia	0.14	0.15	n/a	2.00
Slovenia	0.00	0.06	0.35	0.65
Spain	0.35	0.38	0.44	2.00
Sweden	1.32	2.28	2.23	3.00
UK	0.026	0.04	0.18	0.19
EU-25	0.5	0.7	1 (estimate)	1.4

Source: European Commission (2007b: 15)

Member States, however, had only set targets for a total combined share of 1.4 percent for 2005 (Table 4.2). A more dramatic outcome was that the share that was actually achieved by 2005 was only 1 percent, with biodiesel predominantly produced within the EU accounting for 80 percent, and bioethanol – mainly imported – for 20 percent. Only two Member States – Germany and Sweden – reached shares of more than 1 percent in 2005 and Germany accounted for two-thirds of total biofuels consumption in the EU. This failure to set appropriate targets was blamed on the 2003 Directive's lack of incentives to Member States to reach the voluntary targets, the uncertain investment environment resulting from the indicative nature of the targets, and the reluctance to use imported bioethanol (European Commission, 2007b, 2007f).

In this context of failing voluntary targets, the idea of introducing mandatory targets resurfaced (European Commission, 2005b; Kavalov and Peteves, 2005). In the 2007 Biofuels Progress Report, the European Commission proposed for the EU as a whole, a mandatory target of 20 percent renewable energy and a minimum target of 10 percent for biofuels in the transport sector by 2020 (European Commission, 2007b, 2007f, 2007g). The 10 percent target, as Sharman and Holmes (2010) have argued and that has been confirmed by several interviewees, was not introduced on the basis of scientific evidence.[9] Rather, it was strongly pushed by the European Commission – in particular, DG Transport and Energy, and DG Agriculture – in support of the interests of EU farmers and the biofuels industry by offering a stable framework for investments. It was expected that the 10 percent target would lead to significant subsidies for the biofuels sector, from an estimated €11 billion annually, up to €23 billion by 2020 (Barber, 2008).

This support for the EU biofuels sector, however, contradicted findings that the economic cost of increasing production in the EU would be higher than the cost of an equal share of imports. Moreover, studies showed that increased EU production would lead to lower GHG emissions reductions compared to an equal share of imports (EESC, 2009; European Commission, 2007c). Many environmental NGOs, furthermore, opposed a 10 percent volume target. Instead, they favored a GHG emissions reductions–based target as was established in the 2009 Fuel Quality Directive, developed in parallel with the Renewable Energy Directive (European Parliament and Council of the European Union, 2009d). The NGOs argued that a volume target would merely result in the cheapest and most easily available biofuels being used, while fossil fuels would also still be used, without taking into account any type of sustainability criteria (BirdLife European Division et al., 2009; BirdLife International et al., 2007). A GHG emissions-reductions target, on the other hand, would incentivize suppliers to go beyond the target and then be rewarded for doing so. This could happen, for example, when biofuels that reduce GHG emissions by 70 percent would get double the benefits of those reducing the emissions by only 35 percent.

European farmers and biofuels producers strongly supported a mandatory biofuels target and wanted it to be reached as much as possible with EU-produced biofuels. The farmers' lobby, for example, supported introducing limits on biofuels imports by requiring non-EU biofuels production to comply with existing European agro-environmental rules and "the implementation of an equivalence system with third countries in connection with ecological and socio-economic standards" (COPA-COGECA, 2006a, 2008a, 2008b, 2008c, 2008d).[10] This position indicates that European farmers believed that imported biofuels performed worse on such standards. However, they were also opposed to any additional sustainability restrictions on the production of biofuels. Similarly, the biofuels industry was supportive of the mandatory target as an instrument to stimulate EU-produced biofuels (EBB, 2007b; eBIO, 2007a, 2007b, 2008a).[11] Yet, the industry was initially also not enthusiastic about sustainability standards that would be stricter than existing rules, fearing that new rules would undermine the still young European biofuels industry.[12] The European Biodiesel Board (EBB), for example, which lobbies for the use of biodiesel as the most widely used type of biofuel, considered existing environmental rules under the CAP sufficiently strict for EU-produced raw materials while it argued that the sustainability of imported biofuels needed more scrutiny (EBB, 2007a).

This focus on limiting biofuels imports fit with a policy the EU had adopted in 2005 – the so-called balanced approach toward biofuels imports. The idea was that imports – while not entirely banned due to international trade rules – had to be limited, despite the fact that they were cheaper. The European Commission, for example, had estimated that domestically produced bioethanol made from agricultural crops was about 25 percent more expensive than bioethanol made from sugarcane in tropical regions (European Commission, 2005a: 39).[13] The balanced approach had been adopted to ensure the survival of the European biofuels industry and the concomitant rural development benefits. Relying too heavily on imports would also undermine the potential environmental benefits of biofuels, it was argued, considering the negative impacts of increased palm oil and soy production on natural habitats and deforestation in countries from the global South

(European Commission, 2005a, 2006d; European Parliament, 2006f). Furthermore, this support for the domestic biofuels industry fit with the reform of the EU sugar regime in 2006. This reform occurred after a WTO panel had ruled that the EU's export subsidies were violating international trade rules (WTO, 2014). To compensate for the income loss of producers, the reform included aid for producing energy crops, the possibility of growing sugar beets on set-aside land, and funding for the conversion of sugar refineries to produce ethanol (Taylor, 2007).

When the European Commission released its proposal for a new directive in early 2008, it included a set of sustainability criteria as well as a reference to "voluntary national or international schemes setting standards for the production of biomass" as possible instruments to verify compliance with the proposed sustainability criteria (European Commission, 2008f). Recall that back in 2005 and 2006, policymakers had anticipated that the EU would develop its own certification scheme to ensure that biofuels complied with minimum sustainability standards. Over time, however, this initial idea developed into a proposal to regulate existing private governance schemes because of the growing market for biofuels certification programs. The European Commission had polled support for this position in the 2007 stakeholder consultation on "biofuel issues in the new legislation on the promotion of renewable energy" (European Commission, 2007a). This consultation contained specific questions on certification as a means of verifying compliance with a sustainability standard. Respondents overall considered the incorporation of private certification in the biofuels policy an efficient and cost-effective way of using existing instruments to verify compliance, provided that the schemes would be reliable and legitimate. Several of the respondents specifically suggested harmonization at the EU level in order to prevent private schemes from adopting divergent approaches, and also suggested the EU have control over the approval of the functioning of private schemes in the EU market.[14] Other stakeholders, such as Greenpeace and Friends of the Earth, criticized private certification schemes for their inadequacy in offering any guarantees that biofuels were produced sustainably. These NGOs challenged whether biofuels could ever be sustainable, called into question the very existence of a sustainable (European) crop-based biofuels industry, and questioned the efficacy of private governance schemes (Friends of the Earth Europe, 2007, 2008; Greenpeace, 2007a, 2007b).

The inclusion of private governance schemes in the EU's policy, as a result, was intended to control the diversity and proliferation of certification schemes. The EU's policy design is based on what is called a "meta-standard" approach (Bauen et al., 2005; Dehue, Meyer, et al., 2007; Lin, 2011). This approach entails the EU developing a broad set of sustainability rules and operators using private certification schemes to show compliance with these sustainability criteria. Prior to being allowed to operate on the European market, the schemes need to be approved by the European Commission contingent on their using a standard that is compatible with the EU's sustainability rules and EU procedural regulation that guarantees the schemes are organizationally equipped to certify against these rules.

The organization that was particularly instrumental in the adoption of the meta-standard approach was WWF. This environmental NGO supported this approach from the very beginning of the discussions on the 10 percent mandatory target and the sustainability criteria. As mentioned, in the context of the 2005 consultation on the Biomass Action Plan, WWF had highlighted the importance of biofuels sustainability certification (WWF, 2005). WWF further outlined the meta-standard approach in extensive responses to the 2006 stakeholder consultation on the review of the 2003 Biofuels Directive and the 2007 consultation on the new renewable energy directive (Londo et al., 2006; WWF, 2007). In 2007, WWF also commissioned a report further investigating the meta-standard approach and it actively participated in various workshops organized by the Commission to promote this idea (Dehue, Meyer, et al., 2007).[15] Considering private certification schemes' experience with compliance verification, WWF argued that the schemes could ensure sustainable production. WWF had a clear organizational interest. Using private governance schemes would ensure continued support for certification programs that were already active or in the process of being established. Not only had WWF over the years played a crucial role in the development of private certification programs in other sectors, most notably in forestry (FSC) and fisheries (MSC), it had also used this experience to help develop several of the main biofuels certification schemes, such as RSPO, RTRS, Bonsucro, and RSB. The EU adopting a meta-standard approach would give an extra stimulus to these schemes and guarantee their continued relevance in the newly created EU market for sustainable biofuels.

The governments of the United Kingdom, the Netherlands, and Germany explicitly supported the meta-standard approach. The United Kingdom had firsthand experience based on its domestic renewable fuels policies. The meta-standard concept had been outlined in the context of the United Kingdom's Renewable Transport Fuels Obligation (RTFO) that was developed from 2004 onward and implemented by the Renewable Fuels Agency (RFA).[16] A public-private partnership, called the Low Carbon Vehicle Partnership (LowCVP), had been in charge of creating a carbon- and sustainability-reporting scheme for the RTFO. In this context, LowCVP had issued feasibility studies on the introduction of a meta-standard approach (Bauen et al., 2005; Dehue, Hamelinck, et al., 2007; LowCVP, 2007). The experience of the United Kingdom showed the potential of this approach, both in terms of setting a standard and delegating verification to independent, private voluntary initiatives. The RFA had also had direct contact with several private certification schemes, such as RSB, RSPO, Bonsucro, and Red Tractor.[17] The schemes recognized the opportunities of being approved under a meta-standard approach and discussed compliance with the meta-standard with the RFA (Richardson, 2014: 210).

In addition to the United Kingdom, the Netherlands supported the meta-standard approach and on the basis of the recommendations of the Cramer Commission, the Dutch government was considering using this approach domestically as well (Cramer Commission, 2007; Government of the Netherlands, 2007). The Cramer Commission regularly consulted with the British government on this issue. This was important, as Richardson (2014: 210) explains, "given that the two countries were the biggest importers of biofuel into the EU, and also home to the bloc's biggest oil companies, BP and Shell." Finally, the German government had also suggested incorporating certification in the reform of its national biofuels policy in 2007. In addition, the government was at the time involved with the development of the ISCC, and supportive of a meta-standard approach.[18]

Harmonization at the EU level would prevent the development of these various national programs causing intra-EU trade barriers, as had happened in the case of organic agriculture (European Commission, 2008f). At the same time, it would control the further fragmentation of the private governance market. Recall that before 2009, the field of biofuels certification schemes consisted of several crop-based programs and a few general ones. In addition, existing certification schemes focused on forestry and agriculture. Since the sustainability criteria the EU institutions were developing were not crop-based, experts envisioned that many more general schemes would emerge with the sole purpose of implementing the EU directive, while existing crop-based schemes would have to incorporate the general sustainability criteria (Vis et al., 2008: ii–xi). At the same time, there were several crops – including wheat, rapeseed, and sunflower – for which no certification scheme had yet emerged, even though these crops were widely used for biofuels production (Vis et al., 2008: 44). Indeed, in 2008, rapeseed oil was the most important feedstock used for biodiesel production in the EU and accounted for 75 percent of transport renewable fuels, of which 26 percent was imported. Wheat, corn, and sugar beet, in contrast, were the main crops used for producing bioethanol, which accounted for 15 percent of EU transport biofuel use, of which 31 percent was imported (Ecofys et al., 2012; European Commission, 2009d: 6; Hamelinck et al., 2011: 1, 28–31).[19] It was uncertain whether certification schemes for these crops would emerge and whether they would be global, regional, or national programs.

European policymakers were overall very receptive to the idea of using certification schemes in the context of a meta-standard approach. This approach would allow for the development of an EU-appropriate sustainability standard, while compliance verification could be delegated to private actors. Policymakers considered such an approach useful, since it could lower policy costs and decrease the administrative burden on Member States. Additionally, private schemes could develop stricter or complementary standards and thus fill gaps in the EU's policy. Furthermore, since the EU sustainability criteria would be applied irrespective of the country of origin, private certification would allow for verifying compliance of non-EU biofuels with the EU sustainability criteria (Dehue, Meyer, et al., 2007; European Commission, 2008d; Vis et al., 2008).[20]

The 2009 Renewable Energy Directive

With the proposal of incorporating private governance in public policy relatively uncontested, much of the ensuing discussion focused on the sustainability criteria. Pressure to develop sustainability criteria that would be stricter than the existing EU rules had been building up for several reasons. First, public and expert opinion on the sustainability and even desirability of biofuels was changing quickly. New scientific evidence questioned the environmental benefits of biofuels, arguing that land-use changes from biofuels production resulted in increased GHG emissions, thereby undoing the initial emissions gains from biofuels use. Indirect land-use change in particular became a contentious issue. ILUC refers to the fact that new land will have to be made available for agricultural production when biofuels production takes place on land previously used for agriculture, which leads to additional carbon emissions (Searchinger et al., 2008; UK Renewable Fuels Agency, 2008).

Relatedly, biofuels were increasingly being chastised because of the "food v. fuel" debate, which emerged in the context of the global food crisis of 2007–2008. Critics alleged that biofuels production had contributed significantly to food shortages and increased food prices when crops were diverted from being used as food, to being used for biofuels production. Jean Ziegler, UN Special Rapporteur on the Right to Food from 2000 to 2008, famously called converting food crops into biofuels a "crime against humanity" (UN News Centre, 2007). For that reason, the European Parliament, for example, suggested adding a specific reference to food security in any proposed sustainability standard, namely that "[t]he use of land for the production of biofuels shall not be allowed to compete with the use of land for the production of foods" (European Parliament, 2008c: 113).

Finally, while the national initiatives in the United Kingdom, the Netherlands, and Germany created incentives to harmonize sustainability rules at the EU level, additional pressure was exerted as a result of policy developments in non-EU jurisdictions, in particular the USA. In 2007, California enacted the low-carbon fuel standard, while at the federal level, the Energy Security and Independence Act introduced binding environmental criteria for biofuels. The European Commission and the European Parliament were closely following these policy developments in the USA (European Commission, 2006c; European Parliament, 2007d). Developing an early-mover advantage was therefore thought to be beneficial.[21]

These pressures contributed to the EU farmers' and biofuels industry lobbies – despite their initial opposition – realizing that they had to agree to at least a limited set of sustainability rules in order to enjoy continued support for biofuels production in the EU. Without sustainability criteria, biofuels would have fallen out of grace entirely. Yet, these lobbies continued to stress that EU biofuels production at that time was already sustainable, due to the strict rules under which EU agricultural production was operating. At the same time, they wanted to prevent at all cost cheaper biofuels imports from countries with less strict or no sustainability criteria from being allowed (COPA-COGECA, 2008c, 2008d; eBIO, 2008a, 2008b; EurActiv, 2011).[22]

Non-EU biofuels-producing countries were concerned about the EU introducing strict sustainability criteria. They were afraid that these criteria would create new trade barriers and threaten their competitive position. In 2008, for example, eight countries – Argentina, Brazil, Colombia, Malawi, Mozambique, Sierra Leone, Indonesia, and Malaysia – threatened to file a complaint with the WTO if the EU adopted overly stringent sustainability criteria (EurActiv, 2008c). Some countries, such as Malaysia and Indonesia, were also actively lobbying the EU institutions against the adoption of specific sustainability criteria.[23] Malaysia, for example, argued that "[c]riteria such as land use change, biodiversity and CO_2 neutrality should be subjected to the environmental laws and regulations of the exporting countries" and not the importing ones (Government of Malaysia, 2007). Richardson (2014: 213) argues that Malaysia was "possibly pacified by the later acceptance of the RSPO as a qualifying certification system in 2012; an organisation co-founded by the Malaysian Palm Oil Association."

The sustainability criteria that were finally agreed to in Article 17 of the 2009 Renewable Energy Directive address GHG emissions savings (35 percent, increasing to 60 percent in 2018) and restrictions on the types of land used for biofuels production (land with high biodiversity value, including primary forests and grassland, and certain types of wetlands and peatland), while requiring that biofuels produced in the EU adhere to the environmental and agricultural rules of the CAP.[24] Biofuels that do not comply with these criteria could still be produced or imported. An important discriminating factor, however, is specified in the Directive. Article 17 states that, irrespective of whether production was within the EU or abroad, only those biofuels that comply with the sustainability criteria would be eligible for financial support or counted toward national targets (which, late in the negotiations, had changed from a 10 percent biofuels target to a 10 percent renewable-energy-in-transport target).[25] In this way, the Directive heavily tipped the balance in favor of biofuels complying with the sustainability criteria, while at the same time circumventing violating WTO rules (in particular the TBT agreement).

To verify compliance with the sustainability standard, the 2009 Directive included three options: a Member State's national authority, a bilateral or multilateral agreement concluded by the EU, and voluntary national or international certification schemes (European Commission, 2010d; European Parliament and Council of the European Union, 2009b). The European Commission was tasked with approving the certification schemes before they could operate in the European market. The procedural rules for such approval were deliberately designed in general terms, since there were concerns about existing schemes being able to meet demanding criteria.[26] In the implementation guidelines issued one year after the promulgation of the 2009 Directive, the Commission highlighted the need for independence of the standard-setting organization, the auditor, and the economic operator that is audited, and for auditors to possess the organizational capacity and skills to perform audits. The procedural rules do not require that the auditors be accredited by an independent accreditation organization, even though it is suggested that auditors conform with relevant ISO guidelines (such as ISO Guide 65, ISO 19011, ISO 14065, and ISO 14064-3), or the International Standard on Assurance Engagements (ISAE) 3000 (European Commission, 2010f: 3–4).[27] The European Commission (i.e., DG Energy or its contracted experts) assesses whether the private certification schemes can provide sufficient evidence in this regard.

While private governance schemes were enrolled to verify compliance with the EU's sustainability standard, policymakers also envisioned them filling gaps in the standard (Ponte and Daugbjerg, 2014). These gaps were quite significant, since criteria relating to social impacts, ILUC, and food security had been discussed but not retained in the sustainability standard. First, the European Commission had argued against including social criteria (such as those related to labor conditions and land rights), since it would be very difficult to "associat[e] such social impacts with individual consignments of biofuel" (European Commission, 2008d: 128). In addition, policymakers were aware that including social criteria would likely violate WTO rules (Ackrill and Kay, 2011; European Parliament, 2008b: 12; Vis et al., 2008: viii–ix, 67–68).[28] It was a topic that was discussed extensively in the European Parliament's Committee on Industry, Research, and Energy

(European Parliament, 2007e) and at both the ministerial and the heads of state and government levels (Council of the European Union, 2008a, 2008b, 2008c). The EESC considered the absence of a focus on social impacts (as well as ILUC) "completely inadequate," and believed the biofuels policy lacked a "well thought-out sustainability strategy" (EESC, 2009: 48). At the request of the European Parliament, however, the Directive did include a reporting obligation for the European Commission on the social sustainability of the EU's biofuels policy (European Parliament, 2008b: 12).

Second, ILUC impacts were not included in the sustainability standard. The European Commission had initially put the issue aside with the simple statement that "it can be expected that the main impact of increased biofuel demand will be a further increase in productivity, not an increase in the quantity of land used for agriculture" (European Commission, 2008d: 144–145). Nevertheless, ILUC remained a contentious issue up to the final negotiations between the European Commission, the Council of Ministers, and the European Parliament in December 2008. The NGO community was especially persistent in its requests to seriously consider ILUC.[29] Partly under the NGOs' influence, the European Parliament asked to include an ILUC factor in the calculation of GHG emissions reductions (EurActiv, 2008b). This proposal was rejected by the Council of Ministers but the compromise was that by 2010, the European Commission would have to examine how to potentially include such a factor into GHG emissions calculations (EurActiv, 2008a). Claude Turmes, who was the European Parliament's rapporteur for the RED, was clearly disappointed with this outcome: "Our planet has limits. We have limited oil resources, but we also have limited agricultural land. This is why we have [to] put a stop to the myth of 'large luxury cars and four-by-fours with pseudogreen petrol' … [and] fight against the arrival on the market of insane agrofuels!" (European Parliament, 2008a).

Finally, the European Commission had argued against including food security criteria in the sustainability standard. Similar to social criteria, the Commission argued that it would not be possible to associate food security impacts with individual consignments of biofuels. In addition, the Commission noted that even though competition with food production could initially lead to lower food availability and an increase in food expenditures for poor families, rural families would benefit from higher prices for produce and higher demand (European

Commission, 2008d: 130). Moreover, the European Commission denied any responsibility for the EU in the food crisis, stating, "[a]s regards the effects attributable to biofuels, in 2007 the supply shortfall of main grain producing countries was four times as large as the increasing demand for biofuels. Moreover, the main source of this increased biofuel demand is the U.S. market and not the European market" (European Commission, 2008d: 131). Other studies have also cast doubt on the allegations that the biofuels demand was largely responsible for rising food prices in 2006–2008, focusing instead on the role of rising energy prices and commodity speculation (Baffes and Haniotis, 2010; Timilsina and Shrestha, 2010; UK Department for Environment, 2010). Nonetheless, the EU did take action to reduce the pressure on food prices domestically as well as internationally (Council of the European Union, 2008c), even though Member States were not willing to include food security criteria in the biofuels policy.

Increased Scrutiny of Private Biofuels Governance: The 2015 ILUC Directive

The share of biofuels in the transport sector steadily grew as a result of the EU's policies. It increased from 0.2 percent in 2000 to 0.8 percent in 2004, 3.4 percent in 2008 and 5.3 percent in 2015 (European Commission, 2005a: 27; 2010b; 2017c: 8). This growth was the result of the development of support systems by Member States, mainly in the form of tax relief and blending targets. By 2010, for example, twenty Member States had developed biofuels obligations, while twenty-four had tax exemptions for biofuels (European Commission, 2011j). After 2010, biofuels consumption growth slowed down because of the economic crisis, on the one hand, and the uncertainty resulting from the inclusion of sustainability criteria in the 2009 RED, on the other. Still, the Commission reported that "75% of all biofuels consumed in the EU were produced within the Union" (79 percent for biodiesel and 71 percent for bioethanol) (European Commission, 2015b: 15). EurObserv'ER reports (2013, 2016) indicated that the share of biofuels certified as sustainable grew from 57 percent in 2012, to an estimated 92 percent in 2015. While figures on the share of this total that is certified by voluntary schemes is not available, it was estimated that "most" of it was certified by such schemes (European Court of Auditors, 2016: 15).

The RED's meta-standard approach resulted in a controlled proliferation of approved private certification schemes, with a total of nineteen schemes approved between 2011 and 2014 (Table 4.3).[30] This was a result of the European Commission recognizing these schemes "regardless of whether another recognised scheme already covers the same type of feedstocks, area, etc." (European Commission, 2010f: 3), and letting the market decide which schemes would survive.[31] The first set of seven programs was approved in 2011. Five of these were linked to programs that existed prior to the promulgation of the 2009 RED: ISCC; Bonsucro; RTRS; RSB; and the "Greenergy Brazilian Bioethanol verification programme." Two additional programs approved in 2007 were the "Biomass Biofuels Sustainability voluntary scheme" (2BSvs), which is a French scheme developed by a consortium of companies led by Bureau Veritas, and the Spanish multinational Abengoa's "RED Bioenergy Sustainability Assurance" (RBSA) (European Commission, 2011a). In 2012, six more schemes were approved: three of them – RSPO, Red Tractor, and SQC – were linked to preexisting programs, while the others emerged afterwards, namely, schemes by bioethanol firm Ensus, the German agricultural and biofuels sector (REDcert), and the Dutch Standardization Institute (NTA 8080).[32] In 2013, the European Commission approved the "Biograce GHG calculation tool," which had been co-funded by the EU's Intelligent Energy Europe program and coordinated by several national research institutes, government agencies, and consultancy agencies. Finally, in 2014, five more schemes were approved by Finnish company Neste Oil (Hydrotreated Vegetable Oil [HVO] Renewable Diesel Scheme), the Grain and Feed Trade Association (Gafta Trade Assurance Scheme [GTAS]), the Polish Oil and Gas Institute (KZR INiG System), and the United Kingdom's Agricultural Industries Confederation (Trade Assurance Scheme for Combinable Crops [TASCC] and the Universal Feed Assurance Scheme [UFAS]).

Despite the European Commission approving all schemes on the basis of the sustainability criteria discussed, the schemes differ in three important ways. First, it is not necessarily the case that each scheme is approved for the full set of sustainability criteria. For example, the Bonsucro standard was approved for all sustainability criteria, except for the provisions on grasslands. Another example is the Biograce GHG calculation tool, which was only approved for the GHG emissions-reductions criterion. The European Commission has furthermore, been

Table 4.3 EU-approved biofuels certification schemes (2014)

Voluntary Scheme	Approval Year	Scheme Type	Feedstock	Scope	2009 RED Sustainability Criteria			
					GHG Emissions (Art. 17.2)	High Bio-diversity Value Land (Art. 17.3)	High Carbon Stock Land (Art. 17.4)	Peatlands (Art. 17.5)
ISCC	2011	Multi-stakeholder	Wide range	Global	✓	✓	✓	✓
Bonsucro EU	2011	Multi-stakeholder	Sugar cane	Global	✓	✓[c]	✓	✓
RTRS EU	2011	Multi-stakeholder	Soy	Global	✓	✓	✓	✓
RSB EU	2011	Multi-stakeholder	Wide range	Global	✓	✓[c]	✓	✓
2BSvs	2011	Multi-stakeholder	Wide range	Global	✓	✓[c]	✓	✓
Abengoa	2011	Firm	Wide range	Global	✓	✓[c]	✓	✓
Greenergy	2011	Multi-stakeholder	Sugar cane	Brazil	✓	✓	✓	✓
Ensus	2012	Firm	Bioethanol	EU	✓	✓	✓	✓
Red Tractor	2012	Industry	Cereals, oil seeds, sugar beet	UK	–[a]			
SQC	2012	Industry	Winter wheat, maize, oil seed rape	UK (north)	–[a]	✓	✓	✓
REDcert	2012	Industry	Wide range	Europe	✓	✓	✓	✓

		Standardization						
NTA 8080	2012	Institute	Wide range	Global	✓	✓[c]	✓	✓
RSPO EU	2012	Multi-stakeholder	Palm oil	Global	✓	✓	✓	✓
Biograce	2013	Multi-stakeholder	Wide range	Global	✓	–	–	–
Neste Oil HVO	2014	Firm	Wide range	Global	✓	✓	✓	✓
GTAS	2014	Industry	Wide range	Global	–[b]	✓	✓	✓
KZR INiG	2014	Research Institute	Wide range	EU	✓	✓	✓	✓
TASCC	2014	Industry	Wide range	UK	–[b]	✓	✓	✓
UFAS	2014	Industry	Wide range	UK	–[b]	✓	✓	✓

[a] The scheme "gives accurate data on two elements necessary for the purposes of … Article 17(2) of Directive 2009/28/EC, in particular, the geographic area the crops come from and the annualised emissions from carbon stock changes caused by land-use change."

[b] The scheme "uses accurate data for purposes of Article 17(2) of Directive 2009/28/EC … in as far as it ensures that all relevant information from economic operators upstream the chain of custody is transferred to the economic operators downstream the chain of custody."

[c] Not approved for Article 17.3.c on highly biodiverse grassland.

Sources: European Commission (2011b, 2011c, 2011d, 2012b, 2012c, 2012d, 2014a, 2014b, 2014c, 2016g)

strict with the certification schemes in terms of the absolute content of their substantive standards. Since none of the schemes had standards containing all the details of each of the relevant EU sustainability criteria, schemes have had to adopt the criteria almost word for word.[33] This has resulted in several of the main preexisting schemes (Bonsucro, RTRS, RSB, and RSPO) developing a specific EU-compliant standard that operates beside their more generic standard that applies to the rest of the world.

Second, the European Commission has not only approved multi-stakeholder schemes, but has also allowed individual companies or industry associations to set up their own schemes. This decision has resulted in a situation in which certification schemes that spent valuable resources on establishing a credible stakeholder-driven initiative are competing with schemes that are more one-sided in terms of interest representation and stakeholder involvement. This difference is even noticeable among multi-stakeholder schemes that are seemingly similar. RSB, for example, is a pluralist initiative, organized in seven chambers representing various interests of all parts of the supply chain. It is also a member of the ISEAL Alliance. The program, however, has had much difficulty in gaining support in the market. The ISCC program, on the other hand, has been the most successful scheme in the EU in terms of the number of certificates it has granted. It is, however, much less pluralist and more business oriented. As Ponte (2014: 8) explains, ISCC developed as an industry-dominated scheme, and only included other stakeholders at a later stage: "This expansion took place *after* the main features of the system had been in place – and had already accepted [sic] by the German Ministry of Agriculture. As a result, although its current governance structure includes a General Assembly, a Board, an Executive Board and Technical Committees, its 'roundtabling' process has been shallow and cosmetic. This process follows Fransen's (2012: 9) observation that organizational change can take the form of window dressing."

Finally, and similarly, important differences exist between those certification schemes that have been developed with the sole intent of implementing the EU Directive and those that are more encompassing and global in nature, many of which predate the 2009 RED. According to studies by the International Union for Conservation of Nature (IUCN) (2013) and WWF (Schlamann et al., 2013), multi-stakeholder schemes such as the global RSPO, RSB, RTRS, Bonsucro, ISCC, and NTA 8080, and the national Greenergy, and schemes not merely established to implement RED, perform better on a range of ecological and social criteria. Yet, even those schemes that exceed the EU sustainability criteria, WWF has argued, have been deficient in many areas, including "social, environmental and water management systems, handling of invasive species, handling of hazardous chemicals, maintenance and restoration of riparian vegetation, waste management, [and] segregation of supply chains in order to offer a non-GMO [genetically modified organisms] option" (Schlamann et al., 2013: 21). These schemes include those in which WWF has been a stakeholder. Likewise, German and Schoneveld (2011) found that of the original seven schemes that were approved in 2011, Abengoa's RBSA and 2BSvs did not incorporate any social criteria, while other schemes did so unevenly.

Despite the fragmentation of the private governance market, harmonization among private schemes has not occurred yet. Early efforts to bring stakeholders together, including attempts by IUCN and Shell, did not conclude successfully (IUCN and Shell, 2010). After the EU RED was promulgated, RSB focused on promoting mutual recognition within the EU market, noting that "[b]iofuels and other biomaterials certified by any EU recognized Voluntary Sustainability Scheme can be accepted by RSB certified operators into their chain of custody" (RSB, 2014c). As mentioned earlier, it was only in 2014 that RSB accepted an EU-approved biofuels-specific scheme, namely Bonsucro, as "*de facto* considered compliant with a majority of RSB requirements" (RSB, 2014a).

Several of these issues related to the implementation of the 2009 RED resulted in the approval of the private schemes becoming a topic of discussion again in the context of the negotiations around a new biofuels directive. In the run-up to the reform, NGOs heavily criticized the European Commission's modus operandi. The NGOs argued that the approval process of certification schemes was not transparent in terms of the degree to which schemes needed to comply with the EU's procedural regulation (Brand, 2011). The European Commission responded that the approval process is technical in nature and that all relevant information, apart from sensitive commercial information, has been publicly available in the approval documents.[34] Nonetheless, the biofuels policy reform process resulted in updated procedural rules for approving private governance schemes.

The reform process started in 2012 when the Commission proposed a new directive to specifically target ILUC, limit the use of first-generation biofuels, and encourage the use of advanced biofuels (European Commission, 2012g). The negotiations of this directive, commonly referred to as the ILUC Directive (European Parliament and Council of the European Union, 2015), were very tense and difficult considering they amounted to a partial reversal of the earlier EU support for crop-based biofuels (Skogstad, 2017). Among other things, the ILUC Directive, which was promulgated in 2015, placed a cap of 7 percent on first-generation biofuels (within the overall 10 percent renewable energy target for transport) and required fuels suppliers and the European Commission to report on GHG emissions related to ILUC.

While the biofuels sustainability criteria did not change, the procedural rules for private certification schemes did. The ILUC Directive intended to increase transparency around the private schemes and make approval processes more stringent. Private schemes were now required to yearly publish the auditors they used and their accreditation information. Moreover, the Directive required schemes to provide the European Commission with information annually on, among other things, their audits, procedures for addressing noncompliance, stakeholder involvement, feedstocks and biofuels that were certified, and rules for accreditation. The Directive also allowed, but did not require, the European Commission to establish mandatory "standards of independent auditing" in the future. Finally, the Directive mandated mutual recognition of private schemes and schemes developed by a country's national agency with respect to the verification of the EU's sustainability criteria.

The original European Commission proposal for the ILUC Directive did not include any of these provisions. Upon discussing the Commission's proposal, however, the European Parliament suggested the Commission establish mandatory minimum procedural rules for private governance schemes. Considering the "lack of criteria that those schemes need to comply with in order to obtain recognition," the European Parliament deemed such criteria necessary to ensure "independence and reliability of audits and the involvement of local and indigenous communities," as well as the availability of "clear and stringent rules on the exclusion of consignments of biofuels and bioliquids from the scheme in case of noncompliance with its provisions" (European Parliament, 2016: 375). In addition, the Parliament suggested mutual recognition of all schemes (both national and private ones). This proposal was based on the idea that a lack of mutual recognition would result in "unfair trade barriers, particularly for smaller companies" and would make national schemes "inferior and discriminated against in comparison with voluntary schemes" (European Parliament, 2015: 86).

The European Commission, however, rejected several of these suggested amendments. It argued that it already had established clear criteria – and made them publicly available – for the approval of private schemes. The Commission also argued that "voluntary schemes should not be forced to recognise national systems" (European Commission, 2013b) and that "[m]utual recognition between Voluntary Schemes approved by the Commission … is also detrimental to the idea that they may certify further sustainability aspects beyond" the EU's sustainability criteria (European Commission, 2014d: 7). In that respect, the European Commission defended the right of private schemes to differentiate themselves based on their own private standards after their approval by the Commission. The Council of Ministers agreed that the automatic mutual recognition suggested by the European Parliament was not warranted. It proposed mutual recognition of national and private schemes, once the national scheme was assessed by the European Commission. Instead of the Parliament's requested mandatory minimum procedural criteria, the Council of Ministers suggested imposing reporting requirements on the private schemes as well as the Commission, which, as mentioned, would be adopted in the final Directive (Council of the European Union, 2015).

These updates to the procedural rules for private schemes were not a big part of the debate on the ILUC Directive. Most of the time was spent on the controversial issues of the cap on crop-based biofuels and the question of whether an ILUC factor needed to be included in measuring GHG emissions. Yet, the updates did deal with some of the problems related to the transparency of the approval process, the organization of the private schemes, and potential trade barriers due to a lack of mutual recognition, while also safeguarding the private schemes' role as policy gap fillers.

Conclusion

While many policymakers, stakeholders, and experts originally considered crop-based biofuels to be an environmentally friendly energy source, this perspective has been completely turned upside down in recent years. In the early 2000s, the EU deliberately created a market for biofuels, based on the rationale that these alternative fuels would contribute to GHG emissions reductions, energy independence, and economic development opportunities for farmers and rural development. Soon after the promulgation of the 2003 Biofuels Directive that established this market, however, concerns over the detrimental environmental impacts of biofuels came to dominate the policy debate. On the road to addressing these impacts, the domestic benefits of market differentiation and the fragmentation of the private governance market resulted in the establishment of both standards and procedural regulations for private governance schemes.

The European Commission and the European Parliament early on promoted the adoption of sustainability rules and, considering the nascent state of the private governance market, a public certification scheme. Industry and farmers' lobbies, however, defended EU-grown crops as sufficiently regulated through existing CAP rules and feared that additional sustainability rules would threaten the EU biofuels market. Instead, these lobbies targeted presumably unsustainable imports. Incentives to develop stricter sustainability criteria came from NGO pressure, new scientific evidence about the environmental impacts of biofuels, and national initiatives in the United Kingdom, the Netherlands, and Germany, as well as the USA. These developments revealed a clear choice for the EU biofuels industry: adopt sustainability rules for biofuels or witness the EU biofuels sector losing credibility and support. Differentiating biofuels based on their sustainability characteristics was, in other words, considered to be in the EU industry's own interests, since only in that way could the sector survive and continue to create economic opportunities for farmers and biofuels producers. Furthermore, concerns about the compliance of the sustainability criteria with WTO rules were circumvented by allowing non-sustainable biofuels onto the market, even though they would not receive tax support or be counted toward national targets.

Transnational private governance schemes had rapidly developed in the meantime and were providing market differentiation by the time EU policymakers considered developing concrete sustainability rules. The existing diversity and the expected future diversity of certification schemes, as well as the lack of harmonized standards and procedures further warranted EU-level control. Moreover, policymakers considered private governance schemes useful instruments to verify compliance with public sustainability rules. They valued private schemes for their potential to reduce policy-implementation costs for Member States; to allow for extraterritorial policy reach through the verification of compliance of non-EU biofuels with the EU's sustainability criteria; and to include in their standards sustainability criteria that had been, for political reasons, excluded from the EU's public standard. These objectives all fit within the context of what has been called a "meta-standard approach," in which certification of biofuels by Commission-approved schemes is considered sufficient to show compliance with the EU's sustainability criteria. Particularly strong support for this approach came from WWF, which had been involved in several of the major private governance schemes, as well as several Member States that were experimenting with a meta-standard approach themselves. Continued problems with the diversity of private governance schemes can be partly blamed on the way the European Commission had been approving private schemes; the problems resulted in somewhat more stringent procedural regulation in the 2015 ILUC Directive.

The future of crop-based biofuels is highly uncertain. Policymakers have continued to debate the sustainability of these types of biofuels and in 2015 shifted EU policy slightly toward stimulating non-crop-based, or "advanced," biofuels that are considered environmentally friendlier. This shift will be further intensified in the future, since it is unlikely the EU will continue to support crop-based biofuels as it has done in the past. Nonetheless, crop-based biofuels are still predominantly used, since advanced biofuels are mostly not commercially available yet. Private sustainability schemes will therefore continue to play their role, both in the EU policy context and independently, including in the future to guarantee the sustainability of advanced biofuels.

5 | Fair Trade

The expectation that trade among nations should be fair seems reasonable. Yet, definitions of the term "fair trade" differ quite significantly depending on the institutional setting. Since the EU's Treaty of Lisbon, which was signed in 2007 and entered into force in 2009, the concept shows up for the first time in Article 3 of the Treaty on European Union, stating that in its external relations, the EU will contribute to "free and fair trade" (European Union, 2010: Article 3(5)). In the context of the international trade regime, fairness refers to equality of opportunity or equal treatment. This is reflected in principles such as "most-favored nation" and "national treatment," which ensure, respectively, that concessions to one trade partner covered under the regime are immediately extended to all trade partners, and that domestically produced and imported goods are treated equally (Article I and Article III of the General Agreement on Tariffs and Trade [GATT]).

Fairness in trade, furthermore, has close connections to issues of distributive justice among rich and poor countries (Brown and Stern, 2012). In some instances, countries have implemented this interpretation of fairness as part of preferential access provisions for countries from the global South, such as through the 2000 Cotonou Agreement between the EU and countries from Africa, the Caribbean, and the Pacific (ACP). Alternatively, and more controversially, some countries have approached fairness from the perspective of demanding that "trade access be made conditional upon protection of labour standards" (Burgoon, 2009: 643).

Civil society definitions of fair trade often include such distributional elements. In that context, fair trade refers to "a critique of the historical inequalities inherent in international trade and to a belief that trade can be made more socially just" (Raynolds and Bennett, 2015: 3). Some private governance schemes in this issue area adopt such a counter-hegemonic focus, highlighting the need to improve the sustainable development dimensions of North–South trade when dealing with commodities such as coffee, tea, and cocoa. In this respect, the term "Fair Trade" (two words, capital letters) is used to refer to the international Fair Trade movement and the way it defines its specific approach to fair trade. The term "Fairtrade" (one word, capital letter) then refers to the private certification scheme and label that this movement has developed and that is operated by Fairtrade International (formerly Fairtrade Labelling Organizations International [FLO]) (Fairtrade International, 2011a; FTAO, s.d.).

Policy discussions on private fair trade governance in the EU initially only focused on Fair Trade and Fairtrade certification. These discussions, which entailed suggestions for developing both standards and procedural regulations, date back to at least the early 1990s, when a diverse set of mainly nationally focused private initiatives had emerged, and FLO was yet to be established. With time, the policy area expanded to include other private governance schemes that were considered competitors of Fairtrade (cf. Conroy, 2007: 250–253). These organizations included Rainforest Alliance and UTZ Certified specifically. While these two organizations in January 2018 announced they would be merging, for the entire time frame of the discussion in this book they were operating independently. This expansion of the policy domain may be surprising to some observers, since these private governance schemes do not claim to share the same ideological or normative underpinnings as Fair Trade. Yet, reflecting the European Commission's encompassing definition of private fair trade governance, these schemes are all covered under this policy area in this chapter.[1]

Unlike the cases of sustainable biofuels production and organic agriculture, on two separate occasions – in 1999 and in 2009 – the European Commission explicitly decided not to intervene in private fair trade governance. This means that despite suggestions for interventions by various EU institutions and private actors, and the European Commission's own interest in exploring possible interventions, the Commission never tabled a concrete legislative proposal to regulate private fair trade governance. This situation stands in stark contrast to the other cases discussed in this book.

The EU's noninterventionist approach is the result of a combination of low domestic benefits of product differentiation and low levels of fragmentation of the private governance market. First, the issue area is characterized by specific North–South trade dynamics and a focus on commodities produced in countries in the global South. The lack of concrete productive opportunities in the EU has prevented interest mobilization in defense of domestic producers. At the same time, the structure of trade relationships in this issue area implies that the EU is, more often than in the other issue areas discussed in this book, confronted with the institutional constraints of the international trade regime when trying to establish standards or procedural regulations. In particular, these constraints have prevented the EU from favoring products imported from certain specific regions, such as Member States' former colonies in ACP countries, based on their fair trade production characteristics. Especially in the 1990s, the European Parliament – that has co-decision competence in the context of trade and development cooperation policies – and several Member States, including the United Kingdom and France, proposed interventions to this effect. The European Commission also explored possible interventions in the context of both the reform of the EU banana import regime, which in the late 1990s was found to be violating international trade rules, and the 2003 Sustainable Trade Action Plan (STAP) that was never formally released. On both occasions, the conclusion was that intervention, in particular in the form of standards regulation, was not feasible.

Second, the Fair Trade movement's successful harmonization of several complementary private governance schemes contributed to the EU's noninterventionist approach. Up to the late 1990s, the movement consisted of various nationally focused labeling programs. This fragmentation raised concerns about a further proliferation of private governance schemes, supply chain confusion, private governance legitimacy problems, and intra-EU trade and competitive distortions. This situation led to proposals, in particular under the influence of the European Parliament, for fair trade harmonization that put pressure on ongoing harmonization efforts by the Fair Trade movement. The successful conclusion of these efforts resulted in the establishment of FLO in 1997, which largely alleviated these concerns and reduced calls for the European Commission to intervene.

Finally, competitive dynamics among fair trade schemes have further curtailed EU interventions. The broadening of the policy issue area in the early 2000s should have led to renewed concerns over a lack of harmonization. Yet, differences among the various schemes – especially among Fairtrade on the one hand, and Rainforest Alliance and

UTZ Certified on the other – were framed as commercial and economic-ideological in nature and not problematized as a fragmentation issue. These differences have also prevented the EU from establishing even a voluntary fair trade standard, since it has proven difficult to define a sensible lowest common denominator. Indeed, private governance schemes actively opposed any EU intervention in that respect. Furthermore, a coalition comprised of representatives of the Fair Trade movement and members of the European Parliament attempted to make the European Commission recognize the specific features of Fair Trade at the expense of the other schemes' approaches. These attempts partly failed due to counter lobbying by Fairtrade's competitors and their associated stakeholders. The European Commission argued that favoring one private governance approach over others would push equally valuable approaches to fair trade out of the market and would not serve the EU's overall goal of promoting sustainable development.

Transnational Private Governance and Fair Trade

The Fair Trade Movement

Fairtrade is the main initiative that is referred to when talking about transnational private governance in this issue area. The origins of what is now the Fair Trade movement lie in the early post–World War II period, when international refugee relief agencies including the Mennonite Central Committee/Ten Thousand Villages, Sales Exchange for Refugee Rehabilitation and Vocation, and Oxfam started trading in crafts produced by refugees and poor communities in the global South. From the 1960s onward, a more political-economic focus on the social injustices of the global trade system and a discourse about "alternative trade" was added, fueled by the emergence of social justice movements. This new perspective resulted in the establishment of fair trade importing organizations in the Netherlands and the United Kingdom, and retail "World Shops" where fair trade products were sold (Fridell et al., 2008; Kocken, 2006; Low and Davenport, 2006). The main goal was to simplify and shorten trade relationships between producer and consumer sites by eliminating middlemen, and to ensure higher incomes for Southern producers (Raynolds and Greenfield, 2015: 26). Besides being engaged in trading products, these organizations also provided assistance, advice, and support to marginalized producers in the global economy with the aim of fostering the development of an alternative economic approach and socioeconomic justice for the poor. This model of importing mainly craft goods and agricultural products such as sugarcane, cocoa, and coffee, and selling them in specialized retail shops, has over time expanded into a broad network of organizations. For example, in 1994 the Network of European World Shops (NEWS!) was established as a network of national associations of World Shops in thirteen countries (NEWS!, 2004a).[2]

A second route to selling fair trade products – through certification and labeling – developed in the 1980s. The Dutch organization Max Havelaar is generally considered the first fair trade certification program. It was established by Dutch priest Frans van der Hoff, who worked in Mexico with a local coffee cooperative, and Nico Roozen of the Dutch NGO Solidaridad. The program started certifying coffee in 1988 (Kocken, 2006; Max Havelaar, 2013). It was initially set up as a means to increase fair trade sales. Early on, the European Fair Trade Association (EFTA) – which informally since 1987 and formally since 1990, has represented fair trade importers in Europe (EFTA, 2015) – approached Max Havelaar with the suggestion to expand the certification program to products other than coffee and to markets beyond the Netherlands. EFTA, however, was unsuccessful in this effort. Max Havelaar argued that it wanted to keep its activities limited, partly based on the reasoning that "each country should develop its own culturally resonant approach, and this idea clashed with EFTA's vision of a unified system" (Bennett, 2013: 50). In 1992, EFTA established its own labeling initiative – TransFair International – with national labeling initiatives operating in Germany, Canada, Japan, the USA, Austria, Italy, and Luxembourg (Bennett, 2015: 86; Reed, 2012: 301–302). This trend of proliferating labeling schemes was a response to the collapse of the International Coffee Agreement in 1989 that led alternative trade associations to look to alternative means to increase sales. According to Bennett (2013: 44), multiple labeling schemes were established as the result of "heated debates between pioneers" on topics such as labeling non-coffee products and whether or not to support labeling of products from plantations. Not long after it had rejected EFTA's request, Max Havelaar did branch out with local organizations emerging in Belgium, Denmark, France, Norway, and Switzerland, yet each with its own distinct logo and policies. Similar schemes with local names also emerged in the United Kingdom ("Fair-trade Foundation") and Sweden ("Rättvisemärkt") (Bennett, 2013: 51; EESC, 1996; European Parliament, 1998b).

From the late 1990s onward, several initiatives were launched to harmonize the various fair trade approaches and organizations. A first initiative focused on the labeling organizations. These organizations established what was called a "Trans-Max" working group to oversee the debates around, and processes of, consolidation of the various fair trade labeling schemes (Bennett, 2015: 87). There were significant differences of opinion among the different programs, such as on the certification of plantations, the participation of producers in governing the schemes, and the degree of coordination, with each private scheme eager to defend its autonomy (Auld, 2014b: 143–145). There were good reasons to attempt harmonization; one reason was to create an umbrella decision-making body that could settle disputes on diverging approaches, including the question of whether all or only the main ingredients of a product needed to be certified (for example, cocoa and sugar in a chocolate bar). Another reason was to overcome adminis-trative complications resulting from the programs sharing producer registers, which were housed by different schemes for each commodity. Finally, producers complained that the existence of various national schemes resulted in the duplication of work and increased inefficiencies (Bennett, 2013: 53–57).

In 1997, this harmonization process resulted in seventeen national labeling initiatives establishing FLO, with the aim of uniting the initia-tives under one umbrella, with one label and harmonized standards and certification systems (Fairtrade International, 2011c). This har-monization effort under FLO led, in 2002, to the launch of the Fair-trade Certification Mark, which has been gradually replacing the different national labels (Fairtrade International, 2011a). Changes were also made to the way certification occurred. Initially, FLO con-sidered certification to be an in-house process, in the sense that there was no strict separation between standard-setting and certification activities. Facing critiques regarding the legitimacy of this type of certification, FLO realigned its practices with ISO Guide 65. In 2003, an independent and ISO-accredited certification organization – FLO-Cert – was established and separated from the standard-setting organ-ization, which was renamed Fairtrade International (while retaining the acronym FLO) (Bennett, 2013: 59–61; FLO, 2003; Wilson and

Mutersbaugh, 2015: 289–290). One important result of this change was that while certification was originally provided at no cost to the producer, regular fees for audits now needed to be paid (Raynolds and Greenfield, 2015: 27). FLO's decision to develop its own certification organization was different from what happened in many other sectors, where it is common to establish an accreditation procedure so that other private auditors can also certify against the private standards. The rationale for developing its own certification body had to do with FLO's mission of assisting marginalized producers in the global South. FLO believed that not many private auditors would be interested in being accredited for what would remain a small niche market for certification (Auld, 2014b: 146).

Besides the product certification and labeling initiatives, the second harmonization effort focused on the trading organizations. In 1989, thirty-six of such fair trade organizations promoting market access for small producers established the International Federation of Alternative Trade (IFAT). In 2004 – by then renamed the International Fair Trade Association – IFAT established the Fair Trade Organization Mark and monitoring system for member organizations that showed a 100 percent commitment to Fair Trade in their operations (WFTO, 2011). At the time, the monitoring system was not a full-fledged third-party certification system. Instead, it was based on a self-assessment report submitted by the organization wanting to obtain membership, which was then checked by the Standards and Monitoring Committee (peer review) and an external Fair Trade expert (Boonman et al., 2011: 16; Cremona and Marin Duran, 2013b: 114). After another name change to the World Fair Trade Organization (WFTO) in 2008, a new Guarantee System was introduced in 2013 to further improve the legitimacy and credibility of WFTO membership, which includes formal audits and a complaint system (WFTO, 2016).[3]

A third harmonization effort was concluded in 2001, when a coalition of FLO, IFAT, NEWS!, and EFTA agreed on a shared definition and the principles of Fair Trade (FTAO, s.d.).[4] On this basis, Fairtrade International and the WFTO adopted a Charter of Fair Trade Principles in 2009. It aimed to "provide a single international reference point for Fair Trade through a concise explanation of Fair Trade principles and the two main routes by which they are implemented" (WFTO and FLO, 2009). The Charter identified five core principles: market access for marginalized producers, sustainable and equitable trading relationships, capacity building and empowerment, consumer awareness raising and advocacy, and Fair Trade as a "social contract."

The EU is an important market for Fairtrade-certified products. In 2009, the EU accounted for more than 60 percent of worldwide Fairtrade sales, which by 2014 had grown to 87 percent of worldwide sales (Boonman et al., 2011: 23; International Trade Center, 2015: 30). However, in a global context Fairtrade represents a niche market. In 2005, Fairtrade was estimated to account for only 0.01 percent of global trade (Riedel et al., 2005). By 2014, it was estimated that Fairtrade-certified areas accounted for 0.06 percent of the global agricultural area, with 45 percent in Africa and the Middle East, 42 percent in Latin America, and 13 percent in Asia and Oceania (International Trade Center, 2015: 25, 27). Looking at individual commodities, however, the perspective is slightly better. In 2015, Fairtrade certified 12.4 percent of the global coffee area, 5.7 percent of global cocoa production, 3.7 percent of global tea production, and 0.8 percent of the global banana production area (International Trade Center, 2017: 71, 79, 87, 121). The value of global Fairtrade-certified goods was estimated at €3.4 billion in 2009, €4.9 billion in 2011, and €7.3 billion in 2015 (Fairtrade International, 2011b, 2016; FLO, 2009). In 2012–2013, these goods originated from 1,149 producer organizations, with over 1.3 million farmers and workers in seventy countries, all located in the global South. The United Kingdom, Germany, France, the Netherlands, Sweden, and Ireland are the largest EU consumer markets in retail value (Fairtrade International, 2013).

Fairtrade Compared to Competing Private Governance Schemes

While the Fair Trade movement is the dominant actor in this issue area, two other organizations are seen as competitors in the context of private fair trade governance. The first one is Rainforest Alliance. This organization was established in 1987 as a New York–based conservation organization. Originally, Rainforest Alliance was engaged in sustainable forest management, for which it developed the first forest certification program, the SmartWood Certification program, in 1989. The program was a response to boycotts of tropical timber by various NGOs, which Rainforest Alliance considered ineffective for both solving the deforestation problem and helping the Southern communities that were dependent on such commodities (Conroy, 2007: 62–63, 68–70; Wille, 2004). The scheme issued the first certificate in 1990 in Indonesia. Also, in 1990, Rainforest Alliance branched out to banana production in Central America to address the adverse effects on tropical forests. It developed the Better Banana Project certification program by engaging with a multinational company, Chiquita, and Costa Rican farmers, NGOs, government agencies, and local community leaders.

The cooperation of Rainforest Alliance and Chiquita emerged from criticism of the multinational regarding its engagement in converting forests into land for banana monoculture production, broader concerns about banana companies' environmental and health impacts in Costa Rica, and the Rainforest Alliance's rejection of boycotts as an appropriate pressure instrument. Rainforest Alliance was criticized for directly working with a multinational like Chiquita, yet the first farms were certified in Hawaii and Costa Rica in 1993 (Rainforest Alliance, 2014a; Taylor and Scharlin, 2004: 32–38; Wille, 2004). Other commodities, such as coffee, cocoa, and flowers, soon followed. In 1995, for example, the first coffee farm was certified in Guatemala, as were, in 1997, the first citrus groves in Ecuador, and in 2000, the first flower and fern farms in Costa Rica (Rainforest Alliance, 2014a).

For all of its activities in Latin America, Rainforest Alliance cooperated with several local NGOs. In 1997, this network of NGOs and Rainforest Alliance formalized their cooperation in the Sustainable Agriculture Network. The ECO-OK label that Rainforest Alliance had been using up until then was replaced by the Rainforest Alliance Certified seal – the now well-known green frog image. In 2007, SAN started separating standard-setting from certification activities by creating an independent International Standards Committee (Sustainable Agriculture Network, 2014). In 2008, SAN and Rainforest Alliance also decided to create an independent accreditation system. Between 2008 and 2010, they partnered with IOAS, which had been established in 1997 to accredit auditors against the organic standards of IFOAM. While SAN and Rainforest Alliance had up to that point only used Sustainable Farm Certification International, IOAS was tasked with accrediting additional auditors (LaChappelle, 2012). Since then, accreditation has been done through the independent SAN Accreditation Body, with the process based on ISO Guide 65 and, since 2012, ISO 17065.

In 2006, the global retail sales of Rainforest Alliance–certified coffee, bananas, and cocoa were more than $1 billion (Sustainable Agriculture Network, 2014). Certified farms are located in over forty countries, most of them in Africa (57 percent in 2014), Latin America (28 percent), and Asia (14 percent) (International Trade Center, 2015: 54). In 2015, Rainforest Alliance reported that it certified 6 percent of global coffee production, 11.8 percent of cocoa production, 15.1 percent of tea production, and 5 percent of banana production (International Trade Center, 2017: 71, 79, 87, 121; SAN/Rainforest Alliance, 2015).

The second important alternative private governance scheme to Fairtrade that was engaged in the EU policy discussions was UTZ Certified. The scheme was established in 1999 and was officially launched in 2002 by the Belgian-Guatemalan coffee grower Nick Bocklandt and the Dutch coffee roaster Ahold Coffee Company (UTZ Certified, 2014c). Until 2007, the program was known as Utz Kapeh, which means "good coffee" in the Mayan language Quiché. As Auld (2014b: 160–161) explains, Fairtrade's specific focus on small-scale farmers and the exclusion of other types of operators provided a niche for Utz Kapeh to fill, and to emerge as a complementary program. With the support of Solidaridad – the Dutch NGO involved with establishing the Max Havelaar program – Utz Kapeh's goal was to create an industry standard "that all coffee companies will accept as standard business procedure, regardless of the extra costs it may involve" (Solidaridad, 2006, as cited in Auld 2014b: 160–161).

As the baseline for its coffee standard, UTZ Certified used the EUREPGAP standard, a standard for Good Agricultural Practice (GAP) that was developed by several European retailers of the Euro-Retailer Produce Working Group, and renamed GLOBALG.A.P. in 2007 (GLOBALG.A.P., 2014). Unlike other programs, UTZ Certified approved audit bodies itself, with the requirement that the auditors had to be accredited by an accreditation body that was a member of the International Accreditation Forum or ISEAL. UTZ also offered monitoring and training programs for auditors (UTZ Certified, 2015a, 2015b). Besides coffee, the scheme developed codes of conduct and certification programs for cocoa and tea.

Commodities certified by UTZ Certified represented 0.04 percent of the global agricultural area in 2014, covering 577,000 producers with 72 percent in Africa, 20 percent in Latin America, and 8 percent in Asia

Table 5.1 *Private fair trade governance and share of global production (%) (2015)*

	Fairtrade	Rainforest Alliance	UTZ Certified	TOTAL
Bananas	0.8[a]	5	–	5.8
Cocoa	5.7	11.8	21	38.5
Coffee	12.4[a]	6	9.3	27.7
Tea	3.7	15.1	1.6	20.4

[a] Based on share of global production area instead of global production volume
Source: International Trade Center (2017)

(International Trade Center, 2015: 63, 65). In 2015, UTZ's global production share was estimated at 21 percent of global production for cocoa, 9.3 percent for coffee, and 1.6 percent for tea (International Trade Center, 2017: 79, 87, 124; UTZ Certified, 2015c: 5, 11).

There are some important differences in the approaches taken by Fairtrade International, Rainforest Alliance, and UTZ Certified. First, while they have all incorporated the three dimensions of sustainable development – the environmental, social, and economic dimensions – they have done so to different degrees. Fairtrade, for example, is considered to be focused more on the social aspects of the production process, on empowering producers in the global South, and on tackling poverty. Rainforest Alliance, on the other hand, places more emphasis on the environmental dimension, while UTZ Certified focused more on farm management, such as farm efficiency and traceability (Bitzer et al., 2008; Rainforest Alliance, 2014b; UTZ Certified, 2014b).

Second, the programs differ considerably in the way they approach compensation for farmers. Fairtrade is the only program that offers advance payments and guarantees a minimum price, which is an above-market-price guaranteed minimum.[5] In addition, it offers a Fairtrade premium, which producer organizations can use as they see fit, such as for education, health care, or farm improvement purposes (Fairtrade International, 2014; Fridell et al., 2008). Rainforest Alliance and UTZ Certified, on the other hand, do not guarantee minimum prices or premiums but rather let demand and supply drive prices (Bitzer et al., 2008; Rainforest Alliance, s.d.). Rainforest Alliance, for example, argues that an approach that focuses too much on prices overlooks other factors, such as crop quality, productivity, and efficiency, which equally influence a farm's economic success (Rainforest Alliance, 2010).[6] Similarly, UTZ Certified argued that its responsibility was to "reinforce the independent position of farmers" by training them in "the professionalization of their agricultural practice and operational management," which improves "the quality of their products and allows them to produce higher volumes at lower costs" (UTZ Certified, 2014a).

Finally, the programs differ with respect to their main trading partners. Whereas Fairtrade deals mainly with smallholder producers that are organized in cooperatives, Rainforest Alliance targets large plantations. Moreover, Rainforest Alliance and UTZ Certified cooperate more directly with large multinationals, such as Mars, Ikea, Walmart, Heinz, Cargill, Unilever, Kraft, or Nestlé, and are therefore considered more "mainstream" or "commercial" initiatives (Conroy, 2007: 250–252; Golden et al., 2010; Rainforest Alliance, 2014b; UTZ Certified, 2011, 2014d).[7] Rainforest Alliance has even been "accused of being in industry's pocket" (Knowles, 2011: 28). This does not mean that large corporations are not involved with Fairtrade. In the coffee sector, for example, activist campaigns have led some of the biggest players in the market, such as Nestlé and Proctor & Gamble, to start purchasing Fairtrade-certified coffee, albeit in small amounts (Fridell et al., 2008). In other instances, large companies have committed to Fairtrade by transforming an entire product's sourcing, such as when Cadbury in 2009 announced that its popular Dairy Milk chocolate bar would be made with Fairtrade-certified cocoa, which led to Cadbury doubling its purchases of cocoa from Southern smallholders (Knowles, 2011: 24).

Besides these three private governance schemes, several other private initiatives are operating in the market, such as industry programs and individual company initiatives. Up until 2016, for example, the 4C Association was a prominent coffee-industry-specific initiative. Established in 2003 as the Common Code for the Coffee Community (4C) project, it developed in 2006 into the 4C Association, with more than 300 members, including coffee farmer organizations, traders (importers and exporters), industry (coffee roasters and retailers), and civil society organizations (4C Association, 2014b). The 4C Association developed a code of conduct and a verification system that is now operated by an independent organization, Coffee Assurance Services. According to Bitzer, Francken, and Glasbergen (2008), the 4C Code

represented a baseline for the three sustainable development dimensions, although several NGOs – including Greenpeace, Naturland, and
TransFair Germany – criticized the code for being too lenient (Auld,
2014b: 162). Fairtrade International, Rainforest Alliance, and UTZ
Certified were all members of the 4C Association as part of the Association's "pre-competitive approach," through which it sought "to foster
cooperation between the standards and unite efforts in the coffee
sector ... by promoting other sustainability standards in the market
and by using the 4C Code of Conduct as a tool for farmers to step up
to more demanding certification schemes" (4C Association, 2014a).
These certification programs are currently still members of the 4C
Association's successor, the Global Coffee Platform.

The Ethical Tea Partnership is another industry-wide initiative that
was established in 1997. Called the Tea Sourcing Partnership until
2004, it was developed as an initiative of several United Kingdom-
based tea-sourcing companies. At the time of writing, it represents
more than forty tea companies and retailers from Europe, North
America, Australia, New Zealand, and Sri Lanka (Ethical Tea Partnership, 2014, 2017a). Much like the 4C Association, it has developed a
standard and a monitoring system that verifies the social and environmental conditions of tea producers to help them achieve certification to
schemes like Fairtrade International and Rainforest Alliance (Ethical
Tea Partnership, 2017b).

Individual companies have also established their own initiatives.
One prominent example is the Starbucks C.A.F.E. (Coffee and Farmer
Equity) Practices, developed with Conservation International in 1999.
For 2012, Starbucks stated that 90 percent of its coffee was verified
under the C.A.F.E. Practices, reaching 99 percent in 2017, while 8.1
percent of its coffee purchases were Fairtrade certified (Starbucks,
2013, 2017). Furthermore, individual brands or specialty stores have
also used alternative concepts to brand their products, such as "fairly
traded," "fair-traded," or similar indications (see e.g., Batsell, 2004).

EU Nonintervention: Private Harmonization and WTO Constraints (1994–1999)

Discussions on fair trade and private governance in the EU started in
the early 1990s. They were a direct response to the various local fair
trade programs that had emerged since Max Havelaar and EFTA

developed certification as a feasible market strategy. Several EU institutions issued calls for more streamlined fair trade approaches and definitions; increased transparency and legitimacy of private governance schemes; and a public fair trade label. Apart from fostering harmonization of the private governance market, these proposals were made in support of banana producers in Member States' former colonies after the EU banana regime was found to violate international trade rules. The discussions concluded in 1999 when the European Commission issued a "Communication on fair trade" in which it adopted a noninterventionist approach.

Initial Calls for Harmonization and Professionalization

One of the first clear calls for action came from the European Parliament, when in 1994, it recommended in a Resolution on Promoting Fairness and Solidarity in North–South Trade that "European coordination and joint representation of alternative trade organizations" should be supported (European Parliament, 1994b: 120). In addition, the Resolution discussed the issue of labels, thereby encouraging the "recognition and protection of a quality label certifying fair trade products" (European Parliament, 1994b: 121). One of the ways in which this coordination could happen was by providing more financial support to fair trade organizations in order to facilitate private harmonization. The European Commission at the time was already involved in fostering such cooperation and coordination by financing organizations linked to the fair trade movement and by organizing conferences and seminars to bring European fair trade organizations, distributors, and Member State representatives into contact (La Malfa et al., 1996).

These efforts to enhance coordination and provide clarity on labels and their underlying substantive standards were accompanied by calls to increase the credibility and transparency of private governance schemes. A 1996 EESC Opinion on the European fair trade movement, for example, stressed the need for developing procedural criteria. The Opinion mentioned that an "authoritative system for developing and verifying standards and for accepting products" should be developed and that "national schemes may unintentionally introduce barriers to trade" (EESC, 1996: 42). The EESC also remarked that to enhance such credibility, auditors could use standard EN 45011. The EESC did,

Table 5.2 *EU policy on private fair trade governance*

Year	Title	Main Elements
1994	European Parliament Resolution on Promoting Fairness and Solidarity in North-South Trade	– Calls for fair trade harmonization and quality label
1996	European Economic and Social Committee Opinion on the European "Fair Trade" Marking Movement	– Calls for procedural criteria, while safeguarding the voluntary nature of private governance
1998	European Parliament Committee on Development and Cooperation Report on Fair Trade	– Laments the lack of a common standard and definition of fair trade – Expresses the need for procedural criteria – Supports European fair trade label
1999	European Commission Communication on Fair Trade	– No regulatory interventions proposed – Support for ongoing private harmonization
2005	European Economic and Social Committee Opinion on Ethical Trade and Consumer Assurance Schemes	– Argues against standards regulation – Proposes list of procedural criteria
2006	European Parliament Resolution on Fair Trade and Development	– Calls for a nonbinding legislative act, mainly favoring Fairtrade – Lists several procedural criteria
2009	European Commission Communication on Contributing to Sustainable Development: The Role of Fair Trade and Nongovernmental Trade-Related Sustainability Assurance Schemes	– Argues against "ranking or regulating criteria" related to private governance schemes – Formally recognizes the definition and principles of Fair Trade – Lists set of possible procedural criteria

however, clearly state that it was important to "maintain the voluntary nature of such labelling, both here and in developing countries" and that the schemes "operate in a free market" (EESC, 1996: 41).

The GATT/WTO Challenges to the EU Banana Import Regime

These early discussions on how to respond to private fair trade governance overlapped with discussions on whether privileges could be offered to fair trade products imported from former colonies of EU Member States. This topic made it onto the policy agenda when the EU's import regime for bananas was challenged at the WTO in 1996.

The main issue in the trade dispute was that the EU's 1993 banana import regime provided special treatment to bananas coming from Member States' former colonies and territories in Africa, the Caribbean, and the Pacific, thereby favoring these ACP countries over non-ACP ones. This regime strongly affected Latin American banana-exporting countries, such as Mexico, Honduras, Guatemala, Ecuador, and Costa Rica. The USA, in addition, had a direct stake in the dispute as US multinationals Chiquita, Dole, and Del Monte were mainly active in Latin America (Salas and Jackson, 2000: 146–147). Chiquita, which at the time was cooperating with Rainforest Alliance to certify its banana farms, and had only limited investments in ACP countries, lobbied US policymakers to file a complaint under the GATT and later the WTO (Taylor and Scharlin, 2004: 32, 137–141). Colombia, Costa Rica, Nicaragua, Venezuela, and Guatemala, with support from the USA, initiated the trade complaint against the EU's preferential treatment of ACP countries.

When the GATT panel concluded that the EU's favorable treatment of ACP countries violated GATT rules, the parties to the conflict negotiated the Banana Framework Agreement to address some of the findings of the panel. Guatemala was the only plaintiff that refused to sign the Agreement. Together with the USA, Mexico, Honduras, and Ecuador, Guatemala initiated a case at the newly established WTO. In May 1997, the WTO Dispute Panel ruled that part of the EU's banana import regime violated WTO rules (European Parliament, 1998c: 22–23; Read, 2001; Wiley, 2008: 182–183).

Even before this verdict, and while the EU was beginning to redesign its banana regime according to the anticipated WTO decision, there were calls to link the banana dispute to fair trade. In

September 1996, the ACP-EU Joint Assembly – which brings together Members of Parliament from the EU and ACP countries and which was originally established under the 1975 Lomé Convention, the precursor to the Cotonou Agreement – issued a Resolution on Trade Based on Fairness and Solidarity (ACP-EU Joint Assembly, 1996). The Resolution asked for support for alternative trade associations and for European distributors to increase the supply of fair trade products. It also called for the recognition of a "quality mark for fair-trade products" to allow for preferential treatment of such products (ACP-EU Joint Assembly, 1996: 61). Following this Resolution, members of the European Parliament in early 1997 again requested that the European Commission consider granting more favorable access to fair trade bananas in order to support products from ACP countries (Agri Service International Newsletter, 1997; European Report, 1997a; Osório-Peters, 1998).

In the wake of the WTO ruling, pressure built further on the European Commission to address the banana dispute from a fair trade perspective. An October 1997 resolution by the ACP-EU Joint Assembly expressed great concern over the impact of the WTO's decision on banana-producing ACP countries and insisted "that the [European] Commission should institute arrangements to promote 'fair trade' bananas" (ACP-EU Joint Assembly, 1997: 49). Around the same time, the United Kingdom expressed interest in developing a fair trade label for ACP bananas, while France offered support for ACP producers as well (European Report, 1997b; LA Times, 1997). The European Commission, however, responded negatively to these suggestions. It stated that it had examined the possibility of establishing a fair trade label for bananas in 1995–1996, although it had abandoned this initiative when it became clear that it was difficult to avoid violating WTO rules when discriminating among products based on their modes of production. Yet, the European Commissioner for Agriculture and Rural Development, Franz Fischler, noted that the European Commission would continue examining the feasibility of an EU fair trade label for bananas (European Report, 1997a, 1997b).

The European Parliament picked up the issue again in the context of the revision of the Common Organization of the Market (COM) in bananas following the WTO ruling. In response to the European Commission's COM proposal, the European Parliament adopted a Resolution requesting increased support for fair trade bananas in

ACP as well as other countries from the global South. The European Parliament argued that while a quota for fair trade bananas would not be compatible with WTO rules, "there is no reason why a Fair Trade label should not be promoted within the context of the EU quality policy" (European Parliament, 1998c: 27). Mirroring the specific attention of the EU's policy on Fair Trade to the exclusion of other private governance schemes, the European Parliament's proposal focused only on "bananas produced in compliance with the conditions laid down by Fair Trade Labelling Organisations International (FLO)" (European Parliament, 1998a: 120). In support of the European Parliament's focus on producers following FLO standards, the Council of Ministers later guaranteed financial and technical support for ACP banana producers. This assistance was geared toward helping to establish producer organizations that aimed to engage in fair trade certification and in helping them to master sustainable production methods to achieve this (Council of the European Union, 1999).

By the same token, the European Parliament's suggestion to regulate the certification process was more remarkable. The Parliament's Resolution proposed to make Member States "responsible for accrediting organisations which provide 'fair trade' certification" (European Parliament, 1998a: 120), and grant accreditation only to certification organizations compliant with EN 45011. While FLO at the time was still fully responsible for certification – since FLO-Cert had not been established yet – this proposal by the European Parliament was intended to ensure greater professionalization and consistency of private certification, and seemingly, also to introduce competition among auditors.

Despite these proposals, the Council of Ministers and the European Commission decided to lift any references to fair trade from the reform of the Common Organization of the Market in bananas. The argument for delinking the discussions on fair trade governance from the banana regime was that a broader and more general response was warranted, given that the topic of fair trade touched on many other issues besides bananas (European Report, 1999). The two institutions agreed that the European Commission would develop a communication on fair trade "accompanied by appropriate measures" by March 1, 1999 (Council of the European Union, 1998). The communication was intended to increase support for fair trade organizations and certified products, generally.

Parallel to these developments that were directly related to the banana dispute, broader calls for the harmonization of private fair trade governance continued to be expressed. These calls both supported and put pressure on ongoing harmonization efforts by the Fair Trade movement. A 1998 report of the European Parliament's Committee on Development and Cooperation lamented the lack of a common standard for fair trade and urged that it was "therefore very important that the fair trade sector should arrive at a common definition of the term 'fair trade'"(European Parliament, 1998b: 6). The report acknowledged that the sector had begun drafting a list of overarching principles and it fully supported this private harmonization effort. Yet, in the absence of such principles, the report specified the criteria that the Parliament's Committee believed should be part of a fair trade definition. These criteria included advance payments for producers, a fair price guaranteeing an appropriate standard of living, and direct buying relationships with the producers.[8] In addition, the report supported "measures to lend further credibility to the fair trade certifying bodies," arguing that "fair trade certification must be separate from trading in fair trade products" (European Parliament, 1998b: 6, 9). The report also recommended accreditation of all fair trade organizations to EN 45011.

Finally, the report suggested the "creation of a common European fair trade label" (European Parliament, 1998b: 9), for which financial support could be provided to the fair trade organizations to facilitate this. The report clearly stated that one of the aims of the suggested actions was to identify ways in which the EU could support fair trade activities while finding a "proper balance between providing institutional support and preserving the movement's independence" (European Parliament, 1998b: 11). This statement thus showed a willingness on the side of the European Parliament to support private harmonization, while also distancing itself from any more direct regulatory interventions.

The 1999 European Commission's Communication on Fair Trade

The European Commission responded to these calls for a harmonization of standards, labels, and procedures and the accompanying professionalization of the fair trade organizations and initiatives with a supportive yet noninterventionist approach in a November 1999 Communication on fair trade. The Communication put a temporary lid on the quest for a European regulatory intervention in that it did not support creating EU standards or procedural regulations for fair trade for three main reasons. First, the European Commission invoked the specific geographic nature of fair trade relations and the lack of domestic interests in regulatory interventions. It argued that fair trade had little relevance for EU producers, considering fair trade specifically deals with North–South trade whereby production takes place in the global South only. Moreover, the Commission referred to the fact that "[a]ll domestic production, producers, and workers already benefit from levels of social and environmental protection at least as high as those established for fair trade products" (European Commission, 1999: 4), which made product differentiation based on such criteria redundant.

Second, the European Commission noted that regulatory interventions would likely violate international trade rules and argued that only a system of voluntary private governance schemes would be compatible with WTO rules:

To the extent that fair trade initiatives remain private initiatives and operate through voluntary participation fair trade is consistent with a non-discriminatory multilateral trading system, as it does not impose import restrictions or other forms of protectionism ... If governments were to introduce regulatory mechanisms based on fair trade concepts they would need to take their WTO obligations into account, so as to ensure in particular the transparent and non-discriminatory functioning of such schemes (European Commission, 1999: 12).

The European Commission substantiated its position by referring to a 1998 study by the New Economics Foundation, which had been executed at the European Commission's request (Zadek et al., 1998). The study argued against public authorities getting involved in the development of regulation for private governance schemes. One of the main reasons for this recommendation was the uncertainty around WTO rules regarding a public scheme's discriminatory nature. In particular, uncertainty remained with respect to the application of WTO rules for labels discriminating against or negatively impacting Southern producers, and to differentiation based on processes or production methods. Instead, the study favored governments supporting and facilitating civil society dialogue and participation, which it considered crucial to the success of private governance schemes.

Third, a crucial factor in understanding the EU's noninterventionist approach is the Fair Trade movement's successful, albeit at the time unfinished, harmonization of a large number of private governance schemes. In the Communication, the European Commission strongly supported this private harmonization attempt and explicitly referred to the efforts of the Fair Trade movement. It expressed concern over the multiplication of fair trade claims, the potential for the abuse of such claims due to the absence of a common fair trade definition or label, and the need for more credibility and consistency of verification claims. Nonetheless, the European Commission argued that "[as] a first step, consideration should be given to supporting NGO efforts to reinforce the capacity of fair trade labelling organisations with respect to criteria development for labelling and certification" (European Commission, 1999: 13).

The remainder of the Communication was largely informational, explaining the concept of fair trade, the functioning of fair trade organizations, and existing EU activities supporting fair trade. These activities mainly related to financial support to fair trade labeling organizations for the promotion of new product lines; support to World Shops and EFTA for capacity building; consumer awareness and promotional campaigns; and support to producer groups in countries from the global South. The Communication also referred to several ways in which the EU had been working toward "achieving a sustainable development" as an overarching policy objective (European Commission, 1999: 10). One of the activities that was mentioned was integrating "environmental considerations into other policies and ... placing more emphasise (sic) on the social aspects of trade globalisation" (European Commission, 1999: 10). Furthermore, the Communication referred to initiatives under the EU Generalised Scheme of Preferences, which provided for "special incentive arrangements in the form of additional preferences to be granted to countries whose domestic legal provisions respect certain minimum social or environmental conditions"(European Commission, 1999: 10). These conditions included standards established by the conventions of the International Labour Organization (ILO) and criteria of the International Tropical Timber Organization.

EU Nonintervention, the Sequel: Expanding the Policy Domain and Private Governance Lobbying (1999–2009)

The European Commission reopened the debate on intervening in private fair trade governance in 2003, not even four years after its 1999 Communication. While several of the same arguments resurfaced, the situation was different than before, since the market and policymakers increasingly recognized private schemes apart from Fairtrade. This new perspective was reflected in the Communication that the European Commission issued in 2009, titled Contributing to Sustainable Development: The Role of Fair Trade and Nongovernmental Trade-Related Sustainability Assurance Schemes. Overall, the European Commission retained its noninterventionist approach.

Reopening the Debate

In 2003, the European Commission reengaged with the private fair trade governance debate when it started working on what was then called a Sustainable Trade Action Plan (Lamy, 2004). The STAP, however, was never officially released and remained an internal working document of the Commission. DG Trade and DG Employment started a consultation process within the Commission on this basis to discuss the possibility of developing guidelines for private fair trade governance.[9] The process was initiated by DG Trade as a follow-up to the 2002 Johannesburg World Summit on Sustainable Development, where corporate responsibility and accountability as well as partnerships among business, civil society, and governments, had been discussed extensively (see, e.g., Pattberg et al., 2012). DG Employment got involved with the STAP as part of its work on CSR.[10]

Initially, the two DGs expected that a commonly agreed fair trade definition and set of criteria could be established (e.g., based on ILO labor standards) to cover the whole policy domain.[11] Several options to increase consumer awareness of and confidence in private fair trade governance were put forward. These options included establishing an accreditation system to approve fair trade schemes that met basic organizational criteria (e.g., transparency regarding their development and functioning); developing a sustainability standard focused on the three sustainable development pillars of economic, environmental, and social criteria; and creating a three-color symbol or logo, which would visualize these three sustainability pillars and convey information about the level of compliance with the three sets of criteria (European Commission, 2004a; FTAO, 2004; Schlegelmilch, 2003).[12]

By late 2004, however, European Commission officials had concluded that any initiative they would develop had to be voluntary and that establishing a substantive standard – even a voluntary one – to harmonize the field was not the best way forward. Similar to the situation in the 1990s, the structure of fair trade as North–South trade and the fear of breaching WTO rules were the main concerns. Internal documents of the European Commission show that DG Trade and several Member States were particularly sensitive to this position.[13] They argued that setting standards and hence endorsing programs that adhere to these standards, could only be done when the commonly agreed criteria or guidelines remained voluntary. A mandatory public standard and label were therefore deemed impossible.[14]

Furthermore, the development of voluntary guidelines and criteria was not considered feasible either. While the focus of policymakers was still strongly on Fair Trade, officials had to acknowledge that besides Fairtrade, several other credible private governance schemes existed, which were engaged in similar sustainable development activities. This broadening of the policy debate to include competitors of Fairtrade, however, did not result in new concerns about a proliferation of private governance schemes. Policymakers considered the fundamental differences among the schemes to signify differences in underlying economic ideologies, rather than an issue of proliferation and fragmentation. Recall that while Fairtrade, for example, heavily focuses on prepayments to farmers, minimum prices, and working with farmer cooperatives, UTZ Certified and Rainforest Alliance defend a more supply-and-demand logic in terms of payments and are working more directly with large multinationals.

The European Commission recognized the value of each of these approaches and did not consider that these differences warranted harmonization. It expected that any attempt to establish guidelines covering all private schemes would result in lowest-common-denominator regulation, which was considered "worthless"[15] and not contributing to the EU's overall goal of supporting sustainable development. The European Commission also did not want to favor one approach over the other, which would in practice likely lead to creating a monopoly situation for Fair Trade. Such a policy was considered discriminatory and a violation of fair competition (Boonman et al., 2011; Lamy, 2004).[16]

The European Commission, therefore, regarded it undesirable to develop standards or procedural regulation, both from a public policy point of view and from the standpoint of the functioning of private governance schemes. Considering the debate on fair trade almost exclusively deals with extra-EU production activities, the European Commission argued that international organizations would be the more appropriate venues for rulemaking. Inside the EU, the focus should be on ensuring corporate respect for environmental, social, and economic standards.[17]

Increased Political Involvement of Private Governance Actors

Alongside the European Commission's attempts to establish a common approach to private fair trade governance, other EU institutions actively supported a noninterventionist approach. In 2005, the EESC issued an Opinion on Ethical Trade and Consumer Assurance Schemes (EESC, 2005). While the Opinion did not only deal with fair trade initiatives, it is particularly relevant to the EU's fair trade policy, as the report on which the Opinion is based was written by Richard Adams, founder of the United Kingdom's fair trade organization Traidcraft, a member of EFTA and WFTO. In the Opinion, the EESC argued that it was not up to national or EU public authorities to prescribe substantive standards, considering the wide-ranging aims of private governance schemes.

In addition to arguing against standards regulation, the EESC's Opinion suggested establishing procedural criteria. The EESC highlighted the need to ensure "authoritative quality assessment" of private governance (EESC, 2005: 75), with specific attention to demonstrating an actual impact on the social, environmental, or economic goals set by private governance schemes. The Opinion listed several criteria to which private governance schemes should adhere, including a multistakeholder composition, clearly defined goals and standards developed with stakeholder input, and an independent review of the private governance scheme's operations. The Opinion envisioned the EU not endorsing any specific private scheme, but rather providing "the authority for an assurance scheme to which all reputable consumer assurance initiatives can subscribe" (EESC, 2005: 79). The

Opinion suggested the EU initiate research to examine establishing quality criteria to assess and potentially accredit private governance schemes, while stopping short of arguing these criteria should be mandatory.[18]

A 2006 European Parliament Resolution on Fair Trade and Development largely aligned with the EESC's Opinion in not demanding mandatory regulation (European Parliament, 2006i). It explicitly called on the European Commission to issue a nonbinding legislative act in order to prevent overregulation. The Resolution praised the availability of the single Fairtrade label, which it regarded as beneficial to both consumers and producers. The Resolution also listed several Fair Trade criteria for private governance schemes, including a fair producer price, prepayments, long-term and stable relationships with producers, and support for marginalized producers and workers. The Resolution did not pay much attention to procedural criteria and merely referred to the work done by the ISEAL Alliance.

While the European Parliament's Resolution supported the EESC's and the European Commission's noninterventionist approach, it did suggest a remarkable step forward. It urged the European Commission, on the one hand, to issue a recommendation on Fair Trade, and on the other hand, to consider issuing a separate recommendation on other similar schemes, which in the Resolution were called "other independently monitored trading initiatives contributing to raising social and environmental standards." This position of the European Parliament, and especially the explicit separation of the Fair Trade movement from any other – and in the Resolution unnamed – private governance schemes, was the result of the significant politicization of the topic and the active involvement of private governance schemes and other interest groups in lobbying the EU institutions. The European Parliament's Resolution was based on a report written by Frithjof Schmidt, a German member of the Group of the Greens/European Free Alliance in the European Parliament. He acted as part of a coalition built around a strong belief in the principles of Fair Trade, which considered Fairtrade's main competing certification programs as inferior and merely "Fairtrade light."[19]

This coalition is composed of two main pillars. One pillar consists of the European Parliament's cross-party Fair Trade Working Group, a group of parliamentarians who lobby specifically for Fair Trade within the EU institutions. The Group was established in 2003 at the request of the Fair Trade movement.[20] Schmidt's efforts in writing the report were part of a broader engagement by this group to foster support for Fair Trade.

The other pillar of the coalition is the Fair Trade Advocacy Office (FTAO), with whom Schmidt worked closely while writing his report.[21] FTAO is the formal lobbying office of the Fair Trade movement in Brussels. While EFTA had already opened an advocacy office in Brussels in 1995, Fairtrade International, WFTO, NEWS!, and EFTA established FTAO in 2004 to further coordinate their advocacy activities. Fairtrade International, WFTO, and EFTA formalized FTAO as an independent foundation in 2010 (Cremona and Marin Duran, 2013b: 99, 101; FTAO, 2008, 2016).

This direct presence in Brussels has offered FTAO a substantial advantage over other private governance schemes in terms of information gathering and direct lobbying opportunities. Rainforest Alliance and UTZ Certified, most notably, had no lobbying offices in Brussels and mainly worked via individually contracted lobbyists. This different mode of operating could be attributed to differences in available financial resources, but also to a different valuation of their roles as interest groups.[22]

The Fair Trade movement had very clear objectives with its lobbying activities. It wanted the European Parliament and the European Commission to recognize the specific features of Fair Trade to the exclusion of the more mainstream private schemes.[23] At the same time, it wanted to avoid overregulation. The Fair Trade movement, therefore, opposed the initial idea of the European Commission developing a substantive standard that would lead to a watering down of criteria and a lowest-common-denominator approach. The movement had seen this happen in the case of organic agriculture and wanted to avoid a similar situation at all costs (Boonman et al., 2011).[24] Yet, the Fair Trade movement did seek formal recognition of the Fair Trade approach at the EU level. At the national level, and in particular in France, Belgium, and Italy, the Fair Trade movement at the time was already involved in policy initiatives through which it hoped to achieve "some form of protection of the Fair Trade concept" (Boonman et al., 2011: 17). In France, formal legislation was developed in the end, making it the first (and as of yet, only) EU Member State to do so. France's 2005 law provided a general definition of fair trade, which was only loosely based on the Fair Trade movement's definition. A National

Commission on Fair Trade was set up in 2010 to look into formally recognizing and accrediting labeling organizations that complied with this definition. In 2015, however, this Commission was dismantled, and the authority for publicly recognizing fair trade schemes was transferred to the Trade Consultation Commission for further consideration (cf. Cremona and Marin Duran, 2013a: 128–131; La Plate-Forme pour le Commerce Equitable, s.d.). Beyond France, not many Member States have supported regulation in this issue area, considering the lack of eligible EU producers, and the absence of consumers' or retailers' organizations lobbying for such regulation.[25]

Throughout the drafting process of the European Parliament's 2006 Resolution, the influence of the Fair Trade movement was evident. In the original draft resolution, only Fair Trade was mentioned, while other programs or approaches to fair trade were not even acknowledged (European Parliament, 2006c, 2006d). This strategic omission was part of the broader attempt to highlight the distinctiveness of Fair Trade and have it recognized as the only approach to fair trade. The final 2006 Resolution, however, did include references to these other private governance schemes, which were added after concerns were voiced about the one-sidedness of the draft. However, these other schemes were not identified by their name, but only referred to as "other independently monitored trading initiatives" (European Parliament, 2006i).

The final Resolution is in several other ways also strongly biased toward Fair Trade. Examples of this bias include the following: The Resolution requests the European Commission to issue separate recommendations on Fair Trade and on other schemes; the European Parliament calls on the European Commission to "liaise with the international Fair Trade movement in supporting clear and widely-applicable criteria against which consumer assurance schemes can be assessed" (European Parliament, 2006i: 869), while no such consultation with other schemes is requested; the Resolution calls on the "Commission and the Council to study and to consider implementing a low VAT [value-added tax] rate for Fair Trade products and to eliminate import duties on Fair Trade products" (European Parliament, 2006i: 869), without mentioning products certified by other schemes; and the European Parliament calls "on public authorities in Europe to integrate Fair Trade criteria into their public tenders and purchasing policies and asks the Commission to promote this by, for example, producing guidelines for Fair Trade procurement" (European Parliament, 2006i: 870), again without mentioning the integration of the criteria of the other certification schemes. One of the main strategic goals of the Fair Trade movement may indeed have been this last item – having Fair Trade recognized for public procurement – a topic to which I will briefly return in the final section of this chapter.

In the wake of the European Parliament's Resolution, the Fair Trade movement was dominant in the policy discussions, with little presence of other schemes. The absence of UTZ Certified and Rainforest Alliance, for example, was evident during the Civil Society Dialogue on Fair Trade that DG Trade organized on June 3, 2008. The Dialogue was organized as a response to issues raised in the Schmidt report and in preparation for the European Commission's position. While the title of the Dialogue specifically referred to Fair Trade, the discussion paper that DG Trade distributed dealt more broadly with "issues related to trade and consumer assurance schemes, including Fair Trade" (European Commission, 2008b). UTZ Certified and Rainforest Alliance were not registered to participate in the meeting and do not show up in the meeting notes. Several of the Fair Trade movement's actors, such as IFAT/WFTO, Oxfam-World Shops, EFTA, and Max Havelaar, did have representatives around the table. In written contributions to the meeting, several of them, along with other participants, noted the discrepancy between the title of the Dialogue and the discussion paper's broader topic, and requested that the discussions focus on Fair Trade only. In addition, they made references to the definition of Fair Trade adopted by the Fair Trade movement and requested the European Commission to officially endorse this definition and the accompanying principles in a recommendation, as suggested by the European Parliament's Resolution. This request was, furthermore, linked to a perceived proliferation of (misleading) fair trade claims and initiatives, and to discussions about recognizing Fair Trade for public procurement (Association For Promoting Fairtrade in Finland, 2008; EFTA, 2008; EURO COOP, 2008; European Commission, 2008e; FLO, 2008; IFAT, 2008).

More active opposition to Fair Trade's dominance was in the end organized by UTZ Certified and to a lesser extent Rainforest Alliance that were represented by Brussels-based lobbyists and companies working with these two private schemes. The opposition was led by a related interest group, the European Coffee Federation (ECF), which

represents coffee roasters and importers. ECF recognized the importance of Fair Trade, but favored "sustainability initiatives aimed at the
mainstream market" (ECF, 2007). All these actors argued against
public intervention, fearing this could lead to market restrictions, while
they also aimed to prevent the European Commission from recognizing
Fair Trade's approach to the exclusion of other approaches.[26] Furthermore, ECF welcomed more transparency on the side of private governance schemes – for example, by making available basic information
about their operations and approaches via EU portals (ECF, 2007).
Overall, these actors found a receptive audience in the European
Commission, which was not keen on regulating the sector either. Yet,
the influence of the Fair Trade movement would also make its way into
the European Commission's policy response.

The 2009 European Commission's Communication on Contributing to Sustainable Development

In May 2009, the European Commission issued a Communication on
Contributing to Sustainable Development: The Role of Fair Trade and
Nongovernmental Trade-Related Sustainability Assurance Schemes
(European Commission, 2009b). Above all, the core message of the
Communication was a general dismissal of any kind of public regulatory intervention. Using language similar to the 1999 Communication,
the European Commission referred to the voluntary character of
private governance as being "consistent with a non-discriminatory
multilateral trading system" and mentioned that public regulatory
interventions, "while not problematic per se, need to take account of
WTO obligations, in particular to ensure their transparent and non-
discriminatory functioning" (European Commission, 2009b: 8). As
well, the Commission argued that public intervention could stymie
the dynamic nature of private governance. It noted that it "should
not take a role in ranking or regulating criteria related to private
trade-related sustainability assurance schemes" since this would "limit
a dynamic element of private initiatives in this field and could stand in
the way of the further development of Fair Trade and other private
schemes and their standards" (European Commission, 2009b: 6). This
position was a clear defense of the plurality of private fair trade
governance schemes, and of the fact that the differences among the
schemes did not create problems that warranted public harmonization.

Due to the lobbying efforts by the Fair Trade interest coalition, however, the Communication did explicitly distinguish "Fair Trade proper" from other approaches, namely, "other 'niche' certified products not participating formally in Fair Trade, but targeting consumers aware of sustainability issues (Rainforest Alliance, Utz Certified)," "products covered by baseline standards that aspire to be 'industry-wide' (e.g. Code for the Coffee Community (4C's [sic]); Ethical Tea Partnership)," and "the rest ('no name' commodity supplies)" (European Commission, 2009b: 5). While lobbying efforts by stakeholders such as ECF, Rainforest Alliance, and UTZ Certified had been successful in preventing a Fair Trade policy monopoly, they were not able to prevent the Commission from highlighting the distinctiveness of Fair Trade. The Communication specifically commended the Fair Trade movement for responding to the European Commission's call in 1999 to further harmonize and develop a single Fair Trade approach, which had prevented potential internal trade barriers and mutual recognition problems.[27] Importantly, the Communication formally recognized the definition and principles of Fair Trade as established by the Fair Trade movement in its 2009 charter. The European Commission did not do anything similar for the other private governance schemes that were explicitly mentioned in the Communication.

Despite its overall noninterventionist approach, and as one means to address potential proliferation and consumer reliability issues, the European Commission did list several procedural criteria with which private governance schemes could comply. These criteria included objective and nondiscriminatory standards, independent monitoring, and transparency around audit processes and outcomes. In an annex, the Communication also referenced the procedural criteria developed in the 2005 EESC Opinion. These criteria were included as a starting point for further discussion, "while continuing to avoid entering into defining appropriate sustainability standards for private schemes" (European Commission, 2009b: 7).

Post-2009 Developments

The 2009 Communication once again put a temporary lid on the discussions around regulating private fair trade governance. The European Commission did not foresee any new initiatives in the immediate future and at the time of writing, the 2009 Communication still stands as its official policy position.[28] The main private governance schemes are also not demanding any additional action at the EU level. In the wake of the Communication, they continued to vigorously defend their programmatic differences (UTZ Certified, 2010).[29] In 2011, Fairtrade International, Rainforest Alliance, and UTZ Certified even issued a joint statement on this topic. They defended the competition between their schemes as a motivator for innovation, cost reductions, and increased effectiveness, and argued against harmonization (Fairtrade International et al., 2011).

These positions by public officials and private governance schemes also reflect the findings of a 2010 report by the Ethical Trade Fact-finding Process (ETFP) on Assuring Consumer Confidence in Ethical Trade. The ETFP was a multi-stakeholder initiative that was established following a workshop organized by ISO in 2007 on "Can consumers rely on fair trade claims?" (Ethical Trade Fact-finding Process, 2010: 1). The WFTO and Fairtrade International were part of the ETFP Steering Group. The ETFP report argued, first, that while it is difficult to prove that inaccurate or unreliable claims are decreasing consumer confidence, the "majority of consumers can perhaps be characterized as skeptical" (Ethical Trade Fact-finding Process, 2010: 16–17). The report acknowledged, however, that this depends on the consumer's individual inclination toward such claims, which also varies from country to country. Second, the report suggested developing procedural rules at the international level. The report lamented the lack of an internationally agreed definition of ethical trade. While it considered it a long-term goal to establish such a common understanding, the report also "recognises the complexity of defining attributes of ethical claims" (Ethical Trade Fact-finding Process, 2010: 6). Instead, the report advocated the establishment of procedural regulation. Given that "a key element to increase consumer confidence in ethical claims is the reliability of the claim," it argued this can be "ensured if the process by which the ethical claim is made is rigorous and transparent" (Ethical Trade Fact-finding Process, 2010: 6). In order to build consumer confidence, the report argued, there is a need for "minimum requirements for 'reliable' ethical claims," and "recognition and promotion of credible multi-stakeholder initiatives, that have been developed by key stakeholders, including consumers" (Ethical Trade Fact-finding Process,

2010: 4). The report suggested that the most appropriate political level to develop such harmonized criteria is the international level. While the main private governance schemes and the European Commission supported this position, concrete rules have yet to be developed.[30]

The EU's sustained noninterventionist approach did not prevent a discussion around private fair trade governance to unfold in the context of another policy area, namely public procurement. The discussion revolved around how public authorities could include social and environmental criteria in public tenders and whether they could refer to specific private governance schemes certifying compliance to these criteria. While the details of the broader policy debate are beyond the scope of this book (see, e.g., Cremona and Marin Duran, 2013a: 140–143, 164–168), one outcome is relevant to our discussion. The 2014 Public Procurement Directive, which was the outcome of these policy debates, allows public authorities to refer to a specific label when requiring compliance with environmental or social criteria that are specified in a public tender. This was a topic for which private governance schemes and the Fair Trade movement specifically, lobbied heavily.[31] The Directive, furthermore, lists procedural criteria to which the labeling programs could adhere, including the requirement that standards be based on "objectively verifiable and non-discriminatory criteria," that stakeholders be included in the development of the labels, that the label be accessible to all interested parties, and that the standard-setter be independent from the economic operator seeking compliance with the standard (European Parliament and Council of the European Union, 2014: 122). While not amounting to full-scale procedural regulation as discussed in this book, these criteria do introduce some level of control over the procedural aspects of private governance schemes when public authorities intend to allow such schemes as voluntary instruments of compliance verification in public tenders. In that respect, the criteria partly reflect the procedural concerns mentioned in the 2009 Communication of the European Commission, which indeed proposed these procedural criteria in its 2011 proposal for the public procurement directive (European Commission, 2011f). An open question for the future is whether this initial step toward something that resembles procedural regulation will provide the basis for a new debate on regulating private fair trade governance.

Conclusion

The persistent noninterventionist approach of the EU toward private fair trade governance stands in sharp contrast to the other issue areas discussed in this book. The analysis of the EU's policy positions since the early 1990s shows that the reasons for this approach have not changed much over the course of more than two decades.

First, the nature of the production relations in this issue area is such that it precludes intra-EU interest mobilization. Fair trade governance deals with North–South trade and commodities produced in countries in the global South, which means that the regulatory targets are producers in Southern countries. This feature of the issue area has resulted in an absence of domestic production opportunities and a concomitant lack of interest group lobbying and policy interest for such opportunities, especially as compared to the organic agriculture and biofuels cases. The attempts in the 1990s to intervene in private fair trade governance in support of the interests of producers from Member States' former colonies stand out in this respect. These attempts were intended to more directly integrate production opportunities in these countries as "domestic" interests into EU policymaking. As such, these actions dovetail with Clift and Woll's (2012) argument about economic patriotism. This concept of patriotism can be extended to include not only national and sub/supranational levels, but also entities with historical political relations with the *patrie*, such as former colonies, that are still considered to be entitled to a special relationship.[32] The obstacle to policy support in this case, however, was the European Commission's uncertainty around violating international trade rules that place institutional constraints on a public authority's freedom to support specific countries' producer interests. More generally, these constraints have precluded EU regulatory interventions due to uncertainty around interventions based on non-product-related production methods.

Second, the successful harmonization efforts by the Fair Trade movement from the 1990s onward have prevented internal trade, mutual recognition, and supply chain confusion problems. Since the policy debate in the 1990s focused on Fair Trade specifically, policymakers lauded this private harmonization effort. The scope of the policy domain broadened from the early 2000s onward, with a growing recognition of other approaches to fair trade, in particular those represented by Rainforest Alliance and UTZ Certified. Considering these few schemes dominated the market, policymakers considered the differences between Fair Trade and the other schemes beneficial to the overall development of the market. In other words, they did not consider the variation in private schemes' approaches as fragmentation in need of public intervention.

Third, interest representation by, and on behalf of, private governance schemes has significantly influenced this perception around the fragmentation of the private governance market. The Fair Trade movement has strong representation in Brussels through FTAO and is part of an influential coalition with members of the European Parliament. Yet, opposition from competing private governance schemes and associated stakeholders to EU intervention in favor of Fair Trade has safeguarded these schemes' specific approaches to fair trade and sustainable development. In that respect, EU officials have recognized the governance space of all private governance schemes. Nonetheless, some observers argue that Fair Trade lobbying was particularly geared toward the policy discussions on the revisions of the EU's public procurement policy. The 2014 Procurement Directive indeed allows for direct references to environmental or social labels, which could give Fair Trade, given its large consumer recognition, a considerable advantage. Whether this is the case should be the topic of a separate study.

The market for private fair trade governance remains a market free of governmental oversight. Considering its growth potential, however, it is not inconceivable that many more businesses will be attracted to the market and that new private governance labels or fair trade claims will emerge. While a public standard may not be foreseeable in this policy field, the development of procedural criteria may still be on the table in the future, especially since the debate around public procurement has resulted in an indirect attempt to introduce such criteria.

6 | Fisheries

The sustainability of fisheries is a topic of global concern considering the world's fish stocks are in dire straits. In 1974, when the Food and Agriculture Organization (FAO) of the United Nations first assessed the situation, 50 percent of global fish stocks were fully exploited, while 10 percent were overexploited. This means that they were at or beyond the level of maximum sustainable production. By 2013, the situation had worsened significantly, with 58.1 percent of global fish stocks fully exploited and 31.4 percent overexploited (FAO, 2016: 38). As a result, the amount of non-fully exploited (or underfished) stocks has decreased dramatically, from 40 percent to a mere 10.5 percent in forty years' time.

In the EU, the situation is critical as well. In the Mediterranean Sea, for example, the European Commission reports that "93% of assessed fish stocks were overfished in 2015," while in the northeast Atlantic about half of the stocks are overfished (European Commission, 2016e: 5). These figures led the European Commission to conclude that "European fisheries are eroding their own ecological and economic basis" (European Commission, 2009c: 7). Aquaculture production, which in the EU accounts for about 20 percent of total seafood production, is dealing with its own sustainability problems. These problems include negative environmental impacts on the surrounding ecosystems, including the destruction of mangroves and wetlands, chemical discharges, and biodiversity impacts from the introduction of alien species; the use of fishmeal and fish oil as feed inputs, which puts even more pressure on marine resources; and social impacts, such as local population displacements (Allsopp et al., 2008; FAO, 2014a, 2014b).

Creating effective public policy to deal with these worrisome trends has been a challenging endeavor. When the EU established its Common Fisheries Policy in 1970, it was initially focused on streamlining the organization of the market, ensuring free access to Member

States' waters, and providing structural aid to assist in modernizing the sector. In the mid-1980s, the conservation of marine resources was incorporated as an important pillar of the policy with the introduction of quotas and total allowable catches (Lequesne, 2005). After recognizing that this policy was failing to sustain or improve fish stocks, the EU placed sustainability front and center in the 2002 reform of the CFP and most recently again in the 2013 reform.

In addition to attempts to incorporate sustainability in existing policies, in the early 2000s the European Commission launched a debate on how to deal with private governance schemes for wild-capture fisheries and aquaculture. Until very recently, all involved stakeholders agreed that the fragmentation of the private governance market needed to be addressed. This market developed from the early 1990s onward and has grown to include several dozen sustainability claims. The lack of successful private harmonization efforts and the possibility of the emergence of national-level regulations provided the rationales for supporting public interventions at the EU level.

The debate, however, has also been characterized by continued differences of opinion on the desirability of publicly supporting product differentiation, considering the costs this would impose on European producers. The European Commission, the Council of Ministers, and many involved stakeholders, including private governance schemes and industry, have consistently been of the opinion that adjustment costs for EU fisheries would be significant considering they already needed to comply with quite stringent CFP sustainability rules. These actors, as a result, were only in favor of creating procedural regulation, in the form of a set of minimum procedural criteria with which private governance schemes should comply. The minimum criteria would function as a benchmarking tool for private schemes. This option would address the fragmentation of the private governance market, while not imposing additional substantive regulation on top of existing CFP rules. Such additional rules would be difficult for EU producers to comply with and would potentially create advantages for non-EU producers that are already producing more sustainably.

In contrast, the European Parliament has since the beginning of the debate favored the creation of both standards and procedural regulations in the form of an EU-wide public certification scheme. Such a scheme would entail standards regulation in the form of a substantive sustainability standard and an EU eco-label, which, according to the Parliament, would benefit EU producers over unsustainable non-EU ones. An EU public certification scheme would also entail procedural regulation in order to further control the market for private governance schemes and potentially allow for the delegation of verification responsibilities to private schemes. This approach, therefore, would be similar to the policies on organic agriculture and biofuels production.

Based on these policy positions that had been expressed in stakeholder position papers, a multi-stakeholder expert group report, and several preparatory policy documents, in 2008–2009 the European Commission developed a proposal for procedural regulation in the form of minimum procedural criteria for private governance schemes. In doing so, it followed the majority position of Member States in the Council of Ministers and most stakeholders, while dismissing the position of the European Parliament, which at the time only had consultative – and not co-decision – competence in fisheries policy. Several factors, however, including difficulties with the pre-legislative impact assessment, the European elections in 2009, and the reform of the EU's CFP, which started in 2009, resulted in the Commission never officially releasing this proposal.

This delay in the decision has made a compromise increasingly difficult. Since the entry into force of the Treaty of Lisbon in 2009, the European Parliament has had co-decision competence for fisheries policy; this means that its divergent position can no longer be easily circumvented. While the debate on private fisheries governance was included in the discussions leading to the 2013 reform of the CFP, no new proposal for dealing with private schemes was developed. The main difficulty remained the potential costs for EU fisheries to comply with a public sustainability standard that would be stricter than existing CFP rules. The 2013 reform of the CFP resulted in a process of incrementally strengthening these rules following a very contentious policy debate. With overall policy positions unchanged, the EU institutions agreed to again postpone a decision and have the European Commission draft a feasibility report on the various available options for potential future action.

This report, finished in 2016, may be changing policymakers' perceptions of the need for public intervention. The report questions the assumption of a fragmented private governance market and highlights ongoing private efforts of harmonization in the form of an overarching benchmarking tool for private governance schemes. At the time of writing, the debate was still ongoing and unresolved, so the status quo – the absence of public regulatory intervention – is the current state of affairs. Unlike the fair trade case, this situation is not the result of a concrete policy decision not to intervene, but rather the result of continuing differences of opinion among the main EU institutions and stakeholders. Yet, if EU policymakers in the Council of Ministers and the European Parliament accept the conclusions of the feasibility report, and continue disagreeing on the benefits of product differentiation, this noninterventionist approach may hold for the near future.

Transnational Private Governance and Fisheries

Transnational private governance dealing with the fishing and aquaculture sectors has emerged since the early 1990s.[1] The overall trend has been to a proliferation of sustainability claims with, until recently, very little effort toward private harmonization. Maybe more so than in other sectors, the private initiatives have emerged along several fault lines, including their focus (wild-capture versus aquaculture; single species versus multiple species), scope (global versus local), participating stakeholders (NGOs, industry, government), and type (certification programs, codes of conduct, or consumer guidance schemes). A recent mapping exercise commissioned by the European Commission, for example, identified fifty-seven schemes, ten of which involved governments as cooperators of the schemes (MRAG, 2016). While a comprehensive review of all these initiatives is beyond the scope of this book, I will discuss several of the most important private governance schemes in the next paragraphs.

Arguably the first eco-label in the fisheries sector was the Dolphin Safe label that was established in 1990 by the Earth Island Institute, a US-based NGO. The scheme aims to guarantee that tuna is caught without harming dolphins (UNEP, 2009: 13). As a result of its rather narrow focus, the program has been criticized for not taking into account the broader sustainability of tuna fisheries, or any other environmental criteria (UNEP, 2009: 49; Washington and Ababouch, 2011: 24). Nonetheless, multiple producers, retailers, and NGOs have imitated the Earth Island Institute's initiative and established other "dolphin-safe" or "dolphin-friendly" logos (Brown, 2005). In a 2005 Communication, for example, the European Commission referred to a WWF study that found no less than twenty-six dolphin-safe/dolphin-friendly claims in eight European countries, while also highlighting that such labeling had become the norm in some markets (European Commission, 2005c: 13).

While initially such single-species labels and targeted campaigns (e.g., focused on shrimp or salmon) were common, from the mid-1990s onward, more encompassing private governance schemes emerged for both capture fisheries and aquaculture (Auld, 2014b). The Marine Stewardship Council is widely considered the main wild-capture private governance scheme. The MSC was established in 1997 by WWF and Unilever and became independent from its founders in 1999. The MSC's fisheries standard covers sustainability from three angles: the targeted fish stock(s), wider ecosystem impacts, and the fishery's management system (MSC, 2014, 2015b; UNEP, 2009: 10–12; Washington and Ababouch, 2011: 24–25). In 2017, the MSC estimated that it had certified 12 percent of marine wild catch globally (MSC, 2017a: 4), making it arguably the largest program of its kind.

One of the main competitors of the MSC is Friend of the Sea. This scheme was established by a European representative of the Earth Island Institute that had initiated the Dolphin Safe label. Officially launched in 2006, Friend of the Sea is unique in covering both wild-capture and aquaculture when certifying products (and not fisheries) against fifteen environmental and social criteria (Friend of the Sea, 2016b). In an attempt to widen its coverage and consolidate the aquaculture sector, in 2014 Friend of the Sea engaged in a mutual recognition agreement with GLOBALG.A.P. Originally called EUREPGAP, GLOBALG.A.P. is a business-to-business program developed by European retailers of the Euro-Retailer Produce Working Group in 1997 (Friend of the Sea, 2014b; GLOBALG.A.P., 2014).

Other industry and NGO programs focus exclusively on aquaculture. The Global Aquaculture Alliance (GAA), for example, was established in 1997 by the aquaculture industry. While initially focused on shrimp certification, the GAA developed the Best Aquaculture Practices

(BAP) program, which addresses environmental, social, animal welfare, and food safety criteria (GAA, 2014; Washington and Ababouch, 2011: 75–76). The Aquaculture Stewardship Council (ASC), on the other hand, was founded in 2010 by WWF in cooperation with the Dutch Sustainable Trade Initiative. The ASC's standards were developed on the basis of the outcomes of eight WWF Aquaculture Dialogues (2004–2015) and cover environmental, animal welfare, and social responsibility criteria (ASC, 2015, 2017a, 2017b).

While all these schemes are explicitly global in nature, other schemes are more locally oriented. KRAV in Sweden, for example, while originally engaged in organic agriculture certification, has established a scheme focused on capture fisheries in the northeast Atlantic (KRAV, 2017: 245–253).[2] Compared to this purely private scheme, in other instances public authorities have been more closely involved in local programs. For instance, from 2007 onward the Icelandic government engaged with industry in developing the Iceland Responsible Fisheries Management scheme (IRFM), which is now run by an independent nonprofit foundation (Iceland Responsible Fisheries, 2017).[3] In the United Kingdom, the Seafish Responsible Fishing Scheme was established in 2006 in a cooperative effort between the British Standards Institute and Seafish, which is a nondepartmental public body, an autonomous arm's-length organization with accountability to Parliament.[4]

Finally, individual companies have also created governance schemes. One prominent example is Pescanova, a Spanish company that is among the largest fishing companies in Europe, with its own wild-capture Certified Sustainable Fishing labeling scheme for a limited range of its products (Washington and Ababouch, 2011: 26). Other examples are logos developed by retailers such as Carrefour that introduced its Responsible Fishing eco-label in 2004, while it also sells MSC and Friend of the Sea-certified products. Other French retailers, such as Intermarché and Casino, followed Carrefour's example (Salla-darré et al., 2010; UNEP, 2009: 19). Besides being involved in creating their own eco-labels, many observers consider retailers the main drivers behind private certification and eco-labeling (Washington and Ababouch, 2011). Large retailers, such as Walmart, Metro, Tesco, Lidl, Marks & Spencer, and Sainsbury's have made commitments to predominantly, or even exclusively, sell sustainably certified fisheries products (Food & Water Europe, 2011: 13–14; MRAG, 2016: 91–97; UNEP, 2009: 17–22). A recent survey in the context of an online stakeholder consultation by the European Commission indicated that "[n]early 70% of retailer and supplier respondents sell ecolabelled products, however only 10% exclusively sell ecolabelled products" (European Commission, 2015c: 7).

The development of this varied set of private governance schemes has resulted in criticism regarding the claims that are made by these programs. A ClientEarth (2011) report, for example, identified seven types of claims in nine main supermarkets in the United Kingdom: sustainably sourced; dolphin-friendly/safe; responsibly farmed/from well-managed farms; environmentally friendly farms; from well-managed fishery; responsibly sourced; and protects the marine environment (ClientEarth, 2011: 3). The report found that claims on 32 of the 100 products examined could be considered "misleading or unverified" (ClientEarth, 2011: 3). The report denounced "the lack of harmonised, detailed and mandatory standards covering environmental claims and information on fish product packaging" (ClientEarth, 2011: v).

This lack of harmonization has been a long-standing problem. Only recently, a private harmonization effort has developed in the form of the Global Sustainable Seafood Initiative (GSSI). This initiative was created in 2013 by seventeen seafood companies from across the supply chain in partnership with the German Development Agency GIZ (GSSI, 2017b). In October 2015, the GSSI released a benchmarking tool for seafood certification programs that includes "Essential Components" that private governance schemes "must meet to be recognized by GSSI," and additional "Supplementary Components, which show a seafood certification scheme's diverse approach and help stakeholders understand where differences exist" (GSSI, 2017a). These components are based on existing FAO documents, including the 1995 Code of Conduct for Responsible Fisheries, and Guidelines on Marine Capture Fisheries (2005/ 2009), on Inland Capture Fisheries (2011), and on Aquaculture (2011), which offer best practices for standard-setting and verification procedures.[5]

The process to develop the first of these FAO Guidelines in 2005 was itself initiated as a response to the proliferation of private governance schemes, a topic to which the final chapter will return (FAO, 2008: 11; OECD and FAO, 2009: 21). Even though the Guidelines are voluntary – a result of disagreement among FAO members on whether the organization would create its own labeling scheme, or merely develop technical guidelines (Gulbrandsen, 2009: 656–657) – they have become an internationally recognized benchmark for private fisheries governance. Many, if not all, of the main private governance schemes have in the past made claims about their compliance with the FAO Guidelines (see, e.g., ASC, 2014; Friend of the Sea, 2014a; Seafish, 2012a, 2012b, 2013).[6] Much controversy exists around such claims, however. A 2009 report by UNEP (2009: 47–50), for example, found that the MSC was "fully compliant" with the FAO Guidelines, while the programs of KRAV and Seafish were considered "broadly compliant," and Friend of the Sea "broadly in line" with the Guidelines. The only scheme that was not considered compliant was the Dolphin Safe program. A 2011 study by consumer NGO Food and Water Europe, on the other hand, concluded that none of the examined certification and eco-labeling programs – including MSC, Friend of the Sea, GAA-BAP, and ASC – fully complied with the FAO Guidelines (Food & Water Europe, 2011). Other research has also raised doubts about FAO-compliant claims. For instance, Froese and Proelss argue that for "stocks with available status information, 19% (FOS [Friend of the Sea]) to 31% (MSC) had overfished stock sizes and were subject to ongoing overfishing" (Froese and Proelss, 2012: 1284).[7] These claims about limited compliance with the FAO Guidelines are reflected in the fact that by late 2017 the GSSI had only recognized four programs: IRFM, MSC, GAA-BAP, and Alaska Responsible Fisheries Management scheme (an Alaskan public-private partnership).

The availability of a benchmarking tool like the GSSI is crucial, considering that the market for certified seafood products continues to grow. Potts et al. (2016: 11) found that between 2003 and 2015, the market grew from 0.5 to 14 percent of global production. This is particularly important for the EU, whose market for fishery and aquaculture products is the largest in the world. In 2015, for example, European trade flows totaled a value of more than €49 billion (45 percent of which were extra-EU imports), with a supply

volume of around fourteen million tons (AIPCE-CEP, 2016; European Commission, 2016a: 1). Growth in EU consumption is estimated to be around 0.5 percent per year until 2030 (European
Commission, 2011e: 76). While recent aggregate data for the EU
are not available, the European Commission estimated that in
2009 between 6 and 8 percent of EU fisheries were certified. Production from these fisheries accounted for about 3 percent of total
consumption in the EU, with the amount of imported certified
fisheries products being at least as high. Consumer demand for
certified products was considered highest in western and northern
Europe, limited in southern Europe, and low in the new Member
States in the east. The United Kingdom and Germany were the
largest markets in this respect, accounting for 80 percent of consumption of certified fisheries products, while the Netherlands,
Sweden, France, and Italy were also experiencing increasing demand
(European Commission, 2011e: 79–80). In 2015, the Commission
stated that "[t]he EU is by far the main market for certified products" (European Commission, 2015c: 2).

A few recent figures, furthermore, highlight European countries'
diverse representation in the various certification schemes. By
November 2015, 106 of the 228 fisheries (46 percent) that had been
certified by the MSC were from EU client countries (including
overseas territories), predominantly from the United Kingdom, the
Netherlands, and Denmark. Another 24 EU fisheries (out of 49)
were in the process of being certified.[8] MSC products are predominantly offered in Germany, the Netherlands, the United Kingdom,
France, and Sweden (MRAG, 2016: 72; MSC, 2015a: 40). For
Friend of the Sea, 14 of the 76 wild-capture fisheries from which
products were certified came from EU countries. By early 2017,
across the supply chain a total of 552 companies from more than
60 countries supplied Friend of the Sea-certified products, 249 (45
percent) of which came from seventeen EU countries, and about
70 percent of these from just four countries: Italy (82), Spain (37),
France (31), and the United Kingdom (22) (Friend of the Sea,
2016a: 6; 2017a, 2017b). The GAA-BAP, on the other hand, is
predominantly used in Asia and the Americas. Of the 1,449 certified
facilities listed on its website in June 2017, only two are from EU
countries, one each from Poland and Greece (GAA, 2017). For the

ASC, finally, of the 388 farms from 36 countries that were listed on the website in June 2017, 51 farms (13 percent) came from nine EU countries, more than half of which (26) from Denmark alone (ASC, 2017d). Another eighty-nine farms were in assessment, fourteen of which were from four EU countries (ASC, 2017e).[9] While being underrepresented in terms of production, however, just five EU countries account for half of the approved ASC products (the Netherlands, Germany, Belgium, Sweden, and France) (ASC, 2017c).

Overall, these figures show that the EU market is relatively well developed in both the production and consumption of certified seafood products. Yet, there exist important regional differences, with a dominance of western and northern Europe. The large variety of private governance schemes and the varied importance of the fisheries sector in Member States have significantly shaped public policy discussions on how to deal with private fisheries governance, to which the chapter now turns.

Launching the EU Policy Debate (1990s–2005)

For over two decades, the EU has been engaged in debates on whether and how to regulate private fisheries governance. These policy discussions started at the same time the EU was trying to put the CFP on a more sustainable path. Having observed the "alarming state of many fish stocks that are outside safe biological limits" (European Commission, 2002c: 3) and unsustainable fishing practices resulting from fleet over-capacity, improving the environmental dimension of the EU's fisheries policy was put front and center at the start of the twenty-first century (European Commission, 2002d). The reform of the CFP in 2002 resulted in a new Regulation on the Conservation and Sustainable Exploitation of Fisheries Resources (Council of the European Union, 2002b). The policy included an ecosystem-based approach to fisheries management and focused on recovery and management plans to keep stocks within safe biological limits, to put limits on catches and on the amount and types of vessels allowed to fish, and technical requirements for fishing gear. By 2007, policymakers had further reoriented the CFP to incorporate the concept of "maximum sustainable yield" (European Commission, 2006e), and to address the reduction of unwanted by-catch and the

Table 6.1 *EU policy on private fisheries governance*

Year	Title	Main Elements
1997	European Commission Communication on the Future for the Market in Fisheries Products in the European Union	– Proposes developing a legal framework to address credibility problems with private certification schemes
2005	European Commission Communication on Launching a Debate on a Community Approach Towards Eco-Labelling Schemes for Fisheries Products	– Reviews three options: (1) nonaction; (2) EU voluntary eco-labeling scheme; and (3) minimum criteria for private governance schemes
2006	Final Report of the Expert Group on Eco-Labelling for Fishery Products	– Offers support for minimum criteria – Identifies overarching principles, objectives, and criteria
2013	Regulation (EU) No. 1379/2013 of December 11, 2013 on the Common Organisation of the Markets in Fishery and Aquaculture Products	– Requests the Commission to submit "a feasibility report on options for an eco-label scheme for fishery and aquaculture products, in particular on establishing such a scheme on a Union-wide basis and on setting minimum requirements for the use by Member States of a Union eco-label"
2016	MRAG Feasibility Report on Options for an EU Eco-Label Scheme for Fishery and Aquaculture Products	– Reviews three options: (1) nonaction; (2) minimum criteria for private governance schemes; and (3) EU voluntary eco-labeling scheme
2016	European Commission Report on Options for an EU Eco-Label Scheme for Fishery and Aquaculture Products	– Summary of the MRAG feasibility report

elimination of discards (European Commission, 2007e). In addition, together with industry they had developed a voluntary European Code of Sustainable and Responsible Fisheries Practices (European Commission, 2004e).

In these efforts to refocus the CFP toward sustainability, private fisheries governance had attracted the attention of the Commission quite early on. In the lead-up to the 2002 CFP reform, the European Commission had first mentioned fisheries certification in a 1997 Communication related to a proposed reform of the Common Organization of the Market for fisheries products. Even though the field of private fisheries governance was in an early stage of development, its credibility was immediately targeted. To encourage more market transparency regarding responsible fishing practices, the European Commission highlighted potential problems with "certification schemes that are biased or poorly controlled" and suggested this credibility problem could be addressed by a legislative framework, "which would determine the circumstances in which voluntary certification schemes, accessible without distinction to operators in the Community and in third countries, could be developed" (European Commission, 1997b: 11). In essence, this was the first proposal toward developing procedural regulation for private governance schemes.

While the European Parliament supported this call from the European Commission, and most Member States agreed on the usefulness of an EU-level approach, no concrete action was taken (European Commission, 2005c; European Parliament, 1998d; European Union, 2006). In a 2002 Action Plan to integrate environmental requirements into the CFP, the Commission further highlighted the need for the EU institutions to consider "the potential for eco-labels to stimulate environmentally sound fishing practices" (European Commission, 2002d: 5). The Committee of the Regions – an advisory body that represents local and regional authorities – also emphasized the usefulness of eco-labels to inform consumers, calling certification of responsible fisheries activities "one of the most promising fisheries management instruments" (Committee of the Regions, 2003: 8). The Committee even encouraged the European Commission to set up a public certification body, even though no details were provided for how this body would operate.

A Failed Proposal for Procedural Regulation (2005–2010)

These early discussions on private fisheries governance formed the basis of a broader debate, which the European Commission launched in 2005. In a Communication on a Community Approach Towards Eco-Labelling Schemes for Fisheries Products, the European Commission reiterated that credible private governance could be complementary to public regulation, since it could "contribute significantly to integrating environmental protection concerns into the fisheries sector" (European Commission, 2005c: 2). The increasing proliferation of private schemes, however, was considered highly problematic. The European Commission specifically highlighted potential negative impacts on trade, competition, and consumer protection due to the creation of trade barriers, the absence of mutual recognition, and consumer confusion as a result of misleading claims (European Commission, 2005c, 2005d).

The 2005 Communication reviewed three ways in which the EU could respond to private governance schemes: (1) nonaction (i.e., sticking to the status quo); (2) creating a public voluntary EU ecolabeling and certification scheme for fish and fishery products, whereby public authorities would be involved in the development, operation, and control of the scheme; and (3) establishing minimum requirements for private governance schemes, with the role of public authorities limited to registering the private schemes and verifying compliance with the minimum criteria.

After reviewing the advantages and disadvantages of each of the three options, the European Commission rejected the first two options. First, while acknowledging the flexibility of private governance schemes, the European Commission argued against nonaction and highlighted problems with the reliability of private schemes and their fragmentation, including the potential emergence of legislation at the Member State level in response to private governance fragmentation. Second, the European Commission did not favor creating an EU ecolabeling and certification scheme. It rejected claims that such a scheme was warranted for public authorities to reclaim authority in fisheries management and to avoid confusion resulting from a fragmented private governance market. Regarding the latter, the European Commission argued that "[c]ompeting eco-labelling schemes would not necessarily have an effect of confusion as long as the assessment is made in a transparent and non-biased manner and the criteria applied are clearly communicated to the consumer" (European Commission, 2005c: 7). In other words, public oversight of the private governance market would suffice to deal with the fragmentation problems.

The main reason the European Commission rejected the option of an EU eco-labeling and certification scheme, however, was that such a scheme would potentially have detrimental impacts on the EU fishing industry. Since an EU certification scheme would contain rules that would be more stringent than existing legislation, the European Commission believed that many EU fisheries would not be able to comply with such rules. For instance, at the time it was estimated that 30 percent of the European fish stocks were "outside safe biological levels," 88 percent of the stocks were being fished beyond maximum sustainable yield, and 93 percent of cod in the North Sea was caught before being able to reproduce (European Commission, 2008g: 2; 2009c: 7). Moreover, the European Commission argued that a public EU certification scheme would benefit imports from countries with a longer history of sustainable fishing. This would come on top of the already heavy dependence of the EU on imports and further undermine the EU fishing industry. Between 1999 and 2007, the EU's self-sufficiency rate in fisheries products – the ratio of EU production to EU apparent consumption – decreased from 57 percent to just below 40 percent, while stabilizing at around 45 percent after 2008. The consumption coverage rate from imports increased from 59 percent to more than 77 percent between 1999 and 2007 (Ernst & Young et al., 2008: 2; 2009: 14; European Commission, 2011e: 75; 2016a: 1; 2016b: 17; 2016e: 12; FAO, 2012: 10, 47). In addition to these trends in production and consumption, retailers were increasingly pressured into offering eco-labeled fishery products. In late 2005, for example, Greenpeace UK issued the first of a series of reports criticizing supermarkets for neglecting the sustainability of seafood products (Greenpeace, 2005). This naming-and-shaming campaign led to a surge in demand for MSC certification when Walmart and its UK affiliate ASDA announced in early 2006 that they would fully commit to purchasing MSC-certified fisheries products (Auld and Renckens, 2019).

Considering these potentially disruptive impacts of an EU public certification scheme on the competitive position of EU fisheries, the European Commission argued in favor of the third option presented in the 2005 Communication, namely, establishing procedural minimum criteria. The European Commission argued that this option would allow for the greatest flexibility for private governance schemes, while also allowing adequate protection to consumers and limiting the policy costs to both public authorities and industry. The minimum requirements were specified as encompassing the following procedural elements: Certification standards should be based on precise, verifiable, and objective criteria; standards and criteria should be subject to the consultation and participation of interested parties; standards should be based on international and/or generally accepted standards; the certification scheme should use independent auditors and ensure tracking throughout the supply chain, with accreditation and audit bodies complying with relevant ISO standards; schemes should not discriminate in terms of producer access to the scheme; and the certification standard should be available to consumers, with the information at the point of sale adequately reflecting the underlying standard and audit procedure.

To further examine the different options put forward in the 2005 Communication, the European Commission established an expert group consisting of representatives of various parts of the supply chain (catch, processing, and retail), as well as fisheries scientists and certification schemes.[10] While the EU institutions had always considered both capture fisheries and aquaculture together, the expert group only dealt with the former. In its final report, the expert group supported establishing minimum criteria. Reflecting the interests of its participants, the expert group argued that a single EU certification scheme would be "too prescriptive given the diversity of fisheries in Europe" and "could not allow the flexibility through which retailers and processors could develop their own brand marks" (Expert Group on Eco-Labelling for Fishery Products, 2006: 3). Overall, the expert group based its recommendations on the FAO Guidelines and Code of Conduct, with which the EU at the time had only partly complied (Churchill and Owen, 2010). On this basis, the experts' report identified twenty-one overarching principles, as well as more concrete objectives and criteria that the private governance schemes were expected to specify in order to achieve on-the-ground behavioral changes.

Several of the EU institutions followed the positions of the European Commission and the expert group. Most Member States in the Council of Ministers favored minimum criteria. They highlighted the need to ensure credibility and limit confusion, emphasizing that schemes should be "transparent, market-driven, nondiscriminatory, voluntary, accessible to operators irrespective of their size and economic contexts, based on sound scientific evidence and fully consistent with WTO rules" (Council of the European Union, 2007a). The EESC was also supportive of minimum criteria. It emphasized the importance of including a monitoring system for agreed accreditation and certification rules, a system of sanctions, information to consumers on the meaning of eco-labels, a corresponding investment program with attention to the economic impact of eco-labeling, and continuous dialogue with stakeholders (EESC, 2006).

In contrast, the European Parliament, which at the time was only to be consulted on fisheries policy and did not yet have co-decision powers, disagreed with the other EU institutions. The Parliament strongly favored the option of establishing an EU-wide public certification scheme, thereby highlighting both consumer and environmental concerns (European Parliament, 2006a, 2006b, 2006g, 2006j).[11] The European Parliament argued that minimum criteria would not adequately address the issue of consumer confusion, considering the increasing proliferation of eco-labeling schemes. The Parliament was also skeptical of the trustworthiness of private governance schemes. It suggested that many eco-labels were used to merely increase sales and that receiving unjustified price premiums amounted to a fraudulent practice. Furthermore, the Parliament argued that when fisheries comply with the CFP, they are by definition sustainable, while acknowledging that an EU certification scheme would need to be based on even stricter sustainability rules. The 2006 Resolution of the Parliament on the topic specified several criteria to which an EU certification scheme should adhere (European Parliament, 2006j). These criteria required that the scheme must be consistent with relevant FAO, WTO, and UN rules; voluntary, and ensuring greater environmental improvements, while not making any claims that non-labeled products were inferior; transparent; nondiscriminatory; promoted and operated by the European Commission; focused on sustainability criteria that are based on sound science; clear to consumers; and based on independent and reliable verification procedures.

The European Parliament was, furthermore, very critical of the European Commission's perceived lack of engagement with the issue. In its Resolution, the Parliament regretted "the delays on the part of the Commission in coming forward with its communication" and "deplores the communication's lack of ambition" (European Parliament, 2006j: 234). The report of the Parliament's Committee on Fisheries had earlier already stressed that it was "very disappointed" with the Communication's "poor analysis and limited content," which was "indicative of the lack of interest that the Commission appears to show in this matter" (European Parliament, 2006g: 8). The European Commission, in turn, reproached the European Parliament for having delivered an inconsistent Resolution, since it called for a single EU certification scheme, while at the same time agreeing that establishing such a scheme was "bureaucratically cumbersome" (European Commission, 2006b: 1). Moreover, the European Commissioner for Fisheries, Joe Borg, mentioned during the debate in the European Parliament that the Parliament's support for an EU certification scheme stood in stark contrast to the positions of the EESC, the Advisory Committee on Fisheries and Agriculture, and "most industry and stakeholders' representatives," who supported minimum criteria (European Parliament, 2006a). Later, the Commission also emphasized that these "more or less unanimous opinions" were shared by the Council of Ministers (European Commission, 2006b).

Considering this strong support across the EU institutions and from stakeholders for the option of establishing minimum criteria, and considering the European Parliament only held consultative competence on fisheries policy, it was expected that the European Commission would put forward a legislative proposal on minimum criteria for private governance schemes. The overall aim of the new piece of legislation would be to "underpin and give legal clarity to certain minimum criteria and procedures for voluntary schemes for labelling sustainable fishing from marine capture fisheries products placed on the Community market" (Advisory Committee on Fisheries and Aquaculture, 2009: 3). The criteria were considered to be based on five elements: (1) precise, objective, and verifiable technical criteria; (2) independent third-party assessment and accreditation; (3) open access to all operators that would want to join; (4) proper controls of certification programs to see whether they were complying with the minimum criteria; and (5) transparency and accurate information to consumers (Bates, 2010; Corréard, 2010). The proposal would be based on the FAO Guidelines, with auditors being accredited by the relevant national accreditation bodies under EU law, and Member

States being responsible for monitoring and sanctioning (Bates, 2010). The goal was to have the Council of Ministers adopt the legislation before the end of 2009 (Bates, 2009; Management Committee for Fishery and Aquaculture Products, 2009).[12]

The legislative proposal on minimum criteria, however, was never officially released. This failure was the result of reasons related to the proposal itself and events external to the policy discussions on private fisheries governance. Due to "insufficient evidence" to complete the impact assessment, the policy process initially stalled at the level of the Impact Assessment Board that examines the economic, social, and environmental impacts of any proposed legislation (MRAG, 2016: 17). Moreover, in early 2010, a new European Commission was installed after the European elections of June 2009, which created additional delays in the decision-making process (Bates, 2010). Finally, in 2009, the Commission started the process of reforming the CFP (European Commission, 2009c). As the next section explains, the debate on private fisheries governance would become an integral part of this reform.

Postponing the Decision: The 2013 Reform of the EU's Common Fisheries Policy (2010–2014)

In July 2011, the European Commission released proposals for the reform of the CFP (European Commission, 2011g, 2011i). Building on earlier reforms, one of the main goals of this reform round was further improving the sustainability of the CFP. Both the 2009 green paper on the CFP reform and the subsequent stakeholder consultation had identified sustainability as a continuing concern (European Commission, 2009c, 2010e).[13] In the run-up to the reform, the European Commission set the tone for what were to become contentious negotiations. It blamed Member States for being "focused on keeping their fleets busy rather than adopting proposals for sustainable fishing policies," while decision-making in the Council of Ministers was blamed for being "dominated by concerns about the short-term economic and social impact of reducing fishing pressure and fishing capacity" (European Commission, 2008g: 5). Such a short-term perspective would come at the "expense of the future sustainability of the industry" (European Commission, 2009c: 7). The key foci of the new reform, therefore, were the exploitation of fish stocks at maximum sustainable yield levels, the elimination of discards, the optimization of multi-annual management plans, the use of sound scientific advice following an ecosystem and precautionary approach, and improving partnerships between scientists and industry for enhancing the quality and availability of data.

The reform package included a proposal for a reform of the Common Organization of the Markets for Fishery and Aquaculture Products, and this provided the context for discussing private fisheries governance (European Commission, 2011h). For the reform of the Common Organization of the Markets, the focus on sustainability included attempts to improve consumer information on the sustainability of fishery and aquaculture products in order to increase consumer confidence. In the background note to the proposal, the European Commission suggested this, among other things, could be pursued by supporting certification and eco-labeling (European Commission, 2011h: 2–3). The proposal itself, however, did not directly include a reference to eco-labeling and certification, but it did include an article (Article 45) that indicated that certain information on a fisheries product's label could be provided voluntarily. This information could relate to environmental information, ethical or social information, information on production techniques, and information on production practices. The European Commission proposed (in Article 46) that it could adopt delegated acts to set minimum criteria for such voluntary information (European Commission, 2011h). By means of this article, the European Commission envisioned it could develop the framework to control and ensure the accuracy of voluntary labeling that would include private governance schemes (European Commission, 2011e: 16, 32). This position built on the results of the stakeholder consultation on the CFP reform, in which most organizations that discussed eco-labels supported the option of establishing minimum criteria for private governance.[14]

In response to the European Commission's proposal, the European Parliament placed the idea of an EU certification and eco-labeling scheme back on the table. Throughout the negotiations, the European Parliament defended this position and felt more confident than before, considering that with the entry into force of the Lisbon Treaty at the end of 2009, the Parliament had gained co-decision competence in fisheries policy. The European Parliament called for establishing an EU public eco-labeling scheme by urging the Commission to submit, by January 1, 2015, "a report, accompanied by a proposal, for the establishment of a Union wide [sic] eco-label scheme for fisheries products. The report shall examine potential minimum requirements for obtaining approval for the use of such eco-label" (European Parliament, 2013: 235).[15] The European Parliament's support for an EU eco-labeling scheme was based on the same rationale the European Commission had used earlier to reject such a scheme and instead opt for minimum criteria: support for the EU fishing industry. The European Parliament's argument was that instead of undermining the EU's fishing industry, an EU eco-labeling scheme would create a level playing field for competition with non-EU products. Such imports were considered to be produced against lower standards than were applied in the EU. Furthermore, the European Parliament's support for an EU scheme was based on a system of verifying compliance with an EU public sustainability standard similar to the meta-standard approach used in the biofuels case. It was suggested that existing private governance schemes, such as MSC or ASC, could be approved to perform the certification against the EU's sustainability standard (European Parliament, 2012b: 12; 2012c: 6–7).[16]

Private governance schemes were not in favor of such an approach and, at most, were supportive of minimum criteria (MSC, 2009; Seafish, 2009; WWF, 2009).[17] Their main fear was that an EU public certification scheme would create direct competition, since private schemes would have to differentiate themselves from the public scheme to remain operational in the market. The public character of an EU scheme would potentially be appealing to producers due to the higher legitimacy of such a scheme in the eyes of the consumer, thereby pushing private schemes out of the market. In addition, these consumer preferences may appeal to retailers with commitments to selling certified products, and as a result, these retailers may want to shift to products certified by the EU scheme, instead of those certified by private schemes. Furthermore, while minimum criteria would weed out the worst-performing private governance schemes, an EU-level scheme would intervene significantly in well-performing schemes and entail control by the EU institutions of how the approved private schemes would operate. An EU scheme would also include the risk of regular updates or changes to the standards, based on a political process that would at least partly be out of the hands of private governance schemes.

In the Council of Ministers, despite some differences of opinion, most Member States were not supportive of an EU eco-labeling scheme. The Council's general approach on the Common Organization of the Markets, which was adopted in June 2012, did not include specific references to eco-labeling or certification (Council of the European Union, 2012d). It merely referred to the minimum criteria for voluntary information that the European Commission could establish, as was suggested in the original proposal for the Common Organization of the Markets. Only in a separately issued Council Statement was it mentioned that "[t]he Council invites the Commission to consider establishing minimum standards for an EU sustainability label for fisheries and for aquaculture products, and to evaluate the appropriate procedure for submitting a proposal" (Council of the European Union, 2012e). This could hardly be interpreted as a firm embrace of such an initiative. In the press release of the meeting, it was mentioned that "[t]he framework allowing the Commission to develop an EU sustainability label is established" (Council of the European Union, 2012b). According to a source close to the negotiations, this was euphemistic language to indicate that this topic could be further discussed, but that not much was to be expected.[18] The positions of Member States in the Council were indeed somewhat divided, which resulted in such unclear language. In some instances, the Council reported that some Member States expressed support for an EU eco-label, without identifying these countries (Council of the European Union, 2012a). On other occasions, however, it became clear that multiple Member States, such as Denmark, France, Spain, Germany, Ireland, and the Netherlands were explicitly supportive of minimum criteria for private governance schemes (Council of the European Union, 2012c; Federal Ministry of Food, 2009; Ministry of Agriculture, 2009; Patz, 2012).

This reluctance of Member States to agree to an EU eco-labeling scheme was linked to the overall difficult negotiations of the CFP reform. While some countries were supportive of an ambitious reform, countries with important fishing interests, in particular France and Spain, were much more reluctant to engage in a drastic and fast deviation from the status quo. These countries had a significant impact on the outcome (Cator, 2011; Council of the European Union, 2011).[19] Issues such as reaching maximum sustainable yield and an elimination of discards by 2015 – as proposed by the European Commission and supported by the European Parliament – were considered very difficult (Naver, 2012). Discussions on these topics proved to be very contentious and the timetable to achieve these goals was, in the final compromise, spread out over multiple years – until 2020 (European Commission, 2013d). Similarly, the reform of the subsidies scheme proved to be very difficult, with the Council of Ministers being much less ambitious than the European Commission and the European Parliament, and more willing to sustain subsidies that were considered to be undermining the sustainability of the CFP (Keating, 2013; Naver, 2012, 2013a, 2013b, 2013c, 2013d, 2014a, 2014b).

Considering the lengthy and difficult negotiations to reach a compromise on the overall reform, it seemed unlikely that similar negotiations could be held to achieve a compromise on a sustainability standard for an EU eco-labeling scheme. This standard, it was understood, would have to be even stricter than the new rules of the CFP reform. The changes demanded from the fisheries sector were already considered significant. Additional adjustments to comply with even stricter rules in order to acquire an EU eco-label would not be received well by producer organizations that already had to bend backward to comply with the newly agreed rules.[20]

Ultimately, the compromise that was reached on private governance reflected the original positions of the various EU institutions. It was agreed that the European Commission would write a "feasibility report on options for an eco-label scheme for fishery and aquaculture products, in particular on establishing such a scheme on a Union-wide basis and on setting minimum requirements for the use by Member States of a Union eco-label" (European Parliament and Council of the European Union, 2013: 12). While the European Parliament's concrete reference to an EU eco-labeling scheme was included in the text, it seemed that the Council came out on top.[21] Neither minimum criteria for benchmarking private governance schemes, nor an EU eco-label was established. The decision on how to respond to private fisheries governance was once again postponed.

Old Wine in New Bottles or Redefining the Debate? (2013–2017)

The feasibility report that the EU institutions agreed on in the context of the 2013 CFP reform was finalized in February 2016, after a public stakeholder consultation was held between May and July 2015. The results of the consultation showed that support for public involvement with private fisheries governance was high and that minimum criteria were most widely supported, especially among key stakeholder groups (European Commission, 2015c: 2933).

Overall, 64 percent of stakeholders supported public involvement and 18 percent opposed. Across stakeholder groups, support was higher than 50 percent. Only retailers and eco-label owners showed lower support: 64 percent of eco-label owners opposed public involvement, with 27 percent supporting, while 30 percent of retailers opposed public involvement and 39 percent supported it. This opposition is understandable, since these are the private actors most closely involved with private governance schemes. Overall support for minimum criteria was particularly high, with on average 72 percent of stakeholders supporting such criteria. Among eco-label owners, opposition was largest, with 36 percent disagreeing with the creation of minimum criteria. Support for minimum criteria was highest among fishery/aquaculture companies (92 percent). Finally, across stakeholder groups 51 percent opposed the creation of an EU eco-labeling scheme. In particular, eco-label owners (73 percent), retailers (70 percent), and NGOs (54 percent) expressed opposition to a public EU certification scheme, while public bodies (67 percent), producer organizations (65 percent), and fishery/aquaculture companies (63 percent) expressed support for such a scheme (European Commission, 2015c: 29–33).

Based on the results of this deliberation, consultancy firm MRAG authored the feasibility report. The report provides an overview of the fisheries and aquaculture eco-label landscape and offers an analysis of three familiar options: operating within the existing regulatory framework; creating minimum criteria for the benchmarking of private governance schemes; and a voluntary EU public eco-labeling scheme (Table 6.2). The feasibility report, however, does not issue a recommendation for a particular option.

In May 2016, the European Commission issued a report that summarized the main findings of the feasibility report regarding the market for eco-labels, legislative developments, and advantages and disadvantages of the three options (European Commission, 2016f). Unlike the 2005 Communication and the 2008–2009 draft legislative proposal, however, the European Commission did not offer a preference for any of the three options, as it did not consider that the 2013 legislation on the Common Organization of the Markets demanded such a

Table 6.2 *Options for EU policy on private fisheries governance*

Option	Advantages	Disadvantages
Existing Regulatory Framework	– Low cost for implementation – European Commission role remains focused on improving resource management – Strengthening control of existing regulations may help address quality and validity of information – EU Member States' competent authorities already have the legal basis to control	– Limited effect on the diversity of scope across eco-labels and resulting supply chain complexity
Minimum Criteria and Benchmarking	– Should help in assessing standards across eco-labels, addressing issues of consistency and validity – Should assist consumers, buyers, and retailers assess credibility of different eco-labels and make choices – Could facilitate control – Limited costs of development	– Duplication of effort due to existing initiatives – Will not be operational in less than three years – Substantial implementation costs if all existing and new schemes and possible allegations are being assessed toward the standard
Voluntary EU Eco-label	– Provides a single public alternative to multiple existing schemes	– High cost of implementation – May increase complexity by introducing another label into the market – European Commission has a dual role improving environmental sustainability and setting criteria for assessing sustainability

Table 6.2 (*cont.*)

Option	Advantages	Disadvantages
		– Will not be operational before 3–5 years and may need an additional 3–5 years to get first certifications, logo recognition, and to develop a market share – No example and evidence of successful public scheme

Source: MRAG (2016: 139)

position.[22] The European Commission's report was forwarded to the European Parliament and the Council of Ministers for further discussion. At the time of this writing, neither the Council of Ministers nor the European Parliament has formally discussed the report.

While the three policy options that are discussed in the MRAG feasibility report and the European Commission's report are essentially the same as the ones that have been discussed since the 2005 Communication, the reports highlight two elements that will potentially influence discussions going forward: the relativity of the fragmentation of the private governance market and the changed policy context.

First, the MRAG and European Commission reports both qualify the observation that the private fisheries governance market is characterized by fragmentation and proliferation. As discussions in the past have shown, the existence of "eco-label noise" (OECD and FAO, 2009: 12) in the fisheries sector has time and again been mentioned as an important rationale for public regulatory intervention. This context led various stakeholders in the past to offer support for establishing minimum criteria for private governance schemes, for the EU recognizing existing schemes, and for the EU acting as an "information broker" (GIZ, 2015). Furthermore, the 2015 public consultation found that across stakeholder groups between 42 and 86 percent of the respondents agree with the statement that "consumers don't know what eco-labels mean" (average of 63 percent), while between 42 and

79 percent agree with the statement that "consumers don't know which eco-label to choose" (average of 61 percent) (European Commission, 2015c: 16–18). Of those stakeholders indicating they do not use (i.e., buy, sell, participate in) eco-labeling schemes, the consultation found that "[b]etween 30% and 38% of participants agree that there are too many eco-labels, and 25% to 29% of relevant participants agree that they do not trust eco-label claims" (European Commission, 2015c: 10) .

The feasibility report, however, qualifies these views on fragmentation. It argues that the existence of a large number of eco-labeling schemes does not "necessarily equate to a proliferation as such" (MRAG, 2016: 2). This large number of schemes is "indicative of a bigger issue" since schemes "are responding to variables in the market such as diversity of businesses, diversity of demands, diversity of requirements, diversity of products" (MRAG, 2016: 2). And while potential consumer confusion is not ignored, the report mentions that "[m]uch of the confusion can be attributed to a lack of communication of the differences between eco-labels themselves, and between eco-labels and other schemes" (MRAG, 2016: 2), such as codes of conduct, consumer guides, and other informational tools. In addition, the report emphasizes that "[s]tandard-setting for eco-labels is generally perceived as credible and transparent" and that "there is no evidence of mislabelling and greenwashing" (MRAG, 2016: 4). Indeed, the European Commission points out that the "EU eco-labelling landscape is concentrated. Few eco-labels concentrate most of the certified products and are complementary in terms of products covered" (European Commission, 2016c).

The MRAG feasibility report and the European Commission's report highlight a second issue as to why the current discussions are different than those in earlier times; the reason is that the policy context has changed in three respects. First, the feasibility report points out that several recent EU policy initiatives address the provision of environmental information and consumer protection, thereby mitigating the need to intervene on this basis. These initiatives include a 2010 European Commission Communication on EU best practice guidelines for voluntary certification schemes for agricultural products and foodstuffs; this features several procedural elements, such as openness of the schemes to all possible participants, stakeholder participation in the development and management of schemes, clarity and transparency of requirements and claims, and impartiality and independence of certification (European Commission, 2010c). Also included are a 2011 Regulation on the provision of food information to consumers showing the need to ensure the credibility of voluntary consumer information (European Parliament and Council of the European Union, 2011); a 2012 European Commission Communication on a European Consumer Agenda incorporating a focus on sustainable consumption (European Commission, 2012f); and a 2013 European Commission Communication on Building the Single Market for Green Products, which includes tools to measure the environmental impact of products (European Commission, 2013a).

Second, in addition to these EU-level initiatives, the feasibility report emphasizes the private harmonization effort that is occurring under the umbrella of the GSSI. As mentioned, the GSSI provides a benchmarking tool for private governance schemes. This initiative may make an EU effort to develop procedural regulation unnecessary, considering the GSSI is perceived to be a credible undertaking (MRAG, 2016: 145–146).

Finally, the CFP itself has gradually changed. As the European Commission mentions, the "CFP is expected to deliver on sustainability by 2020 at the latest, partially reducing the need for a public label as a driver of sustainability" (European Commission, 2016f: 10). In that context, the feasibility report argues that "an EU ecolabel would be limited to a role in assurance rather than driving improved environmental performance" (MRAG, 2016: 4). Mere compliance with existing EU fisheries legislation would then suffice to grant certification and an EU label, which in the past had also been proposed by some stakeholders as a rationale for the development of an EU label.[23] Such a label, however, would resemble an indication of origin, rather than a sign of sustainability and market differentiation. It would support consumer recognition of EU products and differentiate them from non-EU products that would not adhere to equally strict rules. In the past, however, the European Commission has argued against such a rationale for an EU label: "If the required standard for a single Community eco-label were mere compliance with Community regulations, it would not provide the product differentiation that consumers are looking for. In actual fact, an eco-labelling scheme would carry with it added value only if it were more demanding than mere compliance with applicable legislation. Otherwise, some might be led to believe that the legislation itself was wanting or even 'sub-standard'" (European Commission, 2005c: 8).

These two elements – a rethinking of the degree of fragmentation of the private governance market, and the changed policy context – could lead policy preferences to shift toward different outcomes than had been contemplated thus far. They could result in stronger support for the status quo of no regulation. This option could be based on the rationale that existing policy developments offer sufficient tools to address remaining fragmentation problems, while public support for market differentiation is still considered too costly for EU producers. Alternatively, even when the fragmentation of the market is no longer considered a problem, market differentiation could still be considered necessary to support EU producers against non-EU producers, as the Parliament has always argued. This rationale would result in standards regulation, but not procedural regulation, when quasi-monopolistic schemes such as the MSC are considered ill-fitted for parts of the EU fisheries. This scenario, however, is not very likely given the entrenched positions of the EU institutions on this topic.

Conclusion

For almost two decades, the EU has been reforming its fisheries policy to place it on a path toward sustainability. These efforts have proven difficult, with many indicators pointing to a failing EU fisheries policy. The difficulties in making the CFP more sustainable have also influenced the debate on private fisheries governance. This debate, which the European Commission announced in 1997 and officially launched in 2005, has yet to conclude.

Overall, throughout most of the debate, there has been quite widespread agreement that the fragmentation of the private fisheries governance market was problematic. Ensuring the credibility of schemes, limiting consumer confusion, and overcoming trade barriers, especially due to the lack of mutual recognition among private schemes, and the potential emergence of national-level regulations, have been put forward as rationales for intervention. However, there is disagreement among the EU institutions about the desirability of public intervention for product differentiation. Throughout the discussions, the European Parliament has consistently supported such differentiation in the form of the creation of a public EU certification and eco-labeling scheme, which would encompass both standards and procedural regulations. The Parliament has argued that such differentiation will benefit EU fisheries that are operating according to stricter sustainability rules compared to non-EU fisheries, and that they will hence reap the competitive benefits of having an EU scheme to differentiate themselves from foreign competition. Several key Member States, the European Commission, and many stakeholders, on the other hand, argue that such differentiation will impose too-high costs on EU producers, who are already struggling to implement the sustainability rules that have been negotiated in the context of the various reforms of the EU's CFP. The EU fisheries would potentially be disadvantaged compared to non-EU fisheries. Instead, these policymakers and stakeholders favor the creation of procedural regulation in the form of minimum criteria to benchmark private governance schemes.

It was this combination of a recognition of the need to address private governance fragmentation, and a reluctance to engage in product differentiation, that led the European Commission to start preparing a legislative proposal on procedural regulation in the form of minimum criteria in 2008–2009. However, due to elements both related to the proposal (a stalled impact assessment) and external to the policymaking process (elections and the start of the reform of the CFP), the proposal for minimum criteria was never officially released. Following this failure, the discussions on regulating private governance became part of the negotiations of the reform of the CFP. Yet, the decision on private fisheries governance was pushed into the indefinite future as a result of the difficulty of the CFP reform negotiations; the unchanged positions of the various institutions and stakeholders with respect to regulations for private fisheries governance; and the fact that the Council of Ministers has since the entry into force of the Lisbon Treaty been confronted with a European Parliament that has co-decision competence in fisheries policy.

In this respect, it remains to be seen whether the 2016 feasibility report will change policy preferences. The context in which the private governance debate occurs has potentially changed, as the feasibility report argues. This is due to several factors, including a questioning of the actual fragmentation of the private governance market; a private harmonization initiative created under the umbrella of the GSSI; the development of EU policy initiatives in areas outside of the specific fisheries context that deal with consumer protection; and the expected sustainability of the CFP in the near future. These changing dynamics in the end mean that all possible options as identified in Table 2.2 are still on the table. Yet, considering that the assumption of the fragmentation of the market has been challenged in the feasibility report, and given the continued differences of opinion on the benefits of product differentiation, the current no-intervention outcome may well remain in place for quite a while.

7 | *Evaluating Public Interventions in Private Governance*

Transnational private governance addressing the environmental and social impacts of global production processes has expanded over the last three decades to cover a wide range of issue areas. While it has largely developed without the authoritative involvement of public policymakers, private governance does not operate outside the boundaries of governments' sovereign authority. When will a public authority intervene to regulate transnational private governance and what form will such regulatory intervention take? This book has addressed these research questions by examining EU interventions in private governance in four issue areas: organic agriculture, biofuels production, fair trade, and fisheries. The EU's regulatory interventions pose a puzzle, since in the former two issue areas, the EU intervened with both standards and procedural regulations, while in the other areas the EU has (so far) not intervened. This variation in interventions, the book argues, can be explained by the interplay of two variables: the domestic benefits of product differentiation, and the fragmentation of the private governance market.

This final chapter will compare the findings from the four issue areas and link them with the theoretical framework presented in Chapter 2. Subsequently, the chapter addresses a question that logically follows from the analysis: Given the EU's interventions, what have been the impacts on the nature and functioning of private governance and the larger policy field? I argue that the regulatory impacts are twofold: The interventions have both restructured the field of private governance schemes and largely retained private governance's governing authority. This dual character of the interventions is important to emphasize. The interventions impose baselines that cannot be undercut and that arguably have resulted in some sustainability improvements. At the same time, the interventions are relatively limited because the standards and procedural regulations represent minimum baselines. They allow private governance schemes sufficient governance space to govern as they see fit, which may result in policy diffusion and spillovers that can subsequently strengthen public policy and governance more generally. The ways in which the public interventions have been designed, however, affect how these interactions play out, with several gaps still evident. Based on these findings, the chapter subsequently discusses the generalizability of the theoretical framework. This is an important concern, given that the EU is a unique polity. To do this, the chapter examines examples of public interventions at both the international and domestic level, highlighting the framework's applicability in these contexts. The book concludes with avenues for further research.

Comparing Public Regulatory Interventions

The cases of organic agriculture and biofuels production show that the combined effect of significant domestic benefits of product differentiation and a high fragmentation of the private governance market resulted in the EU establishing both standards and procedural regulations (Table 7.1). In both cases, the European Commission introduced both types of regulation in its legislative proposals, after which the policy discussions focused on the content of the regulations and the degree of intervention (i.e., the stringency of the regulations). The Commission's proposals were derived from input from a wide range of stakeholders and based on consultations, workshops and conferences, and direct lobbying. Private governance schemes and associated stakeholders played particularly crucial roles in directly shaping the public interventions.

Table 7.1 *Situating the cases in the theoretical framework*

		Domestic Benefits of Product Differentiation	
		Low	High
Fragmentation of the private governance market	Low	Fair Trade Fisheries	*Fisheries post-2017?*
	High	*Fisheries 2008–2009 proposal* *Fisheries post-2017?*	Organic Agriculture Biofuels

In the case of organic agriculture, offering support for and increasing the production opportunities of European farmers provided important incentives for the EU to engage in 1991. The organic products market was considered a growth market due to increasing consumer interest. The intervention coincided with crucial reforms of the CAP that policy-makers wanted to steer away from direct price support to farmers and to present a greener image. Publicly regulating organic agriculture – long since governed by private standards – would contribute to creating new economic opportunities for farmers and serve rural development objectives. The organic movement – including private governance schemes and local producers – played a crucial role in initiating the EU's regulatory intervention, since it expected an intervention would open up new markets and provide EU financial contributions for conversion to organic practices. The absence of a strong involvement of the traditional farmers' lobby further facilitated public support for organic agriculture, which was also promoted by several Member States that had already developed national organic regulations (such as the United Kingdom and France). Finally, the fact that foreign jurisdictions, such as the USA, were looking into regulating organic farming provided an additional incentive to support domestic producers with the aim of developing a first-mover advantage.

Problems resulting from the fragmentation of the private governance market offered other rationales for the EU to intervene. The organic movement had achieved the international harmonization of organic standards through IFOAM. However, the Basic Standards that resulted from this harmonization effort comprised overarching principles that private governance schemes had to interpret and adapt to local cultural and climatic circumstances. Furthermore, the fraudulent uses of the term "organic" and a lack of differentiation among concepts used to identify the quality of food products, including "natural" and "wholesome," resulted in supply chain confusion and problems of legitimacy for private governance more broadly. Eight EU Member States, moreover, had engaged with organic agriculture to address some of these issues, which created intra-EU market problems that EU-level public intervention could overcome.

The combined effect of these rationales for intervention led the EU to develop both standards and procedural regulations that contributed to a level playing field and increased opportunities for producers, and a harmonization of private governance standards and procedures.

Policymakers based the legal definition of organic farming on IFOAM's Basic Standards, for which IFOAM and organic producers had actively lobbied. The organic movement succeeded in retaining significant governance space for private standard-setters that could continue to certify against their own standards and use their own private labels. In addition, the EU Organic Agriculture Regulation allowed for the delegation of the verification of compliance with the EU's standard to private auditors, many of whom at the time also certified against their own standards or had close relationships with private standard-setters. The EU designed this delegation to take advantage of private expertise that was not available in many national administrations.

The continued fragmentation of the private governance market – in particular the lack of mutual recognition among private schemes and the ambiguities around the separation of standard-setting from verification functions in many private governance schemes – created incentives for the EU to further harmonize the market. In 2005, the European Commission proposed strict limitations on private governance, in essence by imposing mutual recognition and limiting private standard-setting capacity. This proposed interference with private schemes' governance space elicited strong opposition from the organic movement and several Member States (such as France and Germany) in defense of their local schemes. As a result, the European Commission's proposals were largely abandoned. Instead, standards regulation was extended by making the EU organic label mandatory for EU-produced prepackaged food and by creating the indications of "EU" and "non-EU" agriculture to more clearly distinguish domestic from imported products. Furthermore, the EU tightened its procedural regulation by mandating auditor accreditation to ensure the independence of standard-setters and auditors.

In the case of biofuels production, EU policymakers developed standards and procedural regulations to provide continued support to the EU's nascent biofuels sector and to address the fragmentation of the private governance market. The 2003 Biofuels Directive, which established the EU's biofuels market, did not include concrete environmental provisions or references to private governance. This was the result of policymakers and many stakeholders at the time believing biofuels were CO_2 neutral and therefore a panacea for reducing GHG emissions. Furthermore, the initial development of private governance schemes dealing with the sustainability of biofuels production coincided with the discussions on this Directive.

In the wake of the 2003 Directive, a heated political debate emerged about the detrimental environmental impacts of biofuels production and the need to differentiate sustainable biofuels in the market. Scientific evidence and NGO pressure increasingly gave the EU's biofuels policy a bad image, in particular since the EU wanted to further stimulate the use of biofuels by introducing mandatory targets. Given that the credibility of the EU's renewable energy policy (which encompassed biofuels) and the survival of the young European crop-based biofuels industry were both at stake, policymakers warmed to introducing sustainability criteria. The criteria were considered necessary in order to provide policy support to the industry, even though farmers and biofuels producers, while heavily supporting mandatory targets, were not supportive of (strict) sustainability criteria. These actors argued that the existing agro-environmental rules sufficiently guaranteed the sustainability of the EU's biofuels, in particular compared to imported biofuels. Overcoming this opposition with the argument that introducing sustainability criteria was in the long-term interests of the biofuels industry was crucial in this respect.

The development of both general and crop-specific private governance schemes, the lack of private harmonization, and the potential development of public interventions at the Member State level to deal with fragmentation and sustainability concerns, further incentivized EU intervention. Moreover, policymakers considered private governance schemes useful instruments to verify compliance with the EU sustainability criteria. They devised a so-called meta-standard approach, implying that compliance with a Commission-approved private scheme equates with compliance with the EU biofuels regime. To be approved, private schemes needed to incorporate the EU's sustainability criteria and comply with a set of procedural criteria. WWF, which was involved in the development of several of the main private biofuels governance schemes, was particularly instrumental in convincing policymakers to adopt this approach, thereby ensuring the continued relevance of private biofuels governance. As well, several Member States (including the United Kingdom, the Netherlands, and to a lesser degree, Germany) had been examining the establishment of a meta-standard approach domestically. EU regulatory intervention with both standards and procedural regulations was warranted, therefore, to reduce information asymmetries in the supply chain, and potential trade and competitive distortions, and to control the further proliferation of schemes that would certify against their own as well as public sustainability criteria.

The European Commission's process of approving private governance schemes resulted in these schemes adopting the EU sustainability criteria almost word for word. As a result, several of the schemes created specific EU-compliant standards, in addition to their regular rest-of-the-world standards. Complaints about the transparency of the approval process and concerns around private schemes' compliance with the procedural rules, however, resulted in updated procedural rules in the 2015 ILUC Directive. The Directive imposed larger transparency requirements regarding the use of auditors, accreditation rules, stakeholder involvement, and noncompliance sanctioning.

In contrast to organic agriculture and biofuels production, the case of fair trade shows that the combination of the absence of the domestic benefits of product differentiation, and a non-fragmented market for private governance results in the absence of public regulatory intervention. The lack of EU fair trade producers and the nearly absent opportunities for producers to become involved in such production – even though possible in principle – have resulted in the absence of sufficient policy interest and interest mobilization around public interventions for this purpose. Such interests were briefly explored in the 1990s when EU policymakers contemplated creating a market for fair trade products from former colonies in the ACP countries. These attempts, however, were stranded on concerns about possibly violating GATT/ WTO rules on trade discrimination, given the specific North–South character of trade in this issue area.

In addition, fragmentation problems in the private governance market have not warranted public intervention. In the 1980s and 1990s, the proliferation of national-level private governance schemes concerned European policymakers. The successful harmonization efforts by the Fair Trade movement, however, largely eliminated asymmetric information problems and prevented trade and competitive distortions from becoming problematic. These private harmonization efforts started in the second half of the 1990s and resulted in the creation of an overarching organization – FLO, now Fairtrade International – and a common definition of Fair Trade and a common label.

Over time, new concerns arose due to the more prominent market position of a couple of private governance schemes – Rainforest Alliance and UTZ Certified – that challenged the Fair Trade model. These competitive dynamics resulted in a broadening of the policy area beyond Fair Trade proper. In the first few years of the new millennium, the European Commission looked to establish a commonly agreed fair trade definition and a set of procedural criteria that could cover all private governance schemes. In this way, policymakers intended to advance EU policy in the areas of CSR and sustainable development in the wake of the 2002 Johannesburg World Summit on Sustainable Development. They quickly realized, however, that the same WTO limitations as before applied, that such an approach to harmonization could not capture fundamental differences in the private schemes' underlying governance philosophies, and that an EU intervention would not significantly contribute to the EU's sustainable development policy. In particular, both policymakers and private governance schemes viewed the differences among the various private schemes as embedded in different commercial and economic-ideological logics, and neither of these actors identified or problematized these differences as fragmentation issues. The European Commission, therefore, has not been willing to stymie these complementary approaches to fair trade. The fact that the functioning of the initiatives has not directly led to trade barriers, and that Member States have not started regulating this issue area, has further influenced the European Commission's decision to not intervene.

While none of the main private governance schemes was in favor of any type of direct public regulatory intervention, the Fair Trade movement did strategically lobby to have its approach to fair trade formally recognized. Its strong Brussels lobby office and close connections to members of the European Parliament contributed to the European Commission explicitly highlighting the unique nature of Fair Trade in the 2009 Communication on the topic. Opposition from the other main private governance schemes and associated stakeholders – even though much less organized than Fair Trade – prevented an exclusive focus on Fair Trade and resulted in a recognition of all of the private governance schemes' commercial approaches.

Finally, the fisheries case is still a case of nonintervention. However, the protracted discussions around possible EU interventions provide direct insights into the skew-diagonal quadrants of Table 7.1. The fragmentation of private fisheries governance in the EU market has been a key element in favor of public regulatory intervention ever since the discussions started in the 1990s. The argument is that because there are too many private schemes and a lack of successful private harmonization efforts, there is supply chain confusion and concern about the legitimacy of private governance. Furthermore, the possibility of the emergence of national-level regulations has provided an additional rationale for EU-level intervention. All relevant stakeholders, including several private governance schemes, have in the past agreed on this stance, as expressed in policy documents, stakeholder consultations, and a 2006 expert group report.

There has been less agreement, however, on the domestic benefits of product differentiation that would result from public intervention. From the very beginning of the debate, the European Commission has objected to standards regulation for this reason. The Commission has argued that such regulation would put the EU fishing industry at a competitive disadvantage, since it would entail developing sustainability rules that surpass existing legislation. EU fisheries would not be able to comply with such rules, while it is feared that some non-EU competitors would. Instead, the European Commission has proposed procedural regulation in the form of minimum criteria for private governance schemes to address the fragmentation problems. Industry, civil society stakeholders, and all EU institutions, apart from the European Parliament, have supported this stance. The European Parliament's argument has been that a public EU certification and eco-labeling scheme, comprising both standards and procedural regulations, could benefit EU producers and properly address private governance fragmentation. Due to the EU's own CFP, the Parliament argues, fisheries are already operating more sustainably than non-EU fisheries and hence could benefit from a formal EU certification scheme, even when this would comprise standards that are more stringent than current CFP rules. Furthermore, the European Parliament has argued that procedural regulation alone would not address unfounded and fraudulent claims by private governance schemes.

Considering that the majority of stakeholders agreed that procedural regulation was the most suitable to deal with the issues at hand, the European Commission started developing a legislative proposal on this basis in 2008–2009. The Commission's proposal was intended to contain procedural regulation in the form of minimum criteria for private governance schemes (lower left quadrant of Table 7.1). The Commission easily circumvented the position of the European Parliament, since the Parliament merely had consultative competence in fisheries policy. The proposal, however, was never formally introduced into the full legislative process. It was delayed due to problems at the stage of the environmental impact assessment, and abandoned at the time of the 2009 European elections and the initiation of the reform of the CFP in 2009. The debate on private fisheries governance would, in the next few years, be included in the CFP reform discussions.

Procrastination and entrenchment have characterized developments in the fisheries case since 2009. Negotiations on the reform of the CFP were arduous and did not allow for much leeway to discuss additional sustainability rules. As before, the European Commission, Member States, and stakeholders (including private governance schemes) preferred procedural regulation to weed out underperforming private schemes and harmonize the market, while considering standards regulation too much of a burden for EU fisheries. The European Parliament, however, still argued in favor of both standards and procedural regulations in the form of a European certification and eco-labeling scheme. These entrenched positions prevented a compromise. Furthermore, the European Parliament has been in a stronger position since the entry into force of the Lisbon Treaty in 2009, which gives the Parliament co-decision competence in fisheries policy. Policymakers, therefore, postponed a decision and requested a feasibility study to again assess future options for intervention.

The feasibility report, which was finalized in 2016, may well restructure the debate. The report questions whether the private governance market is actually fragmented, considering the dominance of just a few private schemes (and one in particular, the MSC). The report also highlights the harmonization effort initiated by the GSSI, which has developed a benchmarking tool for private governance schemes. If this argument of limited market fragmentation is accepted and the GSSI's effort is considered credible and successful, the status quo is a likely outcome (upper left quadrant of Table 7.1) and the result of both the fragmentation and the domestic benefits of product differentiation being considered low. However, the new interpretation of a limited fragmentation of the private governance market may also result in the development of standards regulation (upper right quadrant of Table 7.1). In particular, this would be the case if the European

Parliament could leverage the larger bargaining power it has gained since the Lisbon Treaty and could push through its interpretation that domestic producers would indeed benefit from public intervention. However, considering most stakeholders have rejected this position, and since the policy positions of the various EU institutions on the domestic benefits of product differentiation have not evolved much over the course of more than a decade, this outcome is not very likely.

Implications of the EU's Regulatory Interventions

An important question to address once we understand why and how the European Union intervened in private governance, is what the impacts of these interventions have been. Have they changed the nature or the functioning of private governance and the larger policy field? And what do these interventions entail in terms of possible improvements in sustainability?

The findings in this book show that the *regulatory* impacts of the EU's interventions in private governance have been twofold. On the one hand, in the cases where the EU intervened, the interventions have been significant in terms of restructuring the private governance field. Private schemes have had to adjust to the EU's interventions, with some schemes having to increase the stringency of their standards and procedures, while others exited the market. Since private schemes had to incorporate the public requirements, they have also affected how private schemes view their function in the market (e.g., as experimenters or gap fillers), as the next section will further discuss. On the other hand, the EU's interventions have not fundamentally challenged or undermined the regulatory or governing authority of private governance. Private schemes have largely retained their private governance space in terms of their capacity to develop standards and to incentivize producers to comply with their program requirements. The EU's interventions have not intended to challenge the regulatory nature of private governance in this respect.

This dual regulatory impact of the EU's interventions (both restructuring the field and retaining private governing authority) has both positive and negative implications, as I will show shortly. Overall, the EU's interventions established minimum baselines. Yet, private governance schemes have not always acted on the opportunities to regulate beyond the public baseline. Nonetheless, allowing private schemes the governance space to do so, instead of curtailing their independent governing authority, offers policymakers the opportunity to learn from and build further on advances in private governance.

These findings about the regulatory impacts of public interventions are important to better understand the potential *sustainability* impacts of such interventions. That is, the design of the public regulatory interventions in terms of how significantly the interventions restructure the field of private governance schemes and how much private governance space they grant has a direct impact on sustainability outcomes. Scholars are increasingly studying the concrete sustainability impacts of private governance, with some finding more evidence of sustainability improvements than others (Kalfagianni and Pattberg, 2013; Lambin et al., 2014; Prakash and Potoski, 2014; Tampe, 2018; van der Ven and Cashore, 2018). To fully examine these sustainability impacts, however, one can no longer rely only on an examination of the effects of private governance schemes in isolation. Due to public interventions in private governance (not only in Europe, but also in other parts of the world), private schemes now govern in a very different institutional environment. A proper understanding of the regulatory interactions between private governance and public policy is, therefore, a precondition for a comprehensive analysis of sustainability impacts. In other words, scholars need to consider public authority as endogenous to the functioning of private governance, and vice versa. This perspective requires an understanding of why a public authority intervenes in private governance and what the regulatory implications of such interventions are.

The remainder of this section will elaborate on these regulatory impacts and indicate implications for policymaking. In addition, it will highlight where the sustainability impacts of the EU's interventions are likely situated. It is beyond the scope of this book, however, to undertake a systematic sustainability analysis of the EU's interventions, in the sense of a comprehensive analysis of direct on-the-ground impacts. This is a topic that future research should cover in more depth.

Minimum Baselines and Private Governance Space

The standards and procedural regulations that the EU established in the issue areas discussed in this book are all minimum baselines. As public baselines, they provide floors for private governance standards and procedures, which schemes cannot undercut. As minima, at the same time, the EU regulatory interventions acknowledge private schemes' governance space, thereby explicitly allowing for upward divergences. The level at which the baseline is set has important distributional and sustainability implications. A higher baseline standard will possibly allow fewer private schemes to remain operational in the market, or at least will require larger changes to existing private standards of underperforming schemes. The same counts for procedural rules: Stricter rules will result in some private schemes exiting the market, while others will adjust their procedural rules to reach the public baseline. Overall, stricter standards and procedural rules result in increased legitimacy of the private governance field. In addition, stricter standards and procedures can have positive sustainability impacts, even though they may be offset by fewer producers being able to comply (Cashore et al., 2007; Gulbrandsen, 2005; Potoski and Prakash, 2009).

Both cases of standards regulations discussed in this book – biofuels and organic agriculture – were considered relatively strict at the time they were introduced. For organic agriculture, the fact that the 1991 EU Regulation was based directly on IFOAM's standards is significant, since at the time these standards were considered the gold standard. Fraudulent and underperforming schemes were either pushed out of the market or had to adjust their standards upwards to comply with the EU standard and continue to operate in the European market. At the same time, the EU's rules benefitted private governance schemes that were already regulating organic practices as defined by IFOAM. Schmid et al. (2007) found that there were few differences anymore between the EU organic standard and private standards in terms of the general concept of organic agriculture. In addition, they found that private standards were often more detailed, and that particularly in countries with a long tradition in organic agriculture, private standards more often included areas not covered under EU rules.

An important feature of the EU's regulation for organic agriculture is that private governance schemes are allowed – and indeed encouraged – to apply stricter rules than the EU's in order to experiment with new practices or to fill policy gaps. This opportunity to go beyond the public baseline has resulted in several instances of regulatory spillovers from the private to the public realm. Private schemes, for instance, were forerunners in developing standards for aquaculture, wine, and the prohibition of genetically modified organisms in organic food. The EU later used these standards to further expand its own regulatory coverage (Arcuri, 2015; IFOAM EU Group, 2010). Moreover, the EU largely integrated into its policy the four main principles of organic farming – health, ecology, fairness, and care – that IFOAM had adopted in 2005 (IFOAM, 2005; Padel et al., 2009). This feature of the EU's original policy – granting private governance space – was indeed one of the arguments the organic movement used in its opposition to the attempts of the European Commission to drastically curtail private schemes' governing authority in the 2007 Regulation. Private standards were expected to "lead the way as sources of innovation, local identity, producer and consumer education, improved public trust and market development ... [P]rivate standards keep driving continual improvement and allow the organic sector to expand its scope" (Blake, 2009: 19).

In addition to the organic agriculture standard, the EU organic logo also represents a minimum baseline approach. While initially the EU introduced the logo on a voluntary basis, the 2007 Organic Agriculture Regulation made the logo mandatory for EU-produced prepackaged goods. Here as well, the regulatory implications for private governance schemes are mixed. Private logos can still be used alongside the EU logo when the product complies with the EU organic agriculture standard. In that sense, the EU logo is not directly in competition with private logos. Since there is limited space on product packages, however, there might be practical objections to displaying multiple logos and in that sense there may exist "competition" between the EU and private logos (Janssen and Hamm, 2011). A more important potential impact concerns consumer recognition. The EU logo has the clear advantage in that it imposes a uniform logo across the EU. Yet, consumers may prefer logos they recognize or that are considered to represent a known or familiar set of standards and organizations. Janssen and Hamm (2012a), for example, hypothesize that the impact of the EU organic logo on consumer preferences may be related to the prior presence of private or governmental logos in a market. They expect positive attitudes toward the EU logo to be higher in markets where no governmental logo and no dominant private logo existed prior to the use of the mandatory EU logo (Janssen and Hamm, 2012b, 2014). These scholars suggest consumer awareness campaigns to encourage further consumer recognition of the EU logo, considering strong consumer loyalties in countries where logos existed prior to the EU's intervention. Once known to consumers, the EU logo may instill larger consumer confidence and thereby contribute to market growth.

As in the organic agriculture case, the biofuels sustainability criteria are relatively strict compared to rules in other important jurisdictions, such as Brazil and the USA (Renckens et al., 2017). The EU sustainability criteria are to a lesser degree than in the organic agriculture case directly based on existing private standards. As a result, private governance schemes have been required to change their standards more significantly. As discussed in Chapter 4, the EU has been strict in making private schemes adopt the EU standard almost word for word, leading some schemes to establish separate EU and rest-of-the-world standards. The fact that in this issue area too, private schemes are allowed to set standards that are stricter or more encompassing than the public baseline, allows them to play the role of standards experimenters and gap fillers. While several schemes have taken up such a role, the results have been quite uneven and the improvements over the EU criteria have been rather limited (German and Schoneveld, 2011; IUCN, 2013; Schlamann et al., 2013). As explained in Chapter 4, this has been partly due to the fact that several of the EU-approved schemes have been established to merely implement the EU standard, that several of the schemes are industry or firm-level schemes, and that even some of the multi-stakeholder schemes are dominated by business.

Similar to the standards regulations, the procedural regulations for both organic agriculture and biofuels production are minimum baselines. Overall, the EU's interventions still allow for significant variation in the way private governance schemes are organized. In the 1991 Organic Agriculture Regulation, the rules were rather limited and much of the responsibility for managing the verification system was delegated to the Member States. The 2007 Regulation expanded the rules at the EU level, including compulsory accreditation to EN 45011 or ISO Guide 65 (both, since 2012, have been replaced by ISO 17065). For biofuels production, the procedural rules are not mandatory, yet since satisfactory compliance with the rules is necessary before the European Commission will formally recognize a private scheme, the rules are in essence quasi-mandatory.

By degree, policymakers have paid particular attention to promoting third-party verification systems by ensuring independence between standard-setter and auditor, and between auditor and the operator being audited. This attention to preventing conflicts of interest and adopting the third-party-audited model reflects a wider trend in the private governance field and a key component of private schemes' credibility and, it is expected, their positive sustainability impacts (Auld et al., 2015; Green, 2014: 103–105; van der Ven, 2015).

The EU, however, has not mandated any other organizational design features that scholars have identified as part of an emerging ideal-typical private governance design. These features include diversity in stakeholder representation, participatory decision-making, or internal "corporate governance" processes (Bernstein, 2011; Dingwerth and Pattberg, 2009). Not imposing these design features is a clear flaw in the EU's policy design, and may reduce the EU interventions' sustainability impacts. As mentioned in Chapter 6, the European Commission in 2010 did issue a Communication on "EU best practice guidelines for voluntary certification schemes for agricultural products and foodstuffs" that outlines several of these design features in more detail (European Commission, 2010c). Even though the guidelines are merely voluntary best practices, they are an important recognition that these features, and stakeholder participation in particular, are important for improving private governance's functioning and impacts.

The standards and procedural regulations that the EU issued were not intended to directly change the functioning of private governance in either the organic agriculture or the biofuels case beyond having schemes adopt the regulations as their new baselines. However, these regulations have done so unintentionally in the biofuels case, which the literature has overlooked. This change to the functioning of private governance has occurred through interactions with another part of the larger biofuels policy. Recall that in the 2009 Renewable Energy Directive, the EU established a 10 percent renewable energy target for transport, with the idea that this target would be reached predominantly with biofuels. In interaction with the adopted standards and procedural regulations, this target has changed the compliance incentives for those approved private governance schemes that are not company-specific (cf. Table 4.3). For these schemes, the compliance incentives are, at the outset, market-based, which is recognized as a key feature of such schemes (Cashore, 2002). It is the market, which includes the supply chain as well as external audiences such as NGOs, that creates the incentives to comply with private governance schemes and that confers legitimacy on these initiatives (Bernstein and Cashore, 2007). A public authority's intervention, however, can change this incentive structure. One way in which this is done is by requiring producers to have their operations certified in order to get access to a market. In such a situation, it is no longer the market that incentivizes a producer to engage with private governance, but a public authority's mandate to have part of, or the entire market, certified.

Biofuels production is the only issue area in this book that has witnessed such a shift in compliance incentives. By mandating a target of 10 percent (again, building on the policymakers' assumption that this target would mainly be reached through biofuels use) and delegating verification responsibilities to private governance schemes, the EU has at least partly changed the market-driven basis of the compliance incentives of private governance in the EU market. The logic is as follows: The creation of a market for certification has resulted in a proliferation of private schemes entering the market. The European Commission is tasked with approving these schemes, some of which were already active and some of which are newly created to implement the EU rules. The schemes differ in the extent to which their private standards and procedures go beyond the public baselines. Once the European Commission formally approves them, however, the schemes are each other's equals in the EU market (at least when approved for the same sustainability criteria; see Table 4.3). Biofuels operators seeking to be certified can freely choose which of the approved private governance schemes to use. To some actors in the supply chain, using stricter or more encompassing private schemes may matter more than for others and influence operators' choice of a private scheme. Yet, the combination of a mandatory target and the granting of equal benefits to operators when they are certified by one of the approved certification schemes, results in a partly reduced market-based nature of the compliance incentives.

The EU's biofuels policy therefore incentivizes firms to get certified by a scheme with less rigorous requirements. The biofuels target leads to a "race to the public baseline" in the sense that several schemes have entered the market with the sole purpose of verifying compliance with the EU criteria and only few schemes have established standards that exceed the public baseline. Price premiums for sustainable biofuels, which could provide incentives to choose higher-performing schemes, have been shown to be low or nearly nonexistent. Pacini et al. (2013), for example, estimated that in 2011–2012 the average premium for certified ethanol was 0.46 percent over regular ethanol, with a peak of 3.93 percent in the second semester of 2011 and with almost no premium afterward. For sustainably certified biodiesel, they estimated a premium of 3.42 percent, which was quite stable, yet expected to dissipate as in the ethanol case.

In summary, the interventions by the EU have had a double effect. On the one hand, they have created baselines for both the substantive standards and the procedural rules with which all private governance schemes have to comply, thereby leveling the playing field. The impact of the EU has arguably been largest in terms of the substantive standards. The baselines were based on IFOAM's standards for organic agriculture and relatively strict in comparative terms for biofuels. Regarding procedural issues, the EU's interventions have made third-party verification the norm for organics and biofuels certification, at the exclusion of first- and second-party certification. Clear gaps in the EU's interventions remain, however, including the absence of social, ILUC, or food safety criteria for biofuels, and a lack of requirements regarding stakeholder participation and representation. Nonetheless, the market for certified products in these two issue areas is arguably larger than it would have been without EU intervention. This is, in particular, the case for biofuels, since almost all of the biofuels on the EU market are now certified under the EU regime, even though NGOs would object to the possibility of crop-based biofuels being sustainable at all.

On the other hand, the baselines, being minima, have not stifled private governance as a novel type of regulatory institution. The EU as a public authority did not impose its sovereign authority in such a way as to threaten or fundamentally change private governance. These interventions, in other words, cannot be characterized as intended to supersede private governance or as a situation of "public authority takeover" (Cashore et al., 2011; Steering Committee of the State-of-Knowledge Assessment of Standards and Certification, 2012). The EU does not require all producers to engage in organic agriculture or in sustainable biofuels production. Producers are also not mandated to comply with a particular private standard and compliance is still voluntary. There may be pressure from the supply chain to choose one or the other scheme, but the EU has not imposed its authority in this respect.

Furthermore, despite the EU's interventions, private governance schemes continue to enjoy the freedom to go beyond the public baseline standards and design governance processes that are stricter or cover additional features. When private governance schemes are incentivized to play the role of innovators and gap fillers – and hence develop standards and practices that are beyond compliance – they can show public policymakers what is possible for and acceptable to producers. With time, learning from private governance innovations can result in revised and updated public standards that incorporate such successful private practices. It is here then that allowing private governance schemes sufficient governance space can have the largest effects. It offers both an argument in favor of intervention and one in favor of avoiding imposing sovereign authority too much. This is even the case for the de facto impact on compliance incentives in the biofuels case, which is the result of an interaction with another part of the broader policy, namely the renewable energy target. This unintended impact was a "race to the public baseline," yet by concretely integrating private governance into the design of its public policy, the EU has ensured private governance's continued relevance. In that respect, these findings corroborate Gulbrandsen's (2014) conclusions about the fisheries and forest sectors. For these sectors, he argued that states' responses to certification programs "have served to legitimize certification as a credible policy tool that companies and consumers can trust" (Gulbrandsen, 2014: 89), while at the same time "the state gains the credibility, expertise, and auditing capacity of the [private governance] scheme; and 'each gain the symbolic resources of the other' (Eberlein et al., 2014)" (Gulbrandsen, 2014: 87).

Policy Exports, Ratcheting Up, and Spillovers

Apart from the direct impacts on private governance schemes and on private governance as a regulatory institution more broadly, public interventions and the development of standards and procedural regulations have broader policy and governance implications. The previous section discussed the policy feedback effects that public interventions can elicit in that innovations in private governance can result in spillovers to public policy (cf. Werner, 2012: 152–154). In addition, public interventions can lead to three other types of policy spillover effects and ratcheting up dynamics that derive from the public-private interactions examined in this book.

First, since the EU's policies apply to both domestic and imported products, cross-jurisdictional policy convergence, harmonization, or coordination may occur, thereby further embedding private standards in public policy. Non-EU producers that want to gain or retain access to the EU market need to comply with the EU's rules. This requirement puts these producers at a competitive disadvantage with respect to their domestic or international competitors when the standard in their home country is not at the same level as the EU's. These producers therefore have an incentive to lobby their home governments to adjust regulation upward to the EU's level in order to level the playing field (Damro, 2012; Holzinger and Knill, 2005; Vogel, 1995). When the USA, for example, was developing its organic standards in the 1990s, US organic farmers and IFOAM significantly influenced the policymaking process. This pressure resulted in standards that were largely convergent with the EU rules, which were initially based on the IFOAM standards, as discussed in Chapter 3. This convergence between US and EU rules was at least partly due to concerns around "the importance of international equivalency in fostering U.S. exports" (Klein and Winickoff, 2011: 166). This convergence also formed the basis for the successful negotiation of a bilateral agreement between the EU and the USA that recognizes their respective organic rules and certification processes as equivalent, and which facilitates trade in organic products across the Atlantic (Carreño, 2012).

In the case of biofuels, it has proven more difficult to export the EU regulatory model and harmonize policies cross-nationally and internationally, despite efforts to this effect (Poletti and Sicurelli, 2016). Factors contributing to this failure include changing trade dynamics, which have made the EU less relevant as an export market, and the fact that the EU was a relative latecomer in developing sustainability standards compared to major competing producer countries such as the USA or Brazil. Furthermore, perceptions by other countries that the EU's rules and procedures correspond to "green protectionism" and favor its own domestic producers at the expense of foreign biofuels producers have prevented the EU from influencing the adoption of EU-like standards in international fora such as ISO and GBEP (Renckens et al., 2017).

Second, the export and ratcheting up of standards can occur through private governance schemes directly. Private standards do not need to be adopted by public policymakers for private schemes' role as innovator to play out. For both biofuels and organic agriculture, private governance is used as an instrument to verify compliance with EU standards of both EU and non-EU producers. Yet, some private schemes not only demand compliance with the EU rules, but also with additional private rules they have developed. For organic agriculture, for instance, this is the case for the Soil Association, and for biofuels production, Bonsucro requires this as well (Bonsucro, 2016; Soil Association, 2018). When non-EU producers want to acquire certification and possibly the logo of these schemes, they have to comply with the additional standards of the scheme. In that way, private schemes export their higher standards to producers in non-EU jurisdictions while certifying against EU rules, and this occurs prior to the EU formally adopting these additional private standards.

Finally, the looming shadow of hierarchy can lead to spillover effects from regulated to nonregulated issue areas. Public interventions in one issue area may signal to private governance schemes in nonregulated areas that certain practices or organizational forms are no longer considered legitimate or acceptable. For example, the fact that the EU's procedural interventions have exhibited a clear preference for third-party-audited private governance schemes may lead private schemes in nonregulated issue areas to act strategically, and to preemptively change the features of their organizational structure to reflect this preference. The EU has at times engaged in facilitative orchestration to achieve this. For example, the EU's policy discussions on private fair trade governance in the 1990s, as analyzed in Chapter 5, included repeated calls to harmonize fair trade standards and governance procedures, and financial assistance to foster cooperation and coordination of the various fair trade organizations and labeling initiatives. While not solely having caused the private harmonization process of Fairtrade, this public engagement by the EU may have played a facilitative role in the background of this process. Moreover, the Fair Trade movement's position in the discussions preceding the European Commission's 2009 Communication showed that it was keenly aware of the lasting impact that EU intervention would have and that it wanted to avoid at all costs what had happened to private governance in the organic agricultural sector. Such an awareness may lead private schemes to anticipate future regulation and change practices accordingly (cf. Cafaggi and Janczuk, 2010; Kinderman, 2012; Lyon and Maxwell, 2008).

Europe and Beyond

Considering that the explanatory framework developed in this book is based on cases operating in the specific EU context, the question is whether the framework can be used to explain public regulatory interventions in cases outside the EU and at different levels of policy-making. After all, the EU is a unique organization, arguably the most advanced example of a regional organization. It exhibits features of an international organization and a federal polity. It has achieved a high level of economic integration and possesses an institutional capacity and rulemaking coverage that continue to grow. Can we expect the logic of the theoretical argument to hold in other political settings? It is not the intention in this final chapter to develop shadow cases and test the explanatory framework. Instead, this section highlights two observations that show the boundaries of the theoretical framework that will assist in devising formal tests of the overall argument.

The first observation deals with the fragmentation variable. Problems related to a fragmentation of the private governance market will likely be more prevalent at higher political levels, such as the supranational and international levels, rather than at the domestic level. Size and integration are what matter here. The size of the EU market and the fact that it combines twenty-eight (and after Brexit twenty-seven) national markets, make fragmentation more likely and hence more easily perceived as problematic. The same logic counts for a globally integrated economy in which private schemes operate that are predominantly transnational or global in character. In this context, fragmentation is more easily perceived as problematic when attempting to coordinate rulemaking at the international level. This is not to say that at the domestic level fragmentation cannot emerge as well, especially in the absence of private efforts to harmonize governance schemes. In particular, private governance schemes emerging at the subnational level with products traded in a nationally integrated market may equally create fragmentation problems. Nonetheless, given that size and integration matter, we can expect that problems related to a fragmented private governance market are more likely at the supranational or international level than at the domestic level.

The second observation pertains to the domestic benefits variable. One can expect that interventions in support of producer interests are more likely at political levels that are situated closer to productive activities and at which such interests can be aggregated more easily. In other words, such interventions are more likely at the domestic level, or as this book has demonstrated, the EU level when the EU has regulatory competences in a policy area and therefore can act like a national government. This type of producer support is less likely to emerge at the international level or in a less fully integrated regional organization. The reason is that reaching agreement on such support is less likely when more diverse interests need to be reconciled and when the political authority to impose an agreement is lacking.

The implications of these observations are important for the explanatory framework developed in this book. They indicate that the skew-diagonal quadrants of Table 2.2 are more likely to be populated by interventions at different levels of policymaking: Standards regulation (upper right quadrant) may be more likely at the domestic level, while procedural regulation (lower left quadrant) may be more likely at the international level. I will discuss each of these possibilities below and provide examples to further illustrate the logics underlying these types of interventions.

First, procedural regulation, resulting from the interaction of low domestic benefits and high fragmentation, may be a more likely outcome at the international level. The fisheries issue area is relevant in this respect. An important public response to private governance at the international level was the development of the 2005 FAO Guidelines for eco-labeling. The FAO initiated discussions on the Guidelines in the late 1990s based on fragmentation problems in the private fisheries governance market (FAO, 2008: 11; OECD and FAO, 2009: 21). In particular, there was a "realisation that the present ecolabelling schemes in the fisheries sector [did] not fulfil the requirements of transparency and credibility" (O'Riordan, 1998: 22). Another important trigger was the development of the MSC and the lack of stakeholder involvement therein. Yet, while some FAO member countries were in favor of a public certification scheme operated by the FAO, Gulbrandsen (2009: 657) mentions that "developing countries were deeply skeptical of an FAO-led labeling scheme, which they believed would limit the market access for their fisheries." Diverging expectations about the benefits for domestic fisheries, combined with a willingness to regulate fragmentation problems, resulted in the FAO Guidelines becoming technical guidelines for the operation of certification schemes, rather than them also including a comprehensive sustainability standard. An unintended consequence, Gulbrandsen (2014: 14) argues, has been that the FAO Guidelines "have consolidated the MSC's position as the leading global certification program in the fisheries sector" considering the close alignment of the MSC's practices with these Guidelines over time.

In the biofuels area, there has been a similar development, as briefly highlighted in Chapter 4. Standard-setting at the international level has proved to be a difficult undertaking. States have discussed harmonized international biofuels standards in different fora, including at the level of the UN International Biofuels Forum, the FAO, and the G8-initiated GBEP. Initially, when little was achieved, scholars called this an area of "non-governance at the global level" (Bastos Lima and Gupta, 2013). Nonetheless, GBEP developed a sustainability tool in 2011. However, instead of a substantive sustainability standard, the initiative developed a set of indicators. The tool indicates the elements that could go into developing a substantive biofuels sustainability standard (GBEP, 2011). GBEP explicitly refrained from defining biofuels sustainability as such. In that sense, GBEP developed procedural rules that can be used by other actors (including private governance schemes) to develop substantive standards. The reason for merely developing procedural rules was political disagreement among participating delegations regarding the impact of a substantive sustainability standard on domestic industries and international trade. While European delegations insisted on creating ambitious sustainability standards, in line with the EU sustainability criteria, they were opposed by delegations from the USA, Brazil, and Canada. These countries accused the EU of green protectionism and of intending to limit international trade in support of its own domestic biofuels industry (Renckens et al., 2017).

Second, standards regulation, resulting from the interaction of high domestic benefits and low fragmentation, may be a more likely outcome at the domestic level. A case in point is the development of a public fisheries eco-labeling scheme in France. At the request of the fisheries sector, the public agency FranceAgriMer was charged in 2007 with exploring the development of such a scheme. In 2008, a feasibility study conducted by the French fisheries sector and consultancy firm Bureau Veritas found that only the MSC, as the dominant scheme in the market, was fully compliant with the FAO Guidelines. The study also concluded that MSC certification was costly and did not fit all French fisheries equally well (Lucbert and Picault, 2009; Pôle

Filière Produits Aquatiques and Bureau Veritas, 2008; Washington and Ababouch, 2011: 27). In particular, many French fisheries were not yet able to comply with the MSC requirements. This situation was viewed as problematic for French fisheries, considering producers from competing countries were engaging with MSC certification and several retailers around that time announced a commitment to MSC. Rather than establishing a private alternative to the MSC, the study suggested establishing a public eco-labeling scheme, which would be geared toward the specific circumstances of the French fishing industry. This option was preferred, since the public character of the scheme would grant it the credibility demanded by customers and retailers. The French eco-label standard, which was developed by a commission composed of representatives from industry, government, NGOs, consumers, and scientists, is based on the FAO's Code of Conduct and Guidelines. Besides environmental criteria, the standard also includes additional social and economic criteria, such as on labor conditions, workplace safety, and product quality (FranceAgriMer, 2014). These additional social and economic criteria were important for industry, since they better balance the three dimensions of sustainable development.[1] The fact that the French government developed its own eco-labeling scheme in close cooperation with industry is an additional reason why France is not favoring an EU-level scheme, in a similar way that it originally opposed a mandatory EU logo for organic agriculture. An EU-level scheme would potentially be less well suited to French fisheries (especially since it would not cover social or economic criteria, but only environmental ones), would impose an additional layer of compliance, and create competition between the national and the EU scheme.

The dynamics in the French fisheries case are corroborated by other examples of governmental intervention in non-EU countries. Several scholars, for example, have studied the emergence of a national state-based certification scheme for palm oil in Indonesia, the Indonesian Sustainable Palm Oil System (ISPO) (Giessen et al., 2016; Hospes, 2014; Schouten and Bitzer, 2015). ISPO explicitly emerged as a response to the RSPO as the dominant scheme for palm oil certification, with the intent to provide more production opportunities to Indonesian palm oil producers. Even though there are similarities between the standards of RSPO and ISPO, the latter is less stringent in terms of requirements around deforestation, production in high-conservation areas, and transparency. Indonesian officials have stated that RSPO was not an appropriate instrument for Indonesian palm oil producers and that the development of ISPO was intended to increase the global competitiveness of the Indonesian industry. In this respect, ISPO was a reaction to what were considered "Northern" interventions, following the initial exclusion of both public authorities and palm oil producers from RSPO discussions. In addition, ISPO was used, as Hospes (2014: 434) argues, to "proclaim the sovereignty of the state as the highest political authority to decide on what is acceptable de-forestation and GHG emission due to expansion of palm oil production on its territory." Furthermore, Giessen et al. (2016) highlight that while engaging in coalitions with industry, specific parts of the Indonesian bureaucracy, such as the Ministries of Agriculture, Forestry, Environment, and Trade, sought to increase their power to create a strong public competitor for the RSPO. Thus, the existence of a single dominant private scheme and significant expected benefits from public intervention by means of product differentiation in support of domestic producers, resulted in the development of standards regulation.

In the field of fisheries, furthermore, Foley and Havice (2016) argue that what they call "territorial" certification programs that include state-based schemes (such as in Alaska or Japan), have developed on a similar basis. These schemes intend to assist local producers with market access by affirming that "existing, geographically bounded production practices and regulatory institutions are environmentally sound and worthy of international recognition" (Foley and Havice, 2016: 25). In addition, these schemes "compete with and offer an alternative to the dominant MSC" (Foley and Havice, 2016: 25). In these cases, therefore, the existence of a single dominant scheme and public support for domestic producers by means of product differentiation also resulted in the creation of domestic standards regulation, often in close collaboration with the domestic industry.

Yet, when such domestic benefits are absent, the status quo is shown to hold. In Canada, for example, a 2009 report by the House of Commons Standing Committee on Fisheries and Oceans recommended that the Department of Fisheries and Oceans explore establishing a Canadian certification system for sustainable fisheries (House of Commons Canada, 2009). The report specifically focused on the MSC as the sole market leader, and the difficulty Canadian fisheries have in being certified; at the time, only two Canadian fisheries had been certified. The Canadian government, however, opposed the recommendation of a public certification scheme, based on an argument that dovetails with the EU's discussions on intervening in private fisheries governance. The government argued that a Canadian certification scheme would not benefit the domestic industry, since market actors, such as buyers and retailers, would not consider a government-run program that certifies its own fishery management regime to be a credible program. Instead, the government opted to help the industry obtain and maintain MSC certification (Government of Canada, 2009).

In summary, these examples highlight the boundaries of the explanatory argument, while also providing useful insights into the applicability of the framework in a non-EU context, and in particular, into the logics of the skew-diagonal combinations of Table 2.2. The examples are, nonetheless, merely initial probes, the insights of which should be used to devise more rigorous tests of the explanatory framework.

Going Forward

The findings of this book about the conditions under which a public authority will intervene in private governance and the form this intervention will take point us toward at least five avenues for further research.

First, some of the examples provided in the previous section point to the importance of other variables that warrant further examination. The ISPO example in particular highlights an interesting interaction between support for domestic economic opportunities, as discussed in this book, and dynamics around explicitly reclaiming public authority. The incentives for reclaiming public authority in response to private governance may be larger at the domestic level than the EU level. The potential for transnational non-state actors to elicit private rule compliance by domestic producers and thereby circumvent domestic politics may sit awkwardly with local political elites, especially in more nondemocratic polities, or in states in the global South where one can rally against "Western" or "Northern" interventions. Such states may be less persuaded to mitigate private governance concerns around retaining their private governance space, especially when the private schemes are considered to be "NGO-driven" (Bartley, 2014;

Buckingham and Jepson, 2013). Moreover, restrictions on the development and functioning of a vibrant civil society in such states may prevent private governance from functioning properly, or prevent civil society actors from providing a check on state interventions to make sure they are in line with concerns about the public good (Distelhorst et al., 2015; Malets, 2015). Accordingly, political elites' true interests may lie in increasing their domestic political authority with respect to transnational private governance, while framing it as offering support to the local industry.

This idea of reclaiming political authority may not only play a role at the domestic level, but at the international level as well. Gulbrandsen (2014), for example, hypothesized that "[s]tates are more likely to reassert authority in assessing credible standards when non-state programs emerge in densely regulated sectors." He based his hypothesis on what has happened at the level of the FAO in the fisheries sector, as described. While the logic behind this hypothesis could certainly be applicable to the EU, I do not find evidence of this dynamic in the cases discussed in this book. While the fisheries sector in particular is a densely regulated area in the EU, there has been no public intervention yet, and the types of interventions that are likely, as I have argued, are driven by the interaction between a fragmented private governance market and support for domestic producers, rather than by an eagerness to impose or reclaim political authority. Nonetheless, further research should examine how the interactions between public support for product differentiation and reclaiming public authority play out, and which of the factors potentially carries a heavier weight in the causal explanation.

Second, the flipside of a focus on public authorities explicitly trying to reclaim authority is questioning the possibility of interventions in the first place. An important assumption in the analysis so far has been that a certain level of state capacity exists so that public interventions are a possibility when so desired (cf. Knill and Lehmkuhl, 2002). Yet, this assumption may not hold under all circumstances. While private governance does emerge and can function properly in "weak states" (Börzel and Risse, 2010), state interventions may not be possible in such countries even when the conditions for intervention, as discussed in this book, are present. A fruitful area for future research, therefore, is to examine the level of state capacity that is necessary for a public authority to intervene, and the form that public-private governance interactions take, considering private governance's potential to reduce policy costs.

A third avenue for further inquiry concerns interest representation by private governance schemes. The fact that public regulatory interventions are a reality implies that private governance actors increasingly need to view themselves as more traditional interest groups, as this book has highlighted. They need to respond to public policy initiatives and lobby policymakers to get their voices heard. This will be difficult at times, depending on the scale at which the schemes are operating. Schemes that operate on a national or subnational level might be better able to engage with a national government intent on interfering in an issue area. One can question, however, to what extent transnational private governance schemes can engage at the country level, unless they have local chapters. Some schemes will be better equipped to do so than others, which not only depends on the resources they have at their disposal, but also their self-image as an organization and their capacities to act strategically. In the fair trade area, as discussed in Chapter 5, the Fair Trade movement has had a well-established lobby office in Brussels since 2004. UTZ Certified and Rainforest Alliance, on the other hand, have never had a permanent presence in Brussels and have also shown little interest in developing that capacity. The Fair Trade movement, moreover, learned from IFOAM, which as discussed in Chapter 3 has been involved with EU lobbying since the late 1980s. One of the reasons why the Fair Trade movement lobbied against interventionist EU regulation was indeed its weariness of being put on the same path that organic agriculture has traveled and that, by degree, has seen increasingly stricter and more encompassing EU interventions.

Analyzing policy strategies of private governance schemes, therefore, is an important avenue for further research. While the structural and discursive power of private governance have been highlighted (Dauvergne and Lister, 2013; Fuchs, 2007: 63–67; Levy and Newell, 2005), its instrumental power – usually the first type of power scholars focus on – has been largely overlooked (Renckens, 2019). While this book has highlighted some of the interest representation activities in which private governance actors engage, we still know very little about this phenomenon. This is at least partly the result of private governance scholars only recently turning their attention to the interactions between public and private governance and studying such interactions predominantly from a rule-based perspective. Interest group scholars, however, have also overlooked private governance as an interest group population. While these scholars have studied several populations of interest groups in great detail – such as firms, labor unions, and NGOs (Coen, 1997; Greenwood, 2017; Long and Lorinczi, 2009) – they have not identified private governance schemes as an interest group population in their own right.

To bridge this gap in the literature, future studies should examine the population of private governance schemes to identify the factors that drive some private schemes to become active interest groups, while other schemes do not engage in interest representation and lobbying activities. This research will include assessing the influence of variables related to the organizational features of private schemes (resources, profit/nonprofit, founding organizations), policy-related factors (scope, salience, level of controversy, type of policy issue), and institutional variables (openness, biases, venue-shopping opportunities) (Bouwen, 2002, 2004; Broscheid and Coen, 2007; Eising, 2007; Klüver et al., 2015; Mahoney, 2008; Princen and Kerremans, 2008). In addition, scholars should compare the population of private governance schemes that engage in interest representation and lobbying activities to other populations, in particular business and NGOs. To what extent do private governance schemes differ from these other types of interest groups in terms of the strategies they employ, the access they have to policymakers, and their influence on policymaking (Berkhout et al., 2015; Dür and De Bièvre, 2007; Dür and Mateo, 2013; Klüver et al., 2015)?

Fourth, the findings of this book offer useful starting points for new research on policy diffusion. There exists a well-established literature that examines why and how public policies diffuse and converge. Mechanisms that this literature has focused on include regulatory competition, learning, coercion, and international cooperation (e.g., Dobbin et al., 2007; Holzinger and Knill, 2005; Meseguer, 2005). Furthermore, scholars have assessed the diffusion of private governance, thereby focusing on, among other things, trade linkages and a country's regulatory environment (Delmas, 2002; Perkins and Neumayer, 2010; Prakash and Potoski, 2006a). The diffusion of rules from private to public governance and vice versa has also received some recent attention. Green and Auld (2017), for example, highlight four types of diffusion mechanisms: private governance functioning as an incubator for new ideas; as a venue to redefine a problem; as a forum to further diffuse public rules; and as a provider of rules that public policy later incorporates. This book's discussion of policy exports and spillovers contributes to this existing research on policy and governance diffusion. Future research, however, should seek to further combine these different research strands and examine the conditions under which policy and governance exchanges between public and private actors occur. For example, what is the impact of regulatory competition and trade relations on the role of private governance as a forum for the diffusion of public rules? Or, what role do policy learning and international cooperation play in the incorporation of private governance into public policy design across countries?

Finally, the findings in this book about the rather limited impact of the EU's regulatory interventions on the governing authority of private schemes will likely fail to alleviate the fears of critics who oppose private governance as a useful governance instrument, as discussed in the introductory chapter. This book has shown that public interventions are able to weed out underperforming or fraudulent private governance schemes and establish useful baselines, while also offering beneficial policy impacts by allowing private schemes their governance space. Critics, however, can argue that the EU in this way has displayed a rather instrumental perspective on private governance. The EU's interventions have overall been supportive of, and at times even deferential to, private governance. The EU supports the use of private, market-based instruments, even integrates them into public policy, and supports the greening of consumer products as an individualized solution to environmental problems (Dauvergne, 2016; Maniates, 2001; Wright and Nyberg, 2014). The cases of nonintervention in this book equally highlight the strategic nature of public responses to private governance. Indeed, interventions in private governance are not the rule yet, not in the EU nor elsewhere, and they are not, in the first place, intended to directly address sustainability problems. That is not to say we may not witness more such interventions in the future, considering the increasing presence of transnational private governance in a wide variety of sectors, and increased attention of governments in the global South to supply chain sustainability (Hidayat et al., 2018; Labruto, 2014; Schouten and Bitzer, 2015). However, the question remains whether such public interventions will be sufficient to address the concerns of those critical of market-based sustainability instruments.

More research is therefore required to assess the concrete sustainability impacts of private governance and of public interventions in private governance. The bottom line, in the end, should be an improvement in the underlying sustainability problems that both private governance and public policy claim to be addressing.

Appendix

Interviews

NR.	Organization/Institution	Date	Place/Type
1	Representative of EEB	July 9, 2010	Brussels
2	Representative of IFOAM EU	July 20, 2010	Brussels
3	Representative of MSC	August 10, 2010	Rotterdam
4	Former representative of IFOAM EU	November 10, 2011	Brussels
5	Representative of Friend of the Sea	November 16, 2011	Skype
6	Representative of IFOAM EU	November 17, 2011	Brussels
7	Representative of the Fair Trade movement	November 17, 2011	Brussels
8	Representative of EEB	November 23, 2011	Brussels
9	Representative of WWF	November 25, 2011	Brussels
10	Representative of Naturland	November 28, 2011	Telephone
11	Representative of Transport & Environment	December 2, 2011	Brussels
12	Representative of Friends of the Earth Europe	December 2, 2011	Brussels
13	Representative of WWF	December 5, 2011	Brussels
14	Representative of the Brazilian Sugarcane Industry Association (UNICA)	December 5, 2011	Brussels
15	Representative of the European Organic Certifiers Council	December 7, 2011	Brussels
16	Representative of EBB	December 16, 2011	Brussels
17	Official of the European Commission	December 19, 2011	Telephone
18	Representative of Birdlife Europe	December 20, 2011	Brussels
19	Representative of WWF International	March 27, 2012	Brussels
20	Official of the European Commission	March 28, 2012	Brussels
21	Representative of COPA-COGECA	April 3, 2012	Brussels
22	Official of the European Commission	April 3, 2012	Brussels
23	Official of the European Commission	April 3, 2012	Brussels

(cont.)

NR.	Organization/Institution	Date	Place/Type
24	Representative of ePURE	April 4, 2012	Brussels
25	Member of the European Parliament	April 26, 2012	Brussels
26	Former coordinator of FTAO	May 2, 2012	Skype
27	Official of the European Commission	May 3, 2012	Brussels
28	Official of the European Commission	May 3, 2012	Brussels
29	Official of the European Commission	May 15, 2012	Telephone
30	Official of the European Commission	May 15, 2012	Telephone
31	Official of the European Commission	May 16, 2012	Skype
32	Representative of the Soil Association	May 18, 2012	Skype
33	Former Member of the European Parliament	June 13, 2012	Skype
34	Former official of the European Commission	July 6, 2012	Brussels
35	Official of the European Commission	July 6, 2012	Brussels
36	Representative of EESC	July 8, 2012	Brussels
37	Former staff of a Member of the European Parliament	July 9, 2012	Utrecht
38	Representative of UTZ Certified	July 9, 2012	Amsterdam
39	Representative of UTZ Certified	July 9, 2012	Amsterdam
40	Representative of AIPCE-CEP	July 10, 2012	Brussels
41	Person involved with the development of RTFO	July 10, 2012	Brussels
42	Representative of the European Association of Fish Producers Organisations (EAPO)	July 11, 2012	Telephone
43	Official of the European Commission	July 12, 2012	Brussels
44	Representative of MSC	July 12, 2012	Telephone
45	Official of the European Parliament	July 13, 2012	Brussels
46	Brussels expert dealing with certification	July 13, 2012	Brussels
47	Representative of the European Community of Consumer Cooperatives (Euro Coop)	August 3, 2012	Telephone
48	Member of civil society closely related to certification issues	September 17, 2012	Skype
49	Member of the European Parliament	September 18, 2012	Brussels
50	Official of the European Commission	September 19, 2012	Brussels

(*cont.*)

NR.	Organization/Institution	Date	Place/Type
51	Representative of ECF	September 20, 2012	Skype
52	Employee at a Permanent Representation to the EU	September 21, 2012	Telephone
53	Official of EESC	September 25, 2012	Brussels
54	Official of the European Commission	September 26, 2012	Skype
55	Official of the European Commission	September 26, 2012	Skype
56	Former official of the European Commission	October 4, 2012	Skype
57	Member of the European Parliament	July 17, 2013	Skype
58	Official of the European Commission	June 8, 2015	Brussels
59	Official of the European Commission	June 10, 2015	Brussels
60	Official of the European Commission	June 10, 2015	Brussels
61	Representative of Oxfam International	June 11, 2015	Brussels
62	Assistant to a Member of the European Parliament	June 12, 2015	Brussels
63	Representative of EEB	June 15, 2015	Brussels
64	Representative of ePURE	June 17, 2015	Brussels
65	Expert with knowledge of the EU lawmaking process and EU seafood eco-labeling	June 23, 2015	Skype
66	Representative of Novozymes	July 14, 2015	Brussels
67	Representative of FuelsEurope	July 14, 2015	Brussels
68	Representative of EBB	July 14, 2015	Brussels
69	Member of the European Parliament	July 27, 2015	Skype
70	Member of the European Parliament	October 12, 2015	Brussels
71	Representative of the Fair Trade movement	October 12, 2015	Brussels
72	Official of the European Commission	October 13, 2015	Brussels
73	Official of the European Commission	October 13, 2015	Brussels
74	Representative of RSB	October 16, 2015	Skype
75	Independent Researcher on Fisheries Sustainability	June 27, 2016	London

Endnotes

1 Introduction

1 As Andonova, Betsill, and Bulkeley (2009) explain, governance encompasses several policy-related functions, such as rulemaking, information sharing, capacity building, and implementation. The private governance schemes discussed in this book have a regulatory purpose since they engage in regulating the negative externalities of economic exchanges, such as the environmental or social impacts of production processes. For other types of private governance, see Büthe and Mattli (2011).

2 Scholars have employed many different concepts to refer to the phenomenon of private governance, such as civil regulation, business governance, private authority, regulatory standard-setting institutions, voluntary clubs, and non-state market-driven (NSMD) governance (Abbott and Snidal, 2009a; Cashore, 2002; Cutler et al., 1999b; Eberlein et al., 2014; Hall and Biersteker, 2002; Potoski and Prakash, 2009; Vogel, 2008).

3 Note that, at the time, the EU as a political entity did not yet exist, so it would be more accurate to talk about the European Economic Community. For reasons of simplicity, however, I will only refer to the EU throughout the book to denote the supranational organization for which policymaking is discussed.

4 I use the concept "fair trade" (lower case) as a generic term to refer to the issue area. The term "Fair Trade" (two words, capital letters) refers to the Fair Trade movement's specific approach to fair trade. The term "Fairtrade" (one word, capital letter) refers to the certification scheme that the Fair Trade movement has established (Fairtrade International, 2011a; FTAO, s.d.). For more on these distinctions, see the section on research design and Chapter 5.

5 In addition, the boundaries of the four issue areas are determined by how they are defined by the EU and not by a private governance scheme's problem definition. Auld (2014a) has argued that the way in which a private governance scheme defines a problem area has direct boundary-creating implications for the scheme's functioning and on-the-ground impact. Similarly, problem definitions influence the scope of a potential

public policy intervention, the private governance schemes that are targeted or impacted by the intervention, and the on-the-ground effects. As a result, for example, the book focuses on organic agriculture and fair trade as separate issue areas and not, for instance, on coffee as a single commodity. While coffee is an important commodity for both organic agriculture and fair trade private governance schemes, the EU has developed policies around these issue areas separately, and not around responsibly produced coffee as a commodity.

6 I have selected issue areas in which the EU legally has policy competences, as assigned by the Treaties, thereby excluding issue areas for which the Member States have retained the exclusive policy authority. By choosing cases of both intervention and nonintervention, the research design adopted in this book intends to overcome the problem of selecting on the dependent variable. Such selection bias is considered problematic, since it does not allow for drawing conclusions about the differences between the chosen cases and cases that have different values of the dependent variable, and as a result may lead to incorrectly identifying a factor common in the chosen cases as an explanatory factor (Geddes, 1990; King et al., 1994; Lijphart, 1975). For alternative perspectives, see George and Bennett (2005), and Collier, Mahoney, and Seawright (2004).

7 https://archive.org/web.

8 In the empirical chapters, interviews are identified by a single number. As a result of a confidentiality agreement with the interviewees, personal names will not be revealed. In a limited number of instances, interviewees provided me with (semi-)confidential documents that in the endnotes are identified as Document "nr."

2 Explaining Public Interventions in Private Governance

1 As an acronym, ISEAL used to stand for "International Social and Environmental Accreditation and Labelling" (ISEAL Alliance, 2014).

2 This attention to public policy is obviously present when a private governance scheme is established as a direct response to a public policy gap. That situation, however, is different from the one discussed here, where the focus is on existing schemes developing interests with respect to the larger policy environment in which they operate.

3 Credence goods are distinct from search goods and experience goods. For a search good, the quality of its features is easily observable even before consumption, given limited efforts to acquire the correct information. For an experience good, these quality attributes can only be determined after consumption (Nelson, 1970).

4 Targets can also be located downstream in the supply chain. This is, for example, the case for private governance schemes dealing with product recycling (Auld et al., 2014; Renckens, 2008, 2015).

5 A proliferation of private meta-governance institutions can create problems of its own, which can be both related to and different from the ones described here (Fransen, 2015).

6 Since process-related regulation (unlike product-related regulation) does not generally disrupt trade, the dynamics among the Member States reflect a prisoners' dilemma or cooperation game, whereby regulatory competition among Member States generally leads to a race to the bottom. Whereas there may be an interest in harmonization at the EU level, there will be distributional conflicts over the level at which the harmonized rules should be set. High-standard Member States will want high standards, while low-standard Member States have no interest in a high-level standard, or any standard for that matter, since this will disadvantage their domestic producers. The status quo is therefore more likely to hold, except when Member States can agree on side-payments or package deals (Pollack, 1997; Scharpf, 1996). For this reason, the European Commission has an important role to play as a policy activist. Ankersmith (2017: 81–95), however, notes that these dynamics may differ depending on the type of process-related regulation. Country-based process regulation (targeting products from specific countries) and producer-based process regulation (targeting products from noncompliant producers) established by Member States will likely violate Article 34 of the Treaty on the Functioning of the European Union (TFEU), which prohibits quantitative or equivalent restrictions on imports between Member States, unless when justified on grounds of public policy (Article 36 TFEU). As a result, there is a clear treaty-based rationale for intervention. Consumer-based process regulation (aimed at changing consumers' behavior) such as organic agriculture rules, on the other hand, does not likely fall under Article 34. However, voluntary or mandatory labeling schemes established by Member States may still fall under this article. This will be the case, for example, when "a labelling measure requires a product to be modified (whether by removing a label or attaching one)" since then "it will be more difficult to market the product" (Ankersmith, 2017: 94). Even for voluntary labeling schemes, this may be the case, since "not all products can be marketed without the risk that some products would require adaptation. If a product is labelled as 'fair trade', for instance, but does not comply with the voluntary labelling scheme regulating the use of 'fair trade' labels, and as a consequence the measure in question prevents the marketing of the products, such a measure is a measure equivalent to a quantitative restriction on imports" (Ankersmith, 2017: 94). In contrast to

process-based measures established by Member States, purely private process-based measures (as discussed in this book) do not seem to fall under Article 34 (Ankersmith, 2017: 105–108). This is the case since "[t]hus far, it appears that the ECJ [European Court of Justice] has been reluctant to extend Article 34 to private process-based measures" (Ankersmith, 2017: 107).

7 This activist role may have been less explicit in recent years, considering the European Commission has adopted a new Better Regulation policy. The policy includes a more careful analysis of new legislative initiatives, with the aim of avoiding and overturning a trend toward EU overregulation (European Commission, 2015a).

3 Organic Agriculture

1 The EU-15 refers to the fifteen Member States as of 1995: Austria, Belgium, Denmark, Finland, France, Germany, Greece, Ireland, Italy, Luxembourg, the Netherlands, Portugal, Spain, Sweden, and the United Kingdom. The EU-27 refers to the EU-15 plus the twelve countries that joined between 2004 and 2007: Bulgaria, Cyprus, the Czech Republic, Estonia, Hungary, Latvia, Lithuania, Malta, Poland, Romania, Slovakia, and Slovenia. The EU-28 entails the EU-27 plus Croatia, which joined the EU in 2013. Data between 2000 and 2011 are for the EU-27 and between 2012 and 2016 for the EU-28.

2 Trade data on organic products are difficult to find. For the EU, for example, no distinction is made between organic and conventional agricultural products (European Commission, 2010a).

3 Interview 32.

4 It would take until 2000, however, before the USA would create the National Organic Program.

5 Interview 32.

6 The Treaty of Lisbon has replaced this consultation procedure with what is now called the "ordinary legislative procedure" (i.e., co-decision of the Council of Ministers and the European Parliament).

7 Interview 31; Interview 43.

8 In 2013, eighteen Member States had a purely private system: Austria, Belgium, Bulgaria, Cyprus, the Czech Republic, France, Germany, Greece, Hungary, Ireland, Italy, Latvia, Portugal, Romania, Slovakia, Slovenia, Sweden, and the United Kingdom. Four Member States had a mixed system: Luxembourg, Malta, Poland, and Spain. Four Member States had a purely public system: Denmark, Estonia, Finland, and Lithuania. In the Netherlands, a private certifier has been given the status of governmental inspection authority by law, and it is considered by the European

Commission as a public system. In Member States with a purely private system or a mixed system, 174 private auditors had been approved as of May 21, 2013 (European Commission, 2013c).

9 The seven countries on the list were: Argentina, Australia, Costa Rica, India, Israel, New Zealand, and Switzerland. Other countries that had appeared on the list before, but were not included after mid-2006 since they had become Member States in 2004, were Hungary and the Czech Republic (European Commission, 2004b, 2006a).

10 Interview 43.

11 For a similar situation in product safety, see Cafaggi and Janczuk (2010).

12 Interview 4; Interview 43.

13 Interview 43.

14 Interview 4; Interview 32; Interview 43; Interview 50.

15 Interview 43; Interview 32.

16 The Commission uses Codex Alimentarius guidelines for assessing equivalence. These guidelines are, much like the IFOAM Basic Standards, a standard-for-standards that provide a framework for establishing more specific local standards. The Codex is developed by the Codex Alimentarius Committee, which was established by the Food and Agriculture Organization of the UN and the World Health Organization in 1963 (Codex Alimentarius, 2016).

17 The original seven countries are Argentina, Australia, Costa Rica, India, Israel, New Zealand, and Switzerland. The four new countries are Canada, Japan, Tunisia, and the USA.

4 Biofuels

1 In developing RSPO, WWF cooperated with business actors such as Aarhus United UK Ltd., Migros, the Malaysian Palm Oil Association, and Unilever (RSPO, 2014b). In RTRS, civil society actors involved in its development included WWF, the Catholic Organisation for Relief and Development Aid (CORDAID), and the Federation of Rural Workers and Family Farmers in South Brazil (FETRAF-SUL/CUT), while business actors included the Grupo Maggi, Unilever, and the Swiss supermarket chain COOP (RTRS, 2014). Bonsucro was developed by WWF in collaboration with sugar retailers, investors, traders, producers, and NGOs (Bonsucro, 2013a, 2013b). RSB was developed at the initiative of the Swiss École Polytechnique Fédérale de Lausanne and with the support of NGOs (including WWF), private companies and industry organizations, and (inter)governmental agencies (RSB, 2014b, 2014d). ISCC, finally, was developed by a German consultancy firm – MEO Carbon Solutions – with support from biodiesel producers, oil companies, the German rapeseed

association, academics, the German Ministry of Agriculture, and WWF (ISCC, 2014; Ponte, 2014).

2 For a general overview, see Schlamann et al. (2013).

3 Greenergy was a member of the Better Sugarcane Initiative when it developed its program. This was done in cooperation with Proforest, a company focused on sustainability management, and the Forest and Agriculture Management and Certification Institute (Imaflora), a Brazilian NGO.

4 Interview 19; Interview 37; Interview 41.

5 In a statement added to the Council of Minister's final vote on the Directive, the governments of Belgium, Germany, Denmark, Ireland, Luxembourg, Portugal, Sweden, Finland, and the United Kingdom stated that while the 2003 Directive included the possibility for the European Commission to propose mandatory targets in case the indicative targets were not reached, "the inclusion of these provisions in this Directive does not imply the consent of these delegations to the principle of mandatory targets, or that they will agree to any proposal from the Commission that may be submitted" in this respect (Council of the European Union, 2003c: 3).

6 Apart from a new Directive on renewable energy sources (European Parliament and Council of the European Union, 2009b), this package consisted of three more legislative pieces: (1) a Decision updating Member States' minimum contributions for GHG emissions reductions (European Parliament and Council of the European Union, 2009a); (2) a Directive on carbon capture and storage (European Parliament and Council of the European Union, 2009e); and (3) a Directive updating the EU emissions trading scheme (European Parliament and Council of the European Union, 2009c).

7 A final part of the EU's so-called 20-20-20 by 2020 targets was increasing energy efficiency by 20 percent. This target was established by the Energy Efficiency Directive of 2012 (European Parliament and Council of the European Union, 2012).

8 Interview 11; Interview 12; Interview 18.

9 Interview 11; Interview 12; Interview 21; Interview 23; Interview 45.

10 Interview 21.

11 Interview 24.

12 Interview 12; Interview 14; Interview 18; Interview 19; Interview 37; Interview 41.

13 Interview 23.

14 All the stakeholder responses for the consultation can be found on the following website: https://web.archive.org/web/20080206102259/http://ec.europa.eu:80/energy/res/consultation/biofuels_en.htm; Interview 37.

15 Interview 9.

16 In 2011, the Department for Transport took over the Agency's functions. See: https://web.archive.org/web/20170424213122/https://www.gov.uk/government/organisations/renewable-fuels-agency.

17 Interview 41.

18 For more on these initiatives, see for example Scarlat and Dallemand (2011).

19 The remaining 10 percent are covered by pure vegetable oils (mostly palm oil) and biogas.

20 Interview 29.

21 Later analysis shows that this early-mover advantage was absent and can be partly blamed for the absence of EU influence on biofuels sustainability policies in other jurisdictions (Renckens et al., 2017).

22 Interview 14; Interview 19; Interview 23; Interview 24; Interview 37; Interview 45.

23 Interview 12; Interview 37.

24 Equivalent criteria were adopted in the 2009 Fuel Quality Directive, the sister Directive of RED (European Parliament and Council of the European Union, 2009d).

25 This change from a 10 percent biofuels target to a 10 percent renewable-fuels target resulted, according to European Commissioner for Energy, Andris Piebalgs, from an inconsistent use of concepts on the side of the European Commission (Eckstein, 2008). Ackrill and Kay (2014: 62), however, imply that through this change Member States also "ensured they retained considerable flexibility over how those targets were to be achieved," including by not differentiating between ethanol and biodiesel, feedstocks, or generations of biofuels. Nonetheless, the objective was still to cover the target largely by biofuels.

26 Interview 20.

27 ISO Guide 65 refers to "General requirements for bodies operating product certification systems," ISO 19011 to "Guidelines for auditing management systems," ISO 14065 to "Greenhouse gases–Requirements for greenhouse gas validation and verification bodies for use in accreditation or other forms of recognition," ISO 14064-3 to "Greenhouse gases–Part 3: Specification with guidance for the validation and verification of greenhouse gas assertions," and ISAE 3000 to "Assurance engagements other than audits or reviews of historical financial information."

28 Interview 11; Interview 14.

29 Interview 8; Interview 11; Interview 12; Interview 14; Interview 18; Interview 37.

30 By late 2017, the approval for five of the schemes (Abengoa RBSA, Greenergy, Ensus, NTA 8080, and RSPO) had expired.
31 Interview 30.
32 The NTA 8080 scheme was developed following the work of the Dutch Cramer Commission (2007).
33 Interview 14; Interview 20.
34 Interview 8; Interview 11; Interview 16; Interview 20; Interview 23.

5 Fair Trade

1 I decided not to use the concept of "ethical trade" to refer to this issue area since it has been used by the EU in a specific way, namely to identify CSR activities by multinational corporations (such as codes of conduct) with respect to labor conditions in countries from the global South (European Commission, 1999: 4–5).
2 These countries were Austria, Belgium, Denmark, Finland, France, Germany, Ireland, Italy, the Netherlands, Spain, Sweden, Switzerland, and the United Kingdom. Since 2008, NEWS! has become part of the World Fair Trade Organization-Europe (NEWS!, 2004b; WFTO, 2008).
3 For an overview of other differences between WFTO and Fairtrade International's approaches to Fair Trade, see Cremona and Marin Duran (2013b).
4 The definition reads as follows: "Fair Trade is a trading partnership, based on dialogue, transparency and respect, that seeks greater equity in international trade. It contributes to sustainable development by offering better trading conditions to, and securing the rights of, marginalized producers and workers – especially in the South. Fair Trade organisations (backed by consumers) are engaged actively in supporting producers, awareness raising and in campaigning for changes in the rules and practice of conventional international trade" (FTAO, s.d.). The principles include a fair price, preproduction financing, securing producers' and workers' rights, and sustainable development.
5 This entails the market price being paid when the market price is higher than the Fair Trade minimum (Prevezer, 2013: 20).
6 Interview 38.
7 Differences within the Fair Trade community exist as well, such as in September 2011, when Fair Trade USA broke away from Fairtrade International. Fair Trade USA has been more willing to engage with producers not (yet) democratically organized in producer organizations, plantations, Northern producers, and large corporations (Raynolds and Greenfield, 2015: 27, 30).

8 Other proposed criteria included: no import or sales monopolies; price transparency; long-term stable relations; respecting International Labor Organization conventions; no gender discrimination; respect for the environment; and respect for indigenous people.

9 Interview 56; Document 1, 2003.

10 Interview 56; Document 1, 2003.

11 Document 1, 2003; Document 2, 2006.

12 Interview 56; Document 2, 2006.

13 Document 1, 2003.

14 Interview 7; Interview 33; Interview 56.

15 Document, 3 2005.

16 Document 2, 2006; Document 3, 2005; Interview 56.

17 Interview 56; Document 2, 2006.

18 Interview 53.

19 Interview 33.

20 Interview 49.

21 Interview 26; Interview 33.

22 Interview 38; Interview 48.

23 Interview 26; Interview 33; Interview 46; Interview 53; Interview 56.

24 Interview 7; Interview 26; Interview 53.

25 Interview 7; Interview 26; Interview 28.

26 Interview 33; Interview 46; Interview 51; Interview 53.

27 Interview 33; Interview 53.

28 Interview 73.

29 Interview 38; Interview 39; Interview 48; Interview 71.

30 Interview 7; Interview 28; Interview 38; Interview 39; Interview 46.

31 Interview 46; Interview 71.

32 Clift and Woll (2012) employ the concept of economic patriotism to refer to market-shielding public interventions that are linked to a particular territory other than the national one. Just as List's ([1841] 1885) economic nationalism "needs to be defined by its nationalist references" (Clift and Woll, 2012: 313), "economic patriotism" is distinct since it "is agnostic about the precise nature of the unit claimed as *patrie*" or homeland (Clift and Woll, 2012: 308). Beyond the national level, it can refer to supranational or subnational levels. By extension, it also applies to entities formerly linked to the *patrie*, with whom a special relationship exists, such as former colonies.

6 Fisheries

1 The section provides a brief overview of several important initiatives, without the intention of being exhaustive. One type of initiative that is not

covered is organic aquaculture. Private governance in this area is regulated by the EU's organic agricultural policy as described in Chapter 3 (Council of the European Union, 2007b; European Commission, 2009a).

2 The certification process encompasses two steps: An assessment of the fishery is first performed by the KRAV Fisheries Committee; once approved, certification of the individual vessel(s) follows.

3 While Iceland is not a member of the EU, it is a member of the European Economic area. The scheme contains a third-party certification program with an accompanying eco-label and an indication of origin logo that can be used by fishing vessels, processing plants, and other supply chain actors.

4 The scheme focuses on certifying vessels. While the scheme does have a logo, it is not in the first instance targeted at end-consumers.

5 The 1995 FAO Code of Conduct for Responsible Fisheries (FAO, 1995) contains principles and guidelines on fisheries management, fishing operations, aquaculture development, the integration of fisheries into coastal area management, post-harvest practices and trade, and fisheries research. The FAO Guidelines for the Ecolabelling of Fish and Fishery Products from Marine Capture Fisheries (FAO, 2005, 2009) and for Inland Capture Fisheries (FAO, 2011a) contain minimum requirements for private governance schemes, which address the management system of the fishery, the stocks under consideration, ecosystem impacts, accreditation, and certification. The FAO Technical Guidelines on Aquaculture Certification (FAO, 2011b) provide minimum principles regarding animal health and welfare, food safety, environmental integrity, and socioeconomic aspects, as well as procedural principles for certification and eco-labeling schemes. Private governance schemes are expected to further develop concrete criteria and measurable performance indicators.

6 Interview 44.

7 This study solicited a strong response from the MSC, which argued that Froese and Proelss used "a definition of 'overfished' that is not consistent with internationally accepted definitions and interpretations" (Agnew et al., 2013: 551), a claim that Froese and Proelss subsequently rejected (Froese and Proelss, 2013).

8 Author's own calculations. See Renckens and Auld (2016).

9 Note that this may be an underestimation. The ASC mentioned elsewhere on the website that it had certified 469 farms by June 2017, while another 105 were in assessment (ASC, 2017c). Yet, due to technical problems, not all farms were listed on the website.

10 The group was comprised of industry representatives from Anfaco, Scapêche, Unilever, Young's/Food and Drink Federation, and ARVI;

certification-scheme representatives from MSC, Seafish, and Bureau Vér-itas France; an NGO representative of the Responsible Fishing Alliance; and experts from Manchester Business School, Nantes University, and the Thünen Institute of Baltic Sea Fisheries.

11 While the debates in the Parliament showed that some Members of Parliament were favoring minimum criteria, the Resolution that the Parliament adopted supported an EU certification scheme.

12 While the European Commission was developing the minimum criteria for eco-labeling schemes, it was also considering expanding the scope of the EU "flower" Eco-label to fishery and aquaculture products. The decision to expand the flower eco-label was postponed, however, since the Council of Ministers and the European Parliament requested add-itional impact assessments, to be finished by the end of 2011 (Agritrade, 2009; Management Committee for Fishery and Aquaculture Products, 2009). However, based on a feasibility report (Sengstschmid et al., 2011) and an Opinion of the European Union Ecolabelling Board (s.d.), the European Commission decided not to develop criteria for food and feed products under the EU Ecolabel (European Commission, 2017b).

13 Contributions of the various stakeholders can be found at: https://web.archive.org/web/20100601181857/http://ec.europa.eu/fisher ies/reform/consultation/received/index_en.htm.

14 See the contributions by the European Fish Processors Association – European Federation of National Organisations of Importers and Exporters of Fish (AIPCE-CEP); Birdlife International; Europêche-COGECA; Greenpeace; WWF; European Consumer Organisation (BEUC); Advisory Committee on Fisheries and Aquaculture (ACFA); MSC; Seafish; the Netherlands Ministry of Agriculture; and the German Federal Ministry of Food, Agriculture, and Consumer Protection. See: https://web.archive.org/web/20100601181857/http://ec.europa.eu/fisher ies/reform/consultation/received/index_en.htm.

15 The debate in the Fisheries Committee shows that several Parliamentar-ians promoted establishing minimum criteria instead of an EU label (European Parliament, 2012a). Similarly, the Parliament's Committee on the Environment, Public Health, and Food Safety also supported controlling eco-labeling schemes on their reliability instead of creating a separate EU label (European Parliament, 2012b: 66, 79).

16 Interview 57.

17 Interview 5; Interview 44; Interview 57.

18 Interview 35.

19 Spain and France, together with the United Kingdom and Denmark, are the most important EU producer countries in terms of volume of wild capture and aquaculture combined. The combined catches by these

countries account for over half of the total EU catches. In aquaculture, the United Kingdom, France, Greece, and Spain dominate in terms of volume, together accounting for about two thirds of the European production. Spain alone accounts for 25 percent of employment in the fishing sector in the EU, while, together with France, it is the largest employer in aquaculture (European Commission, 2016e: 16–31). In terms of consumption expenditures, France and Spain together account for more than one third (European Commission, 2016a: 16).

20 Interview 57; Interview 59; Interview 65.
21 Personal communication with a member of the staff of a Member of the European Parliament.
22 Interview 59.
23 See, for example, contributions by the European Association of Fishing Ports and Auctions, the Flemish Government, and the Belgian Central Economic Council to the 2009 consultation on the reform of the CFP: https://web.archive.org/web/20100601181857/http://ec.europa.eu/fisher ies/reform/consultation/received/index_en.htm.

7 Evaluating Public Interventions in Private Governance

1 Interview 65.

References

4C Association. 2014a. Cooperation with Other Standards. https://web .archive.org/web/20140314124145/http://www.4c-coffeeassociation.org :80/our-services/cooperation-with-other-standards.html (accessed March 14, 2014).

2014b. History of the 4C Association. https://web.archive.org/web/20140 328194809/http://www.4c-coffeeassociation.org/about-us/history.html (accessed March 28, 2014).

Abay, Canan, Özlem Karahan Uysal, Bülent Miran, Murat Boyaci, Beate Huber, and Matthias Stolze. 2011. Report on Evaluation of the Revision of Council Regulation (EEC) No 2092/91, Import Regime in Two Exporting Non-EU Countries (TR, CH) and on an International Level. https://web.archive.org/web/20120610030817/http://www.certcost.org/ Lib/CERTCOST/Deliverable/D2.2_D19.pdf (accessed November 30, 2017).

Abbott, Kenneth W. 2012. The Transnational Regime Complex for Climate Change. *Environment and Planning C: Government and Policy*, 30(4), 571–590.

Abbott, Kenneth W., and Duncan Snidal. 2000. Hard and Soft Law in International Governance. *International Organization*, 54(3), 421–456.

2009a. The Governance Triangle: Regulatory Standards Institutions and the Shadow of the State. In Mattli, Walter and Ngaire Woods, eds. *The Politics of Global Regulation*. Princeton: Princeton University Press, 44–88.

2009b. Strengthening International Regulation through Transnational New Governance: Overcoming the Orchestration Deficit. *Vanderbilt Journal of Transnational Law*, 42(2), 501–578.

2010. International Regulation without International Government: Improving IO Performance through Orchestration. *The Review of International Organizations*, 5(3), 315–344.

Abbott, Kenneth W., Jessica F. Green, and Robert O. Keohane. 2016. Organizational Ecology and Institutional Change in Global Governance. *International Organization*, 70(2), 247–277.

Abbott, Kenneth W., Philipp Genschel, Duncan Snidal, and Bernhard Zangl. 2015. Orchestration: Global Governance through Intermediaries.

In Abbott, Kenneth W., Philipp Genschel, Duncan Snidal, and Bernhard Zangl, eds. *International Organizations as Orchestrators*. Cambridge: Cambridge University Press, 3–36.

Ackrill, Robert, and Adrian Kay. 2011. EU Biofuels Sustainability Standards and Certification Systems: How to Seek WTO-Compatibility. *Journal of Agricultural Economics*, 62(3), 551–564.

2014. *The Growth of Biofuels in the 21st Century: Policy Drivers and Market Challenges*. New York: Palgrave Macmillan.

ACP-EU Joint Assembly. 1996. Resolution on Trade Based on Fairness and Solidarity. OJ 1997 No. C62/60.

1997. Resolution on Bananas. OJ 1998 No. C96/48.

Advisory Committee on Fisheries and Aquaculture. 2009. Summary Record of the Meeting of Working Group 3 (Markets and Trade Policy) of the Advisory Committee on Fisheries and Aquaculture. July 8, 2009. On file with author.

Agnew, David J., Nicolás L. Gutiérrez, Amanda Stern-Pirlot, Anthony D. M. Smith, Christopher Zimmermann, and Keith Sainsbury. 2013. Rebuttal to Froese and Proelss "Evaluation and Legal Assessment of Certified Seafood." *Marine Policy*, 38, 551–553.

Agri Service International Newsletter. 1997. Bananas: MEPs Fight on for Concessions on Regime Update Proposals. On file with author.

Agritrade. 2009. Update on EU Policy and Actions on Eco-Labels for Fish. https://web.archive.org/web/20170907064534/http://agritrade.cta.int/en/layout/set/print/Fisheries/Topics/Market-access/Update-on-EU-policy-and-actions-on-eco-labels-for-fish (accessed September 24, 2017).

AIPCE-CEP. 2016. Finfish Study 2016. EU Is the Biggest Trading Bloc and Consumption Is Growing. Press Release, December 13, 2016. https://web.archive.org/web/20171209212552/https://www.aipce-cep.org/wp-content/uploads/2017/04/Press-Release-Finfish-Study-2016.pdf (accessed December 9, 2017).

Akerlof, George A. 1970. The Market for "Lemons": Uncertainty and the Market Mechanism. *The Quarterly Journal of Economics*, 84(3), 488–500.

Alemanno, Alberto. 2009. Regulating Organic Farming in the European Union: Balancing Consumer Preferences and Free Movement Imperatives. *European Consumer Law Journal*, 1, 83–108.

Allsopp, Michelle, Paul Johnston, and David Santillo. 2008. *Challenging the Aquaculture Industry on Sustainability*. Amsterdam: Greenpeace International.

Andonova, Liliana B., Michele M. Betsill, and Harriet Bulkeley. 2009. Transnational Climate Governance. *Global Environmental Politics*, 9(2), 52–73.

Ankersmith, Laurens. 2017. *Green Trade and Fair Trade in and with the EU: Process-Based Measures within the EU Legal Order*. Cambridge: Cambridge University Press.

Arcuri, Alessandra. 2015. The Transformation of Organic Regulation: The Ambiguous Effects of Publicization. *Regulation & Governance*, 9(2), 144–159.

Areté. 2010. Inventory of Certification Schemes for Agricultural Products and Foodstuffs Marketed in the EU Member States. http://web.archive .org/web/20130626052717/http://ec.europa.eu/agriculture/quality/certi fication/inventory/inventory-data-aggregations_en.pdf (accessed November 30, 2017).

ASC. 2014. ASC Certified Seafood Now Available. https://web.archive.org/ web/20140630014121/http://www.asc-aqua.org:80/upload/ASC_flyer_ ENG_feb2014_def.pdf (accessed June 30, 2014).

2015. Creating the ASC Standards. https://web.archive.org/web/201511 17131234/http://www.asc-aqua.org/index.cfm?act=tekst.item&iid=2& iids=386&lng=1 (accessed November 17, 2015).

2017a. 16 Facts About ASC. https://web.archive.org/web/2017070500 2601/http://www.asc-aqua.org/index.cfm?act=tekst.item&iid=2&iids= 288&lng=1 (accessed July 5, 2017).

2017b. About the ASC. https://web.archive.org/web/20170701182631/http:// www.asc-aqua.org/index.cfm?act=tekst.item&iid=2&lng=1 (accessed July 1, 2017).

2017c. Certification Update: June 2017. http://mailchi.mp/asc-aqua/xr162 vrjvq-1760481?e=9ebd51a70d (accessed June 9, 2017).

2017d. Certified. https://web.archive.org/web/20170701182610/http:// www.asc-aqua.org/index.cfm?act=tekst.item&iid=4&iids=204&lng=1 (accessed July 1, 2017).

2017e. In Assessment. On file with author.

Aschemann, Jessica, Ulrich Hamm, Simona Naspetti, and Raffaele Zanoli. 2007. The Organic Market. In Lockeretz, William, ed. *Organic Farming: An International History*. Wallingford: CAB International, 123–151.

Aspinwall, Mark, and Justin Greenwood. 1998. Conceptualizing Collective Action in the European Union: An Introduction. In Greenwood, Justin and Mark Aspinwall, eds. *Collective Action in the European Union. Interests and the New Politics of Associability*. London: Routledge, 1–30.

Association for Promoting Fairtrade in Finland. 2008. Contribution to 3 June 2008 Fair Trade Meeting. https://web.archive.org/web/201504 09104531/http://trade.ec.europa.eu/doclib/docs/2008/june/tradoc_139 327.pdf (accessed October 14, 2016).

Assured Food Standards. 2014. The History of Red Tractor. https://web
.archive.org/web/20140326074309/http://www.redtractor.org.uk/the-
history-of-red-tractor (accessed March 26, 2014).

Audet, René, and Corinne Gendron. 2012. IFOAM and the Institutionaliza-
tion of Organic Agriculture. In Reed, Darryl, Peter Utting, and Ananya
Mukherjee-Reed, eds. *Business Regulation and Non-State Actors:
Whose Standards? Whose Development?* London: Routledge, 264–276.

Auld, Graeme. 2014a. Confronting Trade-offs and Interactive Effects in the
Choice of Policy Focus: Specialized Versus Comprehensive Private
Governance. *Regulation & Governance*, 8(1), 126–148.

2014b. *Constructing Private Governance: The Rise and Evolution of
Forest, Coffee, and Fisheries Certification.* New Haven: Yale University
Press.

Auld, Graeme, Benjamin Cashore, and Stefan Renckens. 2014. Governance
Components in Private Regulation: Implications for Legitimacy, Authority and Effectiveness. In Kanie, Norichika, Steinar Andresen, and Peter M.
Haas, eds. *Improving Global Environmental Governance: Best Practices
for Architecture and Agency.* London: Routledge, 152–174.

Auld, Graeme, Cristina Balboa, Steven Bernstein, and Benjamin Cashore.
2009. The Emergence of Non-State Market Driven (NSMD) Global
Environmental Governance: A Cross Sectoral Assessment. In Delmas,
Magali A. and Oran R. Young, eds. *Governance for the Environment. New Perspectives.* Cambridge: Cambridge University Press,
183–218.

Auld, Graeme, Steven Bernstein, and Benjamin Cashore. 2008. The New
Corporate Social Responsibility. *Annual Review of Environment and
Resources*, 33(1), 413–435.

2015. Transnational Private Governance between the Logics of Empowerment and Control. *Regulation & Governance*, 9(2), 108–124.

Auld, Graeme, and Stefan Renckens. 2017. Rule-Making Feedbacks through
Intermediation and Evaluation in Transnational Private Governance.
The ANNALS of the American Academy of Political and Social Science,
670(1), 93–111.

2019. Micro-Level Interactions in the Compliance Processes of Transnational
Private Governance. In Wood, Stepan, Rebecca Schmidt, Kenneth W.
Abbott, Burkard Eberlein, and Errol Meidinger, eds. *Transnational
Business Governance Interactions: Advancing Marginalized Actors
and Enhancing Regulatory Quality.* Cheltenham: Edward Elgar.

Avant, Deborah D., Martha Finnemore, and Susan K. Sell. 2010. Who
Governs the Globe? In Avant, Deborah D., Martha Finnemore, and
Susan K. Sell, eds. *Who Governs the Globe?* Cambridge: Cambridge
University Press, 1–34.

Bach, David, and Abraham L. Newman. 2007. The European Regulatory State and Global Public Policy: Micro-Institutions, Macro-Influence. *Journal of European Public Policy*, 14(6), 827–846.

Baffes, John, and Tassos Haniotis. 2010. *Placing the 2006/08 Commodity Price Boom into Perspective*. Washington, DC: World Bank.

Bailer, Stefanie. 2011. Structural, Domestic, and Strategic Interests in the European Union: Negotiation Positions in the Council of Ministers. *Negotiation Journal*, 27(4), 447–475.

Bailer, Stefanie, Mikko Mattila, and Gerald Schneider. 2015. Money Makes the EU Go Round: The Objective Foundations of Conflict in the Council of Ministers. *Journal of Common Market Studies*, 53(3), 437–456.

Baillieux, Patrice, and Alberic Scharpé. 1994. *Organic Farming*. Luxembourg: Office for Official Publications of the European Communities.

Barber, Tony. 2008. EU Urged to Use Taxes in Climate Struggle. *Financial Times*, January 21, 2008, 4.

Baron, David P. 2009. Clubs, Credence Standards, and Social Pressure. In Potoski, Matthew and Aseem Prakash, eds. *Voluntary Programs: A Club Theory Perspective*. Cambridge: MIT Press, 42–66.

Bartley, Tim. 2003. Certifying Forests and Factories: States, Social Movements, and the Rise of Private Regulation in the Apparel and Forest Products Fields. *Politics & Society*, 31(3), 433–464.

2007a. How Foundations Shape Social Movements: The Construction of an Organizational Field and the Rise of Forest Certification. *Social Problems*, 54(3), 229–255.

2007b. Institutional Emergence in an Era of Globalization: The Rise of Transnational Private Regulation of Labor and Environmental Conditions. *American Journal of Sociology*, 113(2), 297–351.

2011. Transnational Governance as the Layering of Rules: Intersections of Public and Private Standards. *Theoretical Inquiries in Law*, 12(2), 517–542.

2014. Transnational Governance and the Re-centered State: Sustainability or Legality? *Regulation & Governance*, 8(1), 93–109.

Bastos Lima, Mairon G., and Joyeeta Gupta. 2013. The Policy Context of Biofuels: A Case of Non-Governance at the Global Level? *Global Environmental Politics*, 13(2), 46–64.

Bates, Richard. 2009. Update on EU Policy and Actions on Ecolabels for Fish. Presentation at the Round Table on Eco-Labelling and Certification in the Fisheries Sector, April 22–23, 2009, The Hague.

2010. Update on EU Policy and Action for Seafood Sustainability Labelling. Presentation at the Workshop Future Environmental Labelling of Seafood, January 19, 2010, Copenhagen.

Batsell, Jake. 2004. Bumper Crop of Coffee Labels. *The Seattle Times*, September 20, 2004, A1.

Bauen, Ausilio, Jo Howes, Adam Chase, Richard Tipper, Aino Inkinen, Jessica Lovell, and Jeremy Woods. 2005. Feasibility Study on Certification for a Renewable Transport Fuel Obligation. https://web.archive.org/web/20160807234736/http://www.lowcvp.org.uk/assets/reports/RTFO%20-%20feasibility%20of%20certification.pdf (accessed August 7, 2016).

Baumgartner, Frank, and Bryan Jones. 1993. *Agendas and Instability in American Politics*. Chicago: University of Chicago Press.

Bell, Stephen, and Andrew Hindmoor. 2012. Governance without Government? The Case of the Forest Stewardship Council. *Public Administration*, 90(1), 144–159.

Bennett, Elizabeth A. 2013. A Short History of Fairtrade Certification Governance. In Granville, Brigitte and Janet Dine, eds. *The Processes and Practices of Fair Trade: Trust, Ethics, and Governance*. London: Routledge, 43–78.

    2015. Fairtrade International Governance. In Raynolds, Laura T. and Elizabeth A. Bennett, eds. *Handbook of Research on Fair Trade*. Cheltenham: Edward Elgar, 80–101.

Berkhout, Joost, Jan Beyers, Caelesta Braun, Marcel Hanegraaff, and David Lowery. 2018. Making Inference across Mobilisation and Influence Research: Comparing Top-Down and Bottom-Up Mapping of Interest Systems. *Political Studies*, 66(1), 43–62.

Berkhout, Joost, Brendan J. Carroll, Caelesta Braun, Adam W. Chalmers, Tine Destrooper, David Lowery, Simon Otjes, and Anne Rasmussen. 2015. Interest Organizations across Economic Sectors: Explaining Interest Group Density in the European Union. *Journal of European Public Policy*, 22(4), 462–480.

Berliner, Daniel, and Aseem Prakash. 2014. Public Authority and Private Rules: How Domestic Regulatory Institutions Shape the Adoption of Global Private Regimes. *International Studies Quarterly*, 58(4), 793–803.

    2015. "Bluewashing" the Firm? Voluntary Regulations, Program Design, and Member Compliance with the United Nations Global Compact. *Policy Studies Journal*, 43(1), 115–138.

Bernhagen, Patrick, and Neil J. Mitchell. 2010. The Private Provision of Public Goods: Corporate Commitments and the United Nations Global Compact. *International Studies Quarterly*, 54(4), 1175–1187.

Bernstein, Steven. 2001. *The Compromise of Liberal Environmentalism*. New York: Columbia University Press.

    2011. Legitimacy in Intergovernmental and Non-State Global Governance. *Review of International Political Economy*, 18(1), 17–51.

Bernstein, Steven, and Benjamin Cashore. 2007. Can Non-State Global Governance Be Legitimate? An Analytical Framework. *Regulation & Governance*, 1(4), 347–371.

Bernstein, Steven, and Erin Hannah. 2008. Non-State Global Standard Setting and the WTO: Legitimacy and the Need for Regulatory Space. *Journal of International Economic Law*, 11(3), 575–608.

Bernstein, Steven, and Hamish van der Ven. 2017. Best Practices in Global Governance. *Review of International Studies*, 43(3), 534–556.

Beyers, Jan, Rainer Eising, and William Maloney. 2008. Researching Interest Group Politics in Europe and Elsewhere: Much We Study, Little We Know? *West European Politics*, 31(6), 1103–1128.

Beyers, Jan, and Bart Kerremans. 2012. Domestic Embeddedness and the Dynamics of Multilevel Venue Shopping in Four EU Member States. *Governance*, 25(2), 263–290.

Biermann, Frank, Philipp Pattberg, Harro van Asselt, and Fariborz Zelli. 2009. The Fragmentation of Global Governance Architectures: A Framework for Analysis. *Global Environmental Politics*, 9(4), 14–40.

BirdLife European Division, European Environmental Bureau, FERN, Friends of the Earth Europe, Oxfam International, and Transport and Environment. 2009. Biofuels: Handle with Care. https://web.archive .org/web/20180209180123/https://www.transportenvironment.org/sites/ te/files/media/2009%2011_biofuels_handle_with_care.pdf (accessed January 23, 2014).

BirdLife International, European Environmental Bureau, and Transport and Environment. 2007. Biofuel Issues in the New Legislation on the Promotion of Renewable Energy, Public Consultation Exercise, April–June 2007. https://web.archive.org/web/20180209175850/https://www.tran sportenvironment.org/sites/te/files/media/2007-06_biofuels_consultation_ response_birdlife_eeb_te_0.pdf (accessed January 20, 2014).

Bitzer, Verena, Mara Francken, and Pieter Glasbergen. 2008. Intersectoral Partnerships for a Sustainable Coffee Chain: Really Addressing Sustainability or Just Picking (Coffee) Cherries? *Global Environmental Change*, 18(2), 271–284.

Black, Julia. 2003. Enrolling Actors in Regulatory Systems: Examples from UK Financial Services Regulation. *Public Law*, Spring, 63–91.

Blake, Francis. 2009. General Analysis of the New Regulation. In Mikkelsen, Camilla and Marco Schlüter, eds. *The New EU Regulation for Organic Food and Farming: (EC) No 834/2007. Background, Assessment, Interpretation.* Brussels: IFOAM EU Group, 18–21.

Bloomfield, Michael J. 2017. *Dirty Gold: How Activism Transformed the Jewelry Industry*. Cambridge: MIT Press.

Bonsucro. 2013a. Fact Sheets. https://web.archive.org/web/20131223121
713/http://bonsucro.com/site/fact-sheets (accessed January 22, 2014).

2013b. A Guide to Bonsucro. https://web.archive.org/web/20140207152
621/http://bonsucro.com/site/wp-content/uploads/2013/02/ENG_WEB_
A-Guide-to-Bonsucro_1.pdf (accessed February 7, 2014).

2016. *Bonsucro Production Standard: Including Bonsucro EU Production Standard. Version 4.2 December 2016.* London: Bonsucro.

Boonman, Mark, Wendela Huisman, Elmy Sarrucco-Fedorovtsjev, and Terya Sarrucco. 2011. Fair Trade Facts and Figures: A Success Story for Producers and Consumers. https://web.archive.org/web/201507261
35703/http://www.european-fair-trade-association.org:80/efta/Doc/FT-E-2010.pdf (accessed July 26, 2015).

Börzel, Tanja A., and Thomas Risse. 2010. Governance without a State: Can It Work? *Regulation & Governance*, 4(2), 113–134.

Boström, Magnus. 2003. How State-Dependent Is a Non-State-Driven Rule-Making Project? The Case of Forest Certification in Sweden. *Journal of Environmental Policy & Planning*, 5(2), 165–180.

Botterill, Linda Courtney, and Carsten Daugbjerg. 2011. Engaging with Private Sector Standards: A Case Study of GLOBALG.A.P. *Australian Journal of International Affairs*, 65(4), 488–504.

Bouwen, Pieter. 2002. Corporate Lobbying in the European Union: The Logic of Access. *Journal of European Public Policy*, 9(3), 365–390.

2004. The Logic of Access to the European Parliament: Business Lobbying in the Committee on Economic and Monetary Affairs. *Journal of Common Market Studies*, 42(3), 473–495.

Braithwaite, John. 2008. *Regulatory Capitalism: How It Works, Ideas for Making It Work Better.* Cheltenham: Edward Elgar.

Brand, Constant. 2011. Green Groups Pressure Commission over Biofuel Data. *European Voice.* May 26, 2011. https://web.archive.org/web/20
171202012040/https://www.politico.eu/article/green-groups-pressure-commission-over-biofuel-data (accessed December 2, 2017).

Broscheid, Andreas, and David Coen. 2007. Lobbying Activity and Fora Creation in the EU: Empirically Exploring the Nature of the Policy Good. *Journal of European Public Policy*, 14(3), 346–365.

Brown, Andrew G., and Robert M. Stern. 2012. Fairness in the WTO Trading System. In Daunton, Martin, Amrita Narlikar, and Robert M. Stern, eds. *The Oxford Handbook on the World Trade Organization.* Oxford: Oxford University Press, 677–696.

Brown, Dana, and Jette Steen Knudsen. 2015. Domestic Institutions and Market Pressures as Drivers of Corporate Social Responsibility: Company Initiatives in Denmark and the UK. *Political Studies*, 63(1), 181–201.

Brown, James. 2005. An Account of the Dolphin-Safe Tuna Issue in the UK. *Marine Policy*, 29(1), 39–46.

Buckingham, Kathleen, and Paul Jepson. 2013. Forest Certification with Chinese Characteristics: State Engagement with Non-State Market-Driven Governance. *Eurasian Geography and Economics*, 54(3), 208–299.

Bunea, Adriana. 2013. Issues, Preferences and Ties: Determinants of Interest Groups' Preference Attainment in the EU Environmental Policy. *Journal of European Public Policy*, 20(4), 552–570.

Burgoon, Brian. 2009. The Distinct Politics of the European Union's "Fair Trade" Linkage to Labour Standards. *European Foreign Affairs Review*, 14(5), 643–661.

Burns, Charlotte, Neil Carter, Graeme A. M. Davies, and Nicholas Worsfold. 2013. Still Saving the Earth? The European Parliament's Environmental Record. *Environmental Politics*, 22(6), 935–954.

Büthe, Tim. 2010. Private Regulation in the Global Economy: A (P)Review. *Business and Politics*, 12(3), Article 2.

Büthe, Tim, and Walter Mattli. 2011. *The New Global Rulers: The Privatization of Regulation in the World Economy*. Princeton: Princeton University Press.

Cafaggi, Fabrizio, and Agnieszka Janczuk. 2010. Private Regulation and Legal Integration: The European Example. *Business and Politics*, 12(3), Article 6.

Campbell, John L. 2007. Why Would Corporations Behave in Socially Responsible Ways? An Institutional Theory of Corporate Social Responsibility. *Academy of Management Review*, 32(3), 946–967.

Carreño, Ignacio. 2012. EU and US Mutually Recognise their Respective Organic Standards and Control Systems as Equivalent. *European Journal of Risk Regulation*, 3(2), 225–227.

Cashore, Benjamin. 2002. Legitimacy and the Privatization of Environmental Governance: How Non-State Market-Driven (NSMD) Governance Systems Gain Rule-Making Authority. *Governance*, 15(4), 503–529.

Cashore, Benjamin, Graeme Auld, Steven Bernstein, and Constance McDermott. 2007. Can Non-State Governance "Ratchet Up" Global Environmental Standards? Lessons from the Forest Sector. *Review of European Community and International Environmental Law*, 16(2), 158–172.

Cashore, Benjamin, Graeme Auld, and Deanna Newsom. 2004. *Governing through Markets: Forest Certification and the Emergence of Non-State Authority*. New Haven: Yale University Press.

Cashore, Benjamin, Graeme Auld, and Stefan Renckens. 2011. The Impact of Private, Industry, and Transnational Civil Society Regulation and their Interaction with Official Regulation. In Parker, Christine and

Vibeke L. Nielsen, eds. *Explaining Compliance: Business Responses to Regulation*. Cheltenham: Edward Elgar, 343–376.

Cashore, Benjamin, Fred Gale, Errol Meidinger, and Deanna Newsom. 2006a. *Conclusion*. In Cashore, Benjamin, Fred Gale, Errol Meidinger, and Deanna Newsom, eds. *Confronting Sustainability: Forest Certification in Developing and Transitioning Societies*. New Haven: Yale School of Forestry and Environmental Studies, 561–592.

Cashore, Benjamin, Fred Gale, Errol Meidinger, and Deanna Newsom, eds. 2006b. *Confronting Sustainability: Forest Certification in Developing and Transitioning Societies*. New Haven: Yale School of Forestry and Environmental Studies.

Cashore, Benjamin, and Michael Stone. 2012. Can Legality Verification Rescue Global Forest Governance? Analyzing the Potential of Public and Private Policy Intersection to Ameliorate Forest Challenges in Southeast Asia. *Forest Policy and Economics*, 18(May 2012), 13–22.

Castells, Manuel. 2000. *The Rise of the Network Society (Volume 1 of The Information Age: Economy, Society and Culture)*, Second Edition. Oxford: Blackwell Publishing.

2004. *The Power of Identity (Volume 2 of The Information Age: Economy, Society and Culture)*, Second Edition. Oxford: Blackwell Publishing.

Cator, Julie. 2011. Mixed Reactions by Member States to CFP Proposal. https://web.archive.org/web/20161204201017/http://cfp-reformwatch .eu/2011/07/mixed-reactions-by-member-states-to-cfp-proposal (accessed December 4, 2016).

Cerny, Philip G. 1997. Paradoxes of the Competition State: The Dynamics of Political Globalization. *Government and Opposition*, 32(2), 251–274.

Churchill, Robin, and Daniel Owen. 2010. *The EC Common Fisheries Policy*. Oxford: Oxford University Press.

ClientEarth. 2011. *Environmental Claims on Supermarket Seafood: Improving Product Labelling & Consumer Protection*. London: ClientEarth.

Clift, Ben, and Cornelia Woll. 2012. Economic Patriotism: Reinventing Control over Open Markets. *Journal of European Public Policy*, 19(3), 307–323.

Codex Alimentarius. 2016. About Codex. https://web.archive.org/web/201 60215222902/http://www.fao.org/fao-who-codexalimentarius/about-codex/en (accessed May 25, 2016).

Coen, David. 1997. The Evolution of the Large Firm as a Political Actor in the European Union. *Journal of European Public Policy*, 4(1), 91–108.

Coen, David, and Alexander Katsaitis. 2013. Chameleon Pluralism in the EU: An Empirical Study of the European Commission Interest Group Density and Diversity across Policy Domains. *Journal of European Public Policy*, 20(8), 1104–1119.

Coen, David, and Jeremy Richardson. 2009. Learning to Lobby the European Union: 20 Years of Change. In Coen, David and Jeremy Richardson, eds. *Lobbying the European Union: Institutions, Actors, and Issues*. Oxford: Oxford University Press, 3–15.

Collier, David, James Mahoney, and Jason Seawright. 2004. Claiming Too Much: Warnings about Selection Bias. In Brady, Henri E. and David Collier, eds. *Rethinking Social Inquiry: Diverse Tools, Shared Standards*. Lanham: Rowman & Littlefield, 85–102.

Commins, Ken. 2003. IFOAM Normative Documents. In Westermayer, Christina and Bernward Geier, eds. *The Organic Guarantee System: The Need and Strategy for Harmonization and Equivalence*. Tholey-Theley: IFOAM, FAO, and UNCTAD, 78–81.

2005. The History of the IFOAM Accreditation Programme. https://web .archive.org/web/20120710203750/http://ioas.org:80/xhistory.pdf (accessed July 10, 2012).

Committee of the Regions. 2003. Opinion on the Communication from the Commission on the Reform of the Common Fisheries Policy ("Roadmap"). OJ 2003 No. C128/6.

Concord, Philip, and Patrick Holden. 2007. The Soil Association. In Lockeretz, William, ed. *Organic Farming: An International History*. Wallingford: CAB International, 187–200.

Conroy, Michael E. 2007. *Branded! How the "Certification Revolution" Is Transforming Global Corporations*. Gabriola Island: New Society Publishers.

COPA-COGECA. 2002a. COPA AND COGECA Answers to the Questionnaire from the Commission on the Action Plan for Organic Farming. https://web.archive.org/web/20171201001053/http://www.copa-cogeca .be/Download.ashx?ID=216617 (accessed December 1, 2017).

2002b. Position Paper on the Proposal for a Directive on the Promotion of the Use of Biofuels for Transport and the Proposal for a Directive Amending Directive 92/81/EEC with Regard to the Possibility of Applying a Reduced Rate of Excise Duty on Certain Mineral Oils Containing Biofuels and on Biofuels (COM(2001)547). http://web.archive.org/web/ 20171202012444/http://www.copa-cogeca.be/Download.ashx?ID=362 549%20 (accessed December 2, 2017).

2005. COPA-COGECA Position concerning the Implementation of the Action Plan for Organic Food and Farming. https://web.archive.org/web/ 20171201001210/http://www.copa-cogeca.be/Download.ashx?ID=3500 60 (accessed December 1, 2017).

2006a. COPA and COGECA Reaction and Proposals to the Biomass Action Plan (COM(2005)628) and EU Strategy for Biofuels (COM(2006)34).

http://web.archive.org/web/20171202012640/http://docs.forumue.de/bio energy/txtpdf/pap_2006_copa.pdf (accessed December 2, 2017).

2006b. COPA and COGECA Remarks on the Proposal for a Council Regulation on Organic Production and Labelling of Organic Products. https://web.archive.org/web/20171201001352/http://www.copa-cogeca .be/Download.ashx?ID=216627 (accessed December 1, 2017).

2008a. The Binding Minimum Objective of 10% for Biofuels in Transport Must be Maintained. http://web.archive.org/web/20130516000154/http:// www.copa-cogeca.be/Download.ashx?ID=393440&fmt=pdf (accessed December 16, 2016).

2008b. Bioenergy: European Production Offers the Best Guarantee of Sustainability! http://web.archive.org/web/20171202012932/http://www .copa-cogeca.be/Download.ashx?ID=348331&fmt=pdf (accessed December 2, 2017).

2008c. Biofuels: A Response to Public Concerns from European Farmers and Their Cooperatives. http://web.archive.org/web/20171202013123/ http://www.copa-cogeca.be/Download.ashx?ID=466328 (accessed December 2, 2017).

2008d. COPA and COGECA Position on the Proposal for a Directive on the Promotion of the Use of Energy from Renewable Sources (COM (2008) 19 final). http://web.archive.org/web/20171202013228/http:// www.copa-cogeca.be/Download.ashx?ID=379924&fmt=pdf (accessed December 2, 2017).

Corréard, Bruno. 2010. European Commission Work on Ecolabel of Responsible Fishing-Summary. https://web.archive.org/web/20110225 042853/http://www.sustainablefood.org/fisheries-/82-europeancommis sion-work-on-ecolabel-of-responsible-fishing-summary (accessed March 15, 2014).

Council of the European Communities. 1985. Council Directive 85/536/EEC of 5 December 1985 on Crude-Oil Savings through the Use of Substitute Fuel Components in Petrol. OJ 1985 No. L334/20.

1986. Council Resolution of 16 September 1986 concerning New Community Energy Policy Objective for 1995 and Convergence of the Policies of the Member States. OJ 1986 No. C241/1.

1991. Council Regulation (EEC) No 2092/91 of 24 June 1991 on Organic Production of Agricultural Products and Indications Referring Thereto on Agricultural Products and Foodstuffs. OJ 1991 No. L198/1.

Council of the European Union. 1995. Council Regulation (EC) No 1935/95 of 22 June 1995 Amending Regulation (EEC) No 2092/91 on Organic Production of Agricultural Products and Indications Referring Thereto on Agricultural Products and Foodstuffs. OJ 1995 No. L185/1.

1998. Press Statement of the Council of Ministers of Agriculture, June 26, 1998. On file with author.

1999. Council Regulation (EC) No 856/1999 of 22 April 1999 Establishing a Special Framework of Assistance for Traditional ACP Suppliers of Bananas. OJ 1999 No. L108/2.

2002a. Common Position (EC) No 1/2003 Adopted by the Council on 18 November 2002 with a View to the Adoption of a Directive 2003/.../EC on the Promotion of the Use of Biofuels or Other Renewable Fuels for Transport. OJ 2003 No. C32E/1.

2002b. Council Regulation (EC) No 2371/2002 of 20 December 2002 on the Conservation and Sustainable Exploitation of Fisheries Resources under the Common Fisheries Policy. OJ 2002 No. L358/59.

2002c. Draft Minutes 2433rd Meeting of the Council (Industry/Energy), Luxembourg, June 6–7, 2002. http://web.archive.org/web/201712020 13341/http://register.consilium.europa.eu/doc/srv?l=EN&f=ST%20970 1%202002%20INIT (accessed December 2, 2017).

2002d. Report from the Special Committee on Agriculture. Organic Farming. https://web.archive.org/web/20171201001506/http://register .consilium.europa.eu/doc/srv?l=EN&f=ST%2012071%202002%20IN IT (accessed December 1, 2017).

2003a. 2476th Council Meeting, Agriculture and Fisheries, Brussels, December 16–20, 2002. Press Release. https://web.archive.org/web/ 20171201002005/http://europa.eu/rapid/press-release_PRES-02-399_en .htm (accessed December 1, 2017).

2003b. Council Directive 2003/96/EC of 27 October 2003 Restructuring the Community Framework for the Taxation of Energy Products and Electricity. OJ 2003 No. L283/51.

2003c. Monthly Summary of Council Acts. April 2003. http://web.archive .org/web/20171202013548/http://data.consilium.europa.eu/doc/document/ ST-10085-2003-INIT/en/pdf (accessed December 2, 2017).

2004. 2611th Council Meeting, Agriculture and Fisheries, Luxembourg, October 18, 2004. Press Release. https://web.archive.org/web/2017120 1002737/http://data.consilium.europa.eu/doc/document/ST-13129-2004- INIT/en/pdf (accessed December 1, 2017).

2006a. 2730th Council Meeting, Agriculture and Fisheries, Brussels, May 22, 2006. Press Release. https://web.archive.org/web/20171201002938/ http://data.consilium.europa.eu/doc/document/ST-9170-2006-INIT/en/ pdf (accessed June 6, 2013).

2006b. Presidency Note. Special Committee on Agriculture, June 28, 2006. https://web.archive.org/web/20100821040931/http://www.ifoam .org:80/about_ifoam/around_world/eu_group/PDF_Revision_Organic/ Compromispaper_AT_FIN_28.06.2006.pdf (accessed March 20, 2013).

2006c. Presidency Note. Special Committee on Agriculture, November 9, 2006. On file with author.

2006d. Presidency Note. Special Committee on Agriculture, November 23, 2006. https://web.archive.org/web/20071029131803/http://www.ifoam.org/about_ifoam/around_world/eu_group/PDF_Revision_Organic/proposals_for_council_regulations.pdf (accessed March 20, 2013).

2006e. Presidency Note. Special Committee on Agriculture, October 25, 2006. On file with author.

2006f. Presidency Note. Working Party on Foodstuff Quality (Organic Farming), April 28, 2006. https://web.archive.org/web/20080820040108/http://www.ifoam.org/about_ifoam/around_world/eu_group/PDF_Revision_Organic/Compromisetext_Council_2006_28.4.06.pdf (accessed March 20, 2013).

2007a. 2793rd Council Meeting, Agriculture and Fisheries, Luxembourg, April 16, 2007. Press Release. https://web.archive.org/web/20171004194956/http://www.consilium.europa.eu/ueDocs/cms_Data/docs/pressData/en/agricult/93679.pdf (accessed October 4, 2017).

2007b. Council Regulation (EC) No 834/2007 of 29 June 2007 on Organic Production and Labelling of Organic Products and Repealing Regulation (EEC) No 2092/91. OJ 2007 No. L189/1.

2007c. Presidency Conclusions of the Brussels European Council, March 8–9, 2007. https://web.archive.org/web/20170107051211/http://www.consilium.europa.eu/ueDocs/cms_Data/docs/pressData/en/ec/93135.pdf (accessed January 7, 2017).

2008a. 2874th Council Meeting, Environment, Luxembourg, June 5, 2008. Press Release. http://web.archive.org/web/20171202013856/http://europa.eu/rapid/press-release_PRES-08-149_en.pdf (accessed December 2, 2017).

2008b. 2875th Council Meeting, Transport, Telecommunications and Energy, Luxembourg, June 6, 2008. Press Release. http://web.archive.org/web/20171202014803/http://europa.eu/rapid/press-release_PRES-08-162_en.pdf (accessed December 2, 2017).

2008c. Presidency Conclusions of the Brussels European Council, June 19–20, 2008. http://web.archive.org/web/20171202014944/http://register.consilium.europa.eu/doc/srv?l=EN&t=PDF&gc=true&sc=false&f=ST%2011018%202008%20REV%201&r=http%3A%2F%2Fregister.consilium.europa.eu%2Fpd%2Fen%2F08%2Fst11%2Fst11018-re01.en08.pdf (accessed December 2, 2017).

2011. 3108th Council Meeting, Agriculture and Fisheries, Brussels, July 19, 2011. Press Release. https://web.archive.org/web/20111027171108/http://www.consilium.europa.eu/uedocs/cms_data/docs/pressdata/en/agricult/123967.pdf (accessed March 18, 2014).

2012a. 3155th Council Meeting, Agriculture and Fisheries, Brussels, March 19–20, 2012. Press Release. https://web.archive.org/web/20171 209221918/http://europa.eu/rapid/press-release_PRES-12-115_en.pdf (accessed December 9, 2017).

2012b. 3174th Council Meeting, Agriculture and Fisheries, Luxembourg, June 12, 2012. Press Release. https://web.archive.org/web/2017120922 2013/http://europa.eu/rapid/press-release_PRES-12-258_en.pdf (accessed December 9, 2017).

2012c. Agriculture and Fisheries. Fisheries I. Tuesday, June 12, 2012 at 10.00. Webcast. https://video.consilium.europa.eu/en/webcast/113d75b a-4946-4a4a-99ef-7df9754bb486 (accessed December 9, 2017).

2012d. Outcome of Proceedings. Proposal for a Regulation of the European Parliament and of the Council on the Common Organisation of the Markets in Fishery and Aquaculture Products: General Approach. https://web.archive.org/web/20171209223725/http://data.consilium .europa.eu/doc/document/ST-10415-2012-INIT/en/pdf (accessed December 9, 2017).

2012e. Outcome of Proceedings. Proposal for a Regulation of the European Parliament and of the Council on the Common Organisation of the Markets in Fishery and Aquaculture Products: General Approach: Council Statement. https://web.archive.org/web/20171209223839/http:// data.consilium.europa.eu/doc/document/ST-10415-2012-ADD-1/en/pdf (accessed December 9, 2017).

2015. Position (EU) No 2/2015 of the Council at First Reading. OJ 2015 No. C50/1.

Cramer Commission. 2007. Testing Framework for Sustainable Biomass. Final Report from the Project Group "Sustainable Production of Biomass." https://web.archive.org/web/20190729025837/http://www .globalbioenergy.org/uploads/media/0703_Sustainable_Production_of__ Sustainable_production_of_biomass__Cramer__-_Testing_framework_ for_sustainable_biomass_01.pdf (accessed February 15, 2014).

Cremona, Marise, and Gracia Marin Duran. 2013a. Fair Trade in the European Union. In Granville, Brigitte and Janet Dine, eds. *The Processes and Practices of Fair Trade: Trust, Ethics, and Governance*. London: Routledge, 122–196.

2013b. The International Fair Trade Movement: Actors and Regulatory Approaches. In Granville, Brigitte and Janet Dine, eds. *The Processes and Practices of Fair Trade: Trust, Ethics, and Governance*. London: Routledge, 96–121.

Cutler, A. Claire. 2003. *Private Power and Global Authority: Transnational Merchant Law in the Global Political Economy*. Cambridge: Cambridge University Press.

2006. Transnational Business Civilization, Corporations, and the Privatization of Global Governance. In May, Christopher, ed. *Global Corporate Power*. Boulder: Lynne Rienner, 199–225.

Cutler, A. Claire, Virginia Haufler, and Tony Porter. 1999a. Private Authority and International Affairs. In Cutler, A. Claire, Virginia Haufler, and Tony Porter, eds. *Private Authority and International Affairs*. Albany: State University of New York Press, 3–28.

Cutler, A. Claire, Virginia Haufler, and Tony Porter, eds. 1999b. *Private Authority and International Affairs*. Albany: State University of New York Press.

D'Hollander, David, and Axel Marx. 2014. Strengthening Private Certification Systems through Public Regulation: The Case of Sustainable Public Procurement. *Sustainability Accounting, Management and Policy Journal*, 5(1), 2–21.

Damro, Chad. 2012. Market Power Europe. *Journal of European Public Policy*, 19(5), 682–699.

Danish Ministry of Food, Agriculture and Fisheries. 2001. Organic Food and Farming: Towards Partnership and Action in Europe. May 10–11, 2001. Conference Proceedings. https://web.archive.org/web/20130909060940/http://www.organic-europe.net/fileadmin/documents/country_information/europe/policy/danish-ministry-2001-proceedings-copenhagen.pdf (accessed September 9, 2013).

Darby, Michael R., and Edi Karni. 1973. Free Competition and the Optimal Amount of Fraud. *Journal of Law and Economics*, 16(1), 67–88.

Daugbjerg, Carsten. 1999. Reforming the CAP: Policy Networks and Broader Institutional Structures. *Journal of Common Market Studies*, 37(3), 407–428.

2012. Globalization and Internal Policy Dynamics in the Reform of the Common Agricultural Policy. In Richardson, Jeremy, ed. *Constructing a Policy-Making State? Policy Dynamics in the EU*. Oxford: Oxford University Press, 88–103.

Dauvergne, Peter. 2016. *Environmentalism of the Rich*. Cambridge: MIT Press.

Dauvergne, Peter, and Jane Lister. 2013. *Eco-Business: A Big Brand Takeover of Sustainability*. Cambridge: MIT Press.

de la Cuesta González, Marta, and Carmen Valor Martinez. 2004. Fostering Corporate Social Responsibility through Public Initiative: From the EU to the Spanish Case. *Journal of Business Ethics*, 55(3), 275–293.

Dehue, Bart, Carlo Hamelinck, Saskia de Lint, Richard Archer, Esther Garcia, and Eric van den Heuvel. 2007. Sustainability Reporting within the RTFO: Framework Report. http://web.archive.org/web/20171202020058/http://iet.jrc.ec.europa.eu/remea/sites/remea/files/sustainability_reporting_rtfo.pdf (accessed December 2, 2017).

Dehue, Bart, Sebastian Meyer, and Carlo Hamelinck. 2007. *Towards a Harmonised Sustainable Biomass Certification Scheme*. Utrecht: Ecofys Netherlands.

Delmas, Magali A. 2002. The Diffusion of Environmental Management Standards in Europe and in the United States: An Institutional Perspective. *Policy Sciences*, 35(1), 91–119.

Delreux, Tom, and Sander Happaerts. 2016. *Environmental Policy and Politics in the European Union*. London: Palgrave Macmillan.

Demeter. 2017. History. https://web.archive.org/web/20170627083630/http://www.demeter.net/what-is-demeter/history (accessed December 1, 2017).

den Hertog, Johan. 2010. Review of Economic Theories of Regulation. Tjalling C. Koopmans Research Institute Discussion Paper Series nr. 10–18. http://ideas.repec.org/p/use/tkiwps/1018.html (accessed August 30, 2012).

Dimitri, Carolyn, and Lydia Oberholtzer. 2005. *Market-Led Versus Government-Facilitated Growth: Development of the U.S. and EU Organic Agricultural Sectors*. Washington, DC: US Department of Agriculture Economic Research Service.

Dingwerth, Klaus, and Philipp Pattberg. 2009. World Politics and Organizational Fields: The Case of Transnational Sustainability Governance. *European Journal of International Relations*, 15(4), 707–744.

Dionigi, Maja Kluger. 2017. *Lobbying in the European Parliament: The Battle for Influence*. Cham: Springer.

Distelhorst, Greg, Richard M. Locke, Timea Pal, and Hiram Samel. 2015. Production Goes Global, Compliance Stays Local: Private Regulation in the Global Electronics Industry. *Regulation & Governance*, 9(3), 224–242.

Dobbin, Frank, Beth Simmons, and Geoffrey Garrett. 2007. The Global Diffusion of Public Policies: Social Construction, Coercion, Competition, or Learning? *Annual Review of Sociology*, 33, 449–472.

Drezner, Daniel W. 2007. *All Politics Is Global: Explaining International Regulatory Regimes*. Princeton: Princeton University Press.

Dür, Andreas, Patrick Bernhagen, and David Marchall. 2015. Interest Group Success in the European Union: When (and Why) Does Business Lose? *Comparative Political Studies*, 48(8), 951–983.

Dür, Andreas, and Dirk De Bièvre. 2007. The Question of Interest Group Influence. *Journal of Public Policy*, 27(1), 1–12.

Dür, Andreas, and Gemma Mateo. 2013. Gaining Access or Going Public? Interest Group Strategies in Five European Countries. *European Journal of Political Research*, 52(5), 660–686.

EBB. 2007a. EBB Comments to the Commission Consultation on Biofuels Issues in the New Legislation on the Promotion of Renewable Energy.

https://web.archive.org/web/20071012015748/http://www.ebb-eu.org/
EBBpressreleases/EBB%20answer%20consultation%20sustainability%
20445PRO07final.pdf (accessed April 24, 2013).

2007b. EBB Welcomes the Conclusion of the European Summit on Energy
and Encourages Rapid Implementation. Press Release, March 19, 2007.
https://web.archive.org/web/20071012015823/http://www.ebb-eu.org/
EBBpressreleases/EBB%20press%20release%20B99%20international
%20biodiesel%20trade.pdf (accessed April 24, 2013).

Ebeling, Johannes, and Maï Yasué. 2009. The Effectiveness of Market-
Based Conservation in the Tropics: Forest Certification in Ecuador
and Bolivia. *Journal of Environmental Management*, 90(2), 1145–
1153.

Eberlein, Burkard, Kenneth W. Abbott, Julia Black, Errol Meidinger, and
Stepan Wood. 2014. Transnational Business Governance Interactions:
Conceptualization and Framework for Analysis. *Regulation & Govern-
ance*, 8(1), 1–21.

Eberlein, Burkard, and Dieter Kerwer. 2004. New Governance in the European Union: A Theoretical Perspective. *Journal of Common Market
Studies*, 42(1), 121–142.

eBIO. 2007a. eBIO Welcomes Binding Minimum Biofuels Target for 2020.
Press Release, November 11, 2007. https://web.archive.org/web/
20111107123920/http://epure.org/pressreleases/2007 (accessed January 23, 2014).

2007b. eBIO: "Great News for the EU Bioethanol Industry." Press
Release, March 9, 2007. http://web.archive.org/web/20070715070512/
http://www.ebio.org/downloads/press/070309_Press_release_eBIO_EU_
Council.pdf (accessed January 23, 2014).

2008a. eBIO Welcomes the 10% Mandate of Biofuels. Press Release,
January 23, 2008. On file with author.

2008b. Gallagher Review Disappointing. Press Release, July 10, 2008. On
file with author.

ECF. 2007. ECF Position Paper. Sustainability, Definitions and Labels.
https://web.archive.org/web/20190729030130/https://www.ecf-coffee.org
/images/stories/ECF_Position_Paper_Sustainability_final.pdf (accessed
February 15, 2014).

Eckstein, Anne. 2008. Informal Energy Council: Ministers "Discover" Biofuels Are Not an Obligation. *Europolitics*, No. 0247.

Ecofys, Fraunhofer, Becker Buttner Held, Energy Economics Group, and
Winrock International. 2012. Renewable Energy Progress and Biofuels
Sustainability. https://web.archive.org/web/20171202023443/https://hub
.globalccsinstitute.com/sites/default/files/publications/115618/renewable-
energy-progress-biofuels-sustainability.pdf (accessed December 2, 2017).

Economist Intelligence Unit. 2003. EU Regulations: Parliament Backs Down on Biofuels. *EIU Viewswire*, April 8, 2003.

EESC. 1990. Opinion on the Proposal for a Council Regulation (EEC) on Organic Production of Agricultural Products and Indications Referring Thereto on Agricultural Products and Foodstuffs. OJ 1990 No. C182/12.

1996. Opinion on the "European 'Fair Trade' Marking Movement." OJ 1996 No. C204/41.

2002. Opinion on the "Proposal for a Directive of the European Parliament and of the Council on the Promotion of the Use of Biofuels for Transport." OJ 2002 No. C149/7.

2005. Opinion on "Ethical Trade and Consumer Assurance Schemes." OJ 2006 No. C28/72.

2006. Opinion on the Communication from the Commission on Launching a Debate on a Community Approach towards Eco-Labelling Schemes for Fisheries Products. OJ 2006 No. C88/27.

2009. Opinion on the "Proposal for a Directive of the European Parliament and of the Council on the Promotion of the Use of Energy from Renewable Sources." OJ 2009 No. C77/43.

EFTA. 2008. Contribution to DG Trade's Civil Society Dialogue Meeting on: "Fair Trade: State of Play." https://web.archive.org/web/20150409102713/http://trade.ec.europa.eu/doclib/docs/2008/june/tradoc_139325.pdf (accessed October 14, 2016).

2015. European Fair Trade Association. https://web.archive.org/web/20161202202426/http://www.european-fair-trade-association.org/efta/index.php (accessed December 5, 2016).

Eising, Rainer. 2007. Institutional Context, Organizational Resources and Strategic Choices. *European Union Politics*, 8(3), 329–362.

2008. Clientelism, Committees, Pluralism and Protests in the European Union: Matching Patterns? *West European Politics*, 31(6), 1166–1187.

Eising, Rainer, Daniel Rasch, and Patrycja Rozbicka. 2017. National Interest Organisations in EU Policy-Making. *West European Politics*, 40(5), 939–956.

Eising, Rainer, Daniel Rasch, Patrycja Rozbicka, Danica Fink-Hafner, Mitja Hafner-Fink, and Meta Novak. 2017. Who Says What to Whom? Alignments and Arguments in EU Policy-Making. *West European Politics*, 40(5), 957–980.

Ernst & Young, AND International, Cogea, and Eurofish. 2008. Evaluation of the Common Organisation of the Markets in Fishery and Aquaculture Products. Executive Summary. https://web.archive.org/web/20171209223955/https://ec.europa.eu/fisheries/sites/fisheries/files/docs/body/evaluation_markets_summary_en.pdf (accessed December 9, 2017).

2009. Study on the Supply and Marketing of Fishery and Aquaculture Products in the European Union. Executive Summary. https://web.archive .org/web/20160602185019/http://ec.europa.eu/fisheries/documentation/ studies/study_market/fap_exec_summary_en.pdf (accessed June 2, 2016).

Espach, Ralph H. 2006. When Is Sustainable Forestry Sustainable? The Forest Stewardship Council in Argentina and Brazil. *Global Environmental Politics*, 6(2), 55–84.

2009. *Private Environmental Regimes in Developing Countries: Globally Sown, Locally Grown*. New York: Palgrave Macmillan.

Ethical Tea Partnership. 2014. Our Partners: Members (Tea Companies). https://web.archive.org/web/20140313011242/http://www .ethicalteapartnership.org/our-partners/tea-company-members/ (accessed March 13, 2014).

2017a. History. https://web.archive.org/web/20170711022822/http:// www.ethicalteapartnership.org/about-etp/history/ (accessed October 10, 2017).

2017b. Monitoring & Certification. https://web.archive.org/web/ 20170710171426/http://www.ethicalteapartnership.org/project/ monitoring-certification/ (accessed October 10, 2017).

Ethical Trade Fact-finding Process. 2010. Assuring Consumer Confidence in Ethical Trade. Summary. https://web.archive.org/web/20171201185631/ https://www.isealalliance.org/sites/default/files/ETFP_Summary.pdf (accessed December 1, 2017).

EurActiv. 2008a. EU Agrees 10% "Green Fuel" Target in Renewables Deal. https://web.archive.org/web/20140301105423/http://www.euractiv .com/transport/eu-agrees-10-green-fuel-target-r-news-220953 (accessed March 1, 2014).

2008b. EU Lawmakers Split over Biofuels. https://web.archive.org/web/ 20130630034555/http://www.euractiv.com/transport/eu-lawmakers- split-biofuels-news-220824 (accessed June 30, 2013).

2008c. EU, Brazil "Deepen" Energy Cooperation. https://web.archive.org/ web/20120417042320/http://www.euractiv.com/energy/eu-brazil- deepen-energy-cooperation/article-177435 (accessed April 17, 2012).

2011. Biofuels for Transport. https://web.archive.org/web/20130916165527/ http://www.euractiv.com/transport/biofuels-transport-linksdossier-188374? display=normal (accessed September 16, 2013).

EURO COOP. 2008. EURO COOP Contribution to the European Commission Civil Society Dialogue on Fair Trade. https://web.archive.org/ web/20150409093539/http://trade.ec.europa.eu/doclib/docs/2008/june/ tradoc_139328.pdf (accessed October 14, 2016).

EurObserv'ER. 2013. Biofuels Barometer. *Systèmes Solaires. Le Journal des Énergies Renouvelables*, 216, 48–63.

2016. Biofuels Barometer. July 2016. https://web.archive.org/web/20171203150254/https://www.eurobserv-er.org/pdf/biofuels-barometer-2016-en/ (accessed December 3, 2017).

European Commission. 1985a. A Future for Community Agriculture. Commission Guidelines following the Consultations in Connection with the Green Paper (COM(85)750). https://web.archive.org/web/20120312052054/http://aei.pitt.edu/930/1/perspective_for_cap_gp_follow_COM_85_750.pdf (accessed May 13, 2013).

1985b. Perspectives for the Common Agricultural Policy (COM(85)333). https://web.archive.org/web/20120311161645/http://aei.pitt.edu/931/1/perspectives_for_cap_gp_COM_85_333.pdf (accessed March 11, 2012).

1989. Proposal for a Council Regulation (EEC) on Organic Production of Agricultural Products and Indications Referring Thereto on Agricultural Products and Foodstuffs. OJ 1990 No. C4/4.

1992a. Commission Regulation (EEC) No 94/92 of 14 January 1992 Laying Down Detailed Rules for Implementing the Arrangements for Imports from Third Countries Provided for in Regulation (EEC) No 2092/91 on Organic Production of Agricultural Products and Indications Referring Thereto on Agricultural Products and Foodstuffs. OJ 1992 No. L11/14.

1992b. Commission Regulation (EEC) No 3457/92 of 30 November 1992 Laying Down Detailed Rules concerning the Inspection Certificate for Imports from Third Countries into the Community Provided for in Council Regulation (EEC) No 2092/91 on Organic Production of Agricultural Products and Indications Referring Thereto on Agricultural Products and Foodstuffs. OJ 1992 No. L350/56.

1993. Proposal for a Council Regulation Amending Regulation (EEC) No 2092/91 on Organic Production of Agricultural Products and Indications Referring Thereto on Agricultural Products and Foodstuffs. OJ 1993 No. C326/8.

1995. An Energy Policy for the European Union (COM(95)682). https://web.archive.org/web/20190729030348/https://eur-lex.europa.eu/legal-content/EN/TXT/PDF/?uri=CELEX:51995DC0682&qid=1512313647605&from=EN (accessed July 23, 2013).

1996a. Energy for the Future: Renewable Sources of Energy (COM(96)576). https://web.archive.org/web/20171203151145/http://aei.pitt.edu/1280/1/renewalbe_energy_gp_COM_96_576.pdf (accessed December 3, 2017).

1996b. Proposal for a Council Regulation (EC) Supplementing Regulation (EEC) No 2092/91 on Organic Production of Agricultural Products and Indications Referring Thereto on Agricultural Products and Foodstuffs to Include Livestock Production. OJ 1996 No. C293/23.

1997a. Energy for the Future: Renewable Sources of Energy (COM(97) 599). https://web.archive.org/web/20180419175217/http://aei.pitt.edu/1130/1/energy_white_paper_COM_97_599.pdf (accessed April 19, 2018).

1997b. The Future for the Market in Fisheries Products in the European Union. Responsibility, Partnership and Competitiveness (COM(97) 719). https://web.archive.org/web/20171209224340/http://aei.pitt.edu/6224/1/6224.pdf (accessed December 9, 2017).

1998a. Amended Proposal for a Council Regulation (EC) Supplementing Regulation (EEC) No 2092/91 on Organic Production of Agricultural Products and Indications Referring Thereto on Agricultural Products and Foodstuffs to Include Livestock Production. OJ 1998 No. C61/6.

1998b. Commission Regulation (EC) No 1726/98 of 22 July 1998 on the Protection of Geographical Indications and Designations of Origin for Agricultural Products and Foodstuffs. OJ 1998 No. L224/1.

1999. Communication on "Fair Trade" (COM(1999)619). https://web .archive.org/web/20190729025101/https://eur-lex.europa.eu/legal-content/EN/TXT/PDF/?uri=CELEX:51999DC0619&from=EN (accessed March 17, 2013).

2000a. Commission Regulation (EC) No 331/2000 of 17 December 1999 Amending Annex V to Council Regulation (EEC) No 2092/91 on Organic Production of Agricultural Products and Indications Referring Thereto on Agricultural Products and Foodstuffs. OJ 2000 No. L48/1.

2000b. Towards a European Strategy for the Security of Energy Supply (COM(2000)769). https://web.archive.org/web/20131224191243/http://eur-lex.europa.eu/LexUriServ/LexUriServ.do?uri=CELEX:52000DC0769:EN:HTML (accessed December 19, 2016).

2001a. Communication on Alternative Fuels for Road Transportation and on a Set of Measures to Promote the Use of Biofuels (COM(2001)547). https://web.archive.org/web/20190729025336/https://eur-lex.europa .eu/LexUriServ/LexUriServ.do?uri=COM:2001:0547:FIN:EN:PDF (accessed July 23, 2013).

2001b. European Transport Policy for 2010: Time to Decide (COM (2001)370). https://web.archive.org/web/20171203152043/https://ec .europa.eu/transport/sites/transport/files/themes/strategies/doc/2001_white_paper/lb_com_2001_0370_en.pdf (accessed December 3, 2017).

2001c. Proposal for a Directive of the European Parliament and of the Council on the Promotion of the Use of Biofuels for Transport. OJ 2002 No. C103E/205.

2002a. Amended Proposal for a Directive of the European Parliament and of the Council on the Promotion of the Use of Biofuels for Transport. OJ 2002 No. C331E/291.

2002b. Analysis of the Possibility of a European Action Plan for Organic Food and Farming (SEC(2002)1368). https://web.archive.org/web/20171201032019/http://orgapet.orgap.org/annexes/annex_A4–7.pdf (accessed December 1, 2017).

2002c. Communication on the Reform of the Common Fisheries Policy ("Roadmap") (COM(2002)181). https://web.archive.org/web/20190729030551/https://eur-lex.europa.eu/legal-content/EN/TXT/PDF/?uri=CELEX:52002DC0181&qid=1512860050858&from=EN (accessed December 9, 2017).

2002d. Setting Out a Community Action Plan to Integrate Environmental Protection Requirements into the Common Fisheries Policy (COM (2002)186). https://web.archive.org/web/20091027125506/http://eur-lex.europa.eu/LexUriServ/LexUriServ.do?uri=COM:2002:0186:FIN:EN:PDF (accessed March 12, 2014).

2004a. Agricultural Commodity Chains, Dependence and Poverty: A Proposal for an EU Action Plan (COM(2004)89). https://web.archive.org/web/20190729031106/https://eur-lex.europa.eu/legal-content/EN/TXT/PDF/?uri=CELEX:52004DC0089&from=EN (accessed April 9, 2014).

2004b. Commission Regulation (EC) No 746/2004 of 22 April 2004 Adapting Certain Regulations concerning Organic Production of Agricultural Products and Indications Referring Thereto on Agricultural Products and Foodstuffs by Reason of the Accession of the Czech Republic, Estonia, Cyprus, Latvia, Lithuania, Hungary, Malta, Poland, Slovenia and Slovakia to the European Union. OJ 2004 No. L122/10.

2004c. European Action Plan for Organic Food and Farming (COM (2004)415). https://web.archive.org/web/20130825045925/http://eur-lex.europa.eu:80/LexUriServ/LexUriServ.do?uri=COM:2004:0415:FIN:EN:PDF (accessed August 25, 2013).

2004d. European Action Plan for Organic Food and Farming. Annex (SEC (2004)739). https://web.archive.org/web/20060507060746/http://www.depa.unina.it/depa/PianoAzioneUE_2.pdf (accessed June 4, 2013).

2004e. *European Code of Sustainable and Responsible Fisheries Practices.* Luxembourg: Office for Official Publications of the European Communities.

2005a. Biomass Action Plan (COM(2005)628). https://web.archive.org/web/20190729031913/https://eur-lex.europa.eu/legal-content/EN/TXT/PDF/?uri=CELEX:52005DC0628&from=EN (accessed June 11, 2017).

2005b. EU Biomass Action Plan External Stakeholders Group Meeting. Minutes of the Meeting. On file with author.

2005c. Launching a Debate on a Community Approach towards Eco-Labelling Schemes for Fisheries Products (COM(2005)275). https://web.archive.org/web/20070714194910/http://eur-lex.europa.eu/LexUriServ/site/en/com/2005/com2005_0275en01.pdf (accessed March 12, 2014).

2005d. Launching a Debate on a Community Approach towards Eco-Labelling Schemes for Fisheries Products. Impact Assessment (SEC (2005)840). https://web.archive.org/web/20190729032146/https://eur-lex.europa.eu/legal-content/EN/TXT/HTML/?uri=CELEX:52005SC0840&from=EN (accessed March 12, 2014).

2005e. Organic Food: New Regulation Will Improve Clarity for Consumers and Farmers. Press Release, December 21, 2005. https://web.archive.org/web/20130221151000/http://europa.eu:80/rapid/press-release_IP-05-1679_en.htm (accessed February 21, 2013).

2005f. Proposal for a Council Regulation on Organic Production and Labelling of Organic Products (COM(2005)671). https://web.archive.org/web/20190729031722/https://eur-lex.europa.eu/LexUriServ/LexUriServ.do?uri=COM:2005:0671:FIN:EN:PDF%20 (accessed March 15, 2013).

2006a. Commission Regulation (EEC) No 94/92 of 14 January 1992 Laying Down Detailed Rules for Implementing the Arrangements for Imports from Third Countries Provided for in Regulation (EEC) No 2092/91 on Organic Production of Agricultural Products and Indications Referring Thereto on Agricultural Products and Foodstuffs. (consolidated version). https://web.archive.org/web/20190729033043/https://eur-lex.europa.eu/legal-content/EN/TXT/PDF/?uri=CELEX:01992R0094–20060706&rid=2 (accessed May 16, 2014).

2006b. Eco-Labelling Schemes for Fisheries Products. Commission Response to Text Adopted in Plenary. https://web.archive.org/web/20171210013704/http://www.europarl.europa.eu/oeil/spdoc.do?i=11329&j=0&l=en (accessed December 10, 2017).

2006c. An EU Strategy for Biofuels (COM(2006)34). https://web.archive.org/web/20190729032434/https://eur-lex.europa.eu/LexUriServ/LexUriServ.do?uri=COM:2006:0034:FIN:EN:PDF (accessed December 19, 2016).

2006d. An EU Strategy for Biofuels. Impact Assessment (SEC(2006)142). https://web.archive.org/web/20171203153139/http://eur-lex.europa.eu/legal-content/EN/TXT/?uri=CELEX:52006SC0142 (accessed December 3, 2017).

2006e. Implementing Sustainability in EU Fisheries through Maximum Sustainable Yield (COM(2006)360). https://web.archive.org/web/

20070714194818/http://eur-lex.europa.eu/LexUriServ/site/en/com/2006/ com2006_0360en01.pdf (accessed March 16, 2014).

2007a. Biofuel Issues in the New Legislation on the Promotion of Renewable Energy. Public Consultation Exercise, April–May 2007. https:// web.archive.org/web/20140725184759/http://ec.europa.eu/energy/res/ consultation/doc/2007_06_04_biofuels/2007_06_04_public_consultation_ biofuels_en.pdf (accessed December 19, 2016).

2007b. Biofuels Progress Report (COM(2006)845). https://web.archive .org/web/20170605050755/http://eur-lex.europa.eu/legal-content/EN/ TXT/?uri=CELEX:52006DC0845 (accessed June 5, 2017).

2007c. Biofuels Progress Report. Review of Economic and Environmental Data for the Biofuels Progress Report (SEC(2006)1721). https://web .archive.org/web/20171203154216/http://www.ipex.eu/IPEXL-WEB/ dossier/files/download/082dbcc530b1bf490130bc6f3c99526f.do (accessed December 3, 2017).

2007d. An Energy Policy for Europe (COM(2007)1). https://web .archive.org/web/20180116065536/http://eur-lex.europa.eu/LexUriServ/ LexUriServ.do?uri=COM:2007:0001:FIN:EN:PDF (accessed January 11, 2014).

2007e. A Policy to Reduce Unwanted By-Catches and Eliminate Discards in European Fisheries (COM(2007)136). https://web.archive.org/web/ 20130130135339/http://eur-lex.europa.eu/LexUriServ/LexUriServ.do? uri=COM:2007:0136:FIN:EN:PDF (accessed March 16, 2014).

2007f. Renewable Energy Road Map. Renewable Energies in the 21st Century: Building a More Sustainable Future (COM(2006)848). https://web.archive.org/web/20190517000120/https://eur-lex.europa .eu/LexUriServ/LexUriServ.do?uri=COM:2006:0848:FIN:EN:PDF (accessed December 19, 2016).

2007g. Renewable Energy Road Map. Renewable Energies in the 21st Century: Building a More Sustainable Future. Impact Assessment (SEC(2006)1719). https://web.archive.org/web/20171203154759/http:// eur-lex.europa.eu/legal-content/EN/TXT/?uri=CELEX:52006SC1719 (accessed December 3, 2017).

2008a. Commission Regulation (EC) No 1235/2008 of 8 December 2008 Laying Down Detailed Rules for Implementation of Council Regulation (EC) No 834/2007 as Regards the Arrangements for Imports of Organic Products from Third Countries. OJ 2008 No. L334/25.

2008b. Discussion Paper for the 3 June Civil Society Meeting on Fair Trade. https://web.archive.org/web/20160626132438/http://trade .ec.europa.eu/doclib/html/138964.htm (accessed October 14, 2016).

2008c. Guidelines on Imports of Organic Products into the European Union. https://web.archive.org/web/20171201033803/https://ec.europa

.eu/agriculture/organic/sites/orgfarming/files/docs/body/guidelines_for_imports_en.pdf (accessed December 1, 2017).

2008d. Impact Assessment. Document Accompanying the Package of Implementation Measures for the EU's Objectives on Climate Change and Renewable Energy for 2020 (SEC(2008)85). https://web.archive.org/web/20170122230915/http://ec.europa.eu/transparency/regdoc/rep/2/2008/EN/2-2008-85-EN-1-0.Pdf (accessed December 3, 2017).

2008e. Minutes of Ad Hoc Meeting – Fair Trade: State of Play, June 3, 2008. https://web.archive.org/web/20160626132438/http://trade.ec.europa.eu/doclib/html/139103.htm (accessed October 14, 2016).

2008f. Proposal for a Directive of the European Parliament and of the Council on the Promotion of the Use of Energy from Renewable Sources (COM(2008)19). https://web.archive.org/web/20190729164747/https://eur-lex.europa.eu/legal-content/EN/TXT/PDF/?uri=CELEX:52008PC0019&qid=1551975248066&from=EN (accessed January 10, 2014).

2008g. Reflections on Further Reform of the Common Fisheries Policy. https://web.archive.org/web/20140207190123/http://www.cfp-reformwatch.eu/pdf/reflection_cfp_08_mid.pdf (accessed March 16, 2014).

2009a. Commission Regulation (EC) No 710/2009 of 5 August 2009 on Laying Down Detailed Rules on Organic Aquaculture Animal and Seaweed Production. OJ 2009 No. L204/15.

2009b. Contributing to Sustainable Development: The Role of Fair Trade and Non-Governmental Trade-Related Sustainability Assurance Schemes (COM(2009)215). https://web.archive.org/web/20171017002405/http://eur-lex.europa.eu/LexUriServ/LexUriServ.do?uri=COM:2009:0215:FIN:EN:PDF (accessed November 2, 2012).

2009c. Reform of the Common Fisheries Policy (COM(2009)163). https://web.archive.org/web/20190611053523/https://eur-lex.europa.eu/LexUriServ/LexUriServ.do?uri=COM:2009:0163:FIN:EN:PDF (accessed March 17, 2014).

2009d. The Renewable Energy Progress Report (COM(2009)192). https://web.archive.org/web/20190729165142/https://eur-lex.europa.eu/LexUriServ/LexUriServ.do?uri=COM:2009:0192:FIN:EN:PDF (accessed January 15, 2014).

2010a. An Analysis of the EU Organic Sector. https://web.archive.org/web/20130511191106/http://ec.europa.eu/agriculture/organic/files/eu-policy/data-statistics/facts_en.pdf (accessed May 11, 2013).

2010b. Commission Sets Up System for Certifying Sustainable Biofuels. https://web.archive.org/web/20171204032235/http://europa.eu/rapid/press-release_MEMO-10-247_en.pdf (accessed December 4, 2017).

2010c. EU Best Practice Guidelines for Voluntary Certification Schemes for Agricultural Products and Foodstufs. OJ 2010 No. C341/5.

2010d. Practical Implementation of the EU Biofuels and Bioliquids Sustainability Scheme and on Counting Rules for Biofuels. OJ 2010 No. C160/8.

2010e. Synthesis of the Consultation on the Reform of the Common Fisheries Policy (SEC(2010)428). https://web.archive.org/web/20151115025421/http://ec.europa.eu/fisheries/reform/sec(2010)0428_en.pdf (accessed November 15, 2015).

2010f. Voluntary Schemes and Default Values in the EU Biofuels and Bioliquids Sustainability Scheme. OJ 2010 No. C160/1.

2011a. Certification Schemes for Biofuels. https://web.archive.org/web/20171204032601/http://europa.eu/rapid/press-release_MEMO-11-522_en.pdf (accessed December 4, 2017).

2011b. Commission Implementing Decision of 19 July 2011 on the Recognition of the "Biomass Biofuels Sustainability Voluntary Scheme" for Demonstrating Compliance with the Sustainability Criteria under Directives 2009/28/EC and 2009/30/EC. OJ 2011 No. L190/77.

2011c. Commission Implementing Decision of 19 July 2011 on the Recognition of the "Bonsucro EU" Scheme for Demonstrating Compliance with the Sustainability Criteria under Directives 2009/28/EC and 2009/30/EC. OJ 2011 No. L190/81.

2011d. Commission Implementing Decision of 19 July 2011 on the Recognition of the "Greenergy Brazilian Bioethanol Verification Programme" Scheme for Demonstrating Compliance with the Sustainability Criteria under Directives 2009/28/EC and 2009/30/EC. OJ 2011 No. L190/85.

2011e. Impact Assessment. Accompanying the Document Proposal for a Regulation of the European Parliament and of the Council on the Common Organisation of the Markets in Fishery and Aquaculture Products (SEC(2011)883). https://web.archive.org/web/20171210014607/http://www.europarl.europa.eu/registre/docs_autres_institutions/commission_europeenne/sec/2011/0883/COM_SEC(2011)0883_EN.pdf (accessed December 10, 2017).

2011f. Proposal for a Directive of the European Parliament and of the Council on Public Procurement (COM(2011)896). https://web.archive.org/web/20190729170124/https://eur-lex.europa.eu/legal-content/EN/TXT/PDF/?uri=CELEX:52011PC0896&from=EN (accessed October 15, 2017).

2011g. Proposal for a Regulation of the European Parliament and of the Council on the Common Fisheries Policy (COM(2011)425). https://web.archive.org/web/20190729165927/https://eur-lex.europa.eu/LexUriServ/

LexUriServ.do?uri=COM:2011:0425:FIN:EN:PDF (accessed March 18, 2014).

2011h. Proposal for a Regulation of the European Parliament and of the Council on the Common Organisation of the Markets in Fishery and Aquaculture Products (COM(2011)416). https://web.archive.org/web/20120906062725/http://eur-lex.europa.eu/LexUriServ/LexUriServ.do?uri=COM:2011:0416:FIN:EN:PDF (accessed March 18, 2014).

2011i. Reform of the Common Fisheries Policy (COM(2011)417). https://web.archive.org/web/20120625132113/http://eur-lex.europa.eu/LexUriServ/LexUriServ.do?uri=COM:2011:0417:FIN:EN:PDF (accessed March 18, 2014).

2011j. Renewable Energy: Progressing towards the 2020 Target (COM (2011)31). https://web.archive.org/web/20170730135845/http://eur-lex.europa.eu/LexUriServ/LexUriServ.do?uri=COM:2011:0031:FIN:EN:PDF (accessed January 16, 2014).

2012a. Agriculture in the European Union. Statistical and Economic Information. Report 2012. https://web.archive.org/web/20180119233117/https://ec.europa.eu/agriculture/sites/agriculture/files/statistics/agricultural/2012/pdf/full-report_en.pdf (accessed January 19, 2018).

2012b. Commission Implementing Decision of 16 July 2012 on Recognition of the "Red Tractor Farm Assurance Combinable Crops & Sugar Beet Scheme" for Demonstrating Compliance with the Sustainability Criteria under Directives 98/70/EC and 2009/28/EC. OJ 2012 No. L187/62.

2012c. Commission Implementing Decision of 24 July 2012 on Recognition of the "Scottish Quality Farm Assured Combinable Crops Limited" Scheme for Demonstrating Compliance with the Sustainability Criteria under Directives 98/70/EC and 2009/28/EC. OJ 2012 No. L198/17.

2012d. Commission Implementing Decision of 31 July 2012 on Recognition of the "NTA 8080" Scheme for Demonstrating Compliance with the Sustainability Criteria under Directives 98/70/EC and 2009/28/EC. OJ 2012 No. L205/17.

2012e. Commission Regulation (EC) No 1235/2008 of 8 December 2008 Laying Down Detailed Rules for Implementation of Council Regulation (EC) No 834/2007 as Regards the Arrangements for Imports of Organic Products from Third Countries. Consolidated Version July 1, 2012. https://web.archive.org/web/20190729170324/https://eur-lex.europa.eu/LexUriServ/LexUriServ.do?uri=CONSLEG:2008R1235:20120701:EN:PDF (accessed July 7, 2013).

2012f. A European Consumer Agenda: Boosting Confidence and Growth (COM(2012)225). https://web.archive.org/web/20190729170618/https://eur-lex.europa.eu/legal-content/EN/TXT/PDF/?uri=CELEX:52012DC0225&qid=1497640516110&from=EN (accessed June 16, 2017).

2012g. Proposal for a Directive of the European Parliament and of the Council Amending Directive 98/70/EC Relating to the Quality of Petrol and Diesel Fuels and Amending Directive 2009/28/EC on the Promotion of the Use of Energy from Renewable Sources (COM(2012)595). https://web.archive.org/web/20190729170510/https://eur-lex.europa.eu/legal-content/EN/TXT/PDF/?uri=CELEX:52012PC0595&from=EN (accessed February 25, 2016).

2012h. U.S. – European Union Organic Equivalence Arrangement. Frequently Asked Questions and Answers. https://web.archive.org/web/20131224235614/http://ec.europa.eu/agriculture/organic/files/news/Website_FAQs_EU-US-equivalence_1_June_2012_EN.pdf (accessed December 24, 2013).

2013a. Building the Single Market for Green Products. Facilitating Better Information on the Environmental Performance of Products and Organizations (COM(2013)196). https://web.archive.org/web/20190729170730/https://eur-lex.europa.eu/legal-content/EN/TXT/PDF/?uri=CELEX:52013DC0196&qid=1497641979138&from=EN (accessed June 16, 2017).

2013b. Commission Position on EP Amendments on 1st Reading. On file with author.

2013c. Control Bodies and Control Authorities Approved on 31/12/2011– Updates 21 May 2013. List of Control Bodies and Control Authorities in Charge of Controls in the Organic Sector Provided for in Article 35(b) of Council Regulation (EC) No 834/2007. https://web.archive.org/web/20161230041412/http://biokont.cz/images/eu_control_bodies_authorities_en_20130521.pdf (accessed June 3, 2013).

2013d. Questions and Answers on the Reformed Common Fisheries Policy. https://web.archive.org/web/20171210015322/http://europa.eu/rapid/press-release_MEMO-13-1125_en.pdf (accessed December 10, 2017).

2014a. Commission Implementing Decision of 3 June 2014 on Recognition of the "Gafta Trade Assurance Scheme" for Demonstrating Compliance with the Sustainability Criteria under Directives 2009/28/EC and 98/70/EC. OJ 2014 No. L165/53.

2014b. Commission Implementing Decision of 17 September 2014 on Recognition of the "Trade Assurance Scheme for Combinable Crops" for Demonstrating Compliance with the Sustainability Criteria under Directives 98/70/EC and 2009/28/EC. OJ 2014 No. L276/49.

2014c. Commission Implementing Decision of 17 September 2014 on Recognition of the "Universal Feed Assurance Scheme" for Demonstrating Compliance with the Sustainability Criteria under Directives 98/70/EC and 2009/28/EC. OJ 2014 No. L276/51.

2014d. Communication concerning the Position of the Council at the First Reading on the Adoption of a Directive of the European Parliament and of the Council Amending Directive 98/70/EC Relating to the Quality of Petrol and Diesel Fuels and Amending Directive 2009/28/EC on the Promotion of the Use of Energy from Renewable Sources (COM(2014)748). https://web.archive.org/web/20190729170823/https://eur-lex.europa.eu/legal-content/EN/TXT/PDF/?uri=CELEX:52014PC0748&from=EN (accessed March 31, 2017).

2015a. Better Regulation Agenda: Enhancing Transparency and Scrutiny for Better EU Law-Making. https://web.archive.org/web/20160611170630/http://europa.eu/rapid/press-release_IP-15-4988_en.htm (accessed June 11, 2016).

2015b. Renewable Energy Progress Report (COM(2015)293). https://web.archive.org/web/20190630004757/https://eur-lex.europa.eu/resource.html?uri=cellar:4f8722ce-1347-11e5–8817-01aa75ed71a1.0001.02/DOC_1&format=PDF (accessed September 20, 2017).

2015c. Summary of the Public Consultation on an EU Ecolabel for Fishery and Aquaculture Products. https://web.archive.org/web/20171210030115/https://ec.europa.eu/info/sites/info/files/consultation-eu-ecolabel-for-fishery-aquaculture-products-summary_en_0.pdf (accessed December 10, 2017).

2016a. *The EU Fish Market*. Brussels: European Commission DG Maritime Affairs and Fisheries.

2016b. *The EU Fishing Fleet: Trends and Economic Results*. Luxembourg: Publications Office of the European Union.

2016c. European Commission Adopts Ecolabelling Report. Press Release, May 18, 2016. https://web.archive.org/web/20171210033149/https://ec.europa.eu/fisheries/european-commission-adopts-ecolabelling-report_en (accessed May 19, 2016).

2016d. Facts and Figures on Organic Agriculture in the European Union. https://web.archive.org/web/20180117212910/https://ec.europa.eu/agriculture/organic/sites/orgfarming/files/docs/pages/014_en.pdf (accessed January 17, 2018).

2016e. *Facts and Figures on the Common Fisheries Policy*. Luxembourg: Publications Office of the European Union.

2016f. Options for an EU Eco-Label Scheme for Fishery and Aquaculture Products (COM(2016)263). https://web.archive.org/web/20171210033359/https://ec.europa.eu/transparency/regdoc/rep/1/2016/EN/1-2016-263-EN-F1–1.PDF (accessed December 10, 2017).

2016g. Voluntary Schemes Overview. https://web.archive.org/web/20161223114413/https://ec.europa.eu/energy/sites/ener/files/documents/

voluntary%20schemes%20overview%20table%20to%20publish_0.pdf
(accessed December 23, 2016).

2017a. *The European Union Explained: Agriculture: A Partnership between Europe and Farmers*. Luxembourg: Publications Office of the European Union.

2017b. Product Groups and Criteria. https://web.archive.org/web/20170617182151/http://ec.europa.eu/environment/ecolabel/products-groups-and-criteria.html (accessed August 18, 2017).

2017c. Renewable Energy Progress Report (COM(2017)57). https://web.archive.org/web/20190628005034/https://eur-lex.europa.eu/legal-content/EN/TXT/PDF/?uri=CELEX:52017DC0057&qid=1488449105433&from=EN (accessed March 31, 2017).

European Court of Auditors. 2016. *The EU System for the Certification of Sustainable Biofuels: Special Report*. Luxembourg: Publications Office of the European Union.

European Parliament. 1980. Written Question No 1181/80 by Mr. Glinne to the Commission of the European Communities (22 September 1980). OJ 1980 No. C352/5.

1981. Report on the Contribution of Rural Development to the Re-Establishment of Regional Balances in the Community. https://web.archive.org/web/20171201034442/http://aei.pitt.edu/5254/1/5254.pdf (accessed December 1, 2017).

1986. Report on Agriculture and the Environment. https://web.archive.org/web/20171201034601/http://aei.pitt.edu/46271/1/A8974.pdf (accessed December 1, 2017).

1994a. Amendments to the Proposal for a Council Regulation Amending Regulation (EEC) No 2092/91 on Organic Production of Agricultural Products and Indications Referring Thereto on Agricultural Products and Foodstuffs. OJ 1994 No. C128/109.

1994b. Resolution on Promoting Fairness and Solidarity in North–South Trade. OJ 1994 No. C44/119.

1997. Amendments to Proposal for a Council Regulation Supplementing Regulation (EEC) No 2092/91 on Organic Production of Agricultural Products and Indications Referring Thereto on Agricultural Products and Foodstuffs to Include Livestock Production. OJ 1997 No. C167/55.

1998a. Proposal for a Council Regulation Amending Regulation (EEC) No 404/93 on the Common Organisation of the Market in Bananas. OJ 1998 No. C210/110.

1998b. Report on Fair Trade. https://web.archive.org/web/20171201192135/http://www.europarl.europa.eu/sides/getDoc.do?pubRef=-//EP//NONSGML+REPORT+A4-1998-0198+0+DOC+PDF+V0//EN (accessed December 1, 2017).

1998c. Report on the Proposal for a Council Regulation Amending Regulation (EEC) No 404/93 on the Common Organisation of the Market in Bananas. https://web.archive.org/web/20171201192247/http://www.europarl.europa.eu/sides/getDoc.do?pubRef=-//EP//NONSGML+REPORT+A4-1998-0220+0+DOC+PDF+V0//EN (accessed December 1, 2017).

1998d. Resolution on the Commission Communication on the Future for the Market in Fisheries Products in the European Union: Responsibility, Partnership and Competitiveness. OJ 1998 No. C210/292.

1998e. Resolution on the Commission Communication: Energy for the Future: Renewable Sources of Energy. OJ 1998 No. C210/215.

1999. Resolution on Organic Livestock Production (Amendment of Regulation (EEC) No 2092/91). OJ 1999 No. C104/127.

2002a. Report on the Proposal for a Directive of the European Parliament and of the Council on the Promotion of the Use of Biofuels for Transport. https://web.archive.org/web/20170604110018/http://www.europarl.europa.eu/sides/getDoc.do?pubRef=-%2F%2FEP%2F%2FNONSGML%2BREPORT%2BA5-2002-0244%2B0%2BDOC%2BPDF%2BV0%2F%2FEN (accessed June 4, 2017).

2002b. Resolution on the Proposal for a European Parliament and Council Directive on the Promotion of the Use of Biofuels for Transport. OJ 2003 No. C271E/482.

2003. Recommendation for Second Reading on the Council Common Position for Adopting a European Parliament and Council Directive on the Promotion of the Use of Biofuels for Transport. https://web.archive.org/web/20190529082046/http://www.europarl.europa.eu/sides/getDoc.do?pubRef=-//EP//NONSGML+REPORT+A5-2003-0057+0+DOC+PDF+V0//EN (accessed January 23, 2014).

2006a. Debates. Eco-Labelling Schemes for Fisheries Products. Wednesday, September 6, 2006, Strasbourg. https://web.archive.org/web/20120405010800/http://www.europarl.europa.eu/sides/getDoc.do?type=CRE&reference=20060906&secondRef=ITEM-015&language=EN&ring=A6-2006-0219 (accessed March 13, 2014).

2006b. Debates. Explanations of Vote. Thursday, September 7, 2006, Strasbourg. https://web.archive.org/web/20120405001122/http://www.europarl.europa.eu/sides/getDoc.do?type=CRE&reference=20060907&secondRef=ITEM-008&language=EN&ring=A6-2006-0219 (accessed March 13, 2014).

2006c. Draft Report on Fair Trade and Development. Committee on Development. Explanatory Statement. https://web.archive.org/web/20171201192514/http://www.europarl.europa.eu/sides/getDoc.do?

pubRef=-//EP//NONSGML+COMPARL+PE-372.118+01+DOC+PDF+ V0//EN&language=EN (accessed December 1, 2017).

2006d. Draft Report on Fair Trade and Development. Committee on Development. Motion for a Resolution. https://web.archive.org/web/ 20171201192713/http://www.europarl.europa.eu/sides/getDoc.do?pub Ref=-//EP//NONSGML+COMPARL+PE-371.982+01+DOC+PDF+V0// EN&language=EN (accessed December 1, 2017).

2006e. Draft Report on the Proposal for a Council Regulation on Organic Production and Labelling of Organic Products. https://web.archive.org/ web/20180209195918/http://www.europarl.europa.eu/sides/getDoc.do? pubRef=-//EP//NONSGML+COMPARL+PE-380.703+01+DOC+PDF+ V0//EN&language=EN (accessed June 12, 2013).

2006f. Report on a Strategy for Biomass and Biofuels. https://web.archive .org/web/20190729171922/http://www.europarl.europa.eu/sides/getDoc .do?pubRef=-%2F%2FEP%2F%2FNONSGML%2BREPORT%2BA6- 2006-0347%2B0%2BDOC%2BPDF%2BV0%2F%2FEN   (accessed June 9, 2017).

2006g. Report on Launching a Debate on a Community Approach towards Eco-Labelling Schemes for Fisheries Products. https://web .archive.org/web/20170605061712/http://www.europarl.europa.eu/sides/ getDoc.do?pubRef=-%2F%2FEP%2F%2FNONSGML%2BREPORT% 2BA6-2006-0219%2B0%2BDOC%2BPDF%2BV0%2F%2FEN (accessed June 5, 2017).

2006h. Resolution on a Strategy for Biomass and Biofuels. OJ 2006 No. C317/890.

2006i. Resolution on Fair Trade and Development. OJ 2006 No. C303E/ 865.

2006j. Resolution on Launching a Debate on a Community Approach towards Eco-Labelling Schemes for Fisheries Products. OJ 2006 No. C305E/233.

2006k. Working Document on the Proposal for a Council Regulation on Organic Production and Labelling of Organic Products. https:// web.archive.org/web/20190629000317/http://www.europarl.europa.eu/ meetdocs/2004_2009/documents/dt/618/618730/618730en.pdf (accessed June 6, 2013).

2007a. Organic Production and Labelling of Organic Products (debate). https://web.archive.org/web/20120128164117/http://www.europarl .europa.eu/sides/getDoc.do?type=CRE&reference=20070328&second Ref=ITEM-016&language=EN&ring=A6-2007-0061 (accessed June 12, 2013).

2007b. Organic Production and Labelling of Organic Products (vote). https://web.archive.org/web/20120128154343/http://www.europarl .europa.eu/sides/getDoc.do?type=CRE&reference=20070522&secondRef=

ITEM-009-06&language=EN&ring=A6-2007-0061 (accessed June 13, 2013).

2007c. Report on the Proposal for a Council Regulation on Organic Production and Labelling of Organic Products. https://web.archive .org/web/20170605141353/http://www.europarl.europa.eu/sides/getDoc .do?pubRef=-//EP//NONSGML+REPORT+A6-2007-0061+0+DOC+PDF+ V0//EN (accessed June 5, 2017).

2007d. Report on the Proposal for Amending Directive 98/70/EC as Regards the Specification of Petrol, Diesel and Gas-Oil and Amending Council Directive 1999/32/EC, as Regards the Specification of Fuel Used by Inland Waterway Vessels. https://web.archive.org/web/ 20170605205717/http://www.europarl.europa.eu/sides/getDoc.do?pub Ref=-%2F%2FEP%2F%2FNONSGML%2BREPORT%2BA6-2007- 0496%2B0%2BDOC%2BPDF%2BV0%2F%2FEN (accessed June 5, 2017).

2007e. Report on the Roadmap for Renewable Energy in Europe. https:// web.archive.org/web/20170605203113/http://www.europarl.europa .eu/sides/getDoc.do?pubRef=-%2F%2FEP%2F%2FNONSGML% 2BREPORT%2BA6-2007-0287%2B0%2BDOC%2BPDF%2BV0% 2F%2FEN (accessed June 5, 2017).

2008a. Debates. Tuesday, 16 December 2008. Strasbourg. Promotion of the Use of Energy from Renewable Sources. https://web.archive .org/web/20170606114201/http://www.europarl.europa.eu/sides/ getDoc.do?type=CRE&reference=20081216&secondRef=ITEM- 010&language=EN&ring=A6-2008-0369 (accessed June 6, 2017).

2008b. EP Seals Climate Change Package. Background Note. https://web .archive.org/web/20171204034223/http://www.europarl.europa.eu/sides/ getDoc.do?pubRef=-//EP//NONSGML+IM-PRESS+20081208BKG44004+ 0+DOC+PDF+V0//EN&language=EN (accessed December 4, 2017).

2008c. Report on the Proposal for a Directive of the European Parliament and of the Council on the Promotion of the Use of Energy from Renewable Sources. https://web.archive.org/web/20170608184652/ http://www.europarl.europa.eu/sides/getDoc.do?pubRef=-%2F%2FEP %2F%2FNONSGML%2BREPORT%2BA6-2008-0369%2B0% 2BDOC%2BPDF%2BV0%2F%2FEN (accessed June 8, 2017).

2008d. Resolution on the Road Map for Renewable Energy in Europe. OJ 2008 No. C219/82.

2012a. Draft Report on the Common Organisation of the Markets in Fishery and Aquaculture Products. Amendments 34–467. https://web .archive.org/web/20171210170947/http://www.europarl.europa.eu/ meetdocs/2009_2014/documents/pech/am/898/898739/898739en.pdf (accessed December 10, 2017).

2012b. Report on the Proposal for a Regulation of the European Parliament and of the Council on the Common Organisation of the Markets in Fishery and Aquaculture Products. https://web.archive.org/web/20141104181118/http://www.europarl.europa.eu/sides/getDoc.do?pubRef=-%2F%2FEP%2F%2FNONSGML%2BREPORT%2BA7-2012-0217%2B0%2BDOC%2BPDF%2BV0%2F%2FEN (accessed November 4, 2014).

2012c. Working Document 2 on the Proposal for a Regulation of the European Parliament and of the Council on the Common Organisation of the Markets in Fishery and Aquaculture Products. https://web.archive.org/web/20161227225718/http://www.europarl.europa.eu/meetdocs/2009_2014/documents/pech/dv/889/889343/889343_en.pdf/ (accessed December 27, 2016).

2013. Position Adopted at First Reading on 12 September 2012 with a View to the Adoption of Regulation (EU) No ... /2012 on the Common Organisation of the Markets in Fishery and Aquaculture Products. OJ 2013 No. C352E/213.

2015. Draft Recommendation for Second Reading on the Council Position at First Reading with a View to the Adoption of a Directive of the European Parliament and of the Council of Amending Directive 98/70/EC Relating to the Quality of Petrol and Diesel Fuels and Amending Directive 2009/28/EC on the Promotion of the Use of Energy from Renewable Sources. Amendments 77–195. On file with author.

2016. Resolution on the Proposal for a Directive of the European Parliament and of the Council Amending Directive 98/70/EC Relating to the Quality of Petrol and Diesel Fuels and Amending Directive 2009/28/EC on the Promotion of the Use of Energy from Renewable Sources. OJ 2016 No. C93/371.

European Parliament and Council of the European Union. 2003. Directive 2003/30/EC of 8 May 2003 on the Promotion of the Use of Biofuels or Other Renewable Fuels for Transport. OJ 2003 No. L123/42.

2009a. Decision No 406/2009/EC of 23 April 2009 on the Effort of Member States to Reduce Their Greenhouse Gas Emissions to Meet the Community's Greenhouse Gas Emission Reduction Commitments up to 2020. OJ 2009 No. L140/136.

2009b. Directive 2009/28/EC of 23 April 2009 on the Promotion of the Use of Energy from Renewable Sources and Amending and Subsequently Repealing Directives 2001/77/EC and 2003/30/EC. OJ 2009 No. L140/16.

2009c. Directive 2009/29/EC of 23 April 2009 Amending Directive 2003/87/EC so as to Improve and Extend the Greenhouse Gas Emission Allowance Trading Scheme of the Community. OJ 2009 No. L140/63.

2009d. Directive 2009/30/EC of 23 April 2009 Amending Directive 98/70/EC as Regards the Specification of Petrol, Diesel and Gas-Oil. OJ 2009 No. L140/88.

2009e. Directive 2009/31/EC of 23 April 2009 on the Geological Storage of Carbon Dioxide. OJ 2009 No. L140/114.

2011. Regulation (EU) No 1169/2011 of 25 October 2011 on the Provision of Food Information to Consumers. OJ 2011 No. L304/18.

2012. Directive 2012/27/EU of 25 October 2012 on Energy Efficiency. OJ 2012 No. L315/1.

2013. Regulation (EU) No 1379/2013 of 11 December 2013 on the Common Organisation of the Markets in Fishery and Aquaculture Products. OJ 2013 No. L354/1.

2014. Directive 2014/24/EU of 26 February 2014 on Public Procurement. OJ 2014 No. L94/65.

2015. Directive (EU) 2015/1513 of 9 September 2015 Amending Directive 98/70/EC Relating to the Quality of Petrol and Diesel Fuels and Amending Directive 2009/28/EC on the Promotion of the Use of Energy from Renewable Sources. OJ 2015 No. L239/1.

European Report. 1997a. Bananas: EU Survey Indicates Support for Fair Trade Label. On file with author.

1997b. Bananas: UK, France, Spring to Defence of ACP Banana Growers. On file with author.

1999. Trade: Commission Clarifies Its View on Fair Trade. On file with author.

European Union. 2006. Debate on the Eco-Labelling of Fisheries Products. http://web.archive.org/web/20140814030926/http://europa.eu/legislation_summaries/maritime_affairs_and_fisheries/fisheries_resources_and_environment/l66027_en.htm (accessed August 14, 2014).

2010. Consolidated Versions of the Treaty on European Union and the Treaty on the Functioning of the European Union. OJ 2010 No. C83/1.

European Union Ecolabelling Board. s.d. Opinion on the Development of EU Ecolabel for Food and Feed Products. http://web.archive.org/web/20190626001948/http://ec.europa.eu/environment/ecolabel/documents/EUEB_position_on_food_final.pdf (accessed August 18, 2017).

Eurostat. 2010. Area under Organic Farming Increased by 7.4% between 2007 and 2008 in the EU-27. https://web.archive.org/web/20130124033326/http://ec.europa.eu:80/agriculture/organic/files/eu-policy/data-statistics/sif_2010_en.pdf (accessed January 24, 2013).

2016. Area under Organic Farming. https://web.archive.org/web/20180119225630/http://ec.europa.eu/eurostat/tgm/table.do?tab=table&init=1&language=en&pcode=sdg_02_40&plugin=1 (accessed January 19, 2018).

Evans, Peter B., Dietrich Rueschemeyer, and Theda Skocpol. 1985a. On the Road toward a More Adequate Understanding of the State. In Evans, Peter B., Dietrich Rueschemeyer, and Theda Skocpol, eds. *Bringing the State Back In.* Cambridge: Cambridge University Press, 347–366.

Evans, Peter B., Dietrich Rueschemeyer, and Theda Skocpol, eds. 1985b. *Bringing the State Back In.* Cambridge: Cambridge University Press.

Expert Group on Eco-Labelling for Fishery Products. 2006. Final Report of the Expert Group on Eco-Labelling for Fishery Products. Guidelines and Minimum Criteria for European Responsible Fishing Certification. On file with author.

Fairtrade International. 2011a. About the Mark. https://web.archive.org/web/20130122004230/http://www.fairtrade.net/about_the_mark.html (accessed January 22, 2013).

2011b. *For Producers, With Producers: Annual Report 2011–12.* Bonn: Fairtrade International.

2011c. History of Fairtrade. https://web.archive.org/web/20130122004303/http://www.fairtrade.net/history_of_fairtrade.html (accessed January 22, 2013).

2013. *Unlocking the Power: Annual Report 2012–13.* Bonn: Fairtrade International.

2014. Benefits of Fairtrade. https://web.archive.org/web/20151206045553/http://www.fairtrade.net:80/about-fairtrade/benefits-of-fairtrade.html (accessed December 6, 2015).

2016. Driving Sales, Deepening Impact. Annual Report 2015–2016. https://web.archive.org/web/20161018155245/https://annualreport15–16.fairtrade.net/en/ (accessed October 18, 2016).

Fairtrade International, SAN/Rainforest Alliance, and UTZ Certified. 2011. Joint Statement Fairtrade, SAN/Rainforest Alliance & UTZ CERTI-FIED. www.utzcertified.org/attachments/article/2174/Joint_statement_rainforest%20alliance_fairtrade%20and_utz_certified.pdf (accessed February 25, 2014).

FAO. 1995. *Code of Conduct for Responsible Fisheries.* Rome: Food and Agriculture Organization of the United Nations.

2005. *Guidelines for the Ecolabelling of Fish and Fisheries Products from Marine Capture Fisheries.* Rome: Food and Agriculture Organization of the United Nations.

2008. *Report of the Expert Consultation on the FAO Guidelines for Ecolabelling for Capture Fisheries: FAO Fisheries Report No. 864.* Rome: Food and Agriculture Organization of the United Nations.

2009. *Guidelines for the Ecolabelling of Fish and Fishery Products from Marine Capture Fisheries: Revision 1.* Rome: Food and Agriculture Organization of the United Nations.

2011a. *Guidelines for the Ecolabelling of Fish and Fishery Products from Inland Capture Fisheries*. Rome: Food and Agriculture Organization of the United Nations.

2011b. *Technical Guidelines on Aquaculture Certification*. Rome: Food and Agriculture Organization of the United Nations.

2012. *The State of World Fisheries and Aquaculture*. Rome: Food and Agriculture Organization of the United Nations

2014a. Impact of Aquaculture on Biodiversity. http://web.archive .org/web/20140105072823/http://www.fao.org/fishery/topic/14853/en (accessed January 5, 2014).

2014b. Impact of Aquaculture on Environment. http://web.archive .org/web/20140105072331/http://www.fao.org/fishery/topic/14894/en (accessed January 5, 2014).

2016. *The State of World Fisheries and Aquaculture: Contributing to Food Security and Nutrition for All*. Rome: Food and Agriculture Organization of the United Nations.

Federal Ministry of Food, Agriculture and Consumer Protection, Germany. 2009. Opinion of the Federal Republic of Germany on the Green Paper concerning the Reform of the Common Fisheries Policy (CFP). https:// web.archive.org/web/20120526221125/http://ec.europa.eu/fisheries/ reform/docs/federal_ministry_germany_en.pdf (accessed December 9, 2017).

Fischler, Franz. 2004. Towards a European Action Plan on Organic Food and Farming. Concluding Remarks. *Proceedings of the European Hearing on Organic Food and Farming: Towards a European Action Plan*, January 22, 2004, Brussels.

FLO. 2003. Shopping for a Better World. Annual Report 03/04. http://web .archive.org/web/20130510123041/www.fairtrade.net/fileadmin/user_ upload/content/AR_03-04_screen_final-1.pdf (accessed May 10, 2013).

2008. Fair Trade: State of Play. https://web.archive.org/web/20150409102844/ http://trade.ec.europa.eu/doclib/docs/2008/june/tradoc_139329.pdf (accessed October 14, 2016).

2009. Growing Stronger Together. Annual Report 2009–10. https://web .archive.org/web/20130821225141/https://www.fairtrade.net/fileadmin/ user_upload/content/2009/resources/FLO_Annual-Report-2009_komplett_ double_web.pdf (accessed August 21, 2013).

Foley, Paul, and Elizabeth Havice. 2016. The Rise of Territorial Eco-Certifications: New Politics of Transnational Sustainability Governance in the Fishery Sector. *Geoforum*, 69, 24–33.

Food & Water Europe. 2011. De-Coding Seafood Eco-Labels: How the European Commission Can Help Consumers Access Sustainable Seafood. http://web.archive.org/web/20140719232620/http://documents

.foodandwaterwatch.org/doc/EUecoLabels-web.pdf (accessed July 19, 2014).

FranceAgriMer. 2014. Référentiel Ecolabel des Produits de la Pêche Maritime. Version du 28/11/2014. http://web.archive.org/web/20171213022734/http://www.franceagrimer.fr/index.php/content/download/33095/299068/file/Referentiel_Ecolabel_peche-2014-11-28.pdf (accessed December 13, 2017).

Fransen, Luc. 2011. Why Do Private Governance Organizations Not Converge? A Political-Institutional Analysis of Transnational Labor Standards Regulation. *Governance*, 24(2), 359–387.

  2012. Multi-Stakeholder Governance and Voluntary Programme Interactions: Legitimation Politics in the Institutional Design of Corporate Social Responsibility. *Socio-Economic Review*, 10(1), 163–192.

  2013. The Embeddedness of Responsible Business Practice: Exploring the Interaction between National-Institutional Environments and Corporate Social Responsibility. *Journal of Business Ethics*, 115(2), 213–227.

  2015. The Politics of Meta-Governance in Transnational Private Sustainability Governance. *Policy Sciences*, 48(3), 293–317.

Fridell, Mara, Ian Hudson, and Mark Hudson. 2008. With Friends Like These: The Corporate Reponses to Fair Trade Coffee. *Review of Radical Political Economics*, 40(8), 8–34.

Friedman, Milton. 1970. The Social Responsibility of Business Is to Increase Its Profits. *The New York Times Magazine*, September 13, 1970, 17.

Friend of the Sea. 2014a. About Us. http://web.archive.org/web/20140316164647/http://www.friendofthesea.org/about-us.asp (accessed March 16, 2014).

  2014b. FOS Aquaculture Recognizes GLOBALG.A.P. Certificates. Press Release, May 2, 2014. http://web.archive.org/web/20171213023123/http://www.friendofthesea.org/news-doc.asp?CAT=1&ID=704&page=18 (accessed December 13, 2017).

Friend of the Sea. 2016a. *Annual Report 2016*. Milan: Friend of the Sea.

  2016b. Scheme Scope and Objectives. http://web.archive.org/web/20161124014035/http://www.friendofthesea.org/public/page/annex%201%20scheme%20scope%20and%20objectives%20fos.pdf (accessed June 9, 2017).

  2017a. FOS Approved Customers & Suppliers & Retailers. On file with author.

  2017b. Friend of the Sea Approved Fisheries and Fleets. https://web.archive.org/web/20170704052248/http://www.friendofthesea.org/fisheries.asp?ID=71 (accessed June 14, 2017).

Friends of the Earth Europe. 2007. Biofuel Issues in the New Legislation on the Promotion of Renewable Energy. Public Consultation Response from Friends of the Earth Europe. https://web.archive.org/web/20111117070013/http://ec.europa.eu/energy/res/consultation/doc/2007_06_04_biofuels/non_og/foee_en.pdf (accessed November 7, 2011).

2008. Sustainability as a Smokescreen. The Inadequacy of Certifying Fuels and Feeds. https://web.archive.org/web/20171204034509/http://www.foeeurope.org/sites/default/files/publications/sustainability_smoke screen_fullreport_med_res.pdf (accessed December 4, 2017).

Froese, Rainer, and Alexander Proelss. 2012. Evaluation and Legal Assessment of Certified Seafood. *Marine Policy*, 36(6), 1284–1289.

2013. Is a Stock Overfished If It Is Depleted by Overfishing? A Response to the Rebuttal of Agnew et al. to Froese and Proelss "Evaluation and Legal Assessment of Certified Seafood." *Marine Policy*, 38, 548–550.

FTAO. 2004. Fair Trade Advocacy Newsletter June 2004. On file with author.

2008. About Us. https://web.archive.org/web/20081024172700/http://www.fairtrade-advocacy.org/aboutus.html (accessed September 30, 2016).

2016. Who We Are. https://web.archive.org/web/20161022060234/http://fairtrade-advocacy.org/about-us-27/who-we-are (accessed September 30, 2016).

s.d. Fair Trade Definition and Principles as Agreed by FINE in December 2001. https://web.archive.org/web/20111121080539/http://www.fair-trade-hub.com/support-files/fair-trade-definition.pdf (accessed October 2, 2012).

Fuchs, Doris. 2007. *Business Power in Global Governance*. Boulder: Lynne Rienner.

Fuchs, Doris, Agni Kalfagianni, and Maarten Arentsen. 2009. Retail Power, Private Standards, and Sustainability in the Global Food System. In Clapp, Jennifer and Doris Fuchs, eds. *Corporate Power in Global Agrifood Governance*. Cambridge: MIT Press, 29–60.

GAA. 2014. BAP Standards. http://web.archive.org/web/20140208010340/http://www.gaalliance.org/bap/standards.php (accessed February 8, 2014).

2017. BAP-Certified Facilities. http://web.archive.org/web/20170622220626/https://www.bapcertification.org/find-certified-facilities/ (accessed June 15, 2017).

Gale, Fred, and Marcus Haward. 2011. *Global Commodity Governance: State Responses to Sustainable Forest and Fisheries Certification*. New York: Palgrave Macmillan.

GBEP. 2011. *The Global Bioenergy Partnership Sustainability Indicators for Bioenergy*, First Edition. Rome: Food and Agriculture Organization of the United Nations.

Geddes, Barbara. 1990. How the Cases You Choose Affect the Answers You Get: Selection Bias in Comparative Politics. *Political Analysis*, 2(1), 131–150.

Geier, Bernward. 1997. A Look at the Development of IFOAM in Its First 25 Years. https://web.archive.org/web/20130127055827/http://ifoam.org/about_ifoam/inside_ifoam/pdfs/First_25_Years.pdf (accessed January 27, 2013).

2007. IFOAM and the History of the International Organic Movement. In Lockeretz, William, ed. *Organic Farming: An International History*. Wallingford: CAB International, 175–186.

George, Alexander L., and Andrew Bennett. 2005. *Case Studies and Theory Development in the Social Sciences*. Cambridge: MIT Press.

German, Laura, and George Schoneveld. 2011. *Social Sustainability of EU-Approved Voluntary Schemes for Biofuels: Implications for Rural Livelihoods*. Bogor: Center for International Forestry Research.

Gibbon, Peter. 2006. *Decoding Organic Standard-Setting and Regulation in Europe (1991–2005)*. Vienna: United Nations Industrial Development Organization.

2008. An Analysis of Standards-Based Regulation in the EU Organic Sector, 1991–2007. *Journal of Agrarian Change*, 8(4), 553–582.

Giessen, Lukas, Sarah Burns, Muhammad Alif K. Sahide, and Agung Wibowo. 2016. From Governance to Government: The Strengthened Role of State Bureaucracies in Forest and Agricultural Certification. *Policy and Society*, 35(1), 71–89.

GIZ. 2015. Panel II: Values and Potential Impacts of EU Eco Label. Presentation at the Public Hearing on "The Single European Eco label: Setting Minimum Criteria," June 16, 2015, Brussels.

Gjølberg, Maria. 2009. The Origin of Corporate Social Responsibility: Global Forces or National Legacies? *Socio-Economic Review*, 7(4), 605–637.

Glasbergen, Pieter. 2011. Mechanisms of Private Meta-Governance: An Analysis of Global Private Governance for Sustainable Development. *International Journal of Strategic Business Alliances*, 2(3), 189–206.

GLOBALG.A.P. 2014. GLOBALG.A.P. History. https://web.archive.org/web/20140315074736/http://www.globalgap.org/uk_en/who-we-are/history (accessed March 15, 2014).

Golden, Jay S., Dan Vermeer, Bob Clemen, Alexandra Michalko, Davie Nguyen, Catherine Noyes, Anita Akella, and Julia Bunting. 2010. *An Overview of Ecolabels and Sustainability Certifications in the Global Marketplace*. Durham: Duke University Corporate Sustainability Initiative.

Gough, Robert. 2002. Biofuel Mandate Hit as Political, Not Environmental, in Nature. *Oxy-Fuel News*, 14(22), 1.

Government of Canada. 2009. Government of Canada Response to the Report of the House of Commons Standing Committee on Fisheries and Oceans: The Canadian Lobster Fishery: Trapped in a Perfect Storm. https://web .archive.org/web/20170608104701/https://www.ourcommons.ca/Document Viewer/en/40-2/FOPO/report-6/response-8512-402-125 (accessed December 18, 2017).

Government of Malaysia. 2007. Public Consultation on Biofuel Issues in the New Legislation on the Promotion of Renewable Energy. Response by the Government of Malaysia. https://web.archive.org/web/ 20140725072520/http://ec.europa.eu/energy/res/consultation/doc/2007_ 06_04_biofuels/third_countries/malaysia_en.pdf (accessed July 25, 2014).

Government of the Netherlands. 2007. Public Consultation on Biofuel Issues in the New Legislation on the Promotion of Renewable Energy. Response by the Government of the Netherlands. https://web.archive .org/web/20140722222835/http://ec.europa.eu/energy/res/consultation/ doc/2007_06_04_biofuels/ms_instistution/netherlands_en.pdf (accessed July 22, 2014).

Green, Jessica F. 2013. Order Out of Chaos: Public and Private Rules for Managing Carbon. *Global Environmental Politics*, 13(2), 1–25.

2014. *Rethinking Private Authority: Agents and Entrepreneurs in Global Environmental Governance*. Princeton: Princeton University Press.

2017. Blurred Lines: Public-Private Interactions in Carbon Regulations. *International Interactions*, 43(1), 103–128.

Green, Jessica F., and Graeme Auld. 2017. Unbundling the Regime Complex: The Effects of Private Authority. *Transnational Environmental Law*, 6(2), 259–284.

Greenergy. 2008. Greenergy and ProForest Develop Bioethanol Sustainability Criteria. Press Release. June 18, 2008. https://web.archive.org/web/ 20171205215208/http://www.greenergy.com/press_archives/2008/ Greenergy_and_ProForest.pdf (accessed December 5, 2017).

Greenhill, Brian, Layna Mosley, and Aseem Prakash. 2009. Trade-Based Diffusion of Labor Rights: A Panel Study, 1986–2002. *American Political Science Review*, 103(4), 669–690.

Greenpeace. 2005. *A Recipe for Disaster: Supermarket's Insatiable Appetite for Seafood*. London: Greenpeace.

2007a. Greenpeace Press Briefing in Advance of the EU "Energy Package" Launch: European Commission to Lay Out Good Intentions but Poor Plans. https://web.archive.org/web/20171205215327/http://www .greenpeace.org/eu-unit/Global/eu-unit/reports-briefings/2007/5/eu-energy-package.pdf (accessed December 5, 2017).

2007b. Greenpeace Responses to the Public Consultation "Biofuel Issues in the New Legislation on the Promotion of Renewable Energy."

https://web.archive.org/web/20111117070239/http://ec.europa.eu/energy/res/consultation/doc/2007_06_04_biofuels/non_og/greenpeace_en.pdf (accessed November 17, 2011).

Greenwood, Justin. 2017. *Interest Representation in the European Union.* Fourth Edition. London: Palgrave Macmillan.

GSSI. 2017a. GSSI Story. http://web.archive.org/web/20170420131233/http://www.ourgssi.org/about-2/gssi-story/ (accessed August 8, 2017).

2017b. GSSI Timeline. http://web.archive.org/web/20170420132808/http://www.ourgssi.org/milestones/gssi-timeline/ (accessed August 15, 2017).

Gulbrandsen, Lars H. 2004. Overlapping Public and Private Governance: Can Forest Certification Fill the Gaps in the Global Forest Regime? *Global Environmental Politics*, 4(2), 75–99.

2005. The Effectiveness of Non-State Governance Schemes: A Comparative Study of Forest Certification in Norway and Sweden. *International Environmental Agreements*, 5(2), 125–149.

2009. The Emergence and Effectiveness of the Marine Stewardship Council. *Marine Policy*, 33(4), 654–660.

2014. Dynamic Governance Interactions: Evolutionary Effects of State Responses to Non-State Certification Programs. *Regulation & Governance*, 8(1), 74–92.

Hall, Peter A., and David Soskice. 2001. *Varieties of Capitalism: The Institutional Foundations of Comparative Advantage.* Oxford: Oxford University Press.

Hall, Rodney Bruce, and Thomas J. Biersteker, eds. 2002. *The Emergence of Private Authority in Global Governance.* Cambridge: Cambridge University Press.

Hamelinck, Carlo, Michele Koper, Goran Berndes, Oskar Englund, Rocio Diaz-Chavez, Emily Kunen, and David Walden. 2011. Biofuels Baseline 2008. https://web.archive.org/web/20171205220310/https://ec.europa.eu/energy/sites/ener/files/documents/2011_biofuels_baseline_2008.pdf (accessed December 5, 2017).

Hart's European Fuels News. 2001. EC Moves on Biofuels. *Hart's European Fuels News*, 5(23), 1.

Haufler, Virginia. 2001. *A Public Role for the Private Sector: Industry Self-Regulation in a Global Economy.* Washington, DC: Carnegie Endowment for International Peace.

Hawkins, Darren G., David A. Lake, Daniel L. Nielson, and Michael J. Tierney, eds. 2006. *Delegation and Agency in International Organizations.* Cambridge: Cambridge University Press.

Heisenberg, Dorothee. 2005. The Institution of "Consensus" in the European Union: Formal Versus Informal Decision-Making in the Council. *European Journal of Political Research*, 44(1), 65–90.

Héritier, Adrienne, and Sandra Eckert. 2008. New Modes of Governance in the Shadow of Hierarchy: Self-Regulation by Industry in Europe. *Journal of Public Policy*, 28(1), 113–138.

Héritier, Adrienne, and Martin Rhodes, eds. 2011. *New Modes of Governance in Europe: Governing in the Shadow of Hierarchy*. Houndmills: Palgrave Macmillan.

Hidayat, Nia Kurniawati, Astrid Offermans, and Pieter Glasbergen. 2018. Sustainable Palm Oil as a Public Responsibility? On the Governance Capacity of Indonesian Standard for Sustainable Palm Oil (ISPO). *Agriculture and Human Values*, 35(1), 223–242.

High Level Panel of Experts. 2013. *Biofuels and Food Security: A Report by the High Level Panel of Experts on Food Security and Nutrition of the Committee on World Food Security*. Rome: Secretariat HLPE c/o FAO.

Holzinger, Katharina, and Christoph Knill. 2005. Causes and Conditions of Cross-National Policy Convergence. *Journal of European Public Policy*, 12(5), 775–796.

Holzinger, Katharina, Christoph Knill, and Ansgar Schäfer. 2006. Rhetoric or Reality? "New Governance" in EU Environmental Policy. *European Law Journal*, 12(3), 403–420.

Hospes, Otto. 2014. Marking the Success or End of Global Multi-Stakeholder Governance? The Rise of National Sustainability Standards in Indonesia and Brazil for Palm Oil and Soy. *Agriculture and Human Values*, 31(3), 425–437.

House of Commons Canada. 2009. The Canadian Lobster Fishery: Trapped in a Perfect Storm. Report of the Standing Committee on Fisheries and Oceans. https://web.archive.org/web/20171218211943/https://www.ourcommons.ca/Content/Committee/402/FOPO/Reports/RP3995091/foporp06/foporp06-e.pdf (accessed December 18, 2017).

Iceland Responsible Fisheries. 2017. About IRF. http://web.archive.org/web/20170625005738/http://www.responsiblefisheries.is/about-irf/ (accessed June 25, 2017).

IFAT. 2008. Submission from IFAT to Civil Society Dialogue on Fair Trade. http://web.archive.org/web/20150409100205/http://trade.ec.europa.eu/doclib/docs/2008/june/tradoc_139324.pdf (accessed October 14, 2016).

IFOAM. 2005. Principles of Organic Agriculture. https://web.archive.org/web/20060207115810/http://www.ifoam.org:80/organic_facts/principles/pdfs/Principles_Organic_Agriculture.pdf (accessed August 16, 2018).

2011. IFOAM Presents the Global Organic Mark. Press Release, February 14, 2011. https://web.archive.org/web/20110514041844/http://www.ifoam.org/about_ifoam/standards/OGS/IFOAMlogomediatext.pdf (accessed March 13, 2013).

2017. About Us. https://web.archive.org/web/20171120040156/https://www.ifoam.bio/en/about-us (accessed November 20, 2017).

IFOAM EU Group. 2004. Response to the European Action Plan for Organic Food and Farming. https://web.archive.org/web/20171201153459/http://orgapet.orgap.org/annexes/annex_A1–7.pdf (accessed December 1, 2017).

2005a. The Revision of EC Regulation 2092/91. On file with author.

2005b. Revision of Regulation No. 2092/91. Letter to Commissioner Mariann Fischer Boel. July 26, 2005. https://web.archive.org/web/20080719042649/http://www.ifoam.org/about_ifoam/around_world/eu_group/PDF_Revision_Organic/Let_FischerBoel_26.07.05.pdf (accessed March 25, 2013).

2006a. Letter to Mariann Fischer Boel, Commissioner for Agriculture. November 21, 2006. On file with author.

2006b. Newsletter, No. 13, Extra Edition, July 2006. On file with author.

2006c. Position Paper on the "Proposal for a Council Regulation on Organic Production and Labelling of Organic Products." On file with author.

2010. *Organic Aquaculture. EU Regulations (EC) 834/2007, (EC) 889/2008, (EC) 710/2009. Background, Assessment, Interpretation.* Brussels: IFOAM EU Group.

International Trade Center. 2015. *The State of Sustainable Markets: Statistics and Emerging Trends 2015.* Geneva: International Trade Center.

2017. *The State of Sustainable Markets: Statistics and Emerging Trends 2017.* Geneva: International Trade Centre.

ISCC. 2014. System Setup. https://web.archive.org/web/20140406180927/http://www.iscc-system.org/en/iscc-system/system-setup/ (accessed April 6, 2014).

ISEAL Alliance. 2014. Our History. https://web.archive.org/web/20140710144418/https://www.isealalliance.org/about-us/our-history (accessed July 10, 2014).

IUCN. 2013. *Betting on Best Quality: A Comparison of the Quality and Level of Assurance of Sustainability Standards for Biomass, Soy and Palmoil.* Amsterdam: IUCN.

IUCN, and Shell. 2010. Workshop Summary: Towards Harmonization for Biofuel Sustainability Standards. https://web.archive.org/web/20150424184303/https://cmsdata.iucn.org/downloads/biofuel_sustainability_standards_workshop_report_final.pdf (accessed April 24, 2015).

Jackson, Gregory, and Androniki Apostolakou. 2010. Corporate Social Responsibility in Western Europe: An Institutional Mirror or Substitute? *Journal of Business Ethics*, 94(3), 371–394.

Janssen, Meike, and Ulrich Hamm. 2011. Consumer Perception of Different Organic Certification Schemes in Five European Countries. *Organic Agriculture*, 1(1), 31–43.

2012a. The Mandatory EU Logo for Organic Food: Consumer Perceptions. *British Food Journal*, 114(3), 335–352.

2012b. Product Labelling in the Market for Organic Food: Consumer Preferences and Willingness-to-Pay for Different Organic Certification Logos. *Food Quality and Preference*, 25(1), 9–22.

2014. Governmental and Private Certification Labels for Organic Food: Consumer Attitudes and Preferences in Germany. *Food Policy*, 49, 437–448.

Jordan, Andrew, Michael W. Bauer, and Christoffer Green-Pedersen. 2013. Policy Dismantling. *Journal of European Public Policy*, 20(5), 795–805.

Jordan, Andrew, David Benson, Rüdiger K. W. Wurzel, and Anthony Zito. 2013. Governing with Multiple Policy Instruments? In Jordan, Andrew and Camilla Adelle, eds. *Environmental Policy in the EU: Actors, Institutions and Processes*, Third Edition. London: Routledge, 309–325.

Jordan, Andrew, Rüdiger K. W. Wurzel, and Anthony Zito. 2005. The Rise of "New" Policy Instruments in Comparative Perspective: Has Governance Eclipsed Government? *Political Studies*, 53(3), 477–496.

Jordan, Andrew, Rüdiger Wurzel, Anthony R. Zito, and Lars Brückner. 2003. European Governance and the Transfer of "New" Environmental Policy Instruments (NEPIs) in the European Union. *Public Administration*, 81(3), 555–574.

Kalfagianni, Agni, and Philipp Pattberg. 2013. Fishing in Muddy Waters? Conditions for Effective Private Governance in Fisheries and Aquaculture. *Marine Policy*, 38, 124–132.

Kavalov, Boyan, and Stathis D. Peteves. 2005. Assessment of the Responses to the Questionnaire on the EU Biomass Action Plan. https://web .archive.org/web/20111108142501/http://ec.europa.eu/energy/res/biomass_ action_plan/doc/results_consultation_bap.pdf (accessed December 19, 2016).

Keating, Dave. 2013. Deal Struck on Fisheries Reform. *European Voice*. May 30, 2013. http://web.archive.org/web/20171209100940/https://www .politico.eu/article/deal-struck-on-fisheries-reform (accessed December 9, 2017).

Keefer, Philip, and David Stasavage. 2003. The Limits of Delegation: Veto Players, Central Bank Independence, and the Credibility of Monetary Policy. *American Political Science Review*, 97(3), 407–423.

Kiewiet, D. Roderick, and Mathew D. McCubbins. 1991. *The Logic of Delegation: Congressional Parties and the Appropriations Process*. Chicago: The University of Chicago Press.

Kinderman, Daniel. 2012. "Free Us Up So We Can Be Responsible!" The Co-Evolution of Corporate Social Responsibility and Neo-Liberalism in the UK, 1977–2010. *Socio-Economic Review*, 10(1), 29–57.

King, Gary, Robert O. Keohane, and Sidney Verba. 1994. *Designing Social Inquiry: Scientific Inference in Qualitative Research*. Princeton: Princeton University Press.

Klein, Kendra, and David E. Winickoff. 2011. Organic Regulation across the Atlantic: Emergence, Divergence, Convergence. *Environmental Politics*, 20(2), 153–172.

Klüver, Heike. 2013a. Lobbying as a Collective Enterprise: Winners and Losers of Policy Formulation in the European Union. *Journal of European Public Policy*, 20(1), 59–76.

2013b. *Lobbying in the European Union: Interest Groups, Lobbying Coalitions, and Policy Change*. Oxford: Oxford University Press.

Klüver, Heike, Caelesta Braun, and Jan Beyers. 2015. Legislative Lobbying in Context: Towards a Conceptual Framework of Interest Group Lobbying in the European Union. *Journal of European Public Policy*, 22(4), 447–461.

Klüver, Heike, and Sabine Saurugger. 2013. Opening the Black Box: The Professionalization of Interest Groups in the European Union. *Interest Groups & Advocacy*, 2(2), 185–205.

Knill, Christoph, and Dirk Lehmkuhl. 2002. Private Actors and the State: Internationalization and Changing Patterns of Governance. *Governance*, 15(1), 41–63.

Knill, Christoph, and Duncan Liefferink. 2013. The Establishment of EU Environmental Policy. In Jordan, Andrew and Camilla Adelle, eds. *Environmental Policy in the EU; Actors, Institutions and Processes*, Third Edition. London: Routledge, 13–31.

Knowles, Sam. 2011. The Commodification of Ethics. In Warrier, Meera, ed. *The Politics of Fair Trade*. Milton Park: Routledge, 24–36.

Knudsen, Jette Steen. 2018. Government Regulation of International Corporate Social Responsibility in the US and the UK: How Domestic Institutions Shape Mandatory and Supportive Initiatives. *British Journal of Industrial Relations*, 56(1), 164–188.

Knudsen, Jette Steen, and Jeremy Moon. 2017. *Visible Hands: Government Regulation and International Business Responsibility*. Cambridge: Cambridge University Press.

Knudsen, Jette Steen, Jeremy Moon, and Reineke Slager. 2015. Government Policies for Corporate Social Responsibility in Europe: A Comparative Analysis of Institutionalisation. *Policy & Politics*, 43(1), 81–99.

Kocken, Marlike. 2006. Sixty Years of Fair Trade. A Brief History of the Fair Trade Movement. https://web.archive.org/web/20120105150537/

http://www.european-fair-trade-association.org/efta/Doc/History.pdf (accessed July 10, 2013).

Kohler-Koch, Beate, and Barbara Finke. 2007. The Institutional Shaping of EU–Society Relations: A Contribution to Democracy via Participation? *Journal of Civil Society*, 3(3), 205–221.

Kollman, Kelly, and Aseem Prakash. 2002. EMS-Based Environmental Regimes as Club Goods: Examining Variations in Firm-Level Adoption of ISO 14001 and EMAS in U.K., U.S. and Germany. *Policy Sciences*, 35(1), 43–67.

KRAV. 2006. KRAV's Response to Request for Comments on the Proposal for Regulation on Organic Production and Labelling of Organic Products. https://web.archive.org/web/20171201155018/http://www.gfrs .de/fileadmin/files/vo-revision/krav_response.pdf (accessed December 1, 2017).

2017. *Standards for KRAV-Certified Production – 2017 Edition*. Uppsala: KRAV Association.

La Malfa, Giorgio, Raimondo Fassa, and Luciano Pettinari. 1996. Written Question E-1966/96 by Giorgio La Malfa (ELDR), Raimondo Fassa (ELDR) and Luciano Pettinari (GUE/NGL) to the Commission (July 16, 1996). Subject: Promotion of Fairness and Solidarity in Trade Relations. http://web.archive.org/save/https://eur-lex.europa.eu/legal-content/EN/ TXT/?qid=1564454468715&uri=CELEX:91996E001966 (accessed July 10, 2013).

La Plate-Forme pour le Commerce Equitable. s.d. Définitions et Cadres Légaux. https://web.archive.org/web/20170606075337/https://www .commercequitable.org/lecommerceequitable/definitions-cadres-legaux .html (accessed October 12, 2017).

LA Times. 1997. Britain Weighs Boycott of Some Bananas. September 29, 1997. https://web.archive.org/web/20151002140217/http://articles.latimes .com/1997/sep/29/business/fi-37380 (accessed October 2, 2015).

Labruto, N. 2014. Experimental Biofuel Governance: Historicizing Social Certification in Brazilian Ethanol Production. *Geoforum*, 54, 272–281.

LaChappelle, Jason. 2012. SAN and IOAS Partnership on Accreditation Moves Forward. https://web.archive.org/web/20150912032408/http:// www.isealalliance.org/online-community/blogs/san-and-ioas-partnership-on-accreditation-moves-forward (accessed October 6, 2016).

Lambin, Eric F., Patrick Meyfroidt, Ximena Rueda, Allen Blackman, Jan Börner, Paolo Omar Cerutti, Thomas Dietsch, Laura Jungmann, Pénélope Lamarque, Jane Lister, Nathalie F. Walker, and Sven Wunder. 2014. Effectiveness and Synergies of Policy Instruments for Land Use Governance in Tropical Regions. *Global Environmental Change*, 28, 129–140.

Lampkin, Nicolas, Carolyn Foster, and Susanne Padel. 1999. *The Policy and Regulatory Environment for Organic Farming in Europe: Country Reports*: *Organic Farming in Europe: Economics and Policy, Volume 2*. Stuttgart: University of Hohenheim.

Lampkin, Nicolas, Carolyn Foster, Susanne Padel, and Peter Midmore. 1999. *The Policy and Regulatory Environment for Organic Farming in Europe*: *Organic Farming in Europe: Economics and Policy, Volume 1*. Stuttgart: University of Hohenheim.

Lamy, Pascal. 2004. What Role for Fair Trade in EU Policies? Statement by Pascal Lamy at Panel: Conference on Fair Trade: A Contribution to Sustainable Development. https://web.archive.org/web/20061121060911/ http://trade.ec.europa.eu/doclib/docs/2004/june/tradoc_116424.pdf (accessed October 1, 2012).

Langman, Mary. 1992. Memories and Notes on the Beginning and Early History of IFOAM. https://web.archive.org/web/20140901002526/ http://infohub.ifoam.org/sites/default/files/page/files/early_history_ifoam .pdf (accessed September 1, 2014).

Le Guillou, Gwénaëlle, and Alberic Scharpé. 2000. *Organic Farming: Guide to Community Rules*. Luxembourg: Office for Official Publications of the European Communities.

Lequesne, Christian. 2005. Fisheries Policy: Letting the Little Ones Go? In Wallace, Helen, William Wallace, and Mark A. Pollack, eds. *Policy-Making in the European Union*, Fifth Edition. Oxford: Oxford University Press, 353–376.

Levi-Faur, David. 2005. The Global Diffusion of Regulatory Capitalism. *The ANNALS of the American Academy of Political and Social Science*, 598(1), 12–32.

Levin, Kelly, Benjamin Cashore, and Jonathan Koppell. 2009. Can Non-State Certification Systems Bolster State-Centered Efforts to Promote Sustainable Development through the Clean Development Mechanism? *Wake Forest Law Review*, 44(3), 777–798.

Levy, David L., and Peter J. Newell. 2005. A Neo-Gramscian Approach to Business in International Environmental Politics: An Interdisciplinary, Multilevel Framework. In Levy, David L. and Peter J. Newell, eds. *The Business of Global Environmental Governance*. Cambridge: MIT Press, 47–69.

Lijphart, Arend. 1975. The Comparable-Cases Strategy in Comparative Research. *Comparative Political Studies*, 8(2), 158–177.

Lin, Jolene. 2011. Governing Biofuels: A Principal-Agent Analysis of the European Union Biofuels Certification Regime and the Clean Development Mechanism. *Journal of Environmental Law*, 24(1), 43–73.

Lindblom, Charles E. 1977. *Politics and Markets: The World's Political Economic Systems*. New York: Basic Books.

Lipschutz, Ronnie. 2005. Environmental Regulation, Certification and Corporate Standards: A Critique. In Dauvergne, Peter, ed. *Handbook of Global Environmental Politics*. Cheltenham: Edward Elgar, 218–232.

List, Friedrich. [1841] 1885. *National System of Political Economy*. London: Longmans, Green, and Co.

Lister, Jane. 2011. *Corporate Social Responsibility and the State: International Approaches to Forest Co-Regulation*. Vancouver: University of British Columbia Press.

Locke, Richard. 2013. *The Promise and Limits of Private Power: Promoting Labor Standards in a Global Economy*. Cambridge: Cambridge University Press.

Loconto, Allison, and Eve Fouilleux. 2014. Politics of Private Regulation: ISEAL and the Shaping of Transnational Sustainability Governance. *Regulation & Governance* 8(2), 166–185.

Londo, H. Marc, Ewout P. Deurwaarder, and Elke van Thuijl. 2006. Review of EU Biofuels Directive. Public Consultation Exercise. Summary of the Responses. https://web.archive.org/web/20080609102209/http://ec.europa.eu/energy/res/legislation/doc/biofuels/contributions/2006_08_23_summary_responses.pdf (accessed January 9, 2014).

Long, Tony, and Larisa Lorinczi. 2009. NGOs as Gatekeepers: A Green Vision. In Coen, David and Jeremy Richardson, eds. *Lobbying the European Union: Institutions, Actors, and Issues*. Oxford: Oxford University Press, 169–185.

Low, Will, and Eileen Davenport. 2006. Mainstreaming Fair Trade: Adoption, Assimilation, Appropriation. *Journal of Strategic Marketing*, 14(4), 315–327.

LowCVP. 2007. Public Consultation on Biofuel Issues in the New Legislation on the Promotion of Renewable Energy. Response by LowCVP. https://web.archive.org/web/20140724125257/http://ec.europa.eu/energy/res/consultation/doc/2007_06_04_biofuels/ms_instistution/low_cvp_en.pdf (accessed July 24, 2014).

Lowery, David. 2007. Why Do Organized Interests Lobby? A Multi-Goal, Multi-Context Theory of Lobbying. *Polity*, 39(1), 29–54.

Lucbert, Anne-Kristen, and David Picault. 2009. A Public Eco-Labelling Scheme under Development. Presentation at the Round Table on Eco-Labelling and Certification in the Fisheries Sector, April 22–23, 2009, The Hague.

Lynggaard, Kennet. 2006. *The Common Agriculture Policy and Organic Farming*. Wallingford: CAB International.

Lyon, Thomas P., and John W. Maxwell. 2008. Corporate Social Responsibility and the Environment: A Theoretical Perspective. *Review of Environmental Economics and Policy*, 2(2), 240–260.

Madelin, Robert. 2004. What Do Consumers Expect from Organic Farming? *Proceedings of the European Hearing on Organic Food and Farming: Towards a European Action Plan*, January 22, 2004, Brussels.

Mahoney, Christine. 2008. *Brussels Versus the Beltway. Advocacy in the United States and the European Union*. Washington, DC: Georgetown University Press.

Mahoney, James, and Gary Goertz. 2004. The Possibility Principle: Choosing Negative Cases in Comparative Research. *American Political Science Review*, 98(4), 653–669.

Majone, Giandomenico. 1994. The Rise of the Regulatory State in Europe. *West European Politics*, 17(3), 77–101.

Malets, Olga. 2015. When Transnational Standards Hit the Ground: Domestic Regulations, Compliance Assessment and Forest Certification in Russia. *Journal of Environment Policy & Planning*, 17(3), 332–359.

Management Committee for Fishery and Aquaculture Products. 2009. Meeting of the Management Committee for Fishery and Aquaculture Products. February 25, 2009. http://web.archive.org/web/20171213030510/http://www.europarl.europa.eu/RegData/docs_autres_institutions/commission_europeenne/comitologie/info/2009/CMTD(2009)0128/COM-AC_DI(2009)S009028-01_EN.doc (accessed December 13, 2017).

Maniates, Michael F. 2001. Individualization: Plant a Tree, Buy a Bike, Save the World? *Global Environmental Politics*, 1(3), 31–52.

Marx, Axel, and Dieter Cuypers. 2010. Forest Certification as a Global Environmental Governance Tool: What Is the Macro-Effectiveness of the Forest Stewardship Council? *Regulation & Governance*, 4(4), 408–434.

Matten, Dirk, and Jeremy Moon. 2008. "Implicit" and "Explicit" CSR: A Conceptual Framework for a Comparative Understanding of Corporate Social Responsibility. *Academy of Management Review*, 33(2), 404–424.

Mattli, Walter, and Jack Seddon. 2015. Orchestration along the Pareto Frontier: Winners and Losers. In Abbott, Kenneth W., Philipp Genschel, Duncan Snidal, and Bernhard Zangl, eds. *International Organizations as Orchestrators*. Cambridge: Cambridge University Press, 315–348.

Mattli, Walter, and Ngaire Woods. 2009. In Whose Benefit? Explaining Regulatory Change in Global Politics. In Mattli, Walter and Ngaire Woods, eds. *The Politics of Global Regulation*. Princeton: Princeton University Press, 1–43.

Mattsson, Eva. 2011. Congratulations to Thirty CBs: The EU Settles on the List of Approved Certification Bodies. *The Organic Standard*, 127 (November 2011), 1–3.

Max Havelaar. 2013. Wie Zijn Wij. https://web.archive.org/web/20140503075233/http://maxhavelaar.nl:80/39/wie_zijn_wij (accessed May 18, 2014).

Mayer, Frederick, and Gary Gereffi. 2010. Regulation and Economic Globalization: Prospects and Limits of Private Governance. *Business and Politics*, 12(3), Article 11.

McBarnet, Doreen, Aurora Voiculescu, and Tom Campbell, eds. 2007. *The New Corporate Accountability: Corporate Social Responsibility and the Law*. Cambridge: Cambridge University Press.

McDermott, Constance, Benjamin Cashore, and Peter Kanowski. 2010. *Global Environmental Forest Policies: An International Comparison*. London: Earthscan.

Meidinger, Errol E. 2001. Environmental Certification Programs and U.S. Environmental Law: Closer Than You May Think. *Environmental Law Reporter*, 31, 10162–10179.

Mena, Sébastien, and Guido Palazzo. 2012. Input and Output Legitimacy of Multi-Stakeholder Initiatives. *Business Ethics Quarterly*, 22(3), 527–556.

Meseguer, Covadonga. 2005. Policy Learning, Policy Diffusion, and the Making of a New Order. *The ANNALS of the American Academy of Political and Social Science*, 598, 67–82.

Michelsen, Johannes. 2001. Recent Development and Political Acceptance of Organic Farming in Europe. *Sociologia Ruralis*, 41(1), 1–18.

Midttun, Atle, Kristian Gautesen, and Maria Gjølberg. 2006. The Political Economy of CSR in Western Europe. *Corporate Governance*, 6(4), 369–385.

Milgrom, Paul R., Douglas C. North, and Barry R. Weingast. 1990. The Role of Institutions in the Revival of Trade: The Law Merchant, Private Judges, and the Champagne Fairs. *Economics and Politics*, 2(1), 1–23.

Mills, Russell W. 2016. The Interaction of Private and Public Regulatory Governance: The Case of Association-Led Voluntary Aviation Safety Programs. *Policy and Society*, 35(1), 43–55.

Ministry of Agriculture, Nature and Food Quality, the Netherlands. 2009. Contribution to the 2009 Consultation on the Reform of the CFP. https://web.archive.org/web/20120526162626/http://ec.europa.eu/fisheries/reform/docs/ministry_agriculture_netherlands_en.pdf (accessed December 9, 2017).

Mol, Arthur P. J., and Gert Spaargaren. 2006. Towards a Sociology of Environmental Flows: A New Agenda for Twenty-First-Century

Environmental Sociology. In Spaargaren, Gert, Arthur P. J. Mol, and Frederick H. Buttel, eds. *Governing Environmental Flows: Global Challenges to Social Theory.* Cambridge: MIT Press, 39–82.

Moschitz, Heidrun, and Matthias Stolze. 2007. *Policy Networks of Organic Farming in Europe: Organic Farming in Europe: Economics and Policy, Volume 12.* Stuttgart: University of Hohenheim.

MRAG. 2016. *Feasibility Report on Options for an EU Ecolabel Scheme for Fishery and Aquaculture Products.* London: MRAG.

MSC. 2009. Marine Stewardship Council's Response to the EU Green Paper on the Reform of the Common Fisheries Policy. https://web.archive.org/web/20120526161901/http://ec.europa.eu/fisheries/reform/docs/marine_stewardship_council_en.pdf (accessed September 23, 2017).

2014. *MSC Fisheries Standard and Guidance v2.0.* London: Marine Stewardship Council.

2015a. *Global Impacts Report 2015.* London: Marine Stewardship Council.

2015b. *MSC Chain of Custody Standard: Default Version.* London: Marine Stewardship Council.

2017a. *Global Impacts Report 2017.* London: Marine Stewardship Council.

2017b. *The MSC at 20. Wild. Certified. Sustainable. Annual Report 2016–17.* London: Marine Stewardship Council.

Naurin, Daniel. 2015. The Councils of the EU: Intergovernmental Bargaining in a Supranational Polity. In Richardson, Jeremy and Sonia Mazey, eds. *European Union: Power and Policy-Making*, Fourth Edition. London: Routledge, 135–157.

Naver, Axel. 2012. Ministers: "We Support MSY, but …" http://web.archive.org/web/20140208052220/http://cfp-reformwatch.eu/2012/05/ministers-we-support-msy-but (accessed March 19, 2014).

2013a. Council and Parliament Start Negotiations on Key Fisheries Reform File This Week. http://web.archive.org/web/20140208055849/http://cfp-reformwatch.eu/2013/03/cfp-reform-negotiations-begin-this-week (accessed March 19, 2014).

2013b. Council Deal on Fisheries Fund Criticised for Boosting Overfishing. http://web.archive.org/web/20140208050248/http://cfp-reformwatch.eu/2012/10/council-deal-on-fisheries-fund-criticised-for-boosting-overfishing (accessed March 14, 2014).

2013c. Parliament Rejects Vessel Construction Aid and Increases Funding for Data Collection. http://web.archive.org/web/20140208165641/http://cfp-reformwatch.eu:80/2013/10/parliament-rejects-fleet-renewal-but-approves-money-for-new-engines (accessed March 26, 2014).

2013d. Parliament Supports More Sustainable Overseas Fishing Practices. http://web.archive.org/web/20140208050258/http://cfp-reformwatch

.eu/2012/11/parliament-supports-more-sustainable-overseas-fishing-practices (accessed March 19, 2014).

2014a. Breakdown in Negotiations on Fisheries Fund. http://web.archive.org/web/20140424032501/http://cfp-reformwatch.eu/2013/12/no-deal-on-european-maritime-and-fisheries-fund (accessed March 26, 2014).

2014b. Parliament and Council Reach Political Agreement on Fisheries Fund. http://web.archive.org/web/20140424034552/http://cfp-reformwatch.eu/2014/01/parliament-and-council-reach-political-agreement-on-fisheries-fund (accessed March 26, 2014).

Nelson, Phillip. 1970. Information and Consumer Behavior. *Journal of Political Economy*, 78(2), 311–329.

NEWS! 2004a. About NEWS! http://web.archive.org/web/20040403163746/http://worldshops.org/news (accessed April 9, 2014).

2004b. Members. http://web.archive.org/web/20040208152334/http://www.worldshops.org/news/members (accessed April 9, 2014).

Nye, Joseph S. Jr., and Robert O. Keohane. 1971a. Transnational Relations and World Politics: A Conclusion. *International Organization*, 25(3), 721–748.

1971b. Transnational Relations and World Politics: An Introduction. *International Organization*, 25(3), 329–349.

O'Riordan, Brian. 1998. Sticky Labels. *Samudra*, 21, 22–25.

OECD, and FAO. 2009. Proceedings of the Round Table on Eco-Labelling and Certification in the Fisheries Sector. April 22–23, 2009, The Hague, the Netherlands. http://web.archive.org/web/20150911001534/http://www.oecd.org/tad/fisheries/43356890.pdf (accessed September 11, 2015).

Olson, Mancur. 1965. *The Logic of Collective Action: Public Goods and the Theory of Groups*. Cambridge: Harvard University Press.

Organic World. 2010. IFOAM Basic Standards. https://web.archive.org/web/20130706002209/http://www.organic-world.net/ifoam-norms0.html (accessed July 6, 2013).

Osório-Peters, Suhita. 1998. *The Goals of Sustainable Development and the Reform of the EU Banana Trade Regime: A Discussion of Different Trade Instruments: Discussion Paper No. 98–31*. Mannheim: Zentrum für Europäische Wirtschaftsforschung GmbH.

Ott, Pierre, and Philippe Desbrosses. 2013. Getting Started: 1984–1991. In IFOAM EU Group, ed. *Making Europe More Organic: 10 Years of Advocacy for Sustainable Food and Farming*. Brussels: IFOAM EU Group, 4–5.

Overdevest, Christine. 2010. Comparing Forest Certification Schemes: The Case of Ratcheting Standards in the Forest Sector. *Socio-Economic Review*, 8(1), 47–76.

Overdevest, Christine, and Jonathan Zeitlin. 2014. Assembling an Experimentalist Regime: Transnational Governance Interactions in the Forest Sector. *Regulation & Governance*, 8(1), 22–48.

Pacini, Henrique, Lucas Assunção, Jinke van Dam, and Rudinei Toneto Jr. 2013. The Price for Biofuels Sustainability. *Energy Policy*, 59, 898–903.

Padel, Susanne, Helena Röcklinsberg, and Otto Schmid. 2009. The Implementation of Organic Principles and Values in the European Regulation for Organic Food. *Food Policy*, 34(3), 245–251.

Pallemaerts, Marc. 2013. Developing More Sustainably? In Jordan, Andrew and Camilla Adelle, eds. *Environmental Policy in the EU: Actors, Institutions and Processes*, Third Edition. London: Routledge, 346–366.

Parker, Charles F., and Christer Karlsson. 2010. Climate Change and the European Union's Leadership Moment: An Inconvenient Truth? *Journal of Common Market Studies*, 48(4), 923–943.

Paterson, Matthew. 2010. Legitimation and Accumulation in Climate Change Governance. *New Political Economy*, 15(3), 345–368.

Pattberg, Philipp. 2006. Private Governance and the South: Lessons from Global Forest Politics. *Third World Quarterly*, 27(4), 579–593.

2007. *Private Institutions and Global Governance: The New Politics of Environmental Sustainability*. Cheltenham: Edward Elgar.

Pattberg, Philipp, Frank Biermann, Sander Chan, and Aysem Mert. 2012. *Public–Private Partnerships for Sustainable Development: Emergence, Influence and Legitimacy*. Cheltenham: Edward Elgar.

Patz, Ronny. 2012. EU Council Meeting on Fisheries of 12 June 2012 (Morning Session). http://web.archive.org/web/20140706054946/ http://polscieu.ideasoneurope.eu/2012/06/12/live-blogging-eu-council-meeting-on-fisheries-of-12-june-2012-morning-session (accessed March 19, 2014).

Peckham, Jack, and Jeremy Glunt. 2003. Euro Parliament Industry Committee Adopts Biofuels Measure. *Hart's European Fuels News*, 7(5), 1.

Peckham, Jack, and Robert Gough. 2002. Industry Committee Supports Biofuel Mandate, but Most of Parliament Doesn't. *Hart's European Fuels News*, 6(13), 1.

Peltzman, Sam. 1976. Toward a More General Theory of Regulation. *Journal of Law and Economics*, 19(2), 211–240.

1989. The Economic Theory of Regulation after a Decade of Deregulation. *Brookings Papers on Economic Activity. Microeconomics*, 1–41.

Perkins, Richard, and Eric Neumayer. 2010. Geographic Variations in the Early Diffusion of Corporate Voluntary Standards: Comparing ISO 14001 and the Global Compact. *Environment and Planning A: Economy and Space*, 42(2), 347–365.

Peterson, John. 2009. Policy Networks. In Wiener, Antje and Thomas Diez, eds. *European Integration Theory*, Second Edition. Oxford: Oxford University Press, 105–124.

Pierson, Paul. 2004. *Politics in Time: History, Institutions, and Social Analysis*. Princeton: Princeton University Press.

Polanyi, Karl. 2001 [1944]. *The Great Transformation: The Political and Economic Origins of Our Time*. Boston: Beacon Press.

Pôle Filière Produits Aquatiques, and Bureau Veritas. 2008. Etude de Faisabilité de la Mise en Place d'un Ecolabel dans la Filière des Produits de la Pêche Maritime. http://web.archive.org/web/20171213033434/http:// www.franceagrimer.fr/fam/content/download/11596/80130/file/ETU DEECOLABEL_080208.pdf (accessed December 13, 2017).

Poletti, Arlo, and Daniela Sicurelli. 2016. The European Union, Preferential Trade Agreements, and the International Regulation of Sustainable Biofuels. *Journal of Common Market Studies*, 54(2), 249–266.

Pollack, Mark A. 1997. Representing Diffuse Interests in EC Policy-Making. *Journal of European Public Policy*, 4(4), 572–590.

Ponte, Stefano. 2014. "Roundtabling" Sustainability: Lessons from the Biofuel Industry. *Geoforum*, 54, 261–271.

Ponte, Stefano, and Carsten Daugbjerg. 2014. Biofuel Sustainability and the Formation of Transnational Hybrid Governance. *Environmental Politics*, 24(1), 96–114.

Potoski, Matthew, and Aseem Prakash. 2004. The Regulation Dilemma: Cooperation and Conflict in Environmental Governance. *Public Administration Review*, 64(2), 152–163.

2009. A Club Theory Approach to Voluntary Programs. In Potoski, Matthew and Aseem Prakash, eds. *Voluntary Programs: A Club Theory Perspective*. Cambridge: MIT Press, 17–39.

Potts, Jason, Ann Wilkings, Matthew Lynch, and Scott McFatridge. 2016. *State of Sustainability Initiatives Review: Standards and the Blue Economy*. Winnipeg: International Institute for Sustainable Development.

Prakash, Aseem, and Matthew Potoski. 2006a. Racing to the Bottom? Trade, Environmental Governance, and ISO 14001. *American Journal of Political Science*, 50(2), 350–364.

2006b. *The Voluntary Environmentalists: Green Clubs, ISO 14001, and Voluntary Environmental Regulations*. Cambridge: Cambridge University Press.

2014. Global Private Regimes, Domestic Public Law: ISO 14001 and Pollution Reduction. *Comparative Political Studies*, 47(3), 369–394.

Prevezer, Martha. 2013. Fairtrade Governance and Its Impact on Local Development: A Framework. In Granville, Brigitte and Janet Dine, eds. *The Processes and Practices of Fair Trade: Trust, Ethics, and Governance*. London: Routledge, 19–42.

Princen, Sebastiaan. 2007. Agenda-Setting in the European Union: A Theoretical Exploration and Agenda for Research. *Journal of European Public Policy*, 14(1), 21–38.

2012. Agenda-Setting and the Formation of an EU Policy-Making State. In Richardson, Jeremy, ed. *Constructing a Policy-Making State? Policy Dynamics in the EU*. Oxford: Oxford University Press, 29–47.

Princen, Sebastiaan, and Bart Kerremans. 2008. Opportunity Structures in the EU Multi-Level System. *West European Politics*, 31(6), 1129–1146.

Przeworski, Adam, and Michael Wallerstein. 1988. Structural Dependence of the State on Capital. *American Political Science Review*, 82(1), 11–29.

Rainforest Alliance. 2010. A Number of Ways to Measure Progress. https://web.archive.org/web/20131205230720/http://thefrogblog.org:80/2010/10/01/a-number-of-ways-to-measure-progress/ (accessed February 21, 2014).

2014a. 25 Years of Conservation. http://web.archive.org/web/20140325154911/http://www.rainforest-alliance.org/about/history (accessed March 25, 2014).

2014b. How Does Rainforest Alliance Certified™ Compare to Fair Trade Certified™? https://web.archive.org/web/20140807181453/http://www.rainforest-alliance.org/agriculture/faq-fairtrade (accessed August 7, 2014).

s.d. The Rainforest Alliance Certified Difference. Sustainable Agriculture Certification. https://web.archive.org/web/20140807203954/http://www.rainforest-alliance.org/agriculture/documents/the_ra_certified_difference_en.pdf (accessed August 7, 2014).

Rametsteiner, Ewald. 2002. The Role of Governments in Forest Certification: A Normative Analysis Based on New Institutional Economics Theories. *Forest Policy and Economics*, 4(3), 163–173.

Raynolds, Laura T., and Elizabeth A. Bennett. 2015. Introduction to Research on Fair Trade. In Raynolds, Laura T., and Elizabeth A. Bennett, eds. *Handbook of Research on Fair Trade*. Cheltenham: Edward Elgar, 3–23.

Raynolds, Laura T., and Nicholas Greenfield. 2015. Fair Trade: Movement and Markets. In Raynolds, Laura T. and Elizabeth A. Bennett, eds. *Handbook of Research on Fair Trade*. Cheltenham: Edward Elgar, 24–41.

Read, Robert. 2001. The Anatomy of the EU–US WTO Banana Trade Dispute. *Estey Centre Journal of International Law and Trade Policy*, 2(2), 257–282.

Reed, Darryl. 2012. Fairtrade International (FLO). In Reed, Darryl, Peter Utting, and Ananya Mukherjee-Reed, eds. *Business Regulation and Non-State Actors: Whose Standards? Whose Development?* London: Routledge, 300–314.

Renckens, Stefan. 2008. Yes, We Will! Voluntarism in U.S. E-Waste Governance. *Review of European Community and International Environmental Law*, 17(3), 286–299.

2015. The Basel Convention, US Politics, and the Emergence of Non-State E-Waste Recycling Certification. *International Environmental Agreements*, 15(2), 141–158.

2019. The Instrumental Power of Transnational Private Governance: Interest Representation and Lobbying by Private Rule-Makers. *Governance* https://doi.org/10.1111/gove.12451.

Renckens, Stefan, and Graeme Auld. 2016. the Compliance Processes in Transnational Private Governance: Explaining Variation in Fisheries Sustainability Certification. Presentation at the Conference on Disclosing Sustainability: The Transformative Power of Transparency?, June 24–25, 2016, Wageningen University, Wageningen.

Renckens, Stefan, Grace Skogstad, and Matthieu Mondou. 2017. When Normative and Market Power Interact: The European Union and Global Biofuels Governance. *Journal of Common Market Studies*, 55(6), 1432–1448.

Rhodes, Roderick A. W., and David Marsh. 1992. Policy Networks in British Politics: A Critique of Existing Approaches. In Marsh, David and Roderick A. W. Rhodes, eds. *Policy Networks in British Government*. Oxford: Clarendon Press, 1–26.

Richardson, Ben. 2014. The Governance of Primary Commodities: Biofuel Certification in the European Union. In Payne, Anthony and Nicola Phillips, eds. *Handbook of the International Political Economy of Governance*. Cheltenham: Edward Elgar, 201–219.

Richardson, Jeremy. 2015. The EU as a Policy-Making State: A Policy System Like Any Other? In Richardson, Jeremy and Sonia Mazey, eds. *European Union: Power and Policy-Making*. Fourth Edition. London: Routledge, 3–31.

Riedel, C. Philip, Amy Widdows, Alim Manji, Federico Manzano-Lopez, and Markus Schneider. 2005. The Impacts of Fair Trade. https://web.archive.org/web/20160318135305/http://www.tropentag.de/2005/abstracts/posters/568.pdf (accessed December 5, 2016).

Rieger, Elmar. 2005. Agricultural Policy: Constrained Reforms. In Wallace, Helen, William Wallace and Mark A. Pollack, eds. *Policy-Making in the European Union*, Fifth Edition. Oxford: Oxford University Press, 161–190.

Rittberger, Berthold, and Winzen Thomas. 2015. The EU's Multilevel Parliamentary System. In Richardson, Jeremy and Sonia Mazey, eds. *European Union: Power and Policy-Making*, Fourth Edition. London: Routledge, 107–133.

Roederer-Rynning, Christilla. 2015. The Common Agricultural Policy: The Fortress Challenged. In Wallace, Helen, Mark A. Pollack, and Alasdair R. Young, eds. *Policy-Making in the European Union*, Seventh Edition. Oxford: Oxford University Press, 196–219.

Rogers, Arthur. 1997. European Parliament Gets Tough on "Organic" Food. *The Lancet*, 349(9065), 1610.

Rosenau, James N., and Ernst-Otto Czempiel. 1992. *Governance without Government: Order and Change in World Politics*. Cambridge: Cambridge University Press.

RSB. 2008. Global Principles and Criteria for Sustainable Biofuels Production. Version Zero. https://web.archive.org/web/20091128123432/http://cgse .epfl.ch:80/webdav/site/cgse/users/171495/public/RSB-brochure-eng.pdf (accessed February 15, 2014).

   2014a. Auditor Checklist for RSB Certification of Bonsucro-Certified Operators. https://web.archive.org/web/20160707023125/http://www .rsb.org/pdfs/Benchmarking%20studies/14-03-05%20RSB-CHK-02-003 %20Auditors%20Checklist%20for%20Bonsucro-certified%20Operators .pdf (accessed March 22, 2017).

   2014b. Previous Versions of the RSB Standard. https://web.archive.org/ web/20140226121818/http://rsb.org:80/archives/previous-versions-of-the-rsb-standard (accessed February 26, 2014).

   2014c. Recognition of Other Certification Schemes. https://web.archive .org/web/20140226122309/http://rsb.org:80/sustainability/recognition-of-other-certification-schemes (accessed February 26, 2014).

   2014d. RSB 1St Phase (2006–2009). https://web.archive.org/web/ 20140226121824/http://rsb.org:80/archives/rsb-1st-phase-2006-2009 (accessed February 26, 2014).

RSPO. 2012. Milestones. https://web.archive.org/web/20121017111851/ http://www.rspo.org/en/milestones (accessed January 22, 2014).

   2014a. About Us. https://web.archive.org/web/20141111174614/http:// www.rspo.org/about (accessed November 11, 2014).

   2014b. Why RSPO Certification. https://web.archive.org/web/ 20140224173635/http://www.rspo.org/en/why_rspo_certification (accessed November 11, 2014).

RTRS. 2014. History. https://web.archive.org/web/20170323150627/http:// www.responsiblesoy.org/about-rtrs/history/?lang=en (accessed March 23, 2017).

Ruggie, John G. 2004. Reconstituting the Global Public Domain – Issues, Actors, and Practices. *European Journal of International Relations*, 10(4), 499–531.

Ruggie, John G., and Tamaryn Nelson. 2015. Human Rights and the OECD Guidelines for Multinational Enterprises: Normative Innovations and Implementation Challenges. *Brown Journal of World Affairs*, 22(1), 99–127.

Rundgren, Gunnar. 2001. IFOAM – A Partnership Model for Developing Organic Agriculture Worldwide. *Proceedings of the European Conference on Organic Food and Farming: Towards Partnership and Action in Europe*, May 10–11, 2001, Copenhagen.

2002. Overview of the Implementation of the EU Organic Regulatory System. *The Organic Standard*, Issue 9(January 2002), 3–10.

2006. The Wrong Thing-Too Late. *The Organic Standard*, Issue 57(January 2006).

2011. A Leap Ahead. *The Organic Standard*, Issue 127 (November 2011), 4.

Sabatier, Paul, and Hank C. Jenkins-Smith, eds. 1993. *Policy Change and Learning: An Advocacy Coalition Approach*. Boulder: Westview Press.

Salas, Mauricio, and John H. Jackson. 2000. Procedural Overview of the WTO EC – Banana Dispute. *Journal of International Economic Law*, 3(1), 145–166.

Salladarré, Frédéric, Patrice Guillotreau, Yves Perraudeau, and Marie-Christine Monfort. 2010. The Demand for Seafood Eco-Labels in France. *Journal of Agricultural & Food Industrial Organization*, 8(1), Article 10.

SAN/Rainforest Alliance. 2015. SAN/Rainforest Alliance Impacts Report. Evaluating the Effects of the SAN/Rainforest Alliance Certification System on Farms, People, and the Environment. https://web.archive.org/web/20161219132932/http://www.san.ag/biblioteca/docs/SAN_RA_Impacts_Report.pdf (accessed December 19, 2016).

Scarlat, Nicolae, and Jean-François Dallemand. 2011. Recent Developments of Biofuels/Bioenergy Sustainability Certification: A Global Overview. *Energy Policy*, 39, 1630–1646.

Scharpf, Fritz W. 1996. Negative and Positive Integration in the Political Economy of European Welfare States. In Marks, Gary, Fritz W. Scharpf, Philippe C. Schmitter, and Wolfgang Streeck, eds. *Governance in the European Union*. London: Sage, 15–39.

Schlamann, Inga, Barbara Wieler, Martina Fleckenstein, Jenny Walther-Thoß, Nina Haase, and Laszlo Mathe. 2013. *Searching for Sustainability. Comparative Analysis of Certification Schemes for Biomass Used for the Production of Biofuels*. Düsseldorf: WWF Deutschland.

Schlegelmilch, Rupert. 2003. A Fair Wind for "Fair Trade." *CSR Magazine*, September 2003, 5.

Schleifer, Philip. 2013. Orchestrating Sustainability: The Case of European Union Biofuel Governance. *Regulation & Governance*, 7(4), 533–546.

Schlüter, Marco, and Francis Blake. 2009. History of the EU Organic Regulation and Its Recent Revision. In Mikkelsen, Camilla and Marco Schlüter, eds. *The New EU Regulation for Organic Food and Farming: (EC) No 834/2007: Background, Assessment, Interpretation*. Brussels: IFOAM EU Group, 8–13.

Schmid, Otto. 2007. Development of Standards for Organic Farming. In Lockeretz, William, ed. *Organic Farming: An International History*. Wallingford: CAB International, 152–174.

Schmid, Otto, Beate Huber, Katia Ziegler, Lizzie Melby Jespersen, Jens Gronbech Hansen, Gerhard Plakolm, Jo Gilbert, Steve Lomann, Cristina Micheloni, and Susanne Padel. 2007. Analysis of EEC Regulation 2092/91 in Relation to Other National and International Organic Standards. http://web.archive.org/web/20070729100112/www.organic-revision.org/dissim/biof07/standards.pdf (accessed June 28, 2013).

Schmitter, Philippe C., and Wolfgang Streeck. 1999. *The Organization of Business Interests: Studying the Associative Action of Business in Advanced Industrial Societies*. MPIfG Discussion Paper 99/1. Cologne: Max-Planck-Institute für Gesellschaftsforschung.

Scholte, Jan Aart. 2005. *Globalization. A Critical Introduction*, Second Edition. New York: Palgrave Macmillan.

Schönning, Marianne. 2007. What Does the New Organic Regulation Imply for Small Farmers? *Proceedings of the European Organic Congress. The Future of Organic Food and Farming within the Reformed CAP. Reviewing the European Organic Action Plan and Future Perspectives*, December 4–5, 2007, Brussels.

Schouten, Greetje, and Verena Bitzer. 2015. The Emergence of Southern Standards in Agricultural Value Chains: A New Trend in Sustainability Governance? *Ecological Economics*, 120, 175–184.

Schuler, Gefion. 2008. Effective Governance through Decentralized Soft Implementation: The OECD Guidelines for Multinational Enterprises. *German Law Journal*, 9(11), 1753–1777.

Scott, Steffanie, Peter Vandergeest, and Mary Young. 2009. Certification Standards and the Governance of Green Foods in Southeast Asia. In Clapp, Jennifer and Doris Fuchs, eds. *Corporate Power in Global Agrifood Governance*. Cambridge: MIT Press, 61–92.

Seafish. 2009. Reform of the CFP: Seafish Response to the European Commission. https://web.archive.org/web/20120526161053/http://ec.europa.eu/fisheries/reform/docs/seafish_en.pdf (accessed September 23, 2017).

2012a. Guide to Seafood Standards. Friend of the Sea. http://web.archive .org/web/20160820055751/http://www.seafish.org/industry-support/ guide-to-seafood-standards/standards/friend-of-the-sea (accessed August 20, 2016).

2012b. Guide to Seafood Standards. Marine Stewardship Council. http:// web.archive.org/web/20160819235435/http://www.seafish.org/industry- support/guide-to-seafood-standards/standards/marine-stewardship- council (accessed August 19, 2016).

2013. Guide to Seafood Standards. Aquaculture Stewardship Council. http://web.archive.org/web/20160820071702/http://www.seafish .org/industry-support/guide-to-seafood-standards/standards/aquaculture- stewardship-council (accessed August 20, 2016).

Searchinger, Timothy, Ralph Heimlich, R. A. Houghton, Fengxia Dong, Amani Elobeid, Jacinto Fabiosa, Simla Tokgoz, Dermot Hayes, and Tun-Hsiang Yu. 2008. Use of U.S. Croplands for Biofuels Increases Greenhouse Gases through Emissions from Land-Use Change. *Science*, 319(5867), 1238–1240.

Sengstschmid, Helmut, Niels Sprong, Otto Schmid, Nina Stockebrand, Hanna Stolz, and Achim Spiller. 2011. *EU Ecolabel for Food and Feed Products: Feasibility Study*. Aylesbury: Oakdene Hollins.

Sharman, Amelia, and John Holmes. 2010. Evidence-Based Policy or Policy-Based Evidence Gathering? Biofuels, the EU and the 10% Target. *Environmental Policy and Governance*, 20(5), 309–321.

Sklair, Leslie. 2001. *The Transnational Capitalist Class*. Oxford: Blackwell.

Skocpol, Theda. 1985. Bringing the State Back In: Strategies of Analysis in Current Research. In Evans, Peter B., Dietrich Rueschemeyer, and Theda Skocpol, eds. *Bringing the State Back In*. Cambridge: Cambridge University Press, 3–37.

Skogstad, Grace. 2017. Policy Feedback and Self-Reinforcing and Self-Undermining Processes in EU Biofuels Policy. *Journal of European Public Policy*, 24(1), 21–41.

Soil Association. 2013. Our History. https://web.archive.org/web/ 20140328114101/http://www.soilassociation.org/aboutus/ourhistory (accessed March 28, 2014).

2018. How Do Organic Standards Work? https://web.archive.org/web/ 20180907025308/https://www.soilassociation.org/organic-standards/ how-do-organic-standards-work/ (accessed September 6, 2018).

Soil Association Standards Board. 2008. Response to the Mandatory EU Logo. Consultation Paper March 31st. On file with author.

Solidaridad. 2006. *Annual Report 2005*. Utrecht: Solidaridad Foundation.

SQC. 2016. About SQC. https://web.archive.org/web/20161021193050/ http://sqcrops.co.uk/about-sqc/about-sqc/ (accessed October 21, 2016).

Starbucks. 2013. Ethically Sourced Coffee: Goals and Progress. https://web
.archive.org/web/20140221095530/http://www.starbucks.com/responsi
bility/sourcing/coffee (accessed February 24, 2014).

2017. Committed to 100% Ethically Sourced. https://web.archive
.org/web/20170929202454/https://www.starbucks.com/responsibility/
community/farmer-support/farmer-loan-programs (accessed October 10,
2017).

Steering Committee of the State-of-Knowledge Assessment of Standards and
Certification. 2012. *Toward Sustainability: The Roles and Limitations
of Certification*. Washington, DC: RESOLVE.

Steinberg, Paul F., and Stacy D. VanDeveer, eds. 2012. *Comparative Environmental Politics: Theory, Practice, and Prospects*. Cambridge: MIT
Press.

Steurer, Reinhard. 2010. The Role of Governments in Corporate Social
Responsibility: Characterising Public Policies on CSR in Europe. *Policy
Sciences*, 43(1), 49–72.

Stigler, George J. 1971. The Theory of Economic Regulation. *The Bell
Journal of Economics and Management Science*, 2(1), 3–21.

Stolze, Matthias, and Nicolas Lampkin. 2009. Policy for Organic Farming:
Rationale and Concepts. *Food Policy*, 34(3), 237–244.

Suranovic, Steven. 2015. The Meaning of Fair Trade. In Raynolds, Laura T.
and Elizabeth A. Bennett, eds. *Handbook of Research on Fair Trade*.
Cheltenham: Edward Elgar, 45–60.

Sustainable Agriculture Network. 2014. About Us. History. https://
web.archive.org/web/20140313142819/http://sanstandards.org/sitio/
subsections/display/2 (accessed March 13, 2014).

Tallberg, Jonas. 2007. Executive Politics. In Jørgensen, Knud Erik, Mark A.
Pollack, and Ben Rosamond, eds. *Handbook of European Union Politics*. London: Sage, 195–212.

Tampe, Maja. 2018. Leveraging the Vertical: The Contested Dynamics of
Sustainability Standards and Labour in Global Production Networks.
British Journal of Industrial Relations, 56(1), 43–78.

Taylor, J. Gary, and Patricia J. Scharlin. 2004. *Smart Alliance: How a
Global Corporation and Environmental Activists Transformed a Tar-
nished Brand*. New Haven: Yale University Press.

Taylor, Simon. 2007. Sowing the Seeds for a Biofuels Market. *European Voice*.
January 31, 2007. https://web.archive.org/web/20190730030331/
https://www.politico.eu/article/sowing-the-seeds-for-a-biofuels-market-2
(accessed December 5, 2017).

Thatcher, Mark. 2015. European Regulation. In Richardson, Jeremy and
Sonia Mazey, eds. *European Union: Power and Policy-Making*, Fourth
Edition. London: Routledge, 307–325.

Thomson, Robert. 2015. The Distribution of Power among the Institutions. In Richardson, Jeremy and Sonia Mazey, eds. *European Union: Power and Policy-Making*, Fourth Edition. London: Routledge, 189–210.

Timilsina, Govinda R., and Ashish Shrestha. 2010. Biofuels. Markets, Targets and Impacts. World Bank Development Research Group. https://web.archive.org/web/20171206002625/https://openknowledge .worldbank.org/bitstream/handle/10986/3848/WPS5364.pdf;sequence=1 (accessed December 6, 2017).

Tosun, Jale, Sebastian Koos, and Jennifer Shore. 2016. Co-Governing Common Goods: Interaction Patterns of Private and Public Actors. *Policy and Society*, 35(1), 1–12.

Truman, David B. 1951. *The Governmental Process: Political Interests and Public Opinion*. New York: Alfred A. Knopf.

Tsebelis, George. 2013. Bridging Qualified Majority and Unanimity Decisionmaking in the EU. *Journal of European Public Policy*, 20(8), 1083–1103.

UK Department for Environment, Food and Rural Affairs. 2010. *The 2007/ 08 Agricultural Price Spikes: Causes and Policy Implications*. London: DEFRA.

UK Renewable Fuels Agency. 2008. The Gallagher Review of the Indirect Effects of Biofuels Production. https://web.archive.org/web/ 20171206002925/https://www.unido.org/sites/default/files/2009-11/ Gallagher_Report_0.pdf (accessed December 6, 2017).

UN News Centre. 2007. UN Independent Rights Expert Calls for Five-Year Freeze on Biofuel Production. https://web.archive.org/web/ 20140524011830/http://www.un.org/apps/news/story.asp?NewsID= 24434&#.Wic6VnlryUl (accessed May 24, 2014).

UNDP. 2016. *The UNDP Green Commodities Programme: Six Years of Innovation and Impact (2009–2015)*. New York: United Nations Development Programme.

UNEP. 2009. *Certification and Sustainable Fisheries*. Geneva: United Nations Environment Programme.

UTZ Certified. 2010. UTZ Certified Position Paper on the Existence of Multiple Sustainability Organizations. www.utzcertified.org/attach ments/article/2174/UTZ%20Certified%20position%20paper%20on% 20Multiple%20Sustainability%20Organizations.pdf (accessed February 25, 2014).

  2011. *UTZ Certified Annual Report 2011*. Amsterdam: UTZ Certified.

  2014a. Frequently Asked Questions about UTZ Certified. https://web .archive.org/web/20140725071319/https://utzcertified.org/en/aboututz certified/faq (accessed July 25, 2014).

2014b. Standard & Certification. https://web.archive.org/web/20140725055223/
https://utzcertified.org/en/aboututzcertified/standardcertification (accessed July
25, 2014).

2014c. The Story of UTZ. https://web.archive.org/web/20140101203608/
https://www.utzcertified.org/en/aboututzcertified/the-story-of-utz (accessed
July 25, 2014).

2014d. What Is UTZ Certified. https://web.archive.org/web/20140102170757/
https://utzcertified.org/en/aboututzcertified (accessed February 21, 2014).

2015a. Assurance Code System Report 2.0. https://web.archive.org/web/
20171201205434/https://www.isealalliance.org/system/files/private/
UTZ%20Certified%20Assurance%20Public%20System%20Report
%202015.pdf (accessed December 1, 2017).

2015b. *Certification Protocol. Version 4.0 July 2015.* Amsterdam: UTZ
Certified.

2015c. *Partnerships Are the Key to Change: 2015 in Achievements.*
Amsterdam: UTZ Certified.

van der Ven, Hamish. 2015. Correlates of Rigorous and Credible
Transnational Governance: A Cross-Sectoral Analysis of Best Practice
Compliance in Eco-Labeling. *Regulation & Governance*, 9(3),
276–293.

van der Ven, Hamish, and Benjamin Cashore. 2018. Forest Certification:
The Challenge of Measuring Impacts. *Current Opinion in Environmental Sustainability*, 32, 104–111.

Verbruggen, Paul. 2013. Gorillas in the Closet? Public and Private Actors in
the Enforcement of Transnational Private Regulation. *Regulation &
Governance*, 7(4), 512–532.

Vis, Martijn W., John Vos, and Douwe van den Berg. 2008. *Sustainability
Criteria & Certification Systems for Biomass Production.* Enschede:
BTG Biomass Technology Group BV.

Vogel, David. 1995. *Trading Up: Consumer and Environmental Regulation
in a Global Economy.* Cambridge: Harvard University Press.

1997. Trading Up and Governing Across: Transnational Governance and
Environmental Protection. *Journal of European Public Policy*, 4(4), 556–571.

2005. *The Market for Virtue: The Potential and Limits of Corporate
Social Responsibility.* Washington, DC: Brookings Institution Press.

2008. Private Global Business Regulation. *Annual Review of Political
Science*, 11, 261–282.

2012. *The Politics of Precaution: Regulating Health, Safety, and Environmental Risks in Europe and the United States.* Princeton: Princeton
University Press.

Vogt, Gunter. 2007. The Origins of Organic Farming. In Lockeretz, William, ed. *Organic Farming: An International History*. Wallingford: CAB International, 9–29.

Vossenaar, René. 2003. Promoting Production and Exports of Organic Agriculture in Developing Countries. In Westermayer, Christina and Bernward Geier, eds. *The Organic Guarantee System: The Need and Strategy for Harmonization and Equivalence*. Tholey-Theley: IFOAM, FAO and UNCTAD, 10–15.

Wallace, Helen, and Christine Reh. 2015. An Institutional Anatomy and Five Policy Modes. In Wallace, Helen, Mark A. Pollack, and Alasdair R. Young, eds. *Policy-Making in the European Union*, Seventh Edition. Oxford: Oxford University Press, 72–112.

Washington, Sally, and Lahsen Ababouch. 2011. *Private Standards and Certification in Fisheries and Aquaculture: Current Practices and Emerging Issues*. Rome: Food and Agriculture Organization of the United Nations.

Werner, Timothy. 2012. *Public Forces and Private Politics in American Big Business*. Cambridge: Cambridge University Press.

WFTO. 2008. World Fair Trade Organization Annual Report 2008. https://web.archive.org/web/20131022014040/http://www.wfto.com/index.php?option=com_docman&task=doc_download&gid=1444&&Itemid=1 (accessed April 9, 2014).

2011. The WFTO Logo. http://web.archive.org/web/20130627073703/http://www.wfto.com/index.php?option=com_content&task=view&id=904&Itemid=310 (accessed July 27, 2013).

2016. WFTO Guarantee System Handbook. http://wfto.com/sites/default/files/Ch%207%20Overview%20and%20components%20april%2016.pdf (accessed September 30, 2016).

WFTO, and FLO. 2009. A Charter of Fair Trade Principles. https://web.archive.org/web/20130119144223/http://www.fairtrade-advocacy.org/images/stories/FTAO_charters_3rd_version_EN_v1.2.pdf (accessed January 19, 2013).

Wiley, James. 2008. *The Banana: Empires, Trade Wars, and Globalization*. Lincoln: University of Nebraska Press.

Wille, Chris. 2004. Certification: A Catalyst for Partnerships. *Human Ecology Forum*, 11(3), 288–291.

Wilson, Bradley R., and Tad Mutersbaugh. 2015. Fair Trade Certification, Performance and Practice. In Raynolds, Laura T. and Elizabeth A. Bennett, eds. *Handbook of Research on Fair Trade*. Cheltenham: Edward Elgar, 281–297.

Wonka, Arndt, Frank R. Baumgartner, Christine Mahoney, and Joost Berkhout. 2010. Measuring the Size and Scope of the EU Interest Group Population. *European Union Politics*, 11(3), 463–476.

Wood, Stepan, and Lynn Johannson. 2008. Six Principles for Integrating Non-Governmental Environmental Standards into Smart Regulation. *Osgoode Hall Law Journal*, 46, 345–395.

Wright, Christopher, and Daniel Nyberg. 2014. Creative Self-Destruction: Corporate Responses to Climate Change as Political Myths. *Environmental Politics*, 23(2), 205–223.

WTO. 2014. Dispute Settlement: Dispute DS265. European Communities: Export Subsidies on Sugar. https://web.archive.org/web/20180201122604/https://www.wto.org/english/tratop_e/dispu_e/cases_e/ds265_e.htm (accessed January 26, 2014).

  2017a. WTO Rules and Environmental Policies: GATT Exceptions. https://web.archive.org/web/20150211043940/http://www.wto.org:80/english/tratop_e/envir_e/envt_rules_exceptions_e.htm (accessed August 10, 2017).

  2017b. WTO Rules and Environmental Policies: Key GATT Disciplines. https://web.archive.org/web/20150519003849/https://www.wto.org/english/tratop_e/envir_e/envt_rules_gatt_e.htm (accessed August 10, 2017).

  2018. Labelling. https://web.archive.org/web/20180609053126/https://www.wto.org/english/tratop_e/envir_e/labelling_e.htm (accessed June 9, 2018).

WWF. 2005. WWF Submission to the EC Public Consultation on the European Biomass Action Plan. https://web.archive.org/web/20181019205657/http://d2ouvy59p0dg6k.cloudfront.net/downloads/ecbiomassconsultation.pdf (accessed May 10, 2017).

  2007. WWF Contribution to the European Commission – Energy & Transport Directorate Public Consultation on the Review of the EU Biofuels Directive. https://web.archive.org/web/20111117070254/http://ec.europa.eu/energy/res/consultation/doc/2007_06_04_biofuels/non_og/wwf_en.pdf (accessed November 17, 2011).

  2009. WWF Response to the 2009 Green Paper: Reform of the Common Fisheries Policy. https://web.archive.org/web/20120526222102/http://ec.europa.eu/fisheries/reform/docs/wwf01_en.pdf (accessed September 23, 2017).

Yandle, Bruce. 1983. Bootleggers and Baptists: The Education of a Regulatory Economist. *Regulation*, 7(3), 12–16.

  2011. Bootleggers and Baptists in the Theory of Regulation. In Levi-Faur, David, ed. *Handbook on the Politics of Regulation*. Cheltenham: Edward Elgar, 25–33.

Young, Alasdair R. 2006. The Politics of Regulation and the Internal Market. In Jørgensen, Knud Erik, Mark A. Pollack, and Ben Rosamond, eds. *Handbook of European Union Politics*. London: Sage, 372–394.

Young, Alasdair R., and Helen Wallace. 2000. *Regulatory Politics in the Enlarging European Union: Weighing Civic and Producer Interests*. Manchester: Manchester University Press.

Young, Oran R. 2011. Effectiveness of International Environmental Regimes: Existing Knowledge, Cutting-Edge Themes, and Research Strategies. *Proceedings of the National Academy of Sciences of the United States of America (PNAS)*, 108(50), 19853–19860.

Zadek, Simon, Sanjiv Lingayah, and Maya Forstater. 1998. *Social Labels: Tools for Ethical Trade*. London: New Economics Foundation and European Commission Directorate-General for Employment, Industrial Relations and Social Affairs.

Zito, Anthony R. 2005. Task Expansion: A Theoretical Overview. In Jordan, Andrew, ed. *Environmental Policy in the European Union: Actors, Institutions & Processes*, Second Edition. London: Earthscan, 141–161.

Index

CPSIA information can be obtained
at www.ICGtesting.com
Printed in the USA
LVHW012123150622
721336LV00009B/356